RXpert SERIES
Student's Companion

Cosmetics and Cosmeceuticals

Rxpert SERIES
Student's Companion

Cosmetics and Cosmeceuticals

Prof. (Dr.) Kamla Pathak
Professor & Dean
Pharmacy College Safai,
Uttar Pradesh University of Medical Sciences, Etawah, Uttar Pradesh, India

Prof. (Dr.) Tarun Virmani
Professor & Principal
Amity Institute of Pharmacy,
Amity University, Greater Noida Campus, Uttar Pradesh, India

Dr. Girish Kumar
Associate Professor
Amity Institute of Pharmacy,
Amity University, Greater Noida Campus, Uttar Pradesh, India

Reshu Virmani
Assistant Professor
School of Pharmaceutical Sciences,
MVN University, Palwal, Haryana, India

Pharma Med PRESS An Imprint of BSP Books Pvt. Ltd.

™ **PharmaMed Press**
An imprint of BSP Books Pvt. Ltd
4-4-309/316, Giriraj Lane,
Sultan Bazar, Hyderabad - 500 001.

Cosmetics and Cosmeceuticals
by **Kamla Pathak, Tarun Virmani, Girish Kumar and Reshu Virmani**

Disclaimer: The authors and the publishers have taken due care to provide the authentic, reliable and up to date information related to the subject. However, neither the authors nor the publisher shall be responsible for any liability for any damage caused as a result of use of this book. The respective user must check the accuracy from other sources too.

Published by:

Pharma Med PRESS
An Imprint of BSP Books Pvt. Ltd.

™ **PharmaMed Press**
An imprint of BSP Books Pvt. Ltd.
4-4-309/316, Giriraj Lane, Sultan Bazar, Hyderabad - 500 001.
Phone: 040-23445688
e-mail: info@pharmamedpress.com
www.pharmamedpress.com/pharmamedpress.net

ISBN: 978-93-49562-76-9 (Hardback)

Preface

The world of cosmetics and cosmeceuticals has witnessed an extraordinary evolution in recent decades, fuelled by advancements in science, technology, and consumer awareness. The increasing demand for safe, effective, and innovative products has necessitated a deeper understanding of the formulation, biological mechanisms, and regulatory frameworks governing the cosmetics and cosmeceuticals industry. This book, titled "Cosmetics & Cosmeceuticals" is designed to address these growing complexities and serve as a comprehensive guide for students, researchers, and professionals involved in this fascinating field.

This book provides a detailed exploration of the fundamental aspects of cosmetics and cosmeceuticals, integrating theoretical and practical approaches. It aligns with the latest Pharmacy Council of India (PCI) curriculum for the M. Pharm program, particularly in the second semester, and covers key topics such as the biological aspects of skin and hair care, the formulation of cosmetic products, regulatory requirements, and the emerging trends in the cosmeceutical market.

The book content is structured to provide clarity and coherence, ensuring that even complex topics are explained in a student-friendly manner. Each chapter addresses critical aspects of cosmetics and cosmeceuticals, from the regulatory requirements for cosmetic products in India to herbal cosmetics, preservatives, and the role of antioxidants and bioactive ingredients. The book also delves into advanced areas, such as the challenges faced in formulating herbal cosmetics and using nanotechnology in modern cosmetic formulations.

In addition to academic knowledge, the book emphasizes the practical application of these principles in the cosmetics industry. It offers insights into product formulation, with step-by-step guidelines for preparing various cosmetics such as moisturizing creams, sunscreens, shampoos, and toothpaste. Moreover, it discusses controversial ingredients like parabens and formaldehyde liberators, fostering a critical approach toward cosmetic safety and efficacy.

The text is enriched with recent research findings, industry case studies, and real-world examples that bring relevance to the theoretical concepts covered. Moreover, self-assessment questions, including higher-order thinking skills (HOTS), are included at the end of each chapter to promote critical thinking and the application of knowledge. These questions will aid students in preparing for exams and provide valuable insights for professionals seeking to enhance their understanding of the latest trends in cosmeceuticals.

It is my sincere hope that this book serves as a useful resource for students, educators, and professionals alike. May it inspire further research and innovation in the exciting and ever-evolving world of cosmetics and cosmeceuticals.

- Authors

Contents

CHAPTER 1

Regulatory Requirements for Labelling and Import of Cosmetics

NEED FOR COSMETICS

The word cosmetic comes from the Greek word "kosmeticos", which meaning "to embellish." Since then, any material used to enhance or beautify one's appearance has been referred to as cosmetics. Cosmetics have become so ingrained in our everyday routine that we can't picture life without them because in today's world, everyone is very sensitive about their appearance. It's because people want to improve their looks and appearance without harming their bodily structure or function, which has led to an increase in the need of cosmetics. When we consider the utility of cosmetics in relation to the portions of the body they are used on, we can see many types of cosmetics we utilize in our daily life. Physiological utility, physicochemical utility, and psychological utility of cosmetics prompt the need for cosmetics. The physiological utility of a cosmetic includes its ability to reduce skin roughness, prevent hair loss, and improve other physiological features of the skin and hair. Physiological utility is one of the most significant utility of cosmetics as our society is aging at rapid rate. Physicochemical utility of cosmetics include protection of skin from effects of U-V radiations using ultraviolet absorbing and scattering agents, covering of spots and fleck, and application of permanent waving and creams to make hair more attractive. Psychological utility includes enhancing the confidence and working capability of a person using the cosmetic by soothing as well as stimulating effect of their aroma or perfume on mind.

Origin of cosmetics

Egyptians are said to have been the first to utilize cosmetics, around 4000 BC. They use a famous eye shadow, an antimony compound termed as *Kohl*. The women painted the upper lid black and the lower lid green, with the space between the upper lid and the brow painted grey or blue. Hair Henna derived from *Lawsonia Inermis* was famous hair dye and additionally used to stain the fingernails and toenails. The

Egyptians used a mixture of incense cake, wax, freshly squeezed olive oil, and cypress folded into fresh milk to the face for 6 days to prevent or lessen wrinkles. The ancient Sumerians, Babylonians and Hebrews also employed the cosmetics for their beautification. Cosmetic use peaked around 1760, but with the arrival of the French Revolution, it all but vanished. In the year 1900, their use was revived, accompanied by the introduction of scientifically based beauty aids in France. Since then, the sector has grown to enormous dimensions, with goods designed for every possible application. By the beginning of the 21st century, the cosmetics industry had mostly been taken over by major corporations and had grown to be a multibillion-dollar business. Modern cosmetic products include skin care preparations, face powder, rouge, eye makeup, foundation, lipstick, shampoo, hair care preparations, hair colors, dyes, nail polishes, and related products include deodorants, antiperspirants, depilatories, astrigents, mouthwashes and bath crystals. In current scenario, the cosmetic products are widely used by people of every country which lead to a large market capital across the world.

DEFINTIONS OF COSMETICS AS PER DIFFERENT REGULATIONS

As per European regulations, cosmetics may be defined as "any substance or preparation intended to be placed in contact with the various external parts of the human body (epidermis, hair system, nails, lips and external genital organs) or with the teeth and the mucous membranes of the oral cavity with a view exclusively or mainly to cleaning them, perfuming them, changing their appearance and/or correcting body odours and/or protecting them or keeping them in good conditions."

As per Japanese regulations, cosmetics may be defined as "articles with mild action on the human body, which are intended to be applied to the human body through rubbing, sprinkling or other methods, aiming to clean, beautify and increase the attractiveness, alter the appearance or to keep the skin or hair in good condition".

As per United States Regulations (FD&C Act), cosmetics may be defined as "articles intended to be rubbed, poured, sprinkled, or sprayed on, introduced into, or otherwise applied to the human body for cleansing, beautifying, promoting attractiveness, or altering the appearance".

As per Canada regulations, cosmetics may be defined as "any substance or mixture of substances, manufactured, sold or represented for use in cleansing, improving or altering the complexion, skin, hair or teeth and includes deodorants and perfumes".

According to Indian regulations (Drugs and Cosmetics Act, 1940), cosmetics may be defined as any substance proposed to be rubbed, poured, sprayed or sprinkled on, or applied to, human body or any part for cleansing, beautifying, enhancing the attractiveness or changing the appearance.

As per Australian regulations, cosmetics may be defined as "A substance or preparation intended for placement in contact with any external part of the human body, including the mucous membrane of the oral cavity, the teeth, with a view to altering the odours of the body; or changing its appearance; or cleansing it; or maintaining it in good condition; or perfuming it; or protecting it".

As per Chinese regulations, cosmetics may be defined as "those daily used chemical products applied on the surface of any part of the human body (such as skin, hair, nails and lips) by way of smearing, spraying or other similar methods to keep the body clean, to get rid of undesirable smell, to protect the skin, to make up the face and to increase the beauty of the appearance".

As per ASEAN regulation, (Having ten countries), the definition of cosmetics is same as under European regulations. ASEAN is made up of ten countries which include Brunei, Darussalam, Indonesia, Cambodia, Myanmar, Malaysia, Singapore, Lao PDR, Philippines, Vietnam and Thailand.

Note: The cosmetics regulations for different countries has been summarized into Table 1.1.

TABLE 1.1: Summary of cosmetics regulations for India, USA and Europe.

CONTENTS	INDIA	USA	EUROPE
Authority	CDSCO	FDA	EMEA
Rules & Regulations	Drugs & Cosmetics Act	Food, Drugs & Cosmetics Act	Council Directive 76/768/EEC
Labelling	Must comply with part XV of Drugs & Cosmetics rules 1945	Must comply with FD&C and FP&L	Based on council directive 76/768/EEC
Pre-market approval	Required under state licensing authority	Not required	Not required
Expiry date	Indicated as 'use before date"	Not required	Date of minimum durability if durability is less than 30 months. Period after opening if durability is more than 30 months

TABLE 1.1: *Contd...*

CONTENTS	INDIA	USA	EUROPE
Post marketing reporting system	NA	Yes (Voluntary Cosmetic Registration Program)	NA

Market capital for cosmetics across the world

The demand for cosmetics is increasing steadily with passing time. The figure 1.1 depicts the market capital for cosmetic products in between 2018-2025 across the world. The market capital for cosmetic products was 507.8 billion US Dollars in 2018 across the world and now it is projected to a market capital of about 758.4 billion US Dollars by 2025 which shows the importance of cosmetic products in today's era across the world. The revenue for cosmetics in India was valued for USD 13191.23 million in year 2020 and expected that it will achieve USD 28985.33 million at 16.39% CAGR rate at 2026. Diversely it is forecasted that global cosmetic market will reach USD 450 billion in year 2025 at 4.3% CAGR rate which shows that India will devote 5% of total world cosmetic market and will become one among the highest five leading global cosmetic markets in terms of revenue

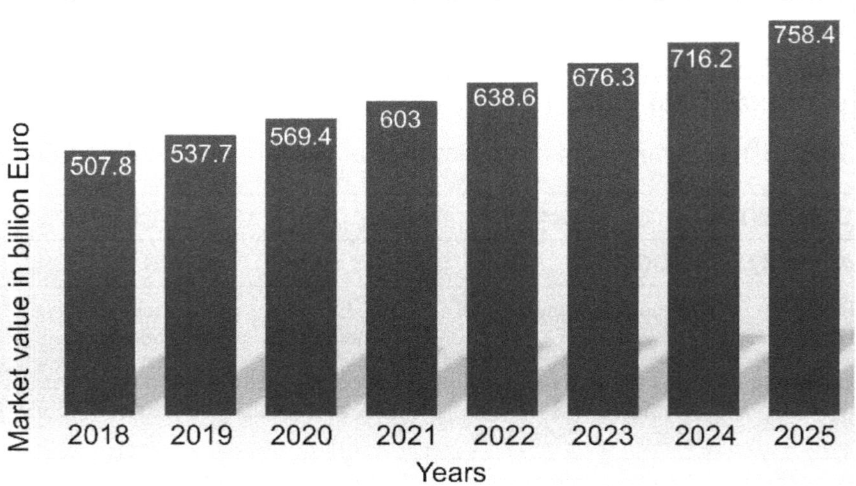

Figure 1.1 Market capital for cosmetics in 2018-2025

INDIAN REGULATORY REQUIREMENTS FOR LABELING OF COSMETICS

A cosmetic product shall carry inner and outer labels having various recognized instructions:

Information on inner and outer labels

1. The name of cosmetic products
2. The name of the manufacturer and the complete address of the establishments where the cosmetic product was manufactured. If the cosmetic product was not made on the firm's premises, the name and entire address of the actual manufacturer should be listed on the label as "Made in......(name of premises)". If the cosmetic product is packaged in a tiny container and the manufacturer's complete address cannot be provided, the name of the producer and his main manufacturing facilities, as well as the pin code, should be listed on the label.
3. Use before or expiry date or date of expiry or use by

Information on Inner label:

For the cosmetic products where hazard exists, following information must be given on inner label:

1. Proper directions for safe use of the product
2. Any consumer-required warnings, specific instructions, or cautions during use
3. A declaration identifying the dangerous or deadly chemicals in the cosmetic product, as well as the amount of each.
4. A unique batch number, which serves as a reference point for recording and inspecting information about the manufacture of a certain batch from which the preparation is taken into the container. The figures representing the batch number beginning with the letter "B" or "Batch no." or "Lot no." shall bear providing this provision does not apply to any cosmetic product with a weight of 10 grams or less in solid or semi-solid form, or a volume of 25 milliliters or less in liquid form. In the case of soaps, instead of a batch number, the month and year of manufacture must be displayed on the label.
5. Manufacturing license number, the number being introduced by the letter “M” or “M.L. No.” or Mfg. Lic. No.” shall bear on the label providing that, in the case of imported cosmetic products, if such a clause is not mandatory in the place of manufacture, these cosmetic items may be allowed to be sold without a manufacturing license number on the label as long as other import laws are followed.
6. If the cosmetic product container has only one label, the inner and outer label information must be combined on that label.

7. The ingredients with a concentration of more than 1% shall be stated in descending order of volume or weight at the time of their inclusion, followed by the ingredients with a concentration of less than or equal to 1%, in any order, introduced by the" INGREDIENTS" heading provided that this information is not required to appear on packs containing less than or equal to 30gm solid or semi-solid items and 60ml liquid products.
8. For cosmetic products included under schedule "S," any labelling requirement stipulated in the appropriate Indian standards framed by the Bureau of Indian Standards shall bear on the label.
9. No cosmetic product may be imported unless it is packed and labelled in accordance with the rules, and the label of the imported cosmetic product must include the cosmetic's registration certificate number, as well as the name and address of the registration certificate holder for marketing purposes in India providing that if Indian-specific labelling instructions are required for imported cosmetic products, these instructions must be pasted on each package at the bonded warehouse.
10. To export the cosmetic product, the labels on the packages of cosmetics must comply with the country's labelling specifications, but the following specifications must appear on the label of the cosmetic product's innermost package and every other outer package in which the innermost package is packed:
    a. The name of cosmetic product
    b. A particular batch number or lot number or serial number introduced by the word “Lot No.”, “Batch No.” or “serial No.” or “B”.
    c. Use before or expiry Date, if any
    d. The name and complete address of the manufacturer along with the address of manufacturing premises
    e. License Number introduced by the “Lic. No.”
    f. Internationally identified symbol in lieu of text, wherever needed providing that if the cosmetic product's consignee is not needed to be tagged with the manufacturer's name and address, the labels on containers or packages must bear a code number assigned by the state Licensing Authority.

Information on outer label:

A statement concerning the container's net contents, stated in fluid measurements for liquids, weight for solids and semi-solid items, and a numerical value if the content is subdivided providing that this disclosure is not required to be printed on the perfume container and that the content of the toilet water does not exceed 30 grams. In the case of solid and semi-solid products, 60ml is required; in the case of liquid products, 60ml is required.

Forbidding against changing the inscription on containers, wrappers or labels of cosmetic products:

No one shall be permitted to change, erase, or deform any inscription or mark made or given by the manufacturer on the container, wrapper, or label of any cosmetic product, provided that nothing in this rule applies to any change in inscription or mark made or recorded on the label, container, or wrapper of any cosmetic product with the permission of the Central Licensing Authority.

Forbidding against misleading or false claims:

Any cosmetic product may not make any claim, pretend, or convey any impression that is untrue or deceptive to the user.

Labelling of hair dyes having dyes, colors and pigments:

- Hair dyes having paraphenylenediamine or other dyes, colors and pigments shall be labelled with the following in english and local languages legends and these legends shall be indicated on both inner as well as outer label of cosmetic product having the caution “This product contains ingredients which may cause skin irritation in some cases and so a preliminary test according to the accompanying directions should first be made. This product should not be used for dyeing of eyelashes, or eyebrows, as such a use may cause blindness”.
- Each package shall also appear following information in English and local languages on the following lines for carrying out the test:

This preparation may cause serious inflammation of the skin in some cases and so a preliminary test should always be carried out to determine whether or not special sensitivity exists. To make the test, cleanse a small area of skin behind the ear or upon the inner surface of the forearm, using either soap and water or alcohol. Apply a small quantity of the hair dye as prepared for use to the area and allow it to dry. After twenty-four hours, wash the area gently with soap and water. If no irritation or inflammation is apparent, it may be assumed that no hypersensitivity to the dye exists. The test should, however, be carried out before each and every application. This preparation should on no account be used for dyeing eyebrows or eyelashes as severe inflammation of the eye or even blindness may result.

Special provisions for toothpaste having fluoride:

1. Content of fluoride in toothpaste shall not be more than one thousand ppm and the fluoride content shall be expressed in terms of ppm on tube and carton.
2. Expiry date shall appear on tube and carton.

REGULATORY PROVISIONS RELATING TO IMPORT OF COSMETICS

No cosmetic may be imported into India unless the Central Licensing Authority or any assigned person has registered the product in accordance with Drugs and Cosmetics rules 2020.

The manufacturer, or his authorized agent, or the importer in India, or the subsidiary in India authorized by the manufacturer, must submit an application for registration of a cosmetic product planned for import into India through the Central Government's online site in Form COS-1.

A manufacturer's authorization to his agent in India must be adequately authenticated either in India before a first class Magistrate or in the place of origin before a competent authority under the laws of that country or by an authority named in the First Schedule.

The applicant referred to above must also provide the following information and documents, which are listed in Part I of the Second Schedule provided however, that in the event of an application for bulk completed formulation ready to fill, the following extra documentation must be provided:

1. A valid manufacturing license from the State Licensing Authority for the finished formulation of the cosmetic ready to fill in finished form.
2. The registered brand owner of the finished product in India.

A copy of the receipt of fee deposited as stipulated in the Third Schedule must be included to the application for registration made.

The fee shall be the same for each cosmetic category and each manufacturing location, with a separate fee for each cosmetic category and variant indicated in the Fourth Schedule.

Until the online portal is operational for this purpose, the manufacturer or his approved agent, the importer in India, or the subsidiary in India authorized by the manufacturer may submit an offline application in Form COS-1 for registration of a cosmetic.

The applicant is responsible for paying testing fees directly to the Central Government-approved testing laboratory for the examination, test, and analysis of imported cosmetics in respect of cosmetics indicated for such examination in the Fifth Schedule.

The applicant shall pay the amount set forth in the Third Schedule in connection with the costs of officers authorized by the Central Licensing Authority inspecting or visiting the manufacturing facilities of cosmetics recognized in other countries, as deemed necessary.

Registration procedure:

The trade mark owner who does not have a manufacturing facility in India but plans to sell his goods through appointed importers/distributors/marketers in India must now get a registration certificate in order to continue their marketing activities in India. The Drugs Controller must receive an application for registration on Form-42, along with all other papers. The Central Licensing Authority may grant import registration certificate in Form COS-2 after examination of documents submitted with the application if satisfied, or may reject the application for reasons to be recorded in writing within six months of the date of application. In the event of refusal, the applicant has 45 days to file an appeal with the Central Government, which may, after conducting any necessary investigation, issue orders within 90 days after the date of the appeal. Before registering the import of a new cosmetic into India, the applicant must get prior authorization from the Central Licensing Authority in Form COS-3, as described in Chapter V. For the import of one or more cosmetics manufactured by the same producer, a single application and a single registration certificate in Form COS-2 may be submitted but if the cosmetics are made in a single plant or multiple factories working together as a single manufacturing unit for cosmetics intended for registration.

If the original registration certificate is disfigured, destroyed, or lost, a charge as stipulated in the Third Schedule must be paid for a duplicate copy.

Validity of import registration certificate:

1. Unless the Licensing Authority suspends or cancels a registration certificate issued by it will remain valid in perpetuity, subject to payment of the registration certificate retention fee as stipulated in the Third Schedule before the end of the five-year period from the date of issue.
2. If the licensee fails to pay the appropriate registration certificate retention fee on or before the due date, the registration certificate holder will be charged a late fee of 2% of the registration certificate retention cost for each month or part thereof within 180 days and the registration certificate will be regarded to have been cancelled if the fee is not paid within that time period.

Fresh application in case of change of constitution:

1. If a registration holder's or an overseas manufacturer's constitution changes after a registration is granted, an application for a fresh registration must be made within 180 days of the date of the change in constitution providing that the present registration will be considered valid until a new registration is issued or the application is denied by the Central Licensing Authority.
2. Within fifteen days of any change in the labelling, composition, or testing of a registered product or its specifications, the Central Licensing Authority must be notified by the manufacturer, an authorized agent, an importer, or a subsidiary in India authorized by the manufacturer, along with an undertaking that the products comply with the Bureau of Indian Standards.
3. After grant of registration, if a registration holder or overseas manufacturer's name or address changes, an application for amendment must be made in the Central Government's online portal for prior approval from the Central Licensing Authority for the said changes in registration certificate within sixty days of the date of the change.

Conditions liable for suspension or cancellation of registration certificate:

If the manufacturer, authorized agent, or importer fails to comply with any of the Registration Certificate's conditions, the Central Licensing Authority may, after giving him an opportunity to show cause why such an order should not be passed, suspend or cancel the registration certificate for such period as it sees fit, by an order in writing, stating the reasons for doing so providing that a person who is aggrieved by a Central Licensing Authority order may appeal to the Central Government within thirty days of receiving the order, and that Government may, after making such inquiries as it deems necessary and after giving the said appellant an opportunity to be heard, pass such orders as it deems appropriate in the facts and circumstances.

Import of cosmetic product already registered for import:

Any person or company may import a cosmetic manufactured in a foreign country that has already been registered for import and sale in India by submitting an application in Form COS-4 to the Central Government's online portal, together with an undertaking as stated in the Sixth Schedule.

After reviewing the documents submitted with the application, the Central Licensing Authority may grant an import registration number in

Form COS-4A if satisfied, subject to the conditions, or may reject the application for reasons to be recorded in writing within six months of the date of application. Unless it is stopped or terminated, an import registration number issued remains valid for three years from the date of issue.

If an importer fails to comply with any of the conditions of the Import Registration Number issued in Form COS-4A, the Central Licensing Authority may, after giving him an opportunity to show cause why such an order should not be passed, suspend or cancel the import registration number for as long as it sees fit, by an order in writing stating the reasons.

Forbidden of import of certain cosmetic products:

No cosmetic may be imported under the same name or any other name if its manufacturing, sale, or distribution is forbidden in the country of origin, except it is for the purpose of examination, test, or analysis. No cosmetics may be imported unless the "Use Before" or "Use By" date on the label, wrapper, or container is more than six months after the date of import.

Imports of hexachlorophene-containing cosmetics are prohibited.

After November 12th, 2014, no cosmetics that have been tested on animals can be imported into the country.

Documents to be present to the commissioner of customs:

Before any cosmetics are imported, the Commissioner of Customs must receive a declaration signed by the manufacturer or on behalf of the manufacturer, or by the importer or on behalf of the importer, stating that the cosmetics comply with the provisions of Chapter III of the Act and the rules made thereunder.

Procedure for import of cosmetic products:

1. If the official nominated by the Central Government at the port of entry has grounds to think that any cosmetic violates any of the Act's or its rules, he may take a sample of the cosmetic from the consignment for inspection.
2. If faults are discovered during the examination of the sample drawn, the officer must notify the Commissioner of Customs.
3. If the suspected violation of the Act or the rules requires a test, the officer shall send the sample to the Laboratory established for the purpose of performing such tests, and the consignment of the said cosmetic shall be held until the test report on that sample is received from the Director of the said Laboratory, or until any other offence is committed provided that the Commissioner of

Customs may make over the consignment to the importer if the importer offers a written promise not to dispose of the cosmetic without the agreement of the Commissioner of Customs and to return the consignment or any portion thereof as may be needed.

4. If the Commissioner of Customs requires the importer who has given a to return the cargo or portion thereof, he must return the consignment or portion thereof within ten days of receiving the notice.
5. If the Director of the Laboratory created by the Central Government for this purpose, or any other laboratory officer authorized by him in this capacity with the Central Government's agreement, reports to the Commissioner of Customs or to the officer that a sample of any cosmetic in a consignment violates the provisions of Chapter III of the Act or rules made thereunder and that the violation is such that it cannot be remedied by the importer, the Commissioner of Customs shall immediately communicate the report to the importer, who, within two months after receiving such communication, shall either return all cosmetics of that sort in the consignment to the nation in which they were manufactured or to the country from which they were imported, or give it over to the Central Government, who shall destroy it provided, however, that the importer may make a representation against the report to the Commissioner of Customs within thirty days of receipt of the report, who shall forward the representation along with a fresh sample of the cosmetic to the Central Licensing Authority, who shall, if necessary, pass orders thereon after obtaining the report of the Director of the Central Cosmetics Laboratory.
6. If the Central Licensing Authority, or any other person empowered by the said authority in this regard with the agreement of the Central Government, reports to the Commissioner of Customs after inspecting the cosmetic sample and, if necessary, making recommendations to the Commissioner of Customs, commissioner of Customs shall immediately communicate the report to the importer and permit him to import the cosmetic on the condition that he gives a written undertaking not to dispose of the cosmetic after obtaining a test report that the sample of the said cosmetic contravenes any provision of the Act or the rules made thereunder and that the contravention is such that it can be remedied by the importer.

Form COS-1
[See rule 12(2), and 12(7)]

Application for issue of registration certificate for import of cosmetics into India

L/We*____________________________________(Name and full address) hereby apply for the grant of registration certificate to the manufacturer, M/s________________(full address with telephone number, fax and e-mail address of the foreign manufacturer) for his manufactured cosmetics meant for import into India.

1. Names of cosmetics along with their brand name and pack size(s) and variants for registration.

Serial Number	Product or Brand of cosmetic	Brand name	Variant name	Pack sizes	Actual manufacturer and its premises

2. I/We* enclose herewith the information and undertaking specified in Part-1 of Second Schedule duly signed by the manufacturer for grant of registration certificate for the premises stated below:-
3. A fee of ……….. for registration of cosmetics for import as specified at serial number 2 above has been credited to the Central Government under the Head of Account--0210-Medical and Public Health, 04-Public Health, 104-Fees and Finest under the Cosmeties Rules, 2020--- Centralvide Challan No................ dated............. (attached in original).
4. Particulars of premises to be registered where manufacture is carried on:

   Address(s): ______________

   Telephone: ______________

   Fax: ____________________

   E-mail: __________________

   I/we undertake to comply with all the terms and conditions required to obtain registration certificate and to keep it valid during its validity period.

   Place:

   Date:

Signature ________________

Name ____________________

Designation ______________

Form COS-2
[See rule 13(1), and 13(4)]

Import registration certificate to be issued for import of cosmetics into India

Registration Certificate No. ______________Date ____________________

M/s ____(Name and full address of registered office) having factory premises at ________________________________ (full address) has been registered under rule 13 as a manufacturer and is hereby issued this Registration Certificate.

2. Name (s) of cosmetics, along with their brand names and pack size(s) and variants which may be imported under this registration certificate.

Serial Number	Product or Brand of cosmetic	Brand name	Variant name	Pack sizes	Actual manufacturer and its premises
1					
2					

3. This registration certificate shall be in force from ________ to _________ unless it is sooner suspended or cancelled under the rules.

4. This registration certificate is issued through the office of manufacturer or his authorised agent or importer in India or by the subsidiary in India authorised by the manufacturer, namely M/s .... (name and full address). .... who shall be responsible for the business activities of the manufacturer, in India in all respects.

5. This Registration Certificate is subject to the conditions, stated below and to such other conditions as may be specified in the Drugs and Cosmetics Act, 1940 and the rules made thereunder, from time to time in this regard.

Place: ___________

Date: ___________

CENTRAL LICENSING AUTHORITY

Seal/Stamp

Form COS-3
[See rule 13(3), 23(3), 32(2) and 32(3)]

Permission to import or manufacture new cosmetics in India

Number of the permission and date of issue. .... M/s. .... having address. .... is hereby permitted to import or manufacture the following new cosmetic under rule 32 of the Cosmetics Rules, 2020.

1. Name of the cosmetic
2. Category or intended use
3. Composition of the product
4. Any special instruction

Dated:

Signature:

Name and Designation of Central Licensing Authority:

Form COS-4
[See rule 17(1)]

Application for issue of Import Registration Number for Import of already registered cosmetics

I/We* ____ (Name and full address of importer) hereby apply for the grant of registration number for Import of already registered cosmetics, meant for import into India.

1. Detail of cosmetics

Serial Number	Name of cosmetic	(Name of manufacturer and address)	Pack sizes	Registration Certificate Number
1				
2				
3				

2. I/We* enclose herewith the information and undertaking specified in Sixth Schedule duly signed.

3. I/we undertake to comply with all the terms and conditions required to obtain registration number and to keep it valid during its validity period.

Address(s): ______________

Telephone: ______________

Fax: ____________________

E-mail: _________________

Place:

Date:

Signature ________________

Name ___________________

Designation ______________

Form COS-4A
[See rule 17(2)

Import Registration Number to be issued for import of already registered cosmetics into India

Import Registration No. _____________ Date _________________

1. M/s ____________________________ (Name and full Address of importer) has been registered under rule 17 as an importer and is hereby issued this Import Registration Number for import of already registered cosmetics into India.

2. Detail of cosmetics

Serial Number	Name of cosmetic (s)	Pack sizes	Name and address of manufacturer
1			
2			
3			

3. This Import Registration Number shall remain valid for three years unless it is sooner suspended or cancelled under the Cosmetics Rules, 2020.

4. This Import Registration Number is subject to the conditions stated below and to such other conditions as may be specified in the rules for the time being in force under the Cosmetics Rules, 2020.

Place: __________

Date: __________

Central Licensing Authority

Seal/Stamp

MISBRANDED AND SPURIOUS COSMETICS

Misbranded cosmetics:

A cosmetic is considered misbranded:

1. If it has a color that is not prescribed, or
2. If it is not labelled in the prescribed manner, or
3. If the label, container, or anything else that comes with the cosmetic contains any statement that is incorrect or deceptive in any way.

Example:

A container having cosmetic claimed to contain 20 grams of a particular ingredient but was almost less than 50% than its claimed amount. Hence in this case, the label on the container was deceptive or misleading in the particulars.

Spurious cosmetics:

A cosmetic is considered spurious:

1. If it's made under a brand name that belongs to another cosmetic, or
2. If the name of an individual or a firm professing to be the cosmetic's maker appears on the label or container, that individual or company is fictional or does not exist, or
3. If it is a deceptive imitation of, substitute for, or resembles another cosmetic in any way, or bears the name of another cosmetic on its label or container, unless it is explicitly and conspicuously marked to reflect its real character and lack of identification with such other cosmetic, or
4. If it claims to be a product of a company for which it is not a true product

Example: Luk for Lux, Sun max for Super master

Note: Offences and penalties related to misbranded and spurious cosmetics has been explained at last of the chapter under the heading of offences and penalties.

CHAPTER 2

Regulatory Requirements for Manufacturing of Cosmetics

Procedure for obtaining the license for manufacturing of cosmetics:

- Any individual who plans to manufacture cosmetics must apply to the state Licensing Authority for a license to manufacture for sale or distribution.
- The applicant must apply online using Form COS-5 for a license and pay the fees listed in the third schedule (Rs. 10000 for 10 items in each category of cosmetic) along with specified documents in part II of schedule second provided that an offline application may be made on Form COS-5 if the online portal is not operational till that time.
- In the event of a novel cosmetic, the applicant must acquire previous approval from the Central Licensing Authority in Form COS-3, as described in Chapter V, and the State Licensing Authority will not provide a license to manufacture any cosmetic without this permission.
- Moreover the documents listed in part II of the Second Schedule, the applicant must submit a self-declaration in Form COS-7 stating that the applicant complies with Good Manufacturing Practices, as well as the requirements for premises, plants, and equipment for the manufacture of cosmetics listed in the Seventh Schedule.
- The State Licensing Authority shall grant a license within 45 days of receiving an application accompanied by the fee and specified documents, after scrutinizing the application and documents and concluding that the Act and rules are met provided that if the State Licensing Authority believes the applicant has not met the Act's and rules' requirements, the applicant will be notified within 45 days of the application's submission.

- The applicant may manufacture cosmetics for sale or distribution after receiving the license and uploading a copy of the license to the Central Drugs Standard Control Organization's website.
- The State Licensing Authority shall inspect the site and verify the information contained in the self-certificate in Form COS-7 within thirty days of the date of award of license.
- The license must be presumed valid for all purposes if the State Licensing Authority or any other person empowered to do so fails to inspect and verify the site of the license.
- If it is found during the inspection that the self-certificate contained any misleading information, the Licensing Authority may cancel the license after giving the licensee an opportunity to show cause provided that if the State Licensing Authority believes that deficiencies can be removed, the said authority may issue directions to the licensee to stop manufacturing until the requirements are met, and when the requirements are met, the applicant must notify the Licensing Authority, and the Licensing Authority, if satisfied, may issue the license.
- If the original license is defaced, damaged, or lost, a duplicate copy may be ordered from the State Licensing Authority for a price as indicated in the Third Schedule.

List of documents required to obtain the license for manufacturing of cosmetics:

1. Application form
2. Fee challan receipt, if payment not made through an online portal
3. A copy of the manufacturing area's approved layout plan.
4. A list of machines and equipment
5. Documents pertaining to the firm's formation, such as the partnership deed, memorandum, and articles of organization, and so on.
6. Full details of the qualified technical employees employed for cosmetics manufacturing and testing, including copies of their educational credentials and experience certifications, as well as a letter of approval as competent staff. A consent letter from the competent technical staff is necessary for full-time employment with the application firm.

7. A list of cosmetics including their composition formulas, and labelling methods in triplicate as well as the project to be submitted.
8. Documents pertaining to the ownership of the cosmetic brand, whether registered or under trademark, if applicable.
9. The full name of the proprietor or partners, as applicable, must be included in the application. The entire name of the Directors who sign the application or the Authorized signatory, if any, must be supplied in the application in the event of private or public limited companies.
10. Form COS-7 self-certification of compliance with Good Manufacturing Practices (GMP) for cosmetics manufacturing.

Undertakings required to obtain the manufacturing license for cosmetics:

1. I/We agree to abide by all terms placed on the license for the manufacture of cosmetics, as required by the Cosmetics Rules, 2020.
2. I/We declare that we are manufacturing the cosmetics listed in this Schedule at the above-mentioned location, and that we will notify you of any changes in the location where manufacturing will take place.
3. I/We will abide by the terms of Chapter IV of the Cosmetics Rules for 2020.
4. Every cosmetic manufactured for sale or distribution in India must meet the criteria set out in the Ninth Schedule by the Bureau of Indian Standards.
5. I/We declare that we have never tested any of our cosmetics on animals.
6. I/We will notify the Licensing Authority within thirty days of any change in the labelling, composition, or testing of the licensed product or its specifications, along with an assurance that the products will meet the standards set forth by the Bureau of Indian Standards as referred to in the Ninth Schedule.
7. I/We will comply with any additional obligations imposed by the Government of India under the Act and the Rules promulgated thereunder.
8. I/We agree to allow the Licensing Authority, or any person authorized by him in that capacity, to take samples of the cosmetics for testing if the Licensing Authority deems it essential.

9. I/We agree that if the State Licensing Authority or any person appointed by the ability discovers any flaw during an inspection, the State Licensing Authority has the complete authority to cancel or provide any direction for improvement in the said premises in respect of the above stated cosmetics. In addition, I shall not seek any damages or other compensation for any actions taken by the State Liquor Authority.

Manufacturing at more than one premises:

If cosmetics are made at more than one premise, a separate application must be submitted for each premise, and a separate license must be secured for each premise.

Issue of license for manufacturing of cosmetics:

The license for manufacturing of cosmetics for sale and distribution is issued in Form COS- 8.

Conditions of license for manufacturing of cosmetics:

A license in Form COS- 8 is subject to the terms and conditions indicated therein, as well as the following additional terms and conditions:

1. Cosmetics must be manufactured under the guidance and personal supervision of competent technical employees, which must include at least one full-time employee with at least one of the following qualifications:
   a. Holds a Pharmacy Diploma from the Pharmacy Council of India, as required by the Pharmacy Act of 1948. (8 of 1948), or
   b. Is registered under the Pharmacy Act, 1948, or
   c. Has passed the Intermediate Examination, which includes Chemistry as one of the subjects, or an examination recognized by the Licensing Authority as equivalent, or
   d. Holds a bachelor's degree in Cosmetic Technology from a recognized institution.
2. The factory must adhere to the standards and circumstances set forth in the Seventh Schedule.
3. The manufacturer shall either:
   a. Establish and maintain enough personnel, facilities, and laboratory equipment for testing cosmetics and the raw materials used in their manufacture.

b. Make arrangements for such tests with a laboratory that has been approved by the Central Licensing Authority under Chapter VIII of the rules and is recognized by the National Accreditation Board for Testing and Calibration Laboratories (NABL).

4. The applicant must keep documentation for the following:
   a. Documentation pertaining to the premises' ownership, rental, or other basis of occupation, as mentioned in the application for license or the license granted,
   b. The firm's constitution, or
   c. Any other document that may be required for verifying the accuracy of the applicant's or licensee's representations made when applying for or after receiving the license, as the case may be.
5. The licensee must follow the provisions of the Act and the regulations promulgated thereunder, as well as any additional requirements that may be specified in future rules promulgated under Chapter IV of the Act.
6. The licensee must keep a record of the specifics of each batch of cosmetics he manufactures, as well as the raw materials used in those batches, as defined in the Eighth Schedule, for a period of three years after the batch's expiration date.
7. If the license issued in Form COS- 8 in respect of manufacturing facilities is cancelled or suspended, the license in Form COS- 9 is presumed to be cancelled or suspended.
8. The licensee must test each batch or lot of raw materials used in the cosmetics manufacturing process, as well as each batch of the finished product, and keep documents or registers detailing the results of such testing. The records or registers must be kept for three years following the date of manufacture.
9. The licensee must allow an Inspector appointed under the Act to enter any premises where the manufacture of a substance for which the license is issued is carried on, inspect the premises, and take samples of the manufactured products for which a receipt shall be issued in Form COS-10, with or without prior notice.
10. The licensee must allow an Inspector to see any registers and records kept under these rules, and must provide the Inspector with any information he may require for the purpose of determining whether the Act's and rules' provisions have been followed.

11. The licensee must keep an Inspection book in Form COS-11 on hand so that an Inspector can record his impressions and any deficiencies found.
12. In the event of a change in labelling, composition, testing, specification, or documentation of any of the cosmetics pertaining to this license, the manufacturer shall notify the Licensing Authority in writing within thirty days, along with an undertaking that the products comply with the standards laid down by the Bureau of Indian Standards as referred to in the Ninth Schedule.
13. Any change in the constitution of the firm operating under the license must be reported to the Licensing Authority in writing. If the firm's constitution changes, the current license will be considered valid for a maximum of six months from the date of the change, unless a new license has been obtained in the interim.
14. After the grant of a license, if a manufacturer's name or address changes, an application for amendment must be submitted to the state government for prior approval from licensing authorities for the said changes in manufacturing license within sixty days of the date of the change.

Grant or refusal of license:

- If the Licensing Authority is satisfied that the requirements of the regulations under the Act have been met and that the terms of the license and the rules under the Act will be followed, he will issue a license in Form COS-8, as the case may be.
- If the Licensing Authority is not satisfied, he will reject the application and notify the applicant of the reasons for the denial as well as the requirements that must be met before a license may be given or renewed. He will also provide a copy of the inspection report to the applicant.

Further apply for license after refusal:

If the applicant informs the State Licensing Authority within six months of the rejection of an application for a license that the requirements laid down in the Act and these rules have been met and deposits the fee as specified in the Third Schedule, the State Licensing Authority may, after further scrutiny and on being satisfied that the requirements for grant of a license have been met, grant the license in Form COS-8.

License Validity:

- Unless it is suspended or cancelled by the State Licensing Authority, a license issued in Form COS- 8 remains valid in perpetuity, subject to payment of the license retention fee as specified in the Third Schedule before the end of the five-year period from the date of issue.

- If the licensee fails to pay the required license retention fee on or before the due date as specified the licensee will be charged a late fee of 2% of the license retention fee for each month or part thereof within one hundred days.

PROHIBITION OF MANUFACTURE AND SALE OF CERTAIN COSMETICS

Manufacturing and / or sale of following cosmetics is prohibited under the Act and rules made thereunder:

1. Any cosmetic that is not of standard quality, is misbranded, or is a forgery.
2. Any cosmetic containing a component that makes it dangerous or harmful to use according to the recommendations specified or recommended.
3. Any cosmetic manufactured in violation of the Act's and rules' clauses.
4. Except for toilet soap containing hexachlorophene, any cosmetic using hexachlorophene is prohibited.
5. Any cosmetic that contains lead or arsenic compounds as a coloring agent.
6. Any cosmetic that contains mercurial compounds.
7. Any cosmetic that contains colors that aren't listed in Act and rules thereunder.
8. A toothpaste or toothpowder having tobacco.

LOAN LICENSE

Loan license is a cosmetic manufacturing license granted by the State Licensing Authority under regulations 25 to a person who plans to use the manufacturing site of another licensee to manufacture the cosmetic made by the licensee at that site.

The rules and regulations to apply for obtaining the loan license and granting the loan license are same as for license for owned premises except the forms which are following:

To obtain the loan license, the applicant must apply online using Form COS-6 and license will be issued using the Form COS-9.

Form COS- 6 [See rule 23(2)]

Application for grant of a loan license to manufacture cosmetics for sale or for distribution

1. I/We .... of..hereby apply for grant of a loan license to manufacture cosmetics, for sale, on the Premises situated at ....C/o.................... the following cosmetics:

2. Details of cosmetic products:

Serial Number	Name of cosmetic	Name of Ingredients	Specifications or Standards or Grade of Ingredients	Percentage of ingredients	Function of ingredients

3. The names, qualifications and experience of the expert staff actually connected with the manufacture and testing of the specified products in the manufacturing premises.

4. I/We enclose

(a) A true copy of a letter from me/us to the manufacturing concern whose manufacturing capacity is intended to be utilized by me/us.

(b) A true copy of a letter from - the manufacturing concern that they agree to lend the services of their expert staff, equipment and premises for the manufacture of each item required by me / us and they will analyse every batch of and maintain the registers of raw materials, finished products and reports of analysis separately in this behalf.

(c) Specimens of labels, cartons of the products proposed to be manufactured.

5. A fee of rupees.....................has been credited to Government under the head of Account..............

Date....................
Signature...............................

Enter here the name and address of the manufacturing concern where the manufacture will be actually carried out and also their license number.

Form COS- 9

[See rule 25, 26(g), 27(1), 27(3), 28 and 30(1)]

Loan license to manufacture cosmetics for sale or for distribution

1. Number of license and date of issue.............................

2. .... of .... is here by granted a loan license to manufacture the following cosmetics on the premises situated at .C/o. .... under the direction and personal supervision of the following technical staff :

a. Names of the technical staff.............................

b. Details of cosmetic products

Serial Number	Name of Cosmetic	Name of Ingredients	Specifications or Standards or Grade of Ingredients	Percentage of Ingredients	Function of Ingredients

3. The licence unless sooner suspended or cancelled shall continue to remain valid. However, the compliance with the conditions of licence and the provisions of the Drugs and Cosmetics Act and Rules shall be assessed at least once in a year.

4. The license is subject to the conditions stated below and to such other conditions as are specified in the rules for the time being in force under the Drugs and Cosmetics Act, 1940.

State Licensing Authority

Date.........................

Signature...................

Designation............

Various forms to be filled related to import and manufacturing of cosmetics

Subject	Forms
Application for registration certificate for import of cosmetics in India	COS-1
Import registration certificate to be granted for import of cosmetics in India	COS-2
Permission to import or manufacturing of new cosmetic in India	COS-3
Application for granting the Import Registration Number for import of already registered cosmetics	COS-4
Granting the Import Registration for import of already registered cosmetics into India	COS-4A
Application for granting the license to manufacture cosmetics for sale or distribution	COS-5
Application for granting the loan license to manufacture cosmetics for sale or distribution	COS-6
Self-certificate of compliance of GMP for manufacture of cosmetics	COS-7
Grant of license to manufacture cosmetics for sale or distribution	COS-8
Grant of Loan license to manufacture cosmetics for sale or distribution	COS-9
Application for granting the permission for new cosmetics for obtaining import registration certificate or manufacturing license	COS-12

Fee to be paid for granting or renewal or license or registration certificate for cosmetics

SUBJECT	FEE
REGISTRATION CERTIFICATES	
a. Fee for granting or maintaining a registration certificate for each category of cosmetic	1000 dollar
b. Fee for granting or maintaining a registration certificate for additional category of cosmetic	1000 dollar
c. Fee for granting or maintaining a registration certificate for each variant of cosmetic	50 dollar
d. Fee for granting or maintaining a registration certificate for each manufacturing premises	500 dollar
e. Fee for issuance of permission for new cosmetic	500 dollar
f. Fee for granting a duplicate copy of the registration certificate in case of damaging or losing the certificate	200 dollar
g. Fee for inspection of each overseas manufacturing site of cosmetics	5000 dollar

Contd....

MANUFACTURING LICENSE	
a. Fee for granting and maintaining the license for manufacturing of the cosmetics for sale or distribution up to 10 items in each category of cosmetics in Form COS-8	10000 rupees
b. Fee for granting and maintaining the license for manufacturing of the cosmetics for sale or distribution of each additional items of the category of cosmetic in Form COS-8	500 rupees
c. Fee for granting and maintaining the license for manufacturing of cosmetics for sale or distribution of 10 items of each additional category of cosmetic in Form COS-8	10000 rupees
d. Fee for granting and maintaining the loan license for manufacturing of cosmetics for sale or distribution up to 10 items of each category of cosmetics in Form COS-9	10000 rupees
e. Fee for granting and maintaining the loan license for manufacturing of cosmetics for sale or distribution of each additional items of the category of cosmetic in Form COS-9	500 rupees
f. Fee for granting the duplicate copy of the license and loan license in Form COS- 8 and Form COS- 9 respectively in case of damaging or losing the original license	500 rupees
g. Fee for subsequent application after rejection	1000 rupees

Various schedules related to import, manufacturing and labelling of cosmetics for sale or distribution included in Cosmetics Rules 2020

S. No.	Schedules	Specifications
1	Schedule-I	Authorization from manufacturer
2	Schedule-II Part I	Information and undertaking required to be furnished by the manufacturer or his authorized importer or distributor or agent with the application form for import registration certificate
3	Schedule-II Part II	Information and undertaking required to be furnished by the manufacturer with the application form for grant of manufacturing license or loan license
4	Schedule-III	Fee to be paid for obtaining the license, permission and registration certificate
5	Schedule-IV	List of categories of cosmetics for import
6	Schedule-V	Fee to be paid for test or analysis by the Central cosmetics laboratories or by the state laboratories

Contd....

S. No.	Schedules	Specifications
7	Schedule-VI	Undertaking for the import of cosmetics to be submitted by the importer with application form for Import Registration Number
8	Schedule-VII	Good manufacturing practices and requirements of premises, plants and equipment for manufacture of cosmetics
9	Schedule-VIII	Manufacturing and raw material records
10	Schedule-IX	Standards for cosmetics
11	Schedule-X Part I	List of colorants allowed for use in cosmetic products as given under IS: 4707 (Part 1) of standards of cosmetics
12	Schedule-X Part II	List of colors permitted to be used in soaps
13	Schedule-XI	Good laboratory practices and requirements of premises and equipment
14	Schedule-XII	Extent and conditions of exemption of various class of cosmetics
15	Schedule-XIII	Word "Cosmetics" is omitted from Drugs and Cosmetics Rules 1945

OFFENCES AND PENALTIES

Offences	Penalties	
	First conviction	**Further conviction**
Offences and penalties related to import of cosmetics		
Import of adulterated or spurious cosmetics or any cosmetic having any ingredient which may render it unsafe or harmful for use under the recommended directions	Imprisonment upto 3 years along with fine upto 5000 rupees	Imprisonment upto 5 years or fine upto 10000 rupees or both
Import of cosmetics other than specified above and whose import is prohibited	Imprisonment upto 6 months or fine upto 500 rupees or both	Imprisonment upto I year or fine upto 1000 rupees or both
Import of any cosmetic in contravention of any notification issued under section 10A	Imprisonment upto 3 years or fine upto 5000 rupees or both	

Contd....

Offences and penalties related to manufacture and sale of cosmetics	
Manufacturing of spurious cosmetic for sale, distribution, stocking	Imprisonment up to 3 years and fine
Manufacturing of any other cosmetic in contravention of this chapter or rules thereunder for sale, distribution, stocking	Imprisonment upto 1 year or fine upto 1000 rupees or both
Not disclose the name of a manufacturer or premises where manufactured cosmetic was kept	Imprisonment up to 1 year or fine up to 1000 rupees or both
Unable to keep the records of manufacturing and sale of cosmetics in specified manner	Imprisonment up to 3 years or fine up to 5000 rupees or both

CHAPTER 3

Biological Aspects of Cosmetics

Skin

Skin is one of the largest organ of the body and accounts about 15% of total body weight of an adult. Skin occupied 2500 cm^2 area at time of birth and 18000 cm^2 in an adult. The weight of skin is 4.8 kg in male and 3.2 kg in female. It is not only a protective wrapper for the body but also serves as frontier in between the body of the organism and external environment. It is not only responsible to control the loss of important fluids from the body but also provides cushions against mechanical injuries to the body, prevents the penetration of toxic material into the body and also regulate the body temperature.

Structure of skin

Skin is made up of three layers having special anatomy and physiology (Figure 3.1)

1. Epidermis
2. Dermis
3. Hypodermis

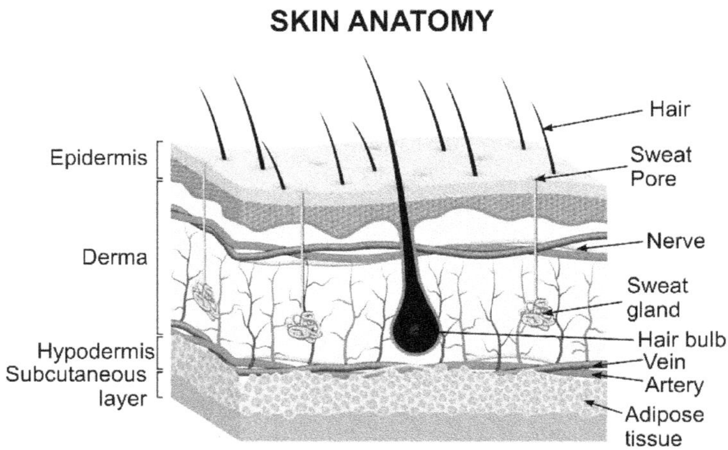

Figure 3.1: Representation of various layers of skin.

Epidermis

It is the outermost layer of the skin serves as barrier for the infections. It is stratified squamous epithelial layer made up of four type of cells namely keratinocytes, melanocytes, Langerhans cells, and merkel cells. Keratinocytes are most abundant type of cells in epidermis accounting for about 90% of the total epidermal cells responsible for production of a protein keratin (tough, protective protein) followed by melanocytes accounting for 8% of total epidermal cells responsible for synthesizing a protein pigment melanin (skin color pigment which absorbs ultra violet radiations), Langerhans cells, a type of immune cells in the skin, and kerner cells responsible for touch. Epidermis is composed of five following layers (Figure 3.2).

1. Stratum basale or stratum germinativum
2. Stratum spinosum
3. Stratum granulosum
4. Stratum lucidum
5. Stratum corneum

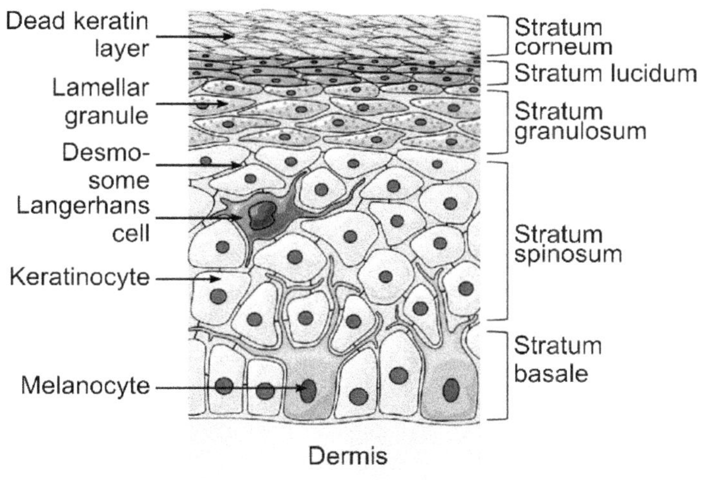

Figure 3.2: Representation of various layers of epidermis.

Stratum basale

It is the innermost layer of the epidermis isolated from the dermis by basal lamina (basement membrane) and attached to it by hemidesmosomes. It contains columnar or cuboidal mitotically active stem cells responsible for continuous production of keratinocytes. In addition, it also contains melanocytes.

Stratum spinosum

It is the layer present just above the stratum basale and is composed of 8-10 cell layers of spiny shape having different structure, shapes, and subcellular properties. It is also termed as prickly cells layer or squamous cell layer. This layer may contains Langerhans cells.

Stratum granulosum

It is the layer present just above the stratum spinosum and most superficial layer having the living cells. It is 3-5 cell layers of diamond shape having keratohyaline granules and lamellar granules. Keratohyaline granules possess keratin precursors that ultimately cluster followed by cross-linking and then formation of bundles. The lamellar granules possess the glycolipids that released to the surface of cells and acts as glue leading to stucking of cells together.

Stratum lucidum

It is 2-3 cell layers, found in thicker skin such as palm skin and soles skin. It is a thin, clear layer of dead skin cells in the epidermis composed of keratinocytes filled with protein “eleidin”. Stratum lucidum is derived from a greek language which means clear layer and it is because when observed under microscope, it is translucent.

Stratum corneum

It is the uppermost layer of the epidermis serves as barrier between the body and external environment. It is composed of 20-30 thin cell layers continuously shedding dead keratinocytes. It is also termed as horny layer because the cells of this layer are very tough like horn of an animal. The cells of this layer are continuously shaded and replaced by newer cells from the deeper layers of the epidermis. This shedding process of cells reduces with age. In this layer, dead keratinocytes release defensins which are the part of first immune defense.

Dermis

This is the deeper, thickest layer of the skin exists between epidermis and hypodermis, linked to epidermis at the level of basal membrane. It is made up of two layers namely papillary layer and reticular layer. The papillary layer is thinner, upper layer made up of loose connective tissues while the reticular layer is thicker, lower layer made up of dense connective tissues. The dermis contains various structure namely connective tissues especially collagen and elastin, lymph vessels, blood vessels, sweat glands, sebaceous glands, nerve endings, and hair follicles. Dermis is mainly composed of three types of tissues which are elastin, collagen, and reticulum. The main functions of the dermis include protection, provide nutrition to the epidermis, wound healing, and cushioning the inner structures of skin from mechanical hazards.

Hypodermis

It is the innermost, thickest subcutaneous layer of skin present beneath the dermis. It mainly consists of fat rich tissues along with some skin appendages such as sensory neurons, hair follicles, and blood vessels. The main functions of the hypodermis include providing structural support to the skin, insulation of the body from cold, and shock absorption.

Biological aspects of skin in relation to dry skin

Dry skin, also known as xerosis, is characterized by rough, scaly, or flaky skin. It also often causes pruritus and a lack of skin elasticity. It can be a common symptom of several skin illnesses, including asteatotic eczema (eczema craquelé), psoriasis, ichthyosis, irritating contact dermatitis, and atopic dermatitis.

The uppermost layer of skin (Stratum corneum) offers a feature termed as barrier function which keeps the moisture inside the skin and harmful chemicals outside the skin on proper functioning. However, when the barrier function is disturbed then moisture inside the skin evaporates leaving the skin susceptible and dry (Figure 3.3).

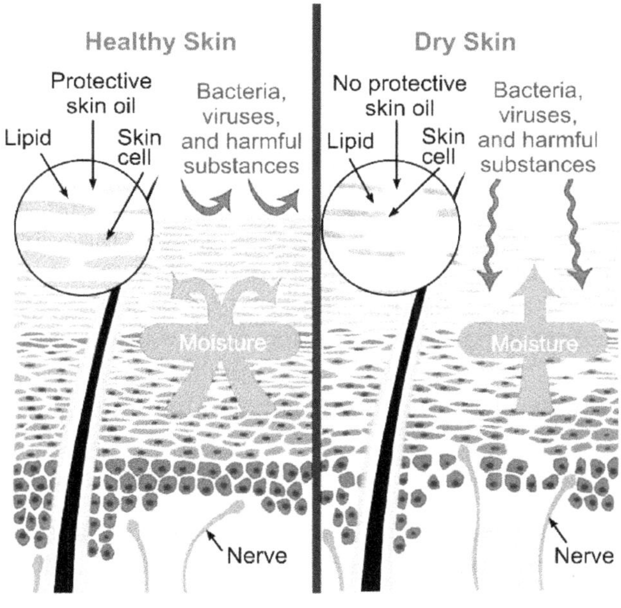

Figure 3.3: Pictorial representation of dry skin verses healthy skin.

Pathophysiology of dry skin

Dry skin originates due to disturbed skin barrier function. This skin barrier is made up of 15 to 20 layers of corneocytes arranged in a regular columnar pattern within the stratum corneum of the skin, and embedded in a lipid intercellular substance. These corneocytes derives from keratinocytes, which gradually differentiate into cells without nuclei and organelles that have a stiff horn protein sheath as they move toward the skin's surface. Any disturbance in the number, size, or arrangement of corneocytes impairs the functioning of skin barrier.

Within keratinocytes in the lower stratum corneum, filaggrin is produced by profilaggrin which have an essential role for fortifying the function of skin barrier by enabling the keratin filaments to crosslink through disulphide bonds. Hence any disturbance in production of filaggrin or mutations in filaggrin leads to dry skin.

For healthy skin, the optimum moisture content preserved by stratum corneum is 10-30%. Low levels of humidity cause the stratum corneum to lose water to the environment, necessitating dermal and lower epidermal layer replacement. Reduced water content in this layer leads to aberrant corneocyte desquamation, which damages the skin barrier and increases transepidermal water loss (TEWL).

To keep the skin barrier intact, sphingolipids, free sterols, and free fatty acids are necessary. Ceramides are one of these elements that make up a large amount of the stratum corneum's weight, making them an important lipid component. Glycosylation of ceramides results in the formation of sphingolipids, which are essential for maintaining the integrity of the skin barrier. An increase in transepidermal water loss acts as a cue to rebuild the skin barrier by inducing a series of cytokine modifications that ultimately result in the creation of ceramides.

Natural moisturizing factors (NMFs) such as lactic acid, sugars, amino acids, and urea are critical to maintain the water retention capacity of skin. NMFs produced by the breakdown of filaggrin make up about 10% of the stratum corneum's dry weight. Alteration in the structure or composition of these elements may result in decreased stratum corneum hydration and dry skin with clinical symptoms such fissuring, dullness, roughness, scaliness, tightness, itching and in extreme situations, bleeding.

Causes for dry skin

There are various causes which can disturbed the above mentioned factors required for smooth functioning of the natural skin barrier. These causes can be categorized as:

External causes

Skin cleansing

Overexposure to water can strip the skin of its natural oils, leaving it dry. The daily activities that leads to dry skin:

- Frequently taking hot showers for longer period
- Extreme scrubbing of the skin
- Hand washing on frequent basis
- Use of tough soaps
- Use of detergents and alkaline soaps
- Use of sanitizers in excessive

Environmental factors

Various environmental factors can lead to dry skin. These factors include

- Overexposure to sunlight and wind
- Use of air conditioning system
- Living in areas where humidity is poor like deserts

Occupational factors

Some persons are exposed to substances that dehydrate the skin on a regular basis, leading to dry skin. This includes those who work in construction, agriculture, hair salons, cleaning, catering, and metalworking, among other industries. Healthcare workers are more likely to experience dry skin since they constantly have to wash their hands.

Internal causes

These are the uncontrollable elements, which include a number of illnesses that might result in dry skin.

Inflammatory skin disorders

Various inflammatory skin disorders which can lead to dry skin include:

- Psoriasis
- Atopic dermatitis
- Irritant contact dermatitis
- Allergic contact dermatitis
- Seborrheic dermatitis
- Dyshidrotic eczema
- Scabies
- Perioral dermatitis

- Nummular eczema
- Lichen planus
- Skin infections
- Cutaneous T cell lymphoma
- Xeroderma pigmentosum
- Urticaria
- Drug eruptions

Infectious dermatose

These are the skin conditions brought on by parasites, fungus, viruses, or bacteria. They can also lead to dry skin in the chronic stage. Scabies and pediculosis are two symptoms of the illness.

Genodermatoses

It refers to uncommon hereditary skin conditions that, depending on the type, might affect the skin's structure, color, and texture. Common examples include ichthyosis, which causes extremely dry skin.

Neoplasms

Certain diseases such as cutaneous lymphoma, a white cell malignancy can also lead to dry skin.

Dietary causes

- Dietary deficiencies of vitamin A, D, zinc, iron etc. can lead to dry skin
- Inadequate fluid intake and extreme perspiration can also lead to dry skin.

Psychiatric disorders

- The patients of obsessive compulsive disorder (OCD) are addict to clean and wash frequently which can lead to dry skin.
- The patients of anorexia nervosa have inadequate intake of essential nutrition required to keep skin healthy due to self-starvation which leads to dry skin.
- The extreme alcohol intake causes dehydration which can lead to dry skin. The excessive alcoholism results in a disorder termed as alcohol use disorder (AUD) which results in various skin disorders such as dry skin, skin infection, and skin cancer.

Endocrine and metabolic disorders

There are some endocrine and metabolic disorders which can lead to dry skin which are following:

- Diabetes mellitus
- Liver disorders such as liver cirrhosis, extrahepatic cholestasis etc
- Malabsorption
- Hypothyroidism
- Hyperthyroidism

Hormonal imbalance

The hormonal imbalance in various conditions such as menopause, pregnancy, and andropause causes loss of skin elasticity which leads to dry skin.

Infections

Various infections like hepatitis B, hepatitis C, diarrheal infections can cause dry skin.

Drug associated causes

The administration of drugs of various categories like beta b ockers, topical corticosteroids, lipid lowering agents, diuretics, calcium antagonists, antirheumatic drugs, contraceptives/antiandrogens, cytostatic agents, radiation dermatitis, immunomodulators can lead to dry skin.

Symptoms of dry skin

There are various symptoms of dry symptoms which has been illustrated in the Figure 3.4.

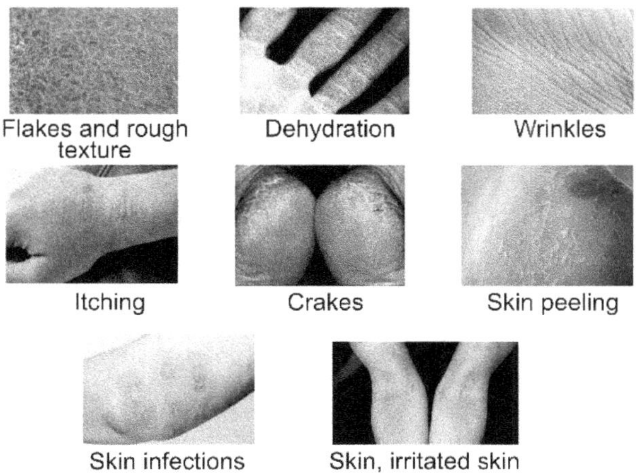

Figure 3.4: Pictorial representation of various symptoms of dry skin.

Diet recommendations

- Intake of foods having omega-3 fatty acid due to their potential to retain moisture and strengthen the skin.
- Intake of vitamin E rich diet due to its powerful anti-oxidant property.
- Intake of fruits having high content of water and low sugar to hydrate and protect the skin.
- Intake of plenty of water to retain the hydration of the skin.
- Intake of green tea due to possession of high amount of antioxidants which help to repair the damaged skin.
- Intake of green vegetables, fishes, eggs, almonds etc. which help to keep the skin soft and shiny.

Biological aspects of Skin in relation to acne

Acne vulgaris is a prevalent inflammatory skin condition of the pilosebaceous unit that has a long-lasting course. It is usually induced throughout adolescence by the bacterial species *Cutibacterium acnes* under the influence of normal circulating levels of dehydroepiandrosterone. Usually on the face, the ailment presents as nodules, pustules, or papules, though it can also affect the upper arms, back, and trunk. A number of interrelated elements combine during the pathophysiology of acne vulgaris to eventually generate the main lesion termed as "comedo". Even though teenagers are the age group most likely to experience acne vulgaris, people of all ages can still be affected. This condition can range in severity from moderate types with few comedones to more severe forms with disfiguring inflammatory symptoms that can cause scarring, hyperpigmentation, and negative psychological impacts (Figure 3.5).

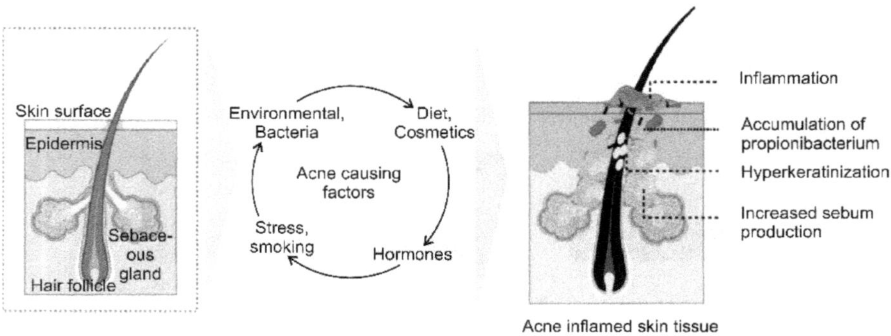

Figure 3.5: Structure of healthy and acne skin.

Pathophysiology of Acne

The four key elements, excessive sebum production, hyperkeratinization of pilosebaceous follicles, inflammation, and hyperproliferation of Propionibacterium acnes play an important role in pathophysiology of acne DNA methylation also play a role in development of acne.

Increased Sebum production

One of the main factors contributing to the development of acne is an increase in sebum production in the hair follicles. Androgen hormones, particularly testosterone and Insulin Growth Hormone (IGH-1), are known to enhance sebum synthesis and release. Higher sebum production is clearly correlated with the frequency and severity of acne lesions. Therefore, it is an important factor that patients with acne vulgaris should take into consideration.

Hyperkeratinization of pilosebaceous follicles

Single-cell keratinocytes are typically shed by healthy follicles into the lumen, where they are eventually removed. However, hyperproliferating keratinocytes that are not shed into the lumen cause acne patients' pilosebaceous follicles to accumulate irregularly desquamated corneocytes together with lipids and monofilaments.

Hyperproliferation of Propionibacterium acnes

Cutibacterium acnes, originally identified as Propionibacterium acnes, is a gram-positive, lipophilic, anaerobic pathogen that thrives in sebaceous follicles due to their high sebum production and ability to serve as an ideal anaerobic growth medium. P. acnes secretes a lipase enzyme that breaks down sebum triglycerides into fatty acids and glycerol, which can cause skin irritation and comedones to form resulting in acne.

Inflammation

In keeping with the previous P. acne process, the inflammatory process starts as soon as the immune system recognizes P. acnes. Strong inflammatory responses to P. acnes can result in the production of chemostatic agents such as neutrophils, macrophages, and lymphocytes. Furthermore, these disorders result in follicular destruction, rupture, and the dermal layer's release of bacteria, fatty acids, and lipids. The inflammatory lesions caused by these mechanistic processes include ulcers (pustules, nodules, cysts, and papules). Compared to inflammatory lesions, non-inflammatory lesions are smaller and less pus-filled.

DNA methylation

In the field of dermatology, DNA methylation is one of the well-studied types of epigenetic modification which is receiving more interest due to its role in the mechanisms behind inflammatory, autoimmune, and malignant skin diseases. Research has demonstrated that DNA methylation contributes to the development and course of inflammatory skin conditions, including psoriasis, hidradenitis suppurativa, and atopic dermatitis. The development of acne vulgaris is significantly influenced by epigenetics, which may also provide light on the disease's molecular causes and possible treatment options.

Types of acne lesions

Acne lesions have been categorized into two categories namely inflammatory (Cyst, nodule, papule, and pustule) and non-inflammatory (White heads and black heads) which have been illustrated in the Figure 3.6.

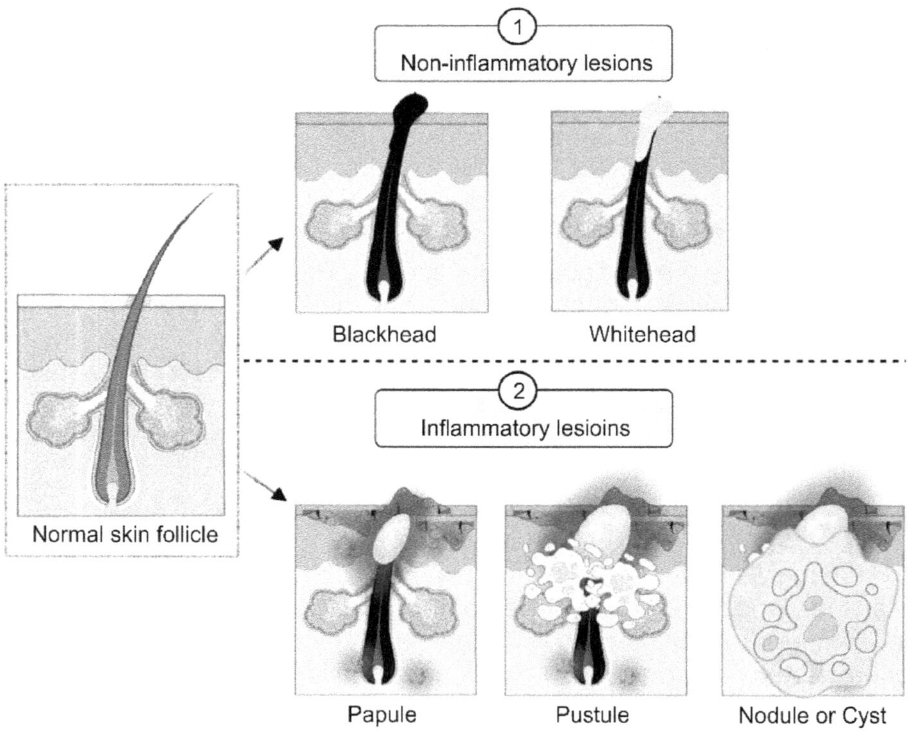

Figure 3.6: Representation of inflammatory and non-inflammatory acne lesions along with their prognosis.

Blackheads

Blackheads are non-inflammatory acne lesions that appear on the skin as a result of blocked hair shafts from dead skin cells and excess oil. The term "open comedo" refers to a blackhead because the skin's surface is still visible and appears dark, like black or brown. Mild acne known as "blackheads" typically affects the face, arms, chest, neck, back, and shoulders.

Whiteheads

Whiteheads are tiny pimples and a type of non-inflammatory acne lesion that appear on the skin when skin cells, oil, and bacteria clog pores in the hair follicles. Because the bumps on a whitehead are closed and white, they are known as closed comedones. Although whiteheads can appear anywhere on the body, the nose, chin, and forehead constitute the T-zone where they most commonly appear.

Pustules

Pustules are tiny pimples and an inflammatory lesion that develop on the skin when dead skin cells and excess oil block the pores. Inflammatory lesions with pus or fluid in the center are called pustules. They frequently appear as white pimples encircled by red, inflamed skin. Although they can appear anywhere on the body, pustules are most commonly found on the shoulders, chest, back, face, neck, pubic area, and hairline.

Papules

Inflammation, which manifests as swelling, heat, redness, and discomfort, is the body's reaction to germs, excessive oil production, and increased androgen activity. Referred to as papules, these inflammatory lesions are thought to represent a transitional stage between non-inflammatory and inflammatory lesions. Papules appear as a tiny pink lump on the skin that is usually smaller than 5 mm in diameter and does not contain pus.

Nodules

When bacteria, excess oil, and dead skin cells block the pores, severe inflammatory acne known as acne nodules results. Infections that damage the pores beneath the skin's surface can also produce redness, swelling, and the appearance of a small bump in the surrounding area. Typically, this combination results in comedones or whiteheads. Over-the-counter drugs alone cannot treat acne nodules, which can persist for weeks or months. Similar to papule acne, nodular acne has a diameter more than 5–10 mm and frequently appears on the chin or jawline of the face.

Cysts

A severe form of inflammatory acne called cystic acne develops beneath the skin as a result of clogged pores brought on by a buildup of oil, dry skin cells, and bacteria. *The majority of those affected are people of various ages with oily skin*. A cyst usually manifests as huge, painful, white or red lesions that are filled with pus and can occasionally leave scars. Although cystic acne can form anywhere on the body, the face, arms, shoulders, back, chest, and neck are the most common areas. The majority of cystic acne sufferers have both inflammatory and non-inflammatory acne manifestations.

Biological aspects of Skin in relation to pigmentation

The term "skin pigmentation" describes the color of the skin. The kind and quantity of melanin, a pigment produced by certain skin cells called melanocytes, determines it. Eumelanin and pheomelanin are two kinds of melanin which are produced at the junction of dermis and epidermis by the melanocytes. Pheomelanin is responsible for lighter skin color whilst eumelanin causes darker skin color. The protection of skin from sunlight is provided by the eumelanin which is brown or black in color. The pheomelanin does not absorb sunlight hence light in color. Pigment disorders including hyperpigmentation (dark spots), hypopigmentation (light spots), and depigmentation (white spots or patches) can be brought on by variations in melanin production (Figure 3.7). Skin pigmentation may result from sun exposure, autoimmune diseases, genetic factors, blisters, wounds, acne, and other skin injury.

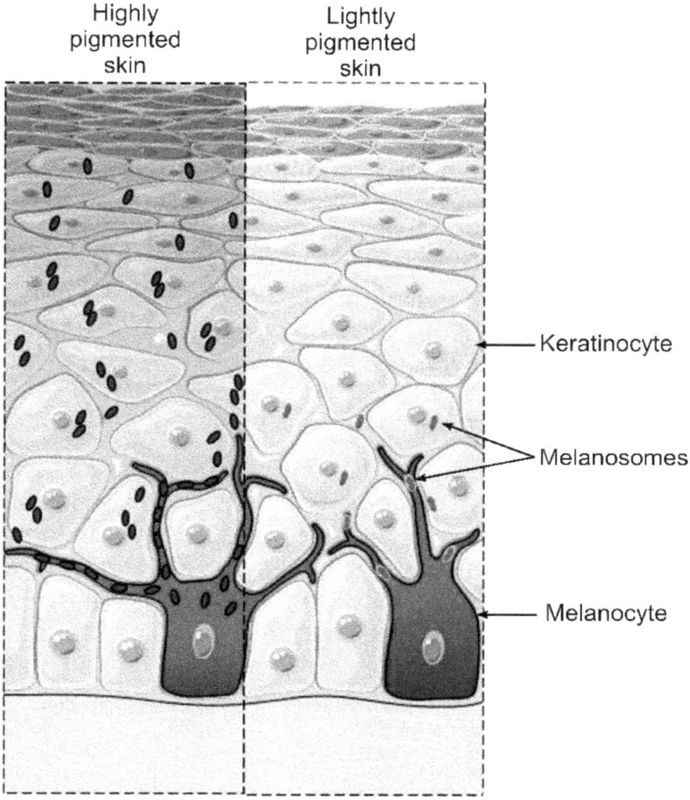

Figure 3.7: Illustration of skin structure in hyperpigmentation and hypopigmentation.

Causes of skin pigmentation

Skin pigmentation is a frequent condition that can be brought on by a number of causes. Genetics, exposure to sunburn, and administration of some drugs are the three main factors that contribute to skin pigmentation.

Types of skin pigmentation

Hyperpigmentation

Hyperpigmentation is the condition in which skin patches becomes darker than surrounding skin. It includes various conditions such as melasma, ephelides, postinflammatory hyperpigmentation, solar lentigines, and café au lait macules (Figure 3.8A). Although these illnesses are usually benign, people may experience distress.

Melasma

Melasma is a sun-exposed skin condition characterized by gradual, macular, non-scaling hypermelanosis, mainly on the face and dorsal forearms. Pregnancy, the use of oral contraceptives, anticonvulsants such as phenytoin, or idiopathic causes are typically linked to it. It is typically bilateral, though not always. Under a Wood Lamp examination, epidermal melasma tends to be light brown in color. Grayish in color, dermal melasma is non-enhancing. Dark brown melasma with varying enhancement is a feature of mixed kinds. Topical treatment does not work for dermal melasma. In these situations, dermatological referral is advised.

Solar Lentigines

Macular, well-circumscribed, hyperpigmented lesions on sun-exposed skin surfaces are known as solar lentigines, sometimes known as liver spots. These are 1-3 cm in size. They frequently have a variegated look and range in color from bright yellow to dark brown. The most typical sites are the shins, hands, forearms, chest, and back. Most frequently impacted are Whites and Asians. The cause of solar lentigines is a localized modest proliferation of basal melanocytes brought on by both acute and long-term UV exposure, which is followed by an increase in melanization.

Ephelides

Small, uniformly colored, strongly defined macular lesions, known as ephelides or freckles, measure 1-2 mm and are typically present on the face, neck, chest, arms, and legs. Color can range from light brown to tan to crimson, and there can be a few to hundreds of them. Usually begins in childhood following sun exposure. Since ephelides have no symptoms, there is no need for treatment. But the undesired lesions can be treated using the same treatment required for lentigines.

Post inflammatory hyperpigmentation

Postinflammatory hyperpigmentation appears as uneven, darkly pigmented skin during laser or light therapy, after cryotherapy, or at the locations of prior injury or inflammation. Melanin synthesis and epidermal melanocyte hypertrophy are caused by inflammation's stimulation of prostaglandin, leukotriene, and thromboxane production. A typical result of trauma or inflammation is postinflammatory hyperpigmentation, which is more prevalent in darker skin types. For certain people, lesions can be mentally damaging and last for months or years.

Café au lait macules (CALM) – Hyperpigmented Skin Patch -Birthmark

Common hyperpigmented and flat skin lesions in the general population are called cafe-au-lait macules. Congenital conditions are those that are present from birth or appear early in life. As they age, their numbers and sizes may increase. They can appear on any area of the body and range in hue from light brown to dark brown, although the trunk and extremities are where they most frequently appear. The French phrase "café au lait" translates to "coffee with milk." These are majorly of two types. One type has cleared margins which is very common and other has irregular margins and uncommon.

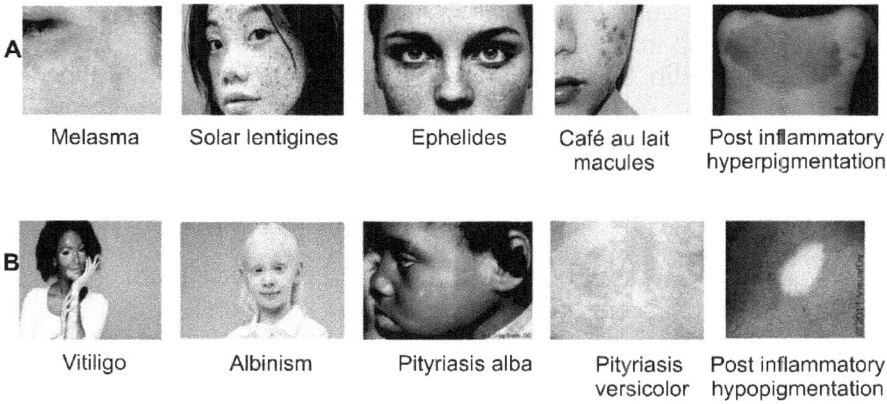

Figure 3.8: A, B representing the types of hyperpigmentation and hypopigmentation respectively.

Hypopigmentation

It is the condition in which skin patches becomes lighter than surrounding skin. It includes various conditions such as vitiligo, albinism, post inflammatory hypopigmentationm, Pityriasis alba, Pityriasis versicolor (Figure 3.8B).

Vitiligo

A chronic (long-lasting) autoimmune condition called vitiligo results in regions of skin losing color and pigmentation. The skin turns milky-white as a result of attacks on and destruction of melanocytes, the skin cells that produce pigment. Segmental and non-segmental vitiligo are the two most prevalent forms. Segmental vitiligo manifests as a unilateral or band-shaped dispersion of hypopigmented macules, often ranging in size from 5 to 50 mm. These macules are coalescent, rapidly stabilize, and appear at a young age. Non-segmental vitiligo usually develops over time and is usually bilateral or dispersed symmetrically.

If it encompasses more than 10% of the body's surface area, it is deemed generalized. The face and distal extremities are usually affected by acrofacial or acraral vitiligo. While lesions on the genitalia and extremities tend to be more resistant to therapy, lesions on the head and neck typically respond to it the best. It is more prone to people who have family history of vitiligo or have some autoimmune diseases like psoriasis, Adddison's disease, thyroid disease, type I diabetes, and pernicious anemia.

Albinism

The term albinism, derived from the Latin albus, which means "white," refers to a set of heritable disorders marked by low or missing melanin in tissues derived from ectoderms, particularly the skin, hair, and eyes, resulting in a distinctive pallor. This condition generates with the birth and does not take severe form along with age. The persons with albinism are more prone to damage by sunburn and skin cancer. Hence these persons are always suggested to avoid the sunrays.

Pityriasis alba

Pityriasis alba is a condition that is frequently linked to atopic dermatitis. In children and young adults, it typically manifests as hypopigmented, asymmetrical patches on the face, head, neck, and forearms. Sometimes there is a fine scale that itches. Unprotected sun exposure in excess could act as a trigger. Pityriasis alba is self-limited, thus treatment is not required.

Pityriasis versicolor

Pityriasis versicolor is a fungal infections caused by *Malassezia spp.* On the neck, chest, back, abdomen, and proximal extremities, it frequently manifests as hypopigmented or pink plaques with fine scale. It can be hyperpigmented sometimes. Frequently, a clinical diagnosis is made, and microscopy using a prepared potassium hydroxide solution confirms the diagnosis.

Post inflammatory hypopigmentation

Post-inflammatory hypopigmentation is an acquired pigmentary condition that is prevalent and more noticeable in skin of color. It denotes an acquired loss of skin pigmentation, either partial or entire, brought on by cutaneous inflammation, the aftereffects of viral or inflammatory dermatoses, or dermatological operations.

Biological aspects of Skin in relation to Wrinkles

Wrinkles occur as natural part of the ageing. It is a fold, ridge, or crease in the skin that results from dehydration, loss of body mass, or the breakdown of the dermis and epidermis junction and it is a natural phenomenon (Figure 3.9). Numerous changes are brought about by the interaction of exogenous (such as toxins, chemicals, pollutants, and UV radiation) and endogenous (such as gene mutation, cellular metabolism, and hormone influences) factors which leads to wrinkles. The wrinkles may be the result of chronological aging and photoaging. In chronological aging, the wrinkles result with passage of time whereas in photoaging, the wrinkles result from exposure to sunlight. The earliest wrinkles on the face of a person usually develop in the places where their skin naturally folds as they make facial expressions. They appear as a result of the skin aging and becoming less elastic. Additionally, areas of the body including the face, neck, backs of hands, and arms that are exposed to the most sun light are more likely to develop wrinkles. Everybody gets wrinkles as they age; they are an inevitable aspect of being older. But a lot of individuals don't like wrinkles due to which the market for anti-wrinkles or anti-ageing products is growing at constant pace. Sometimes, premature wrinkles also occur which might be due to various lifestyle and environmental factors.

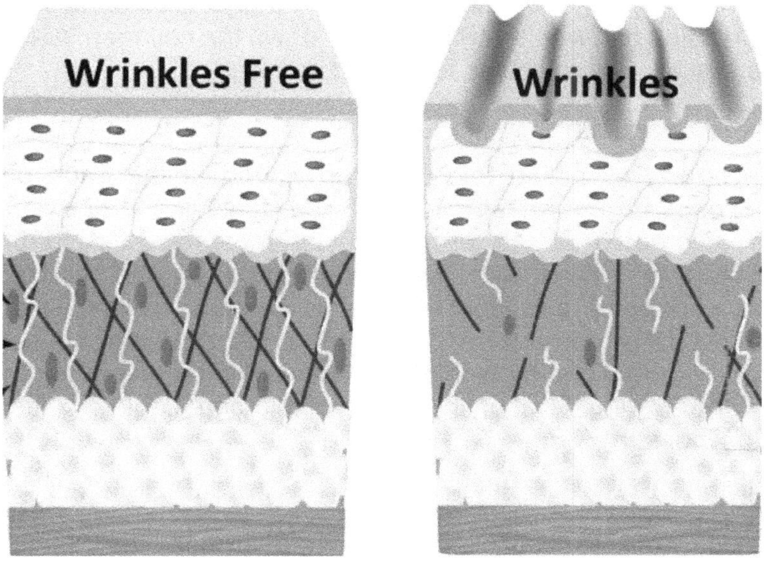

Figure 3.9: Representation of skin structure in wrinkles.

Causes of wrinkles

Various intrinsic factors such as ageing, hormonal balance, intercurrent diseases and extrinsic factors like smoking, exposure to sunburn cause wrinkles. These elements play a part in skin fragility, wrinkles, elasticity loss, and epidermal thinning. The type of skin, which includes skin color and tanning ability, affects how severe photodamage is. It is becoming more and more obvious that the ordinary person's daily exposure to UV radiation is greatly increased by short unintentional solar exposures that happen during routine activities.

Mechanism of wrinkles

Various molecular mechanisms are responsible for wrinkles or ageing of skin comprising oxidative stress and 'Matrix metalloproteinase' (MMP), telomere shortening, cytokines, and autophagic control.

Oxidative stress and MMP

With increase in age, ATP formation is reduced and reactive oxygen species (ROS) production is increased along with decrease in antioxidant defense mechanism. Elevated ROS trigger the nuclear factor kappa B (NF-κB) and mitogen-activated protein kinase (MAPK) signaling pathways, which are the two primary regulatory signaling routes for SASP by senescent cells. This trigger ultimately increases the expression of MMP. MMP can break down the collagen, elastin and other extracellular molecules leading to wrinkles.

Talomere shortening

Protein structures called telomeres are found at the ends of each chromosomal arm of eukaryotic DNA. By identifying double-stranded breaks, telomeres at the end of a chromosome help to prevent degradation or fusion with the chromosome around it. Telomere shortening denotes a malfunction of this defense mechanism, which triggers the DNA damage response and causes cellular senescence and aging symbolized by wrinkles. Hence, an increase in telomerase activity and slowing down of shortening of telomere could provide some rid from wrinkles.

Cytokines

Cytokines are essential for the appearance of aging skin characteristics. Tumor necrosis factor-alpha, a pro-inflammatory cytokine, increases MMP-9 production, which in turn promotes collagen breakdown by inhibiting collagen synthesis. Additionally, it reduces skin immunity, which raises the possibility of cutaneous infections as one ages.

Autophagy control

Autophagy (ATG) is an evolutionarily conserved method of cell self-digestion which transport undesired or damaged proteins, lipids, and other cellular components to the lysosome for breakdown. Skin cells produce significantly more ROS when exposed to UV light over an extended period of time, especially UVA and UVB radiation. Thus, mitochondrial dysfunction and oxidative stress results from an imbalance between oxidant and antioxidant systems. Generally, high ROS generation triggers the activation of autophagy. When autophagy is activated, it breaks down and gets rid of oxidized proteins and lipids and stops ROS from building up. As a result, oxidative damage is reduced and metabolic homeostasis is restored, slowing the progression of photoaging. On the other hand, in photoaging skin cells, an excessive buildup of ROS inhibits autophagy and reduces its clearance effectiveness. In turn, these consequences intensify oxidative damage and play a role in the emergence of wrinkles, roughness, hyperpigmentation, and other signs of photoaging.

Biological aspects of skin in relation to Prickly heat

It is a severe inflammatory skin condition caused by clogged eccrine sweat glands and ducts. This obstruction causes eccrine sweat to backflow into the dermis or epidermis, resulting in a rash that appears as vesicles filled with sweat beneath the skin (Figure 3.10). They are appeared in red bumps on skin along with prickly and itchy sensation. It is also known as heat rash, miliaria and sweat rash. It s most prevalent in warm and humid areas mainly in summer season. These skin conditions are self-limited and disappear within few days without any treatment. Any part of the body can be affected by prickly heat but mostly affected parts are face, neck, back, abdomen, and elbows.

Pathophysiology

A blockage of the eccrine sweat glands or ducts is the primary cause of prickly heat. This may be caused by bacteria like *Staphylococcus epidermidis,* which forms biofilms, or by cutaneous debris. The blockage causes sweat to seep into the dermis or epidermis, which causes edema, overhydration of the cells, and further duct occlusion. Ruptures of the eccrine gland or duct may result from deeper involvement of these structures. The most common cause for the prickly heat is exposure to sunlight for prolonged time in summer season.

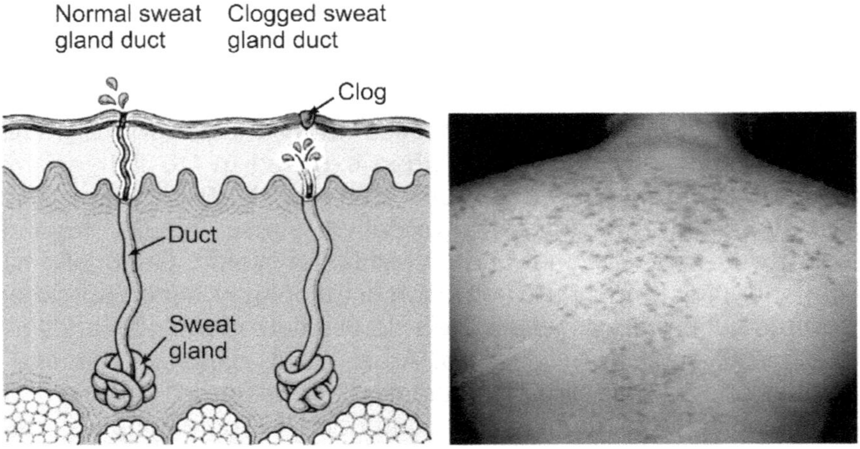

Figure 3.10: Skin structure in Prickly heat.

Types of prickly heat

There are mainly four kinds of prickly heat which are as following:

- Miliaria rubra (Red)
- Miliaria crystalline (Clear)
- Miliaria pustulosa (White/yellow)
- Miliria profunda (Deep)

Miliaria rubra (Red)

Miliaria rubra is most common type of heat rash which causes small and inflamed bumps on the skin along with itching or prickly sensation. It is mainly occur due to the clogging of the deeper layers of the epidermis.

Miliaria crystalline (Clear)

Miliaria crystalline is the mildest type of heat rash which occurs due to clogging of the sweat ducts at closest surface of the skin. It causes small clear pumps filled with fluid which can be break easily.

Miliaria pustulosa (White/yellow)

In this type of heat rash, the formed bumps become infected with the microorganisms present on the surface of the skin. The bumps have pus which can be break easily.

Miliaria profunda (Deep)

Miliaria profunda is uncommon type of heat rash which occur due to clogging of the sweat ducts at the level of dermis. This kind of heat rash has hard, uncomfortable, or itchy pimples that resemble goose bumps. They might crack open.

Biological aspects of skin in relation to body odor

The odor that results from perspiration coming into touch with skin microorganisms is known as body odor. Perspiration has no fragrance by itself; rather, odors are produced when perspiration and skin germs combine. The smell of body odor might be onion-like, sour, sweet, or tangy. The level of perspiration has no bearing on how your body smells. This explains why someone can smell bad from the body without perspiring. On the other hand, someone can perspire a lot without smelling. This is due to the fact that sweat itself does not generate body odor; rather, the type of bacteria on your skin and how those bacteria interact with perspiration do. Sweating is the fluid secreted onto the surface of the skin by sweat glands. There are two types of sweat glands namely apocrine and eccrine glands. The apocrine glands are in charge of generating body odor whilst eccrine gland is responsible for maintenance of body temperature. Aprocrine glands open in at the hair follicles, hence the males are more prone to body odor than female due to high content of hairs on their body.

Mechanism for body odor

Body odor occurs when the bacteria present on the surface of skin come in the contact of perspiration. This body odor can be good, bad, or no smell depending upon the various factors. The factors which affects the body odor include the food intake, exercise, stress, anxiety, summer season, genetics, obesity, and administration of various drugs. Eating sulfur rich foods like garlic, onions, red meat, broccoli, and cauliflower cause increase in body odor. The presence of various diseases or disorders like diabetes, menopause, gout, liver cirrhosis, kidney problem, and any other infectious disease may intensity the body odor.

Care for body odor

The use of antiperspirants can decrease the intensification of body odor by reducing the volume of sweat along with changing the amount and activity of odor producing bacteria. The covering of the body using proper clothing can reduce the intensity of body odor. The washing of the body with soaps regularly can reduce the body odor. The male candidates can reduce the body odor by using the shaving.

Cosmeceuticals for addressing the skin problems

The skin is exposed to numerous intrinsic and extrinsic factors which result into the various skin problems such as dry skin, hyperpigmentation, hypopigmentation, wrinkles and miliaria etc. The natural microbiota of skin, which is made up of a variety of microorganisms including bacteria, viruses, fungus, and micro-eukaryotes, is also greatly impacted by both intrinsic and extrinsic causes. Skin microbiota not only builds a physical barrier against pathogenic bacteria through a variety of antagonistic processes, but it also strengthens the host's defenses against them. Nonetheless, the destruction of natural microbiota (dysbiosis) has been connected to a number of skin illnesses like psoriasis, acne, atopic dermatitis, and chronic wounds.

The cosmeceutical sector is growing quickly as a result of the never-ending need to seem younger and avoid aging. These are the naturally derived products having cosmetic as well as therapeutic potential. Because of the efficacious claims made for their ability to treat various skin diseases and symptoms of aging, these are in high demand. Because cosmeceutical products are more easily available and more reasonably priced than prescription products, consumers frequently include them into their skin care routines. These possess a variety of advantageous characteristics, such as antioxidant, anti-inflammatory, and antibacterial action. They are often derived from natural sources (plants, animals, or microorganisms), however synthetic derivatives are also employed. Various ingredients employed as cosmeceuticals have been described in preceding section.

Vitamins

Vitamins are frequently included in a variety of cosmeceutical products since they are crucial for preserving skin health and treating skin conditions. The most important vitamins for skin problems include vitamin A,B,C,D and E. Along with performing various essential functions within the body, these vitamins have role in addressing various skin problems such as acne, wrinkles, pigmentation etc. Various vitamins used in skin problems has been summarized in the Table 3.1.

Table 3.1: List of vitamins used to address various skin problems.

Vitamin	Analogue	Indication
Vitamin A	Retinyl acetate and palmitate	Antiaging
	Retinol	Antiaging
	Retinal	Antiaging
	Tretinoin	Acne vulgaris
	Tazarotene	Acne vulgaris
	Adapalene	Acne vulgaris
	Trifarotene	Acne vulgaris
	Alitretinoin	Kaposi's sarcoma
Vitamin B	Niacinamide	Hyperpigmentation, Photoaging, Acne vulgaris, Inflammatory skin conditions
	Dexpanthenol	Xerosis, Atopic dermatitis, Diaper rash, Wound healing, Scar management, Alopecia
Vitamin C	L-ascorbic acid	Photoaging and hyperpigmentation
	Sodium L-Ascorbyl-2-phosphate	Acne vulgaris
	Magnesium ascorbyl phosphate	Depigmentation
	Ascorbic 2-phosphate 6-palmitate	Antiaging
	Ascorbyl tetraisopalmitate	Depigmentation
	3-O-Ethyl ascorbic acid	Wrinkles, hyperpigmentation
Vitamin D	Calcitriol	Atopic dermatitis
	Calcipotriene	Psoriasis
	Tacalcitol	Psoriasis
	Maxacalcitol	Antiaging, psoriasis
Vitamin E	α-Tocopherol	Hyperpigmentation
	Tocopheryl succinate	Melanoma, atopic dermatitis, psoriasis
	Tocopheryl acetate	UV protection, antiaging, photoaging
	Tocopheryl phosphate	UV protection
	Tocopheryl nicotinate	Antiaging, hyperpigmentation, skin tone
	Tocopheryl linoleate	Skin moisturizer

Coenzyme Q10

Coenzyme Q10 is an endogenous, hydrophobic co-factor present in biological membranes in both its reduced (ubiquinol) and oxidised (ubiquinone) forms. It is a vital natural antioxidant that promotes the development of collagen and elastin, which helps to achieve youthful-looking skin. Its advantages include protecting against aging, minimizing wrinkles, and improving moisture content of the skin. In addition, it exhibits anti-inflammatory, photoprotective and skin brightening potential. In UV-irradiated cells, coenzyme Q10 decreases the synthesis of interleukin (IL)-1α, reactive oxygen species (ROS), and (MMP)-1 while increasing the expression of the genes for collagen and elastin. It also suppresses tyrosinase activity in melanoma cells, which in turn hindered melanogenesis.

Acids

Various acids mainly hyaluronic acid, hydroxyl acids, ferulic acid, trichloroacetic acid, kojic acid have proved their potential in addressing various skin problems.

Hyaluronic acid, or hyaluronan, is a glycosaminoglycan that is one of the primary constituents of the extracellular matrix (ECM). One of the major characteristic of hyaluronic acid is its string water retention capacity which imparts hydration and stability to the dermal and epidermal layers of the skin. But with passage of the age, the production of hyaluronic acid decreases resulting in loss of moisture, elasticity, decreased skin volume and appearance of wrinkles on the skin. Hence, hyaluronic acid has been added in various skin products to impart moisture and protection against oxidative stress. Sodium hyaluronate, a derivative of hyaluronic acid is used in commercial products due to its higher stability and reduced size allowing deep penetration through the skin. Sodium hyaluronate has also provided its efficacy in balancing the skin microbiota. Various hyaluronic acid based commercial products are available to restore the skin volume and decrease the wrinkles.

Hydroxy acids are a family of organic acids that occur naturally and are mainly divided into four groups: bionic acids (BAs), β-hydroxy acids (βHAs), polyhydroxy acids (PHAs), and α-hydroxy acids (αHAs). In order to promote collagen and elastin manufacturing and epidermal cell turnover, hydroxy acids are frequently utilized as exfoliants in anti-aging products. These enhance the general tone, texture, and pigmentation of the skin. Higher doses of hydroxy acids are used to treat keratoses, psoriasis, acne, and photodamage using chemical peels. αHAs are hydrophilic acids which include lactic, citric, malic, glycolic, and mandelic acids. αHAs are generally used at the concentration less than 10%. PHAs and βHAs are structurally similar to the αHAs. Due to possession of large size, PHAs and βHAs can only penetrate the superficial layers of the skin causing less skin irritation than αHAs enabling their use for the very sensitive skin. Salicylic acid is frequently categorized as a βHA, although other people classify it as a phenolic aromatic acid because of how differently its structure and function from those of standard βHAs. Salicylic acid is miscible with the lipophilic stratum corneum and the sebaceous glands because of its lipophilic nature, which makes it perfect for treating acne in those with oily skin types. Salicylic acid not only exfoliates skin but also lowers the production of sebum, has anti-inflammatory and antibacterial qualities, and an anesthetic action that makes salicylic acid peels more bearable. Salicylic acid for cosmetic products is used in concentration of 0.5%-50%. Topically applied salicylic acid formulations are well tolerated by all kinds of skin but higher concentration of salicylic acid may lead to crusting, erythema, dryness and dyspigmentation.

Ferulic acid is a natural based antioxidant mainly employed in antiaging skin care products. This antioxidant stabilizes other antioxidants (including L-ascorbic acid and α-tocopherol) and strengthens intracellular antioxidant systems in addition to scavenging free radicals and chelating catalytic metal ions. It also inhibits enzymes involved in the formation of ROS. The antioxidant action of ferulic acid also shields skin from UV-induced damage, hence avoiding photoaging. Apart from its antioxidant properties, ferulic acid exhibits anti-inflammatory, angiogenesis inhibiting, skin lightening, and wound healing properties. Ferulic acid is therefore used to treat atopic dermatitis, hyperpigmentation, and symptoms of photoaging. Ferulic acid concentrations in topical skincare products range from 0.5% to 1%, and in ferulic acid peels, they can reach 12%.

Kojic acid is a well-known fungal metabolite that lightens skin and used in various pigmentation issues like melasma, age spots, freckles, and post-inflammatory hyperpigmentation. The mechanism of kojic acid in skin products is inhibition of tyrosinase activity responsible for melanogenesis. kojic acid alos exhibits antibacterial, anti-inflammatory, antioxidant, and antiproliferative properties. Kojic acid is commonly found in topical formulations at concentrations of up to 1%, which is thought to be secure and well tolerated for extended use. Those with sensitive skin may develop contact dermatitis from using products containing kojic acid.

Cannabinoids

Cannabinoids are a class of structurally related substances that are produced by the *Cannabis sativa* plant (phytocannabinoids) and the human body (endocannabinoids), as well as cannabinoid derivatives that are synthesized. The endocannabinoid system (ECS) is one of the several molecular targets via which cannabis mediate their biological effects. It is found all over the body including the skin and is involved in many physiological functions. Skin derived cannabinoid signaling controls immunological response, homoeostasis, barrier function, melanogenesis, cell division, and proliferation. Hence imbalance in this cannabinoid signaling leads to various skin disorders like acne, psoriasis, atopic dermatitis, wrinkles etc. Tetrahydrocannabinol (THC, a psychoactive cannabinoid) and cannabidiol (CBD) are the two most prevalent phytocannabinoids. CBD is the main ingredient in over-the-counter cannabis medicines. It can be found alone, as pure CBD, or combined with other plant chemicals and phytocannabinoids, like terpenes, flavonoids, and polyunsaturated fatty acids. The possession of various biological effects like anti-inflammatory, antimicrobial, antioxidant, and antiproliferative, the cannabinoids have been utilized for various dermatological disorders. Various scientific studies have been proved that topical cannabinoids are more effective in skin disorders along with minimum adverse effects.

Allantoin

Allantoin is a naturally occurring substance derived from the *Symphytum officinale* plant, although it can be chemically synthesized for cosmetic uses. The possession of keratolytic, emollient, anti-inflammatory, and moisturizing properties, allantoin is frequently used to relieve dry, irritated skin. It is a healing and moisturizing substance that can help to remove dead skin cells from the skin and leave it looking radiant. It may promote wound healing through controlling inflammation, eliminating necrotic tissue, acting as an antibacterial to prevent infection, and promoting the growth of fibroblasts, epithelialization, and the production of extracellular matrix (ECM). It has been added in various cosmetic products such as shampoo, creams, toothpastes, mouthwashes, lotions, anti-acne creams etc. It is mainly used in 0.1%-0.2% concentration topically which is safe even for sensitive skin.

Urea

Urea is the primary endogenous humectant that keeps the stratum corneum hydrated. It also improves the function of the skin's barrier, possibly through controlling the expression of genes related to keratinocyte development and the manufacture of antimicrobial peptides and epidermal lipids. Topical formulations with low urea concentrations (<10%) are commonly utilized for their moisturizing properties in skin disorders such psoriasis, xerosis, ichthyosis, and atopic dermatitis while formulations with higher urea concentrations (10%–40%) also show keratolytic actions, which remove the skin's outer layers and promote the growth of new skin cells. This is notably helpful for hyperkeratosis prone skin and nail disorders such psoriasis, ichthyosis, dermatitis, and onychomycosis. Urea has shown promise both as a monotherapy and in combination therapies in increasing the absorption of corticosteroids and antifungal medications. Topical treatments are usually well tolerated but, in sensitive skin areas (such as the area around the eyes and lips) and at greater dosages, erythema, burning, and irritation may occur.

Caffeine

Caffeine is the key ingredient of various topical antiaging, anti-cellulite, and anti-hair loss products. Because of its antioxidant property and capacity to block the enzymes collagenase and elastase, which cause the breakdown of ECM, caffeine is thought to provide antiaging benefits. Caffeine may also offer extra ultraviolet B (UVB) protection when used as a sunscreen adjuvant, lowering the risk of skin cancer and photoaging. Numerous effects of caffeine encourage lipolysis, which may help to reduce cellulite. This involves the suppression of phosphodiesterase in adipocytes, which raises cyclic adenosine monophosphate (cAMP) levels and activates lipase. Caffeine also promote hair growth hair by blocking 5-α-reductase and the subsequent translation of testosterone to dihydrotestosterone, the hormone responsible for hair loss. Topical caffeine formulations have been found to have a few side effects, including as moderate discomfort and erythema (caused by increased blood circulation).

Zinc

Zinc is a necessary trace mineral which acts as a co-factor for many enzymes and transcription factors. Zinc and its derivatives have been included in a variety of skin and hair care products due to possession of antibacterial, anti-inflammatory, antioxidant, and wound healing properties. Skin care products containing zinc have the ability to relieve irritated skin and show promise in treating inflammatory skin disorders like psoriasis, rosacea, acne, and eczema. Zinc oxide creates a barrier that protects against moisture, infection, and irritation and is frequently found in diaper rash treatments and ointments. Zinc oxide has been added in mineral based sunscreen formulations due to its broad spectrum UVA and UVB protection. Due to its fungicidal effect against *Pityrosporum* (*Malassezia*), zinc pyrithione is a common active component in shampoos. Certain deodorants also contain zinc derivatives, such as zinc oxide, which block bacterial growth or inhibit the bacterial enzymes that create odorants (such as zinc glycinate and ricinoleate). The antifungal, antibacterial, and deodorizing qualities of zinc derivatives, such as zinc propionate, caprylate, and undecylenate, make them popular ingredients in foot care products. All stages of the wound healing process require zinc-dependent enzymes (such alkaline phosphatase and MMPs) and transcription factors (like zinc finger regulatory proteins). Zinc paste bandages, stockings, and other dressings infused with zinc have been recommended for the management of wounds resulting from various causes.

Green tea extract

Green tea is the natural substance derived from *Cammelia sinesis* plant and possess potent polyphenols termed as catechins namely epicatechin, epigallocatechin, epigallocatechin-3-gallate, and epicatequinagalato. These catechins have demonstrated their antioxidant, anti-inflammatory, and anticancer potential due to which they have been utilized in various cosmetic products like anti-acne, and anti-wrinkles products. The green tea polyphenols that are used into cosmetic products exhibit good skin penetration and retention. Some characteristics that may improve skin function include the prevention of acute impacts of UVB radiation, the decrease of inflammation and as a result, erythema and immunosuppression brought on by sunlight. The antioxidant property of green tea extract reduce photoaging and lipid peroxidation by neutralizing reactive oxygen species. Various other constituents like amino acids, proteins, lipids, vitamins (B, C and E), pigments such as chlorophyll and carotenoids, caffeine, and minerals are present in green tea extract which provide additional benefits to skin like moisturizing effect and protective effects.

Botulinum toxin

It is commonly recognized that botulinum toxin can be used cosmetically to lessen the appearance of wrinkles and creases on the face. This neurotoxic causes acetylcholine release inhibition at the neuromuscular junction, which leads to a transient paralysis of the face muscles. Five injections of botulinum toxin type A have been approved by the FDA so far for use in cosmetic procedures. Among them are daxibotulinumtoxinA (DAXI), prabotulinumtoxinA (PRA), incobotulinumtoxinA (INCO), onabotulinumtoxinA (ONA), and abobotulinumtoxinA (ABO). The formulation, molecular potency, and clinical effects of these products vary, although having the same active component and mechanism of action. Products containing botulinum toxin type A may have different clinical effects depending on a number of criteria including as tissue distribution, molecular potency, and individual patient reaction. Different formulations and manufacturing processes result in varying molecular potencies (i.e. amounts of free, active neurotoxic accessible for binding) in commercial products. Each manufacturer's method of measuring molecular potency is proprietary, making it impossible to directly compare the potency of various brands of botulinum toxin. The injection technique, volume, depth, number of injection sites, and muscle density of the patient can all impact the neurotoxin's tissue distribution. To have the intended therapeutic effect and avoid paralyzing nearby muscles, the neurotoxin must be precisely localized to the target region. Due to intrinsic characteristics (e.g., age, gender, muscle mass, and type) that affect neurotoxic receptor density, clinical consequences can also differ throughout patients. Clinical effectiveness and neurotoxic binding will both decrease with a decrease in neurotoxin receptor density. The duration of action of botulinum toxins is typically 3–4 months, however DAXI formulations have the potential to extend up to 9 months. Pain, erythema, oedema, hypoesthesia, and bruises at the injection site are common side effects of botulinum toxin injections. A toxin's undesired spread to other regions may cause ptosis and facial weakness. Rarely, severe side effects like anaphylaxis, dysphagia, and breathing issues could happen.

Peptides

Bioactive peptides are protein fragments which assist cellular communication during a variety of biological activities such as growth, homoeostasis, immunological response, and stress response. Bioactive peptides, both natural and synthetic are employed as cosmeceutical agents to address a range of skin disorders. Bioactive peptides are categorized as neurotransmitter inhibitor, signal, and carrier peptides based on how they work. Carrier peptides aid in the passage of co-factors through the epidermal barrier, including manganese and copper. Both cofactors are necessary for a number of enzymatic processes related to wound healing and anti-aging. Examples of carrier peptides that have been effectively used to reduce fine lines, wrinkles, and hyperpigmentation related to photoaging are copper tripeptide-1 and manganese tripeptide-1. Signal peptides or matrikines peptides are specifically produced from ECM proteins like collagen, elastin, and fibronectin. These peptides induce ECM synthesis, repair, and remodeling by interacting with certain receptors.

These also control the activity of some important age-related enzymes, including hyaluronidase, collagenase, elastase, tyrosinase, and MMPs. Several topical healthcare formulations for skin rejuvenation (better skin firmness, elasticity, hydration, and wrinkle reduction) contain signal peptides. Palmitoyl tripeptide-1 (Biopeptide CL™), Palmitoyl hexapeptide-12 (Biopeptide EL™), Palmitoyl pentapeptide-4 (Matrixyl®), Palmitoyl tripeptide-5 (Syn®-Coll) Palmitoyl tripeptide-38 (Matrixyl Synthe'6™), Tripeptide-10 citrulline (Decorinyl®), Heptapeptide (Perfection Peptide P7™), Decapeptide (SA1-III or KP-1) and Oligopeptide-68 (β-WHITE™) are the the examples of signal peptides. Neurotransmitter inhibitor peptides provide inhibition of release of acetylcholine responsible for muscle contraction. These peptides share a sequence with the synaptic protein SNAP-25 (synaptosome-associated protein, 25 kDa), which mediates the acetylcholine release signaling cascade. Fine lines and wrinkles are prevented from forming by inhibiting this process, which relaxes the muscles in the face. These peptides have fewer possible adverse effects than the conventional Botulinum toxin therapies, making them a safer option. Acetyl hexapeptide-3 (Argireline®), Pentapeptide-18 (Leuphasyl®), Pentapeptide-3 (Vialox), and Tripeptide-3 (Syn®-Ake) are the examples of neurotransmitter inhibitor peptides. Table 3.2 has a list of cosmeceuticals used in commercial cosmetic products.

Table 3.2: A list of commercial cosmetic products having cosmeceutical ingredients.

Commercial product	Cosmeceutical ingredient	Manufacturer	Application
Super light gel (Oil free moisturizer)	Hyaluronic acid	Pond's	Imparts moisturization effect
Revitalift serum	Hyaluronic acid	L'Oreal	Deeply hydrate and visibly plump skin
Lotus professional PhytoRx serum	Hyaluronic acid	Lotus	Anti-wrinkles and moisturizer
Lakme Absolute Hydro Pro serum	Hyaluronic acid	Lakme	Strengthening of skin barrier and moisturizer
Calming soothing face cream	Hyaluronic acid, Biotin and Niacinamide	Hindustan Multi Cosmetics	Intense hydration, protection of skin barrier and soothing effect

Table 3.2 *Contd....*

Commercial product	Cosmeceutical ingredient	Manufacturer	Application
Pond's bright beauty	Niacinamide	Pond's	Anti-pigmentation
Pond's Rejuveness anti-wrinkle cream	Alpha hydroxy acid	Pond's	Antiaging and anti-wrinkle
Glycolic bright cream	Glycolic acid (type of alpha hydroxy acid)	L'Oreal	Reduction of dark spots
Glycolic illuminate serum	Glycolic acid	Lakme	Reduces dullness and improve skin texture
Oil-free daily face wash	Hyaluronic acid and glycolic acid	Derma Co	Removes oil, facilitate exfoliation and hydration
Retinol contour serum	Retinol and vitamin C	Lakme	Antioxidant
Revitalift triple action day cream	Hyaluronic acid, Retinol and vitamin C	L'Oreal Paris	Antiaging
Revitalift laser cream	Retinol and niacinamide	L'Oreal Paris	Anti-wrinkle and improves the skin tone
Rivela Derma Science	Allantoin and salicylic acid	Cipla	Provides long lasting moisturizing effect
UV squad soothing after-sun gel	Allantoin	Hindustan unilever limited	Moisturization and quick recovery of skin
Ponds bright beauty	Niacinamide	Pond's	Provides moisturizing effect
2% Kojic acid face cream	Kojic acid, vitamic C and glycolic acid	Derma Co	Antipigmentation
Kojic acid Cream	Kojic acid	LA Organo	Skin brightening and lightening
Deep wrinkle facial serum	Coenzyme Q10	AG Industries	Anti-wrinkle

CHAPTER 4

Hair Cosmetics

Hair

Hair is simple in structure and is distinguishing characteristic in mammals. Hair is also known as protein filament which propagates from dermal follicles. Our entire body is covered in hair with the exception of a few spots like the soles of our feet or the palms of our hands. Hairs are mainly of two types namely vellus hairs and terminal hairs (Figure 4.1). Vellus hairs also termed as peach fuzz and are shorter and thinner than terminal hairs which include the hairs of face, stomach, arms, and legs. The thick, coarse hair that makes up eyelashes and eyebrows and grows on scalp is known as terminal hair. After puberty, terminal hair may also begin to grow on belly, chest, armpits, and pubic area. It covers about 30% of body surface in female whilst about 90% body surface in male candidates.

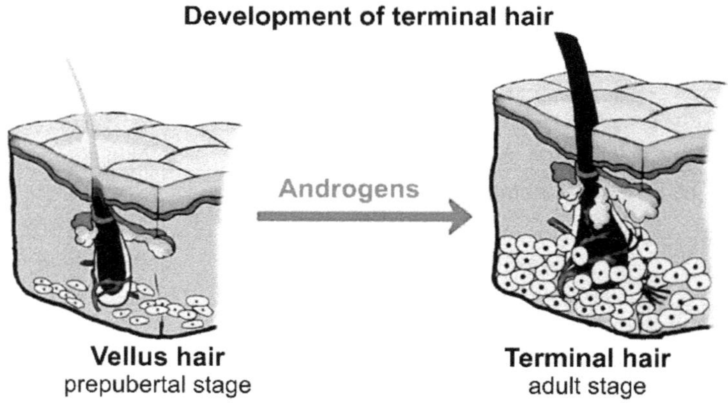

Figure 4.1: Types of hair.

Hair structure

Each hair consists of a **hair root** and a **hair shaft**. The visible portion of the hair that protrudes from the skin is called the shaft. The hair root is located in the skin and extends into the deeper layers of the skin. The hair follicle which is encased in a sheath of connective tissue and skin surrounds it and is joined to a sebaceous gland. Each hair follicle is connected to arrector pili, a small muscle that can cause the hair to rise up. Numerous nerves also terminate in hair follicles. These nerves are sensitive to even the smallest draught and can detect hair movement. Hair is composed of a hard protein known as keratin which provides strength to the hair. Keratin is a large molecule which is further composed of smaller molecules known as amino acids which link together to form a chain. The structure of hair is mainly composed of following two different layers (Figure 4.2).

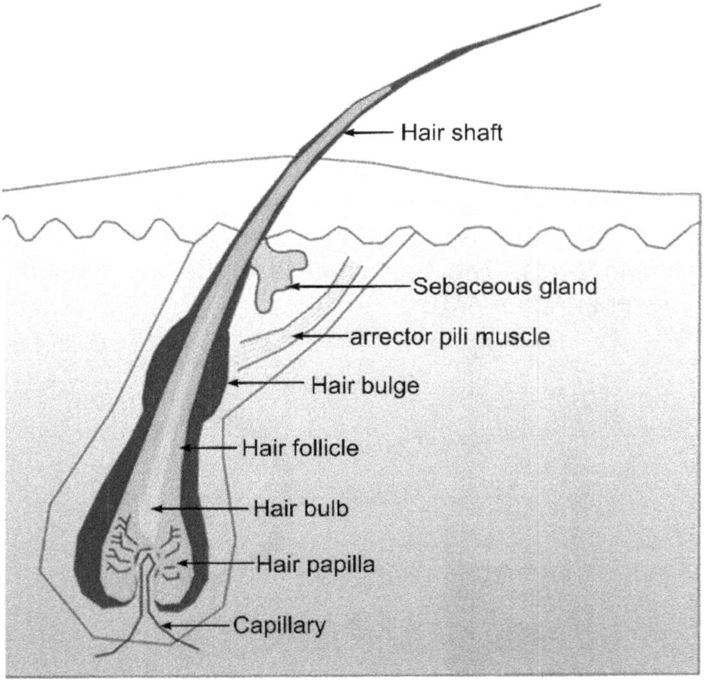

Figure 4.2: Structure of hair.

Hair follicle

A hair follicle is a pore-like structure that encloses the root and strand of the hair. The top two layers of human skin are home to hair follicles. Over 5 million hair follicles are present in our body at time of birth amongst over a million follicles are present on our head. Various biological activities such as promotion of hair growth, pigmentation of hair, formation of new blood vessels, formation of new neuron cells of nervous system and repairing of skin after wound takes place in hair follicle. It is the place where hair grows and is club like structure in the skin. A network of blood arteries that get nutrients to nourish the hair and support its growth are found at the end of the follicle which is termed as papilla. A bulb surrounds the papilla and the base of the hair follicle is made up of hair bulb. The living cells divide and expand in the hair bulb to form the hair shaft. Blood vessels feed the cells of hair bulb and carry hormones responsible to regulate the growth and shape of hair at various stages of life. There are glands just next to the hair follicle including sebaceous gland which secretes oil and aids in the skin protection. Various specialized cells namely melanocytes are found in the hair bulbs which are responsible for producing the melanin. The hair follicle in the skin is protected by internal and external root sheaths. Along with the epidermis, outer roots of hair follicle go through a continual growth cycle.

Hair shaft

It is the portion of the hair that is visible above the skin. Small amounts of water and binding materials as well as dead cells that have transformed into the protein keratin make up the hair shaft. Hair is made strong and flexible by the keratin. Keratin is also composed of a chain of amino acids. The hair shaft is further composed of three distinctive layers (Figure 4.3).

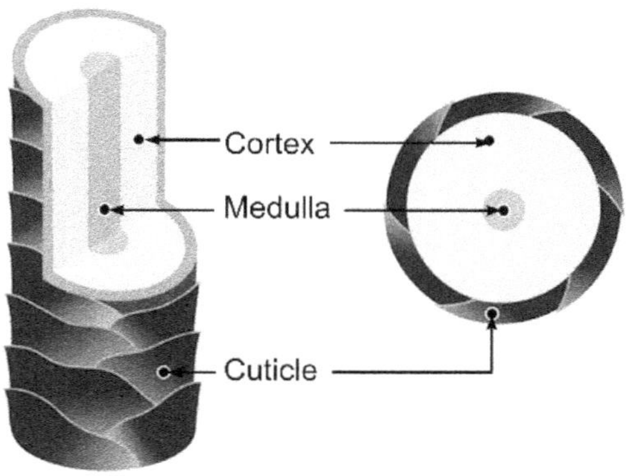

Figure 4.3: Hair shaft.

Cuticle: It is the protective or outermost layer of the hair which is comprised of overlapping cells like tiles of a roof. It provides shine to the hair and guards the inner layers of the hair shaft. It retains the hydration capacity of the hair by reducing the movement of moisture in and out of the cortex. Sometimes, various chemical processes and weather conditions can lift the cuticle causing distraction of the functions of cuticle leading to dryness and brittleness of the hair.

Cortex: It comprises the middle layer of the hair shaft and responsible to provide pigmentation, texture, and strength to the hair. It is made up of elongated keratin filaments held together by hydrogen and disulphide bonds. The strengthening of cortex depends upon the reliability of the cuticle guarding it. It also has a color pigment called as melanin responsible to impart color to the hair.

Medulla: It is the innermost or deepest layer of the hair shaft which is also known as core of the hair shaft. It is not present in all hairs of the body but present only in the large and thick hairs like the hairs of scalp. The cuticle is responsible to guard the medulla from harmful environmental conditions, chemicals and other type of toxic materials. Medulla cannot maintain its structure if cuticle is damaged or destroyed. It resembles to honeycomb in structure having air spaces inside it.

Hair growth cycle

The growth of hair starts from the follicle that lies beneath the skin. The hair is nourished by the blood arteries present at the follicle's base required for growth of the hair. Each hair goes through four stages namely anagen, catagen, telogen and exogen between the beginning to grow and eventually falling out years later (Figure 4.4). Recently another stage namely kenogen also has been identified. The growth cycle of each hair is at different stage. The anagen stage gets shorter as time goes on resulting that after each cycle, the hair may weaken and thin. Hence to maintain regular, healthy hair growth it is crucial to guarantee a diet rich in particular nutrients. Excessive shedding and observable thinning of the hair can occur if hair enters the resting phase too soon.

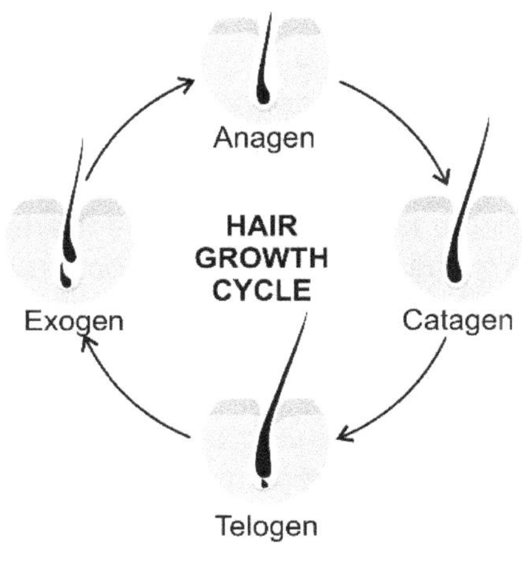

Figure 4.4: Sequential representation of hair growth cycle.

Anagen phase

The initial stage of hair growth is known as anagen phase which lasts roughly one thousands days. It starts in the papilla and continues for 2-6 years. Approximately 80-90% of all hairs of human are in this phase. This phase also can be divided further into two phases namely proanagen phase and metanagen phase. Proanagen phase starts the differentiation process when it notices the dividing hair progenitor cells of the hair follicle and the metanagen phase is identified by the appearance of the new hair shaft on the surface of the skin. The Asian people typically experience lengthier anagen phases which can last up to 7 years and allow for hair growth of up to 1 meter. Genetics determines how long the hair will stay in this stage of growth. The length of growth of hair depends on how long it spends in the anagen phase.

Catagen phase

Hair enters the catagen phase at the end of the anagen phase. It is a brief phase of transition that lasts around 10 days. The stoppage of synthesis of melanin in the hair bulb and the apoptosis of follicular melanocytes are the first sign of this phase. The hair follicles can regenerate during this phase which is also known as transitional phase. The hair follicle shrinks due to disintegration during this period of about two weeks and the papilla separates and rests serving the hair strand from its nourishing blood supply. When the hair follicle is finally $1/6^{th}$ of its initial length the hair shaft is forced upward. The length of terminal fibres lengthens even though the hair is not actively growing at this stage. This phase accounts for about 2% of all hair growth and development.

Telogen phase

The final stage of hair growth cycle is telogen phase which is also known as resting phase. During this phase, the hair follicle is latent and the hair shaft does not grow. Approximately 10-15% of all body hairs are in this resting phase at any given moment and depending on the location of hair, this phase can last anywhere from a few weeks for eyelashes to almost a year for scalp hair.

Exogen phase

Long hair shedding was once thought to be a feature of the telogen phase, however it has now been proven that the exogen phase is separate phase during which shedding truly happens. According to recent study, the shedding of the hair fibre is an extremely active and controlled process. As a result, the process is different from the typical quiescence of telogen phase. According to earlier studies, hair loss is influenced by the freshly generated hair fibre pushing the resting shaft outward. The shape of hair root shows that a proteolytic event happens during the exogen process between the moving cells of the telogen shaft base. It is still unclear what allows for this shedding process. Desmoglein and proteolytic activities have been proposed as potential contributors. According to a different view, the exogen process involves at least two steps: the follicular base cells receive a signal or set of signals that initiate exogen are received by the follicular base cells after varying amounts of time in telogen. In the latter, the shedding effectors are activated.

Kenogen phase

This phase is also termed as interval phase. This phase states to the interval during which the hair follicle remains empty. It depicts the period of time following hair shedding and before the beginning of the new hair growth cycle. Extension of kenogen phase is observed in men and women having androgenetic alopecia.

Each hair follicle is liberated and completes the growth cycle at altered times, otherwise all the hair would fall out at once. Which hairs on the head are in which stage at any one time do not follow any pattern. A specific number of hairs up to 80 hairs are shed every day from a healthy head. The disturbance in hair growth cycle can lead to hair loss, hair thinning and growth related issues. Conditions including metabolic imbalance, sickness, or inadequate nourishment can cause this.

Antidandruff Shampoo

Dandruff

Dandruff is a non-inflammatory and infectious disease characterized by excessive shedding of the scalp epidermis followed by scalp redness and itching (Figure 4.5). There are about 195,785,036 cases of dandruff in India. It is accounting for about 50% population and characterizes about 25% of total scalp diseases. Nearly half of prepubescent people regardless of gender or race suffer from dandruff. The intensity of dandruff might change with the season because it frequently gets worse in the winter.

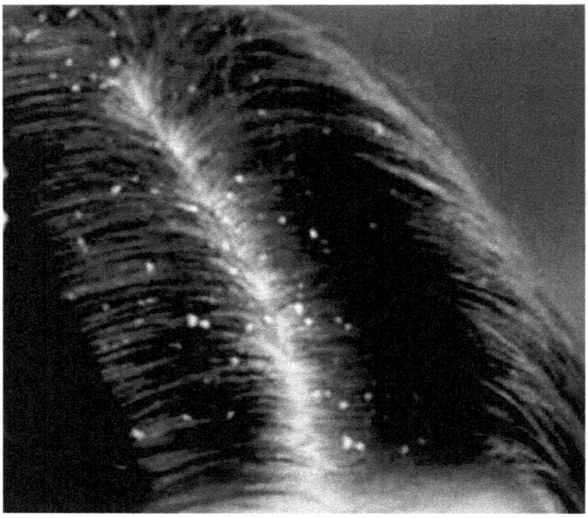

Figure 4.5: Dandruff.

Pathophysiology of dandruff

The main organism behind the progression of dandruff is lipophilic yeast species Pityrosporum including seven species *M. restrica, M. globasa, M. furfu, M. obtuse, M. sloofiae, M. pachydermatis* and *M. sympodialis* which was first demonstrated by Eichstedt in 1846. These species are main component of the typical skin flora living on the scalp of the hair and feeding on oil produced by the hair roots but during dandruff these organisms increased by 1.5-2 times to reach its usual level. There are several etiopathologic routes with complicated mechanisms that cause dandruff (Figure 4.6).

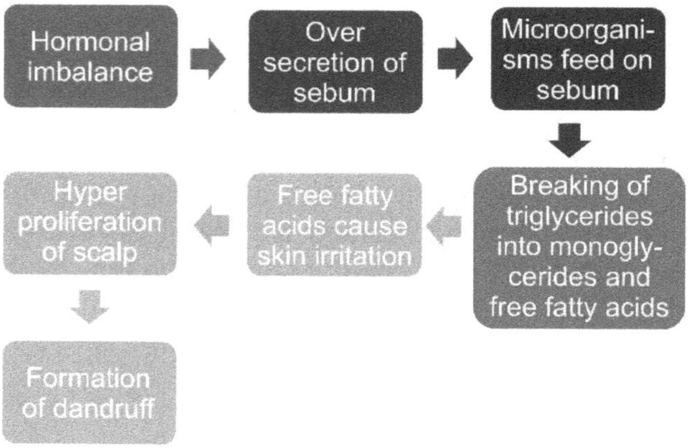

Figure 4.6: Sequential representation of pathophysiology of dandruff.

Types of Dandruff

Dry skin dandruff

It began when the scalp became dry and started to exfoliate the dry skin cells. The majority of the flakes are tiny and white. It mostly happens in the season of winter when the temperature is low and humidity is high.

Oily skin dandruff

Under the surface of skin, sebum is produced by glands whose primary function is to hydrate and protect the skin but if it is secreted in excess then it make hair greasy and cause dandruff. Seborrheic dermatitis can also cause oil skin dandruff.

Fungus related dandruff

This type of dandruff is caused by fungus species *Malassezia* which is present on the skin of each person. Conversely in some people it may cause seborrheic dermatitis.

Disease associated dandruff

Several skin conditions including eczema, psoriasis and seborrheic dermatitis can also cause dandruff to appear. When scalp psoriasis flares up, it can cause a white buildup of skin cells, irritation, scaling and eventually disease related dandruff. Thus in order to control this type of dandruff, underlying skin conditions must be treated.

Antidandruff ingredients

Antidandruff ingredients have been classified into various following classes:

- Antifungal agents
- Cytostatic agents
- Corticosteroids
- Keratolytic agents
- Anti-proliferative agents

Antifungal Ingredients

Ketoconazole

It is a popular antifungal drug. Chemically, it is imidazole analogue that prevents the formation of ergosterol in the membrane of fungal cells by blocking the activity of the Cyp-450 enzyme. It has been used for a variety of fungal infections on the skin including seborrheic dermatitis, tinea, dandruff and cutaneous candidiasis. Ketoconazole has been used as an active agent in shampoos to treat dandruff and the resulting hair loss issue in the concentration of 0.25-2% w/v. Additionally, it has been used to treat hair loss problems either on its own or in combination with other active ingredients. Dry skin and skin redness are the negative effects of shampoo containing ketoconazole.

Zinc pyrithione

The most popular bacteriostatic and fungistatic agent is zinc pyrithione. It is an ingredient that is beneficial in treating seborrheic dermatitis and dandruff because of its complex with zinc present in zinc pyrithione. Due to its limited water solubility, it lingers on the scalp even after rinsing. Due to its relative affordability it quickly rose to the top spot among materials used to treat dandruff on a global scale. Since 1960 it has been the antidandruff ingredient most frequently used in USFDA shampoo formulations. In order to stop fungal development, it relies on the ionophore characteristics of pyrithione and ultimately raises zinc levels in mammalian cells.

Climbazole

It is an antifungal ingredient that is applied topically to treat a variety of skin fungi including eczema, dandruff. It is preferred treatment for dandruff and it is effective in concentration of 0.25-2% w/v as antidandruff agent. The mode of action is comparable to ketoconazole in that it interferes with membrane function by preventing the synthesis of ergosterol and thereby increases drug permeability which in turn affects the normal functioning of the cell membrane and exhibits antifungal activity. The negative effects of climbazole include rashes, redness, irritation and sometimes ecotoxic.

Clotrimazole

It is another imidazole derivative used as antifungal ingredient in 1960. Being a broad spectrum antifungal agent it has demonstrated encouraging results in treating a number of illness including skin conditions and vaginal infections. Dandruff can be effectively treated with clotrimazole. It has a 1% concentration recommendation for anti-dandruff therapy. It prevents the synthesis of ergosterol by causing increase in permeability through cell membarne demonstrating its antifungal potential. It has no potential negative effects however overuse may cause erythema, stinging, blistering, skin irritation and burning sensation.

Selenium sulphide

Another antifungal ingredient that is suggested for dandruff and other fungal infections is selenium disulphide. For the treatment of cutaneous fungal infections it is offered as a shampoo and lotion to apply directly to the affected area. It was approved by United States in 1951 and listed on the essential drug list of the WHO. Later, it was made generic and is currently a drug that may be purchased without a prescription. It is used in 1-2.5% w/v concentration in shampoos to treat dandruff. It acts in two ways. Firstly, it acts as antifungal agent like zinc pyrithione and secondly it prevents the cell regeneration of skin. Due to which it can be effective in treating both seborrheic dermatitis and psoriasis induced dandruff. It can also be used to relieve the itching related to both above conditions of skin. But the use of selenium sulphide in excess can lead to oily hair and scalp.

Ciclopiroxolamine

Another effective antifungal ingredient used to treat dandruff is ciclopiroxolamine. It is hydroxy pyrimidine ring derivative. Ciclopirox has been prepared for clinical use as ciclopiroxolamine and olamine salts. It is also available in creams and lotions for treating a variety of fungal infections. It is more effective than oxiconazole, econazole and 2.5% hydrocortisone. The broad spectrum antifungal activity and anti-inflammatory activity of ciclopiroxolamine will able to cause clinical development in dandruff.

The antifungal mechanism of ciclopirox is less clear than that of other azole analogues. However it was thought that the antifungal activity was caused by the inactivation of enzymes such as catalase and peroxidase. It alters the DNA of fungus and leads to prevention of fungal cells from dividing. It is effective in concentration of 1.5% as antidandruff ingredient. It is equally effective as ketoconazole to treat seborrheic dermatitis still it is preferred over ketoconazole due to possession of anti-inflammatory activity also.

Corticosteroids

Fluocinolone

It is obtained from hydrocortisone which has antibacterial and antipruritic properties and is used to treat various skin infections. In was initially synthesized in 1959 in the research center of Syntex laboratories. Due to its reputation as strongest topical corticosteroid, fluocinolone may be urgently advised depending on how severe the scale infection is. Both shampoo (Carpex) and 0.01% solution (Synalar) of fluocinolone can lessen the scalp itching and inflammation. As a result they are helpful in treating mild to severe dandruff problems. To get rid of dandruff related problems, fluocinolone (0.01%) has been sold as cream, oil, gel. However it may cause skin atrophy, hyperpigmentation and dryness of skin.

Its mechanism is not well understood but it functions by causing the skin's own chemicals to be activated thereby reducing inflammation, itching and redness. Fluocinolone acetonide shampoo was found to be more effective and potent than the other therapies for seborrheic dermatitis in a double blind placebo controlled multicenter study.

Keratolytic agents

Coal tar

Coal tar is thought to comprise a complicated mixture of phenol, polycyclic aromatic hydrocarbons and heterocyclic substances. Its primary role is that of a keratolytic agent showing the pace of skin cell development and keratinization. Although the exact mechanism of action of coal tar is unknown, it causes massive proliferation epidermal cells by suppressing DNA synthesis in hyperplastic skin which then reduces the activity of mitotic protein synthesis in the lower layer of the epidermis. Because of this, it is used to treat a variety of scalp conditions namely eczema, psoriasis, sunburn and dandruff. However the prolonged use of coal tar may cause hyperpigmentation, telangiectasias and squamous cell carcinoma. It is available in form of shampoo in concentration of 0.5-3% in market.

Salicylic acid

It is the most common and oldest antidandruff ingredient which is a chemical exfoliant. It eliminates dead skin cells from the epidermis of the skin. It is recommended treatment for dandruff caused by mild or moderate psoriasis and it slows down the regeneration of skin cells. It is not only a fantastic ingredient for acne but also for removing dandruff flakes from scaly scalps due to its kerotoplastic properties. For those who have buildup on their scalp due to oiliness, pimples, or scalp acne, this is quite beneficial. While salicylic acid anti-dandruff shampoo may not be widely available in India, there are a tonne of salicylic acid face washes that you can use on your scalp without harm.

Anti proliferative agents

Topical calcineurin inhibitors

These include tacrolimus and pimecrolimus which offer potential in treating the skin conditions because of their innate immunosuppressive properties. They are frequently advised for skin eczema. These are effective calcineurin from fungi. These have proven antifungal effect on Malassezia species. Therefore, when given topically these drugs have the ability to fight both fungal and immune-suppressive conditions. However, to support these effects clinical research must be investigated.

Combinational treatment

It might be challenging to treat severe dandruff with just one anti-dandruff ingredient. Hence, in these conditions, taking two or more anti-dandruff ingredients is advisable to effectively treat dandruff. Typically, antifungal ingredients are combined to have a synergistic effect on dandruff. To address complex fungal problems of the scalp, keratolytic agents can be used with antifungal ingredients. Various studies have employed combination of anti-dandruff ingredients having superior action than their individual action. In a study, the combination of zinc pyrithione (1%w/w) and climbazole (0.5%w/w) was used to treat dandruff effectively.

Various commercial anti-dandruff shampoos having synthetic anti-dandruff ingredients have been summarized in Table 4.1.

Table 4.1: List of anti-dandruff shampoo with synthetic anti-dandruff ingredients.

Anti-dandruff agent	Marketed anti-dandruff shampoo
Zinc pyrithione and ciclopiroxolamine	Cipla-8X
Zinc pyrithione	Dove shampoo, Head & Shoulder shampoo, Pantene pro-v shampoo, Garnier fructis shampoo
Salicylic acid	Neutrogena
Piroctone Olamine	Sebamed shampoo
Coal tar	Denorex shampoo
Ketoconazole	Nizoral shampoo
Salicylic acid and ketoconazole	Protar shampoo
Zinc pyrithione and ketoconazole	Kezele plus shampoo

Herbal anti-dandruff ingredients

As Ayurveda gains more and more importance, several floral and herbs have been recognized for their influence on the beauty and cosmetic business. This market has been dominated by herbal cosmetics including conditioners, shampoos, soaps and face washes. On the other hand, numerous herbal remedies have demonstrated efficacy in treating conditions of scalp. Historically, aqueous preparations of *Ocimum sanctum, Acacia, Azadirachta indica, Aloe vera* have been employed to provide glossiness to hairs, to remove dandruff and to treat various other scalp conditions. Various herbal remedies employed as anti-dandruff ingredient have been summarized in Table 4.2.

Table 4.2: List of herbal remedies used as anti-dandruff agent.

Scientific name	Common name (Indian)
Mangefira indica	Mango
Lawsonia inermis	Mehndi
Zingiber officinalis	Ginger
Aloe vera	Aloe
Nyctanthes arbor-tristis	Harsingar
Camellia sinesis	Tea
Hibiscus rosa sinesis	Gurhal
Citrus aurantifolia	Nimbu
Acacia concinna	Shikakai
Eclipta alba	Bhringraj

CHAPTER 5

Cleansing Cosmetics

Over many millennia, the practice of cleansing has advanced greatly from the simple act of scraping the skin to a modern relaxing technique that enhances both the appearance and health of the skin. The fundamental cleaning agent, soaps, have evolved dramatically as well, gaining several variations and modern ingredients. Along with other therapeutic approaches, occupational dermatosis cleansers may be helpful in the treatment of dermatological conditions such as acne, rosacea, atopic dermatitis, photoaging, and "sensitive skin." The importance of cleaning and using different cleansing agents before cosmetic operations has increased with the development of aesthetic dermatology.

Cleansing and Care Needs for Face

Removing oil, grime, and other undesired detritus from the face is a common benefit of facial cleansing. The skin of face is continuously covered in dirt, bacteria, viruses, pollutants, and dead skin cells throughout the day. These pollutants are eliminated by daily face cleansing, leaving the skin looking radiant. In order to allow other things to fully permeate through the skin, it is need to wash the skin because it would be heavily coated in dirt and grime. Various home remedies are available to clean the face but the fast running world depends on cosmeceutical products for cleansing the face. The cosmetic products used for facial cleansing are following:

- Face wash
- Face cleansers
- Face creams
- Face masks
- Face moisturizers

Face wash

A face wash is a gentle cleanser that fulfills the essential tasks of keeping skin clear, smooth, germ-free, and fresh. It also hydrates the horny layer of the skin without being too harsh on it resulting in youthful and vibrant skin of the face. It can be used to provide skin-fairness, moisture, anti-wrinkle, and anti-acne qualities. It is believed that skin-lightening agents function by inhibiting the production of melanin in melanocytes, hence lowering the amount of melanin on the skin's metabolism and production of melanin. Ingredients that inhibit the production of melanin, such as propanediol, evodia rutaecarpa fruit extract, arbutin, kojic acid, and vitamin C and its derivatives, are utilized in whitening cosmetics since they are not harmful to melanocytes. It is best choice for oily and acne sensitive skin. It is believed to have at least four distinct mechanisms, including bringing the skin back to normal, producing more sebum inside the pores to avoid blockage, getting rid of the propioni bacteria that cause acne, being anti-inflammatory, and influencing hormone levels. It is available in various forms depending upon the physical form:

- Liquid face wash
- Gel face wash
- Cream face wash
- Powder face wash

A cream face wash leaves your skin feeling moisturized and clean. Typically, a cream based face wash is rich, creamy, and packed with vital hydrating ingredients like plant oils. It will assist you in eliminating any debris, perspiration, makeup, or microorganisms. For dry skin, cream-based facewashes and creamy cleansers are ideal. They eliminate all pollutants from the skin without depriving it of its natural oils.

Gel facewash is a type of face wash that is based on water and has a gel-like texture. It is usually formulated with essential oils and flower extracts. Gel facewash that can assist in pH balance for your skin. For skin types that are sensitive, irritated, or itch, gel facewash is advised. While many gel facewashes remove excess oil, they don't completely strip your skin of its oil, which makes them suitable for dry skin types as well. If you want a face cleanser that really cleans your skin, go for gel. In addition to thoroughly cleaning your pores, it also gets rid of extra oil and debris from the surface of your skin by unclogging them with a gentle formula that doesn't irritate your skin too much.

Liquid facewashes have become a common sight in the cosmetic industry because of their rapid onset of action, great dosage flexibility, and simplicity of swallowing. They are usually divided into two major categories: biphasic and monophasic formulations, which include a wide range of dose forms. In a monophasic liquid, the active pharmaceutical ingredient (API) dissolves entirely in the vehicle; in a biphasic liquid, the API is suspended or disseminated in the vehicle, creating two phases instead of a total dissolve. The kind of API and the intended therapeutic effect are thought to be the two main determining variables when selecting a liquid dosage form.

Powder facewashes are desirable for the human beings having sensitive skin and want to remove dead cells of the skin without extensive scrubbing.

Composition of Face Wash

There are various ingredients which are used to formulate face wash and face cleansers. With the use of these ingredients, the skin can be made to look healthier and less prone to flaking by clearing blocked pores and removing dirt and debris. Various ingredients used in formulation of face wash are following:

Active Ingredients

In skincare products, active ingredients are used to treat a variety of skin conditions and problems, such as eczema-prone skin, dry or oily skin, and wrinkles and fine lines. Presently, practically every kind of skincare product available on the market contains them, and their usage in natural cosmetics is growing in popularity. Active ingredients used in face wash include antioxidants such as Vitamin A, C, and E, probiotics such as hyaluronic acid, alpha-hydroxy acid, and coenzyme Q10 etc. However, the incorporation of active ingredients in face wash provides relief from various skin problems but overexposure of these ingredients can damage the skin in areas of thinner skin. Various active ingredients used in face wash along with their function has been compiled in the Table 5.1.

Table 5.1: Compiled list of active ingredients used in face wash

Ingredient	Function
Vitamin C	Antioxidant
Vitamin E	Antioxidant
Retinol	Anti-aging
Alpha-hydroxy acid	Exfoliant
Hydroquinone	Whitening agent
Hyaluronic acid	Hydrating agent
Niacinamide	Anti-inflammatory agent
Peptides	Collagen booster and anti-wrinkles
Ceramide	Buildup skin barrier

Humectants

Agents known as humectants draw in and retain molecules of water. To keep the skin hydrated and supple, they function by absorbing moisture from the surrounding environment and deeper layers of the skin. These can be synthetic like urea and glycerin or naturally occurring like hyaluronic acid. Whatever their origin, their purpose is the same: to retain moisture and ward off flakiness, roughness, and dryness. They draw water molecules to the surface of the skin when they come into touch with it. After being absorbed, these water molecules might form bonds with the humectant molecules in the top layers of the skin. The skin remains hydrated and smooth as a result of the moisturizing impact of this technique. Various humectants added in face wash include glycerin, propylene glycol, urea, aloe vera, and honey.

One of the most widely utilized humectants in skincare products is glycerin. The skin naturally contains glycerin, a humectant that aids in attracting and retaining moisture from the surroundings. It's one of the best humectants for your skin because it's mild, non-irritating, and works for all skin types. It can be utilized in various skin cosmetics such as face wash, skin conditioner, skin protectant, and as humectant. It decreases skin flaking when employed as skin conditioner and reduces skin irritation when employed as skin protectant. It can be found naturally and can be synthesized artificially.

Propylene glycol is extensively used personal care and cosmetic ingredient which organic alcohol in nature. According to the Cosmetic Ingredient Review (CIR), it is safe upto concentration of 50%. It is added in face wash to decrease flaking of the skin and to maintain the moisture level of the skin. It prevents dull, dry skin damage and keeps water in the skin.

Our skin cells contain urea, a chemical that exists naturally. Its superior moisturizing qualities have led to decades of use in skincare products. It aids in increasing the skin's moisture content and exfoliating dead skin cells. Products that address dry, rough, or cracked skin frequently contain it.

For ages, people have used aloe vera, a naturally occurring humectant, to soothe and moisturize their skin. It moisturizes the skin without making it feel oily or heavy while also assisting in the reduction of irritation and redness. Aloe vera is one of the greatest humectants for skin that needs some TLC because it works well for people with sensitive or acne-prone skin.

Honey is a fantastic humectant for the skin in addition to tasting nice in tea. In addition to having antibacterial and antioxidant qualities, honey aids in attracting moisture from the atmosphere and retaining it in the skin. It can help to minimize the appearance of fine lines and wrinkles while providing hydration that lasts, making it perfect for anyone with dry or mature skin.

Buffers

These agents are added to adjust the pH of the face wash resulting in stabilization of formulation. Tritehanolamine (TEA) is the agent which has been reviewed by CIR as safe and is used in various skin care products to control the pH of the formulation and an emulsifier. 5% concentration of triethanolamine is safe for cosmetics. It helps in reducing the interfacial tension between oil phase and water phase enabling mixing of them. It is important to remember that, depending on their skin type, certain people may be sensitive to triethanolamine. Therefore, in order to ascertain the compatibility of a product containing TEA, it is advised to conduct a patch test on a small region of skin, such as the neck.

Surfactants

Nowadays, almost all face wash and body cleansers include one or more surfactants. They perform various functions including cleansing, emulsification, solubilization, and conditioning effect. Additionally, some special functions like preservation, reduction of irritation and thickening property are also provided by the surfactants. But the excessive use of surfactants can damage to the barrier of skin. These have the capacity to pass through the stratum corneum and harm the lipids that make up the permeability barrier, reducing the levels of proteins, ceramides, and natural moisturizing factor, among other lipids causing oxidative stress, dryness, and inflammation. Using high pH cleaners can lead to considerable increases in desquamation, increased protease activity, and trans-epidermal water loss (TEWL). Various surfactants used in face wash include sodium lauryl sulphate (SLS), Sodium lauriminodipropionate, cocamidopropylamine oxide, cetyl alcohol, and steryl alcohol etc. SLS is the most widely utilized surfactant in face wash which belongs to category alkyl ether sulphates. They aid in production of foam and provide cleansing property to the face wash. They are used majorly in skin products which are meant for skin having high mineral.

Skin protectant

These agents protect the skin by boosting the effect of skin barrier and avoid the skin irritations. Various ingredients including allantoin (0.5-2%), calamine (1-25%), cocoa butter (50-100%), aluminium hydroxide gel (0.15-5%), lanolin (12.5-50%), zinc oxide (1-25%), zinc carbonate (0.2-2%), zinc acetate (0.1-2%) and kaolin (4-20%) are utilized as skin protectants in face wash.

Gelling agents

These agents improve the thickness of face wash which enables the increase in contact time of face wash with stratum corneum. Various ingredients like xanthan gum, carboxymethyl cellulose, agar, carrageenan, pectin, propylene glycol, carbopol etc. are used as gelling agents in face wash. Xanthan gum is extensively used natural gelling agent in various cosmetic products which is derived from fermentation process of plant bacteria *Xanthomonas campestris.* Because it is easily obtainable, adaptable, and compatible with the majority of substances used in cosmetics, xanthan gum is utilized extensively.

Organoleptic ingredients

These ingredients are added in any formulation to provide desired color, fragrance, and inhibition from microorganisms. Various shades of colors such as creamy, peach, green, pink, red etc. are used to get the final color of the product. Various essential oils, fragrance oils, and other fragrances are added in formulation to get desired perfume. Various preservatives like phenol, benzyl alcohol, parabens, benzoic acid etc are added to inhibit the growth of microorganisms in the final product resulting in prolonged stability.

Herbal ingredients used in face wash

Following herbal ingredients are added in face wash:

Peach extract

Owing to its purported benefits for skin texture and appearance, peach extract has gained popularity as an ingredient in skin care products. The extract may also aid in preventing wrinkles and other indications of aging, according to anecdotal evidence. This is most likely because of the ingredients, which are known to support good skin, including antioxidants and vitamins A and C. Peach extract not only offers these advantages but has also been demonstrated to have anti-inflammatory qualities, which may lessen the visibility of imperfections. Peach fruit is renowned for having a wealth of nutritional advantages. Antioxidants, which scavenge dangerous poisons and byproducts that might damage cells, are found naturally in peach extract. By promoting a young complexion and minimizing wrinkles and age spots, these antioxidants can help the skin seem better. Additionally, peach extract has moisturizing qualities that can maintain skin supple, hydrated, and healthy.

Cucumber extract

Cucumbers provide a long range of remarkable skin care advantages, so their advantages go beyond just the dinner table. Cucumbers are rich in vitamins, minerals, and other nutrients. It reduces skin irritation and maintains clear, healthy pores. Additionally, it aids in detoxifying the skin cells and removing stress. It helps in removal of pimples and acne from the skin due to balancing the sebum production. The possession of antioxidant in cucumbers provides relief from wrinkles. It keeps the skin healthy and hydrated due to possession of 96% water. It also relieves fatigue and under eyes bags.

Pea extract

Commercial facewashes often contain pea extract due to its well-known benefits for the skin. Peas are high in zinc and essential fatty acids, two nutrients that are good for skin health and help keep the skin hydrated, prevent dryness and flakiness, and protect against environmental damage. Peas are also a good source of vitamin A, which is necessary for the growth and repair of body tissues, including the skin.

Turmeric extract

Turmeric extract is one natural substance that is gaining popularity. Strong antioxidants like turmeric extract can help shield the skin from harm from free radicals. It may also aid in promoting healing and lowering inflammation. Moreover, the antibacterial qualities of turmeric extract might aid in maintaining clear, acne-free skin. In addition, turmeric has been a part of traditional Indian medicine for generations. According to recent research, turmeric extract possesses antioxidant and anti-inflammatory qualities, which may make it useful for usage in skin care products. According to a recent study that was published in the journal Phytotherapy Research, turmeric extract can effectively lower the amount of melanin produced by human skin cells as well as inflammation. Since melanin is what makes skin pigmentation darker, decreasing melanin synthesis may aid in lightening skin tone.

Neem extract

Neem extracts have been introduced to a wide range of products including facewash. Neem extract is a popular ingredient in face washes. Among these advantages include skin tone lightening, acne relief, and inflammation reduction. The advantages of neem extract in facewash are not well known. An all-natural antibacterial and antifungal that can calm and shield skin is neem. Additionally, it contains anti-inflammatory qualities that may aid in lowering acne-related redness and irritation. Neem extract is a mild and efficient substitute for the harsh chemicals present in a lot of facewashes sold in stores.

Tulsi extract

Tulsi extract is a beneficial ingredient in facewash. It is a naturally occurring antiseptic that aids in skin cleansing and guards against bacterial infections. Additionally, it contains anti-inflammatory qualities that aid in the reduction of swelling and inflammation. Tulsi extract also keeps the skin moisturized and helps to maintain a pH balance. Tulsi extract is a key ingredient in several Ayurvedic medications. Tulsi extracts are also a useful and natural skincare product, according to recent studies.

Aloe vera extract

Aloe vera is a plant that resembles a cactus that grows in desert areas all over the world. Vitamins A, C, E, and B12 are abundant in the gel that is produced by its leaves. It provides various skin benefits including anti-inflammatory property, support and production of collagen, wound healing property, antioxidant effect, reduction in skin burning, Moisturization property, and antibacterial or antifungal property. The possession of huge potential in skin problems makes, aloe vera a best ingredient to formulate face wash.

Apricort

Apricort contains various vitamins like vitamin A, C, E and minerals. Due to possession of these constituents, apricort provides various skin benefits like skin moisturizer, improving the skin elasticity, anti-wrinkles, and removal of blackheads and treatment of various skin disorders such as eczema, scabies, itching, and dry skin. It also serves as exfoliating agent to remove skin dead cells resulting in glowing skin.

Witch Hazel extract

The numerous advantages that witch hazel extract provides have led to its widespread use as an ingredient in face wash. Its anti-inflammatory and antioxidant qualities, which help to tone and clean the skin while also preventing aging signs, are the main advantages. Witch hazel extract is a popular option for those with oily or acne-prone skin because of its proven capacity to reduce pores and minimize the appearance of imperfections.

Lavender oil

This oil can be used to treat a variety of skin conditions, including acne, eczema, wound healing, and restoring the skin's natural radiance. The possession of anti-inflammatory property by lavender oil helps to provide glowing skin. The antibacterial property of this oil provides relieve from acne. The antibacterial and antifungal property of the oil cause inhibition of *Staphylococcus aureus* bacteria resulting in prevention of eczema. It also serves as wound healer and sun burn healer in various cosmetic products.

Various face washes available in market has been summarized in the Table 5.2.

Table 5.2: A summarized list of commercial face washes.

Brand name	Key ingredients	Applications	Manufacturer
Garnier Men Acno Fight	Salicylic acid	Uprooting of blackheads, removal of pimples, and freshening of face	Garnier
Garnier Men Turbo Bright Double Action	Vitamin C, black charcoal	Decrease the dullness, cleanses the skin deeply, remove the oil and dust, and remove pollution	Garnier
Garnier Men Oil Clear	Menthol, mineral clay	Removal of excessive oil from skin, impart freshness to the face and clean the face	Garnier
Clear & Clean	Lauric acid, Glycerin, and Benzophenone-4	Controls oil and remove pimples	Johnson & Johnson
Himalaya Herbals Purifying Neem Face wash	Turmeric extract,	Anti-acne and cleansing of the face	Himalaya
Himalaya Dark Spot Clearing Turmeric Face Wash	Turmeric, licorice, and niacinamide	Reduction of dark spots on face	Himalaya

Table 5.2: ***Contd....***

Brand name	Key ingredients	Applications	Manufacturer
Himalaya Men Active Sport Face Wash	Menthol, orange, and red ginseng	Removal of sweat, oil and dirt from face, reenergizes and brighten the face	Himalaya
Fair & Lovely Fairness Face Wash	Vitamin B3, C and E	Impart glow to face and deep cleansing of face	Fair & Lovely
Fair & Lovely Instant Brightness Rapid Action Facewash	Vitamin B3, C, E and icy cool menthol	Provides fresh, glowing skin	Fair & Lovely
POND'S Bright Beauty Spot-less Glow Face Wash	Lauric acid, Niacinamide, glycerin and menthol	Remove dullness by exfoliating the dead skin cells	POND'S
Ponds Pure Detox pollution clear	Lauric acid, Niacinamide, glycerin, and activated charcoal	Treat the problems like wrinkles, pimples, acne dullness etc. caused by pollution	POND'S
Patanjali Saundarya Face Wash	Niacinamide, Lauric acid, tocopheryl acetate, aloe vera, pearl, honey and retinyl palmitate	Removal of dirt and grime along with deep cleansing, healing and rejuvenation of the skin	Patanjali
Patanjali Saundarya Neem Tulsi Face wash	Aloe vera, tulsi, neem, vitamin E, and honey	Provide glow and freshness to face, prevent pimples and provides hydration to skin	Patanjali
Lakme Blush & Glow Hydrating Face Wash	Strawberry extract, glycerin, menthol, and vitamin C	Rejuvenation of the skin, and provides soft and glowing feel to the face	Lakme
Nivea Men Dark Spot Reduction Face Wash	Liquorice, Vitamin C, E, ginkgo leaves extract, ginseng leaves extract, and glycerin	Deep cleansing, refined and refreshed skin	Nivea
Nivea Purifying Face Wash	Fucus Vesiculosus Extract, tocopheryl Acetate, and glycerin	Retention of moisture, vitalization of the skin, and deep cleansing	Nivea

Face cleanser

Like face wash, face cleanser is also used to remove dirt, debris, pollution, and grime from the skin of the face but it removes only from upper layers of the skin while face wash removes from deeper layers of the skin. These are mainly used to remove facial make up or any other impurities present on the surface of the skin. It occurs in cream or lotion form and mainly applied for cleansing of the sensitive skin. Various differences between the face wash and face cleanser has been compiled in the table 5.3.

Table 5.3: Compilation of differences in between the face wash and face cleanser.

Properties	Face cleanser	Face wash
Application	Remove the dirt, debris, and pollutants from skin's surface only	Remove the dirt, debris, and pollutants from deeper layers of skin
Suited skin	Sensitive skin	Oily skin
Gentleness	Gentler than face wash	Gentler than soap bar
Time for use	Night	Morning
Rinsing	Rinsing can be done or not	Rinsing is required
Texture	Gel and foam	Cream, lotion, oil and powder

Types of Cleansers

Foaming cleansers

Foaming cleansers are advised for oily skin types, however they can also be highly drying. The cleansers that foam the longest are those that take a minimal quantity of cleanser to produce a thick lather and thoroughly clean the entire face. If you have dry or inflamed skin, foaming cleansers may be too drying for you. These can be purchased as creams or gels. While cream foamy cleansers might not be as stripping as gel foaming cleansers, they do contain oils and emollients.

Non-foaming cleansers

The majority of non-foaming cleansers are mild gel or lotion formulas designed for people with delicate or eczema-prone skin. These are gentle cleansers that don't foam and don't appear to accomplish much cleaning. These don't take away sunscreen or makeup. Cleaners that don't foam can be wiped away with water or only with a tissue. Additionally, they could leave a thin coating on the skin. These cleansers work well for dry skin types or for use in the morning.

Cleansing balms

Tissue-off cleansers with an oil or cream base are known as cleansing balms. Those with very dry skin or as makeup removers typically use them. Oil washing balms have a viscosity similar to petroleum jelly, while cream cleansing balms are thick, cold creams. When exposed to body heat, they liquefy from their solid state at room temperature. These cleansers work well for getting rid of sunscreen, stage makeup, and other waterproof items. After tissuing off, they typically leave behind an oily residue that can be removed with a second cleaner.

Micellar

Cleaning waters are another name for micellar cleaners. They resemble a toner that is cleaning virtually. Using a cotton pad, apply the cleansing solution to a micellar cleanser; the liquids in the cleanser will dissolve any dirt, oil, or other substance due to the micellar particles in the cleanser. Micellar cleansers represent an incredibly gentle alternative for people whose skin is easily irritated by anything, including tap water.

Oil cleansers

Oil cleansers are divided into two categories. One is known as the Oil Cleansing Method, and the other is an oil cleansing product.

Makeup and water-resistant sunscreen can be removed by cleansing oil, although regular cleanser cannot. Dry skin is covered with the washing oil, which is then rubbed and washed (turms milky white). Because of the emulsifiers in the cleansing oil, it may be removed with merely water.

With a few minor exceptions, the Oil Cleansing Method (OCM) is comparable to cleansing oils. The OCM involves applying basic oil—such as castor, olive, jojoba, safflower, or vaseline—to dry skin, wiping it off with a warm, but not hot, washcloth, and steaming it. It is optional to use a non-cleansing oil cleanser afterward. If not, just use a good foaming cleanser to remove the oil after washing it off rather than using a wash towel. While the skin can be washed, the OCM leaves behind trace amounts of oil to nourish and hydrate. Using oils is based on the idea that "oils dissolve oils or likes dissolve likes." Oils are also useful for eliminating sunscreen and waterproof makeup.

Medicated cleansers

Any of the aforementioned cleansers—but mostly in the form of foam cleansers—are advertised as medicated cleansers for those with acne-prone skin. The active chemicals in the cleansers are either benzoyl peroxide, which helps to fight bacteria, or salicylic acid, which helps to unclog pores. But after washing with a simple but light cleanser, the majority of medicated cleansers are too strong and ought to be used as an additional acne treatment solution.

Soap free cleansers

Cleaners sans soap are those that don't use sodium lauryl, sodium laureth sulphate or sodium sulphate. Some people find soap-based cleaners to be harsh or irritating. For others, a cleanser without soap may be required prior to receiving a chemical peel. The skin will be better prepared and the peel will work better if you use a cleanser without soap for a few days prior to the procedure.

Face masks

Face masks are an excellent way to tackle particular skin care issues and are a terrific addition to any skincare program. Masks provide a calming, spa-like experience at home while hydrating skin, eliminating excess oil, and improving the appearance of pores. Facial masks are readily available, simple to use, and have immediate benefits for the skin. To give the masks their rejuvenating qualities, bioactive ingredients with various mechanisms are added, such as exfoliants, moisturizers, herbal and lightening ingredients, growth factor (GF), various types of vitamins, proteins, and minerals, and additional materials like honey and coenzyme Q. It is anticipated that the mask would eliminate sebum, properly and deeply moisturize the skin, and revitalize it. The skin masks often have convenient application due to their pseudoplastic qualities. They come in a variety of forms, including gel, emulsion, sheet, and paste.

Types of Face Masks

Sheet mask

The sheet mask is an older style of mask that is more widely accessible than other varieties because of its availability from prolonged time. The main issues with sheet masks are the various synthetic perfumes and colors, parabens, and phthalate esters that are utilized, all of which can be bad for the skin. Because there are more bacteria on the skin's surface, some doctors think that sheet masks aren't usually made for those with oily or acne-prone skin. Additionally, a sheet mask delays the rate at which the water phase evaporates and increases the amount of time needed for the chemicals to deeply permeate the skin. Depending on the company, sheet masks can include everything from standard components like vitamin C and *Aloe vera* to uncommon ones like pearl, snail extract, and seaweed. Sheet masks can be of different types depending on the type of fabrics like pulp masks, hydrogel masks, foil sheet masks, ampoule sheet masks, bubbling masks, knit cotton masks, and bio-cellulose masks.

Rinse-off masks

There are numerous varieties of rinseable masks, including mud, waxy, cleansing, toning, exfoliating, and moisturizing ones. For dry skin, waxy masks are typically used to control the epidermal hydration level and limit transepidermal water loss. One major component of skin appearance is the equilibrium of water content between the stratum corneum and skin surface lipid. In this sense, polyherbal supplements have great promise due to their natural organic origins and moisture-retaining properties. Moisturizers also contain synthetic ingredients, however these have certain disadvantages. For instance, the humectant propylene glycol might result in eczema, rashes, and allergic reactions. As an occlusive and emollient, petroleum-tum can have adverse effects such as chopping and dryness. Although paraben has antibacterial properties, it can also result in skin rashes and allergic reactions. Diazolidinyl urea, imidazolidinyl urea, and benzalkonium chloride are employed as preservatives, however they cause contact dermatitis as a side effect. Diethanolamine is used as an emulsifier but irritates the skin.

Herbal moisturizers include soy lecithin, glycerin, and Aloe vera (which contains barbaloin, aloe-emodin, aloesin, amino acids, enzymes, and vitamins) as humectants; triple-distilled water, *Triticum sativum*, and *Trigonella foenum graecum* as occlusive/emollients; *Cucumis sativus* (which contains silica, vitamin C, and folic acid) as adhesives/emollients; Acacia as an emulsifier; *Azadirachta indica* (Neem) as a preservative; *Santalum alba* (sandal oil) for fragrance; and rose water for a cooling effect. Herbal mask is a non-toxic and non-allergic rinse-off mask.

Peel-off mask

Certain materials, like clay, which is commonly used in cosmetic preparations, cannot be applied properly or conveniently; as a result, they are immobilized on the substrate for easy application. These kinds of masks leave a film on the skin that is simple to remove. The majority of peel-off masks are made using polyvinyl alcohol (PVA) or polyvinyl acetate (PVAc), which result in tensor effect and occlusion. The mask can contain a variety of ingredients, including moisturizer, herbal soap, plasticizer, fragrances, and preservative. Masks come in a variety of compositions, but drying agents like alcohol and matrix concentration usually determine how well they work. Owing to its lower vapour pressure than water, alcohol is widely utilized as a drying agent to regulate the duration of application. The less time needed for drying, higher the alcohol content. The viscosity, film formation, and application thickness are all determined by the matrix concentration. This concentration needs to be adjusted to create the right mask for the application.

Different herbals have been used in masks for different reasons: beetroot reduces acne, orange peel acts as an astringent and toner, apples provide antioxidants, walnuts act as emollients, and cucumbers soothe. Based on tretinoin (an acne drug), glycerin (a humectant that promotes skin hydration), and sodium metabisulfite (an antioxidant in PVA matrix), a mask for treating acne vulgaris was created.

Hydrogel mask

A hydrogel mask is a form of sheet mask that, in contrast to conventional cotton masks, has a gel-like texture that is incredibly calming and pleasant to the skin. Its distinct texture not only makes the mask more comfortable, but it also makes sure that it sticks to the skin evenly and smoothly for the best possible touch. As a result, the skin-boosting elements in the mask are delivered more effectively. The way hydrogel masks function is by sealing your skin. The skin is better able to absorb a higher concentration of nutrients because of this physical barrier, which seals in the treatment and stops it from evaporating. These masks' gel texture, which is typically colder than that of regular sheet masks, has a revitalizing and calming impact that makes it ideal for healing inflamed skin and minimizing puffiness. Hydrogel masks provide improved hydration of skin, improved skin texture, soothing effect, cooling effect, and anti-acne property. Various ingredients used in face masks have been compiled in the Table 5.4.

Table 5.4: Various ingredients used in face masks

Category	Example	Application
Vitamins	Vitamin A	Treatment of acne and wrinkles, protection from UV rays and regulation of keratinization
	Vitamin B3	Anti-inflammatory effect, enhanced lipid synthesis and skin lightening effect
	Vitamin C	Antioxidant, anti-wrinkles, wound healing property, and protection from sun burn
	Vitamin E	Antioxidant, protection from sun burn and treatment of eczema

Table 5.4: ***Contd....***

Category	Example	Application
Exfoliant	Alpha hydroxy acids (Glycolic acid, hyaluronic acid)	Anti-wrinkles, improvement of skin texture and tone, unclogging and cleansing pores and adjustment of skin pH
	Beta hydroxy acids (Salicyclic acid)	Anti-inflammatory effect
Moisturizers	Glycerin, lecithin, propylene glycol, jojoba oil	Retention of skin hydration or moisture
Honey		Antioxidant, anti-inflammatory, wound healing, emollient and humectant
Brightening ingredients	Vitamin C, Vitamin E, Alpha hyroxy acids, hydroquinone (widely used), azelaic acid, Kojic acid, and retinoids	Depigmentation of skin
Proteins	Collagen, Epidermal growth factors	Moisturizing, regenerating and film forming ability
Minerals	Clay	Skin cleansing and moisturizing property, reduction of cellulite and acne
	Zinc oxide	Protect from environmental pollutants, irritants and allergens
	Gold, silver	Antibacterial, antifungal and antiviral property
Herbal ingredients	Aloe vera	Removal of dead skin cells and moisturizing effect
	Rice bran	Antioxidant
	Green tea	Antioxidant and anti-inflammatory effect
	Parsley	Control of sebum
	Coenzyme Q10	Facilitate the penetration through stratum corneum

Moisturizing cream

Dry skin is dehydrated, and there are several ways cosmetic formulas can temporarily make up for this by moisturizing the skin. The stratum corneum, or non-viable epidermis, can have its water content increased by a preparation. To relieve the symptoms and indications of dry skin and leave it feeling smooth and soft, moisturizers are applied. Based on the idea that fats and oils keep the skin smooth, lipids were the main ingredients in earlier moisturizer formulations. Actually, it is hard to say how much skin water content is necessary for proper moisturization. About 70% of the keratinocytes in the basal layer are made of water. The stratum comeum diminishes to approximately 15% when it reaches the desquamating layers. The current moisturizing technique is to:

1. Increase the ability of the stratum comeum to retain water with the use of humectants, which are hydrophobic substances applied externally. These compounds function similarly to the skin's natural moisturizing factor (NMF), including lactic acid and urea.
2. By depositing an oily substance that is insoluble in water on the skin's surface, occlusive agents can trap water in the stratum comeum. Oily materials have an effect similar to the skin's natural lipid bilayers, which limit evaporation from the petrolatum-covered surface.

There are various ways to get moisturized, but using emollients and humectants is the most common one. Preserving normal skin and restoring inadequate components are alternative strategies.

Emollients

Skin feels smooth and velvety once a small layer of occlusive materials, like oil or wax, is applied. These substances, usually referred to as emollients, frequently lessen TEWL (transepidermal water loss), which tends to raise the water content of stratum corneum, such as lanolin alcohols and hydrocarbons.

Humectants

Although humectants are intended to increase skin hydration, in certain situations they may actually cause the skin to lose water. Water loses its activity coefficient when it is sorbed by a humectant. Water molecules will not be transported to the skin if the water activity of the skin tissue is not lower than that of the surrounding humectant-water blend. For this reason, glycerin is often the humectant of choice.

Restoration of Deficient Materials

Preservation of normal skin

Moisturizers protect sensitive skin, cure and prevent dry skin, enhance skin tone and texture, and conceal flaws. To keep the skin from getting overly dry or oily, apply moisturizers. Light, non-greasy moisturizers with a water base work well. These moisturizers frequently include silicone-derived components like cyclomethicone or light oils like cetyl alcohol. The kind of skin may influence the moisturizer choice.

Moisturizer for dry skin

The best moisturizers for treating dry skin are thicker formulas with substances like dimethicone, grape seed oil, or antioxidants. Petrolatum based treatments work better than creams for dry, cracked skin because they last longer and keep water from evaporating.

Moisturizer for oily skin

Moisturizers can still be helpful for oily skin following actions that lead to sundryness, including utilizing care products and washing. Water-based moisturizers are better for oily skin.

Moisturizer for ageing skin

Oil-based moisturizers with petrolatum as the foundation work well to keep aging skin hydrated and smooth. They can also contain alpha hydroxy acids or antioxidants to help prevent wrinkles.

Moisturizer for sensitive skin

Use moisturizers with calming elements like aloe vera and that reduce potential allergens like scents or colors as well as irritants like acids on sensitive skin, which is otherwise prone to skin irritation, redness, itching, or rashes.

Classification of moisturizing creams

Moisturizing cream can be classified into four types namely day cream, night cream, hand and body lotions, and all-purpose creams which has been summarized in the Table 5.5.

Table 5.5: Classification of moisturizing creams

Ingredients	Night cream	Day cream	Hand & Body lotion	All-purpose cream
Petroleum jelly	8.0	-	-	10.0
Mineral oil	38.0	4.0	10.0	60.0
Paraffin wax	1.0	-	-	24.0
White bees wax	15.0	-	-	-
Cetyl alcohol	15.0	3.0	2.0	-
Lanolin	2.0	-	2.0	-
Stearic acid	-	-	20.0	-
Glyceryl monostearate	-	12.0		-

Table 5.5: *Contd....*

Ingredients	Night cream	Day cream	Hand & Body lotion	All-purpose cream
Sorbitan sesquioleate	-	-	2.0	-
Glycerol	-	12.0	7.5	-
Borax	2.0	-	-	-
Propylene glycol	-	-	5.0	-
Sorbitol	-	-	2.5	-
Preservative	q.s.	q.s.	q.s.	q.s.
Water	35.0	69.0	-	-
Antioxidant	q.s.	-	-	q.s.
Perfume	q.s.	q.s.	q.s.	q.s.

Disadvantages of moisturizers

- The safety of the ingredients contained by the moisturizers
- The chances of bacterial degradation
- Some peoples are allergic or sensitive to various chemicals used in moisturizers which can cause rashes, or other allergic reactions.

Moisturizers as Cosmeceuticals

Due to the fact that moisturized skin bends to release sebum that has accumulated inside pores, it is crucial to treat acne. The use of clogging substances such as mineral oil, petroleum, or silicones like dimethicone in a face moisturizer for skin prone to acne is not recommended. Avoid using moisturizers with alcohol in them since this can exacerbate inflammation because it dries out the skin, which is why controlling oil production can make it worse. Gel, oil-free, or water-based moisturizers are good options. Benzoyl peroxide and salicylic acid are two components that can be included in a moisturizer to manage acne. A moisturizer can also contain humectants, such as glycerin and hyaluronic acid, which draw moisture to the skin to maintain its natural moisture content, and mild exfoliants, such lactic and glycolic acid, which assist to lighten any remaining dark or red patches. Combining benzoyl peroxide and salicylic acid-based acne treatments with alpha hydroxy acids (glycolic and lactic) can cause imitation and dry skin. Various cosmeceuticals as skin moisturizers have been added in the Table 5.6.

Table 5.6: Various cosmeceuticals used as moisturizers.

Ingredients	Formulation	Application	Positive attributes	Negative attributes
Salicylic acid	Lotion	Anti-acne	Avoid the drying of skin, oil free	Has no sun protection factor
Soy complex	Lotion	Skin toner	Oil free and non-comedogenic	Has no sun protection factor
Witch hazel	Cream	Anti-acne	Natural	Unsuitable for oily skin
Oligopeptide-10		Anti-acne	Improves skin complexation	
Lemon grass	Lotion	Soothing the skin	Non-comedogenic	More viscous
Hyaluronic acid	Lotion	Makes the skin plumper and supple	Useful for acne prone skin	Doesn't clear blemishes
Lactic acid	Lotion	Exfoliating the skin	Makes skin more clear	-
Tea tree & cucumber extract	Lotion	Reduction of redness and soothing of skin	Hydration	-
Macadamia nut oil	-	Reduction of itching and inflammation	Non-greasy feel	Can sting eyes
Avobenzone	Lotion	Soothing of dry skin	Non-greasy, non-irritating and non-comedogenic	-

Face creams

Face creams such as cold cream, vanishing cream has been discussed in chapter 7 in detail, so kindly refer chapter 7 for details of face creams.

Care needs for face

There are following essential phases to a regular skin care program, which you can perform once in the morning and once before bed.

Cleanser

Wash the face lightly, being careful not to scrub too vigorously using cleanser. After that, give the skin a warm water rinse because hot water strips away natural oils and dehydrates the skin. Use one without alcohol or fragrance if one has dry skin. Persons with oily skin, should seek for an oil-free product and maybe think about using a toner as well.

Toner

After cleansing the face, use a toner to help relax, soften, and smooth the skin. Toners can help reduce redness and dry areas on the skin by including substances that replenish and restore nutrients to the skin.

Moisturizer

Moisturizers are universally suitable and ought to be applied after every facial wash. Similar to cleansers, finding the ideal product may take some trial and error; oily skin, for instance, responds better to lightweight, oil-free, or gel solutions. By keeping the skin hydrated and smooth, moisturizers shield it from drying out. When applied while your skin is still slightly damp, they work best to seal in moisture.

Sunscreen

Certain moisturizers come with SPF, but if the moisturizer doesn't have an SPF of at least 30, it does not hurt to use sunscreen twice as often. By now, you ought to be familiar with the lines: Even in gloomy or chilly weather, and even when one is covered up, remember to use sunscreen every day. Reapply after every two hours if exposed to sun. Make sure the UVA and UVB rays are blocked by your sunscreen. UV exposure is the leading cause of wrinkles, uneven skin tone, loss of firmness, and aging indications.

Exfoliation

Exfoliation helps remove flaky skin by promoting skin cell turnover; it can be used before moisturizer but after cleanser. Although exfoliating dead skin and buildup might result in smoother skin and clearer pores, most physicians advise against using scrubs in favor of chemical exfoliants to preserve the skin's protective layer.

Serum

Serums are an additional optional component of your face care regimen that include components like retinol or antioxidants that support the health of your skin in a variety of ways, like reducing redness and enhancing firmness and texture.

Cleansing and care needs for lips

The lips, which are frequently regarded as one of the most attractive elements of the face, have a structure that is both delicate and complex that transcends simple beauty. These structures, made up of thin skin layers, are more vulnerable to outside forces because they lack the outer layer of protection that covers the majority of our skin. Various lip care products include lip scrubs, lip balms, lip sticks, and lip gloss.

Lip scrub

A lip scrub is a mixture of particles in a semi-liquid or other soft-solid basis that removes dry, flaky skin cells and leaves the skin smooth. Lip scrubs are a form of mechanical exfoliation, which means that dead skin cells are physically removed as opposed to chemically. Lips that have been properly exfoliated are more receptive to protectants and moisturizers like lip balm. The majority of lip scrubs also come in a lipstick-like formula that may be used straight out of the container. For a more even application of color, use either version to prepare your lips before applying lipstick.

Oily or creamy bases are typically used in lip scrubs. These bases contain emollients, which are compounds that aid in soothing, moisturizing, and softening the skin. Typical emollients consist of cocoa butter, jojoba oil, coconut oil, avocado oil, shea butter, grapeseed oil, and pure vitamin E oil. Additionally, humectants that draw water to the surface of the skin to improve moisture retention are found in several lip scrubs. Hemp, glycerin, and aloe vera are common humectants. Raw honey is said to possess inherent qualities. Lastly, exfoliants are the small solid particles that are used with the base ingredients to genuinely brush away dead skin. Coarse oats, coffee grounds, and fine-granule white or brown cane sugar are examples of gentle exfoliants.

Lip balms

Lip balms comprise a moisturizing balm that is applied to the lips for protection and nourishment. Depending on the components, the balm may have a flavor, taste, or be natural. A quality lip balm will both treat dry or chapped lips and replenish moisture. Its viscosity is similar to that of wax. Nutritious elements included in lip balms, such beeswax, shea butter, and natural oils, act as a moisturizer and shield your lips from harm. Lip balm can assist in replenishing the essential moisture that is lost from the lips due to exposure to wind, cooler temperatures, and dry air. Because our lips have such thin skin, they are more vulnerable than other areas of our body. Compared to other regions of the body, the skin of our lips frequently becomes much drier. Naturally derived components are used to make natural lip balm, which is typically a better option for people with sensitive skin or lips. Natural lip balm is made from nutritious elements sourced from nature, including beeswax, coconut oil, vitamin C, and E.

The common ingredients used in formulation of lip balm include various bases (cocoa butter, bees wax, shea butter, white bees wax, carnauba wax, candelilla wax, avocado butter, jojoba butter), oils (almond oil, olive oil, coconut oil, peanut oil, arachis oil, avocado oil, lemon oil, jojoba oil, sunflower oil, vitamin E oil), coloring agents (beet root extract, pomegranate, tomato, honey, saffron, strawberry, carrot, lemon, cherry), and flavoring agents (strawberry, honey, saffron, rose oil, sandalwood oil, apple, lemon, pineapple, jasmine, cherry).

Lipsticks

Lipstick is a cosmetic product that women mostly use to give their lips a lovely color, glossy aspect, and youthful appearance. Essentially, these are coloring matter dispersions on a base consisting of an oil and wax mixture that has been appropriately scented, formed into the shape of a stick, and sealed in a case. Various essential characteristics possessed by lipsticks include:

- These should make the lips soft and be able to cover the lips correctly with a hint of gloss and last for a long time.
- The film should not be hard or brittle; it should stick to the lips.
- The color intensity should be retained to a great degree without changing in shade.
- It must be non-toxic and grittiness free.
- It should not cause irritation or dryness of the lips.

The formulation of lipsticks include various ingredients namely structuring agents, oils, bromo mixtures, coloring agent, preservatives, flavoring agents, antioxidants, and surfactants. In addition, various other ingredients like sunscreen agents, silicon fluid, and isopropyl linoleate may also be included in their composition. The formulation of a lipstick has been given in the Table 5.7.

Table 5.7: Various ingredients used in formulation of a lipstick.

Ingredients	Quantity
Carnauba wax	2.5 gm
Candelilla wax	6 gm
Ozokerite wax	2.5 gm
Bees wax	6 gm
Lanolin	8 gm
Castor oil	55 gm
Isopropyl myristate	4 gm
Halogenated fluorescein	3 gm
Lake colour	12 gm
Preservative	0.20 gm
Perfume	0.80 gm

Lip gloss

Lip gloss is a type of makeup that is mostly used to give lips a glossy sheen, though it can also be used to subtly tint lips. It is sold as a liquid or a soft solid (not to be confused with lipstick, which is typically a solid, cream-like product that imparts a highly pigmented color, or with lip balm, which typically has medicinal or soothing properties). The product can have frosted, sparkly, glossy, or metallic qualities, and its opacity ranges from translucent to solid. Lip gloss is made of a blend of waxes, oils, and pigments, just like lipstick. But there are fewer pigments in lip gloss, and the ones that exist are frequently thinly diluted (<3%) or have a light color. Moreover, less wax is used because the product flows naturally. The main ingredients are polybutene and lanolin, which feels nice on the lips because of its moisturizing properties and gloss. Various lip care products available in market has been compiled in the Table 5.8.

Table 5.8: List of commercial lip care products in the market

Brand name	Benefits	Product type
Lip Love scrub	Smoothening	Lip scrub
Nicolips	Hydrating	Lip scrub
Glow lip scrub	Moisturizing	Lip scrub
Vilvah lip scrub	Exfoliation and reduction of dryness	Lip scrub
mCaffeine	Reduction of dark lips and pigmentation, exfoliation and moisturization	Lip scrub
Plix	Hydrating, exfoliating and brightening	Lip scrub

Table 5.8: ***Contd....***

Brand name	Benefits	Product type
Pink Grapefruit	Exfoliating	Lip scrub
Bio Morning Nectar	Lightening and flawless	Lip balm
Himalaya Lip balm	Relief from chapped and sore lips	Lip balm
Nivea Strawberry	Nourishing and hydrating the lips	Lip balm
Blistex	Sunburn prevention	Medicated lip balm
Maybelline	Hydrating	Lipstick
Elle18 Lip Gloss	Moisturizing	Lip gloss
Glossed lip gloss	Hydrating	Lip gloss
Lakme Absolute Plump & Shine	Moisturizing, shine and smoothening	Lip gloss
SUGAR POP High shine	Hydrating, nourishing, smoothening, and long lasting	Lip gloss
RENEE Hot Lips	Hydrating	Lip gloss

Care needs for lips

A straight forward yet effective strategy to maintain the health and appearance of your lips is to follow a regular lip care regimen. Every action counts toward maintaining the delicate character of this face feature, from washing to sun protection. Let's examine a thorough daily lip care regimen, emphasizing the significance of every action for hydrated, silky, and healthy lips.

Cleansing the lips

Throughout the day, the lips, like the rest of face, gather debris, oils, and pollutants from the outside world. Keeping up a good lip care regimen starts with cleaning the lips. To remove any debris, use a moderate, fragrance-free soap or a gentle, moisturizing lip cleanser. For a little exfoliation during the cleansing procedure, think about using a soft, damp towel or a toothbrush with soft bristles. This encourages a smoother lip texture and aids in the removal of dead skin cells.

Exfoliation of lips

A crucial first step toward having soft, smooth lips is exfoliation. It facilitates the removal of dead skin cells, encouraging cell turnover and exposing brand-new skin. For a more natural solution, try making your own lip scrub with sugar and honey or selecting a product with fine exfoliating particles. After gently massaging the scrub in circular motions onto the lips, rinse it off. Because the skin on lips is fragile, try not to overdo it when exfoliating them twice a week. To seal in moisture, use a hydrating lip balm afterward.

Moisturization of the lips

Keeping the lips moisturized is essential for good lip care. Because the lips' thin skin is devoid of oil glands, it is more vulnerable to dryness and chapping. Choose a premium lip balm with nutritious components like vitamin E, shea butter, almond oil, or beeswax. Throughout the day, liberally use the lip balm, especially after washing and exfoliating. Before going to bed, apply a thicker layer of lip balm for maximum hydration. This enables the cream to do its magic overnight, leaving the lips feeling smooth and renewed when wake up.

Sun protection of the lips

When it comes to lip care, sun protection is frequently disregarded. But the lips are particularly vulnerable to sun damage, which can result in sunburn and early aging. After eating or drinking, use a lip balm with a broad-spectrum SPF of at least 30, or more frequently if necessary. For complete coverage, use a moisturizer or sunscreen with SPF to extend the face's protection from the sun.

Including these four actions in the regular lip care regimen offers a comprehensive approach to maintaining healthy lips. Exfoliation encourages smoothness, moisturizing keeps skin from becoming dry, and sun protection shields skin from damaging UV rays. Cleaning gets rid of impurities.

Cleansing and care needs for eyelid

Due to their vital function in our existence, the eyes are among the most valuable organs in our bodies. It's important to clean your eyes every day for sanitary as well as cosmetic reasons. But it can be difficult to select the best product with so many possibilities accessible. Various cleansing products like eyelid wipes, eyelid foam, eyelid spray, and eyelid solutions are available to clean the eyelids.

Eyelid wipes

Wipes are among the most common and practical kinds of eyelid cleaners. These pre-moistened, individually wrapped wipes are a convenient solution for on-the-go use. People with sensitive skin can use wipes because they are mild and soft on the skin. However, they should only be used for daily cleansing as they lack the strength to remove stubborn makeup or dirt. All cleansing eye wipes have the same main purpose, which is to thoroughly clean the region around the eyes. However, there are several varieties with varied purposes, and some can be more suitable than others. For instance, makeup-specific eye wipes are usually made to gently remove eye makeup without the use of water. If you use waterproof mascara, though, you might want to opt for a stronger remover than someone who uses a non-waterproof variety. Cleaning eye wipes appear like a convenience when compared to other methods of cleaning the face and eyes because each wipe is essentially a combination of washcloth and soap. Moreover, no-rinse washing eye wipes eliminate the need for water or even a restroom. No-rinse wipes can be useful if there is need to remove the makeup before leaving work or school, or if you have an eye ailment (like allergies) that requires to clean the eye area throughout the day. For those who frequently travel or go camping and do not always have easy access to restrooms. Alternatively, utilizing no-rinse wipes can be a simpler and faster approach to clean your face before bed.

Eyelid foam

One more well-liked choice for contact lens wearers is the foam cleanser. Despite being mild, this kind of cleanser may effectively eliminate extra oil, makeup, and dirt from your eyelids. Because it is gentle and does not irritate skin or clog pores, it may also be used as face cleanser.

Eyelid sprays

Another alternative to eyelid cleaners is to use cleaning sprays. They do not need to be rinsed or rubbed, and they are simple to use. The calming combination of vitamins, antioxidants, and glycerin in the sprays helps to nourish and revitalize the skin around the eyes.

Gel cleansers

An increasingly common choice for those with dry eyes is gel cleansers. Because they moisturize the skin, they are hydrating and can aid to relieve sore eyelids. Those with sensitive skin or those who have had eye surgery can use gels because they are mild.

Eyelid cleansing oils

Oils for cleaning the eyelids have many advantages for those with dry eyes. These specialty oils offer relief and hydration while delicately cleansing and soothing the eye area. They get rid of dirt, leftover makeup, and extra oil, all of which cause dryness. These oils' nourishing qualities restore moisture, lessen pain, and improve eye health. By include them in your routine, you can benefit from revitalized and refreshed eyes.

Various special ingredients used for eyelid cleansing and care are following:

Tea tree oil

Tea tree oil (TTO) is taken from *Melaleuca alternifolia* leaves. TTO is an effective detergent for maintaining good lid hygiene because of its antiparasitic, antibacterial, antifungal, and anti-inflammatory qualities. It was reported that a Demodex infection can be successfully treated with TTO diluted to the proper concentration. It was also observed that treating patients with Demodex blepharitis with 5% TTO produced positive clinical outcomes. Many reports state that utilizing TTO products to clean the lid margin has resulted in improvements in symptoms, the removal of eyelash scales, and a decrease in Demodex. Nowadays, 5% TTO lid scrub pads are commercially available. TTO is considered a well-rounded eyelid detergent because of its medicinal value in treating Demodex ectoparasite infections; however, at high concentrations or after prolonged exposure, the strong odor of TTO may cause irritation and discomfort. Many patients, particularly the elderly and young, who often have more sensitive skin, reported mild to severe discomfort when using TTO products. Since TTO at a concentration of 0.02% cleaning foam is a relatively mild substance, skin irritations are less prone to occur. Its effectiveness in removing Demodex is not as effective as that of other high concentration TTO treatments, despite the fact that research indicates that patients prefer it.

Terpine-4-ol

The most prevalent and potent ingredient in TTO is terpine-4-ol (T4O), which is also the most irritating. T4O also has a remarkable ability to kill Demodex. T4O eyelid cleansing wipes are available in the market, and they have the ability to kill mites by preventing the production of superoxide and boosting the body's natural defenses. More pro-inflammatory mediators, like IL-8 and IL-12p70, may be produced by it. By competitively inhibiting acetylcholinesterase (AChE), a parasitic neurotransmitter terminator enzyme, these media can eradicate Demodex. T4O also possesses anti-inflammatory, antibacterial, and antifungal properties. T4O compounds exhibit good acaricidal activity at doses as low as 0.5%.

Hypochlorous acid

Low concentration hypochlorous acid, which typically has a concentration of 0.7%–0.9%, is regarded as a secure and efficient disinfectant. Research has demonstrated that it possesses potent antiviral and antibacterial qualities as well as the ability to eliminate biofilm. It is highly susceptible to *Staphylococcus aureus*. In injured skin, it can also lessen the expression of inflammatory factors such histamine, matrix metalloproteinase-9, interleukins-1 (IL-1) and IL-6; nevertheless, it has no effect on Demodex death. Bacterial buildup in the ocular skin can be decreased with a hypochlorous acid solution. Numerous studies have shown that hypochlorite eyelid washing is effective in reducing the degree of conjunctival and lid border congestion, relieving ocular symptoms, and stabilizing the tear film in various forms of blepharitis.

Boric acid

Boric acid solution is a clear, colorless disinfectant that has a mildly antibacterial effect and minimal irritation. While it is not easily able to penetrate the entire skin layer, it can penetrate the damaged skin mucosa. It is commonly used for disinfecting skin, mucosa, and wounds, particularly for vesicular exudative skin diseases. Boric acid solution, at a concentration of 3%, is widely used in dermatology because of its anti-inflammatory, anti-swelling, astringent, and anti-itching properties. It can be applied wet or rinsed in a wet manner. In ophthalmology, boric acid solutions are used for eye irrigation in eyelid wounds and acute chemical injuries.

Okra oil

It has been shown that okra has anti-inflammatory properties because it inhibits the Akt-mediated NF-κB pathway in mouse BV2 microglia cells. Okra is effective at removing peristomal mites and lid border scales from eyelid wipes, which helps to alleviate blepharitis symptoms, according to a study on the product. It is less irritating and has better patient compliance than TTO. Table 5.9 has various cleansing and care products for eye.

Table 5.9: Compiled list of cleansing products for eye

Brand name	Key ingredients	Form	Benefits
Oculeaf	Tea tree oil	Wipes	Removal of debris, germs, oils, and contaminants from eyelids
Evolve Pure	Sodium Chloride, Potassium Chloride, Calcium Chloride Dihydrate, Magnesium Chloride, Hexahydrate, Sodium Acetate, Sodium Citrate Dihydrate, Water Purified	Wipes	Refreshing and reviving the tired eyes

Table 5.9: ***Contd....***

Brand name	Key ingredients	Form	Benefits
Systane	PEG-200 Hydrogenated, Glyceryl Palmate, Disodium Laureth Sulfosuccinate, Cocamido Propyl Amine Oxide, PEG-80 Glyceryl Cocoate, Benzyl Alcohol and Edetate Disodium, purified water	Wipes	Cleansing the eye lids
Ocusoft	Polyaminopropyl biguanide, cocamidopropyl hydroxysultaine	Foam	Clean, comfort, and refresh the eye lids
Naviblef	D-Pantenol, Aloe Vera, Taurine, Tea Tree Oil, Anthemis Nobilis, Aroma Camomile and purified Water	Foam	Removal of ocular secretions and debris from eye lids
Noveha	Hyaluronic Acid, Tea Tree Oil Extract, and Vitamins B5, E, and C	Foam	Hydration for dry eyelids, reduction of redness and discomfort
Blephadex	PEG-40 Hydrogenated Caster Oil, Glycerin, Aloe vera, salicylic acid, coconut oil, and sorbic acid	Foam	Removes extra oil and debris from eye lids
OCuSOFT HypoChlor	Hypochlorous acid (main ingredient)	Spray	Removal of oil and debris from eye lids
Optase protect	Hypochlorous acid (main ingredient)	Spray	Cleansing of dry eye lids
Avenova	Hypochlorous acid (main ingredient)	Spray	Removes dust and debris from lashes and lids
Hypoclin	Oxidized water and Hypochlorous acid (main ingredient)	Solution	Prevention of dryness of the eyes
Lid clean	Sodium chloride solution (Main ingredient)	Solution	Moisturization of the eye lids
Heyedrate	Hypochlorous acid (main ingredient)	Solution	Soothing the irritated and inflamed eye lids and lashes
Blephagel	Poloxamer 188, PEG-90, sodium borate, carbomer, methylparaben, and water	Gel	Refresh and soothing the sensitive eyelids
Optase	Tea tree oil, hyaluronic acid, and pro-vitamin B5	Gel	Removes dust, debris and other impurities from eye lids

Table 5.9: *Contd....*

Brand name	Key ingredients	Form	Benefits
Ilast	Glycerin, Polysorbate 20, Hydroxyethyl Acrylate / Sodium Acryloyldimethyl Taurate Copolymer, Sodium Hyaluronate, Allantoin, Sodium Hydroxide, and water	Gel	Removes pollutants, germs, dust and debris from eye lids

Cleansing and care needs for hands

Hand care is essential for preserving proper hand hygiene, stopping the spread of pathogens and diseases, and encouraging hands that are comfortable, functional, and healthy. You may preserve attractive, well-groomed hands and safeguard your general health and well-being by including hand care into your daily routine and practicing good hand hygiene. Various cleansing and care products for hands include:

- Hand moisturizers
- Hand sanitizers
- Hand wash
- Hand wipes

Hand wash

Hand wash is a cleansing product intended to get rid of or lessen bacteria on the hands. These cleaning supplies include hand wash liquid, non-antimicrobial soap, and antimicrobial soap. Non-antimicrobial soap comes in bar, leaflet, tissue, powder, and liquid forms. The detergent qualities of non-antimicrobial soaps allow for the physical removal of dirt, organic matter, and passing germs from hands. Non-antimicrobial soaps do not, however, include antimicrobial ingredients, in contrast to antimicrobial soaps. Antimicrobial soaps contain antimicrobial active ingredients like triclosan (bacteriostatic activity), hexachlorophene (inactivation of essential enzymes), chloroxylenol (inactivation of bacterial enzymes and alteration of cell walls), and quaternary ammonium compounds, like benzalkonium chloride. The ingredients used in formulation of a liquid hand wash has been summarized in the Table 5.10. The composition of Dettol hand wash include water, Sodium laureth sulfate, Cocamidopropyl Betaine, Glycerine, Sodium Chloride, Glycol Stearate, Salicylic acid, Polyquaternium-7, Parfum, Chloroxylenol, Tetrasodium EDTA, Acrylates/PEG-10 Maleate/Styrene copolymer, Citric acid, Sodium Hydroxide, Methylchloroisothiazolinone, Methylisothiazolinone, CI 17200. Various herbal ingredients like neem, aloe vera, tulsi, and turmeric are used in hand washes to avoid the adverse effects of chemical ingredients used in hand washes.

Table 5.10: List of ingredients used in the formulation of liquid hand wash.

Category	Example	Application
Surfactant	Sodium lauryl sulfate, sodium laureth sulfate	Removal of dirt, debris and other impurities from the hands
Co-surfactant	Cocamidopropyl betaine	Increase the activity of surfactant
Emollients	Coconut oil, jojoba oil	Keep the skin hydrate
Preservatives	Parabens, methylisothiazolinone	Inhibit the growth of microorganisms
Colors	D & C approved colors	Impart characteristic color
Fragrance	-	Impart pleasant color
Thickening agents	Xanthan gum, carrageenan	Improve viscosity
Buffers	Citric acid, sodium hydroxide	Adjust the pH

Hand moisturizers

It is important to have healthy skin because a poor appearance might lower one's self-esteem. A patient's social life, psychological well-being, and overall quality of life may all be enhanced by using moisturizers, which are frequently used to smooth out fine wrinkles on the skin and hydrate it. Furthermore, using moisturizers correctly can assist people with normal skin as well as those with dermatoses that cause symptoms of dry skin. Along with providing skin moisturizing, moisturizers offer various other functions such as anti-inflammatory, antimitotic, antipruritic, and wound healing property.

Moisturizers function as humectants, emollients, and occlusives, each with a unique mechanism of action, to help restore the skin barrier and preserve the integrity and appearance of the skin. By directly supplying water to the skin from their water phase and increasing occlusion to reduce trans-epidermal water loss, moisturizers improve skin hydration and increase the water content of the stratum corneum. They also cover small skin fissures, provide a soothing protective film, and shield the skin from friction. Additionally, using a moisturizer restores the ability of the intercellular lipid bilayers to absorb, retain, and redistribute water and smoothes the surface of the skin by filling up the spaces between partially desquamated skin flakes.

The key ingredients used in formulation of hand moisturizers include humectants, occlusives, emollients, and antioxidants which has been compiled in the Table 5.11. Various humectants serve as emollients. Hydration of the stratum corneum is mostly dependent on natural moisturizing agents, which are a combination of low molecular weight soluble hygroscopic compounds like lactic acid, pyrolidone carboxylic acid. In order to improve the function of the epidermal barrier and promote moisture, humectants can also increase trans-epidermal water loss by boosting the absorption of water from the dermis into the epidermis, where it quickly evaporates. As a result, their combination with occlusives is frequently necessary. Occlusives contribute to the inter-corneocyte matrix and have the greatest impact when applied to damp skin because they form a hydrophobic barrier over the skin. The effectiveness of occlusives is attributed to their diffusion into the intercellular lipid regions. Emollients play a significant role in improving skin healing and permeability, influencing skin physiology and pathology through a variety of impacts on skin barrier function, including eicosanoid synthesis, membrane fluidity, and cell signaling. Antioxidants are added in moisturizers to prevent the cell damage due to oxidation.

Table 5.11: Compiled list of ingredients used in hand moisturizers.

Category of ingredient	Examples
Emollients	Isopropyl palmitate, isostearyl alcohol, decyl oleate, propylene glycol, castor oil, jojoba oil, glyceryl stearate, dimethicone, octyl octanoate, isopropyl myristate, Isopropyl isostearate, diisopropyl dilinoleate
Humectants	Glycerin, sorbitol, honey, hyaluronic acid propylene glycol, butylene glycol, glycolic acid, lactic acid, urea, gelatin, panthenol, sodium pyrrolidine
Occlusives	Paraffin, mineral oil, lanolin acid, stearic acid, cetyl alcohol, stearyl alcohol, propylene glycol, squalene, caprylic/capric triglyceride, beeswax, cholesterol, carnauba, Candelilla
Antioxidants	Tocopherol, ascorbic acid, citric acid, tartaric acid, butylated hydroxytoluene, retinol, salicylic acid, hyaluronic acid, EDTA

Hand sanitizers

Despite the fact that frequent hand washing with soap and water is an inexpensive hand hygiene measure that can be used to stop the spread of pathogenic microorganisms, alcohol-based and non-alcohol-based hand sanitizers (ABHS and NABHS) have emerged as the preferred substitute, especially in situations where the practice is impractical or water is not available. Two types of hand sanitizers namely alcohol based sanitizers (ABHS) and non-alcohol based hand sanitizers (NABHS) are available to impart hand hygiene. ABHS have one or more types of alcohol along with additional excipients and humectants, for the purpose of eliminating microorganisms and temporarily inhibiting their growth. Without water or towel drying, ABHS may rapidly and efficiently eliminate microorganisms with a wide range of germicidal properties. However, ABHS's effectiveness is not without its drawbacks. These include its short antibacterial action and poor activity against certain non-lipophilic viruses, bacterial spores, and protozoa. Conversely, the antibacterial effects of the NABHS are achieved by the use of compounds like chlorhexidine, chloroxylenol, triclosan, and iodine that possess antiseptic qualities. Based on their chemical functional groups, these compounds have various modes of action and functions. Compared to ABHS, they are generally safer for children to use because they are non-flammable and are frequently used at low doses. ABHS are available in liquid, foam, and gel form. But the gel and foam form of ABHS is widely accepted than liquid form in terms of easy handling, shorten the time for drying, and more cleansing. Various ingredients used in both ABHS and NABHS have been illustrated in the Figure 5.1. Table 5.12 has United State Pharmacopeia expert committee and WHO approved alcohol based hand sanitizers.

Table 5.12: United State Pharmacopeia expert committee and WHO approved ABHS (Alcohol based sanitizers)

Ingredients	**Formulation 1 Ethanol antiseptic-80% topical solution**	**Formulation 2 Isopropyl alcohol antiseptic-75% topical solution**	**Formulation 3 Isopropyl alcohol antiseptic-75% topical solution**
Ethanol 96%	833.3 mL	-	-
Isopropyl alcohol 99%	-	757.6 mL	-
Isopropyl alcohol 91%			824.2 mL
Hydrogen peroxide 3%	41.7 mL	41.7 mL	41.7 mL
Glycerol 98%	14.5 mL	14.5 mL	14.5 mL
Water q.s	1000 mL	1000 mL	1000 mL

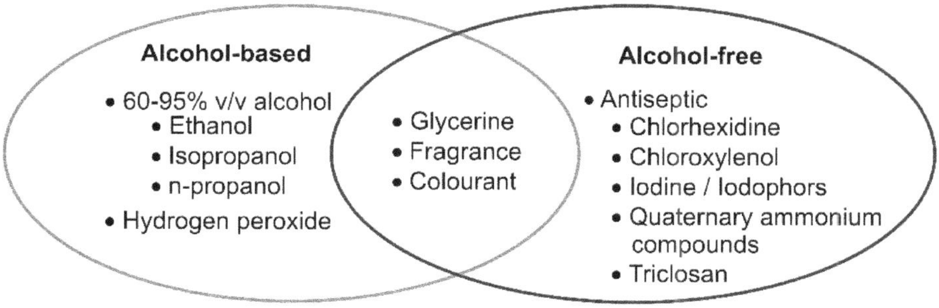

Figure 5.1: Composition of ABHS and NABHS.

Despite their effectiveness, hand sanitizers have a number of toxic effects. Exposure to ethanol results in redness, skin cracking, eye irritation, skin irritation, and contact dermatitis. Another risk associated with prolonged usage of hand sanitizers is isopropyl toxicity. Hand sanitizers contain hydrogen peroxide, which has been shown to be extremely dangerous when ingested in large quantities. Hand sanitizers pose a serious danger of injury to children as well. Children can suffer major consequences if they consume hand sanitizers. Hand sanitizers are most commonly applied to skin. Hand dermatitis and hand eczema are likely to result with frequent usage of hand sanitizers. Commercially available hand hygiene products has been summarized in the Table 5.13.

Table 5.13: List of commercial hand hygiene products.

Brand name	Application	Type
Dettol Original Germ Defence	Fight against germs	Hand wash
Dettol Skin care Everyday Protection	Skin care	Hand wash
Savlon Moisture Shield Germ protection	Protects from million germs along with hydration of skin	Hand wash
Savlon Professional	Fight against germs	Hand wash
Dove Nourishing	Nourishing and smoothing the skin	Hand wash
Santoor	Cleansing the skin	Hand wash
Himalaya Pure hands	Moisturizing and antibacterial	Hand wash
Lifebuoy 99.9% Germ Protection	Fights against bacteria and virus	Hand wash
Lifebuoy Total 10	Fights against germs	Hand wash
Lifebuoy with Vitamins	Fights against germs	Hand wash
Koparo Clear	Prevention of hand dryness	Hand wash

Table 5.13: ***Contd....***

Brand name	Application	Type
Fem Safe Handz	Moisturizing	Hand wash
Nivea Hand cream	Moisturizing	Hand moisturizer
Vaseline Intensive Care Hydra Replenish	Nourishing and moisturization	Hand moisturizer
Vaseline Radiant Hand Butter Deep Nourishment	Hydration	Hand moisturizer
Vaseline Clinical Care Hand Cream + Anti-Bac	Moisturization and killing of bacteria	Hand moisturizer
Curel Extreme Dry Hand Relief	Hydration, soft and smooth feel	Hand moisturizer
Eucerin Advanced Repair Hand Cream	Moisturization, anti-aging	Hand moisturizer
Purell Advanced	Kills 99.9% germs	Hand sanitizer
Lifebuoy Total	Kills 99.9% germs	Hand sanitizer
Dettol Instant	Kills 99.9% germs	Hand sanitizer
Himalaya Pure Hands	Kills 99.9% germs	Hand sanitizer
Equate	Kills 99.9% germs and moisturization	Hand sanitizer
Germ-X moisturizing	Kills 99.9% germs and moisturization	Hand sanitizer
Dove Nourishing	Kills 99.9% germs and moisturization	Hand sanitizer

Cleansing and care needs for feet

Our feet are a frequently neglected part in the wide world of skincare. We tend to overlook their upkeep in favor of our faces and hands, even though they are always in need of repair. But complete well being depends on having healthy feet. If our feet are not properly cared for, they might develop fungal infections or damaged heels, among other difficulties. Various feet care products like feet cream, foot wash, and feet wipes are available.

Foot creams

Foot creams facilitate the cleansing of the foot by removing dead skin and helps in restoring the foot cells resulting in prevention of dry, chopped and cracked foot skin. These are widely accepted preparations for cleansing and care of feet. Various functions performed by foot cream include:

Hydration and moisturization

One of the key benefits of foot cream is that it is hydrating and nourishing. Our feet have thicker, drier skin than other parts of our body, which makes it more prone to dryness and roughness. Shea butter, avocado butter, and argan oil are a few of the components used in the composition of the foot cream since they deeply permeate the skin and provide a substantial amount of moisture. By keeping the skin on your feet hydrated, smooth, and supple, foot cream helps to avoid soreness and cracks.

Dead skin and callus removal

Frequent use of foot cream exfoliation reduces the thickness of calluses and smoothes out rough areas, exposing younger, healthier skin. Calluses and dead skin can be removed with a foot cream's exfoliating components.

Control of odor

The foul smell on feet might be attributed to perspiration and microorganisms. Foot lotions with antibacterial components, such as peppermint oil, assist control foot odor by eliminating the germs responsible for the unpleasant odor. Beautiful scents that can leave your feet smelling amazing and revitalized are additional advantages of foot care cream.

Relaxation and self-care

Foot cream application is a delightful self-care practice that promotes wellbeing and relaxation. We can improve blood circulation in addition to nourishing the skin by rubbing the lotion over our feet. It is a relaxing and restorative experience because massage stimulates nerve endings. A wonderful way to unwind and pamper yourself after a demanding day is to treat yourself to some foot cream.

Foot washes

Foot washes remove the dirt from the foot and make the skin smoother by imparting the soothing action. These are mainly used by the diabetic patients.

Foot wipes

These are instant moistened tissue wipes used to clean the dirt of foot. These are easy to carry than other foot care products. Various cleansing and care products for feet available in the market has been summarized in the Table 5.14.

Table 5.14: List of commercially available feet cleansing and care products

Brand name	Application	Type of product
Himalaya Herbals	Foot care	Foot cream
CeraVe Renewing	Moisturize, exfoliation, and cleansing	Foot cream
VLCC Clinic	Hydrate, reduce dryness, exfoliation	Foot cream
Vilvah	Moisturization	Foot cream
Oriflame Feet up Comfort	Moisturization, soft and smoothness	Foot cream
Cipla Evexpert	Smoothness of cracked feet, deep moisturization,	Foot cream
Freeman Feet	Smoothing the dry skin, refreshing the tired legs	Foot lotion
Krack Heel Repair Cream	Repairing of the cracked heels	Foot cream
Amlactine Foot Repair	Moisturization and exfoliation of dry and cracked skin	Foot Cream
Varco DiaFoot Cream	Used for dry and cracked feet	Foot cream
Dr Foot Antiseptic and Antibacterial	Removal of germs and bacteria from foot skin	Foot wash
Dr Foot Scrub Soap	Nourishment, moisturization, exfoliation, and soothing	Foot wash
Earth Scrub	Removal of dead skin and impurities, relaxing of aching and tired feet, and soothing the heels	Foot wash
Footvital Deep Cleansing Concentrate	Indicated for smelly, dirty, polluted, dry and calloused feet,	Foot wash
Yogafy Beauty	Pain reliever, relaxation of muscles, removal of toxins, and rejuvenation of feet	Foot wash
DiaFC	Diabetic foot care	Foot lotion
Pedifix Tea Tree Ultimates	Clean, deodorize, and refresh	Foot wipes
pHeet	Clean, moisturize, and prevent microbial growth	Foot wipes

Cleansing and care needs for nails

The nail, as an anatomical structure, shields the digit's terminal phalanx from harm. It has been used historically as a tool for survival and protection. It gained the added use of decoration as civilizations advanced. Nowadays, there is a large market around nail beauty. Products include nail hardeners, polishes, extensions, artificial/sculpted nails, and manicure decorations.

Nail bleachers and stain removers

These preparations are used to whiten the nails and to remove discolorations. These preparations were widely used before commencement of nail lacquers. These are generally prepared using oxidizing agents like sodium perborates and hydrogen peroxides. The formulation of nail bleacher include zinc peroxide (7%), talc (23%), petroleum jelly (25%), titanium dioxide (20%), and mineral oil (20%).

Nail polish

Nail polish serves the purposes of beautification, strengthening the weak brittle nails, and masking the surface imperfections. Various desirable characteristics like harmless to skin and nails, ease in application, stability on prolonged storage, satisfactory film formation must be possessed by an ideal nail polish. Various ingredients used in composition of nail polish have been given in the Table 5.15.

Table 5.15: Formulation of nail polish.

Category	Ingredients	Application	Concentration
Film formers	Nitrocellulose, cellulose acetate, ethyl cellulose, methacrylate polymers	Provide hardness, toughness, and resistance of abrasion	16 gm
Resins	Shellac, benzoin (Natural), Sluphonamide-formalodehyde (Synthetic)	Provide adhesion, enhance gloss, and facilitate dispersion of insoluble color pigments	9 gm
Solvents	Ethyl alcohol, benzene, ether, acetone	Serve as vehicle	60.5 gm
Plasticizers	Castor oil (Non-solvent plasticizer), butyl acetyl ricinolate (Solvent plasticizer)	Impart plasticity to the film over nail surface	4.8 gm
Colors	Eosin, carmosine, and erythrosine	Impart desired color to the formulation	0.5 gm
Pearlescent agents	Titanium dioxide, chrome oxide green	Impart pearly appearance	-
Perfume	-	Provide fragrance	q.s.

Cleansing and care needs for neck

The neck region is particularly delicate and moves a lot every day, which can lead to aging symptoms. Furthermore, it is well known that sedentary lifestyles and prolonged mobile use have been linked in recent years to the development of wrinkles and fine lines, either vertically or horizontally. The neck typically exhibits indications of aging earlier than the face since its skin is two to three times thinner than the face's. This is because sebaceous glands are less numerous in neck skin than in face skin, which makes drying and dehydration easier to deal with.

Care needs for neck

Selection of appropriate product

It's critical to search for specialized neck care items that satisfy your requirements. You can select the forms and active substances that work best for you, either in a cream or gel texture. Hyaluronic acid and peptides, which are well-known in anti-aging treatments and enhance skin texture, are included in certain product compositions for the neck and décolleté area. Use neck care products as part of your regular beauty regimen for a more polished look and youthful appearance.

Sun protection

Sun protection is essential throughout the year for the neck region. It is required to use sunscreen products with high protection index on face and neck, as these are highly sensitive areas of the body.

Care of the back of the neck

When treating neck skin, we frequently concentrate exclusively on the region just beneath the face. The back of the neck, however, requires equal attention and should be given special attention. Sun protection, hydration, and skin washing are all included in this.

Avoidance of exfoliation

As the neck is highly sensitive area, always use mild cleanser products to escape the skin irritation and avoid the use of products with high exfoliating activity.

Avoidance of perfumes on neck during expose to sun

Alcohol is a common ingredient in colognes and perfumes, and it is advised to stay away from them right before going outside. When combined with the sun, alcohol can exacerbate the appearance of freckles or spots on the skin, so it's best to avoid wearing your best perfume on sunny days.

Application of make-up remover

Cleansers should also be used on your neck if you plan to paint over any blemishes in this area. To ensure there is no makeup residue, it is very crucial to apply your makeup remover regimen on the neck as well.

Cosmetic products for neck

There is no special requirement of cosmetic products for the care of neck. The cosmetic products used for the care of face can been employed for the neck. Cosmetic products for the care of neck mainly include moisturizing cream, cleansing cream, fairness cream, and face wash. All these cosmetic formulations has been discussed in this chapter earlier.

Cleansing and care needs for scalp

Normal, healthy hair development depends critically on maintaining a clean and healthy scalp. Dandruff and other problems, including inflammation and extreme itching, can arise from the accumulation of sweat, grime, and excess oils in the scalp.

Care tips for scalp

Hair Washing

Washing the hair at least twice a week is recommended, and even more if you have very greasy hair or have recently exposed it to a lot of dust, pollution, etc.

Cleaning

The scalp and hair must be kept clean to prevent dandruff, flaking, itching, and other related issues. The shampoo specifically designed for scalp cleaning should be used to avoid drying out the hair and to stop the dandruff. It will also soothe and relieve an itchy scalp.

Moisturization

The hairs require an adequate quantity of moisture to be healthy and function effectively. The conditioners should be used after every wash of the hair, and a hair mask can also be used at least once every two weeks.

Massage

The massage provides great benefit to the scalp because it increases blood flow. The increased blood flow nourishes the cells and promotes the development of healthier hair. The grime and dirt present in the hair can be removed by a gentle massage for a few minutes during bathing. It also increases the blood flow to the scalp.

Diet

Scalp and hair are impacted by diet as well. Eating a well-balanced diet is crucial to preserving the health of your scalp. To guarantee optimal feeding of the scalp, diet should ideally consist of a lot of fruits and vegetables as well as healthy fats and proteins. The scalp need a lot of fluid to stay healthy, as water is essential for good health.

Cleansing and care products for scalp

The cleansing and care products for scalp include antidandruff shampoos, hair oils, and scalp scrub.

Antidandruff shampoo

Dandruff is a non-inflammatory and infectious disease characterized by excessive shedding of the scalp epidermis followed by scalp redness and itching. It is the main problem of the scalp which must be treated otherwise results in various other serious problems such as psoriasis and eczema. The details about the antidandruff shampoo has been given in the Chapter 4.

Hair oils

Humans have a variety of hair kinds, ranging from deep black to blazing red to silver blonde. The physical characteristics of hair are also significant since they enhance its beauty. Hair health and physical characteristics affect the texture and sensory qualities of hair, or how it looks and feels. It is well known that regular oil application makes hair stronger and keeps it from breaking. Hair oils with a coconut base also aid in lining up the hair's cuticles. Hair appears healthier and has more luster when the cuticles are aligned. To untangle hair, force is applied when combing. Frequently, this results in hair breakage. Using oil lubricates hair, lessens the force needed to comb it, and keeps it from breaking.

Depending on the season, hair behaves differently. Summertime heat causes the hair to lose essential moisture, leaving it brittle and dry. By applying oil, hair is kept pliable and soft and moisture loss is avoided. The high humidity during the monsoon season causes hair to absorb a lot of moisture from the air. Rain can also commonly cause hair to become moist. When hair is damp, water seeps into the hair shaft and is expelled when the hair dries. Frequent repetition of this cycle of water absorption and release causes hydral fatigue, which weakens hair. When oil is applied to hair, it creates a protective layer that stops water from being absorbed and lost and lessens hormonal exhaustion.

A variety of hair style methods, including coloring, straightening, and perming, are frequently employed. The hair shaft may sustain significant damage from the chemicals, blow dryers, or hot irons utilized in these treatments. However, frequent hair oiling can stop this damage from getting worse. It has been demonstrated that frequent hair oiling keeps chemically treated hair from losing protein and helps keep the hair strong even after treatment. It is also said that massaging the scalp with oil improves blood flow, ensuring that the hair receives all the essential nutrients. Using hair oils with a coconut basis also promotes hair growth and stops hair loss.

Classification of hair oils

Hair oils are a type of hair tonic that are used to treat hair conditions like dryness, dandruff, and hair loss. Frequent application of hair oil makes hair shiny and resilient to breakage, prevents split ends, and hydrates the scalp. In addition, hair oils serve as a conduit for the delivery of vital nutrients to the hair root, ensuring healthy growth. The base oil can be any of the following, but it must be a non-sticky oil. Small-scale businesses often produce and sell three kinds of hair oils. These include:

- Vegetable hair oils
- Mineral hair oils
- Mixture of vegetable oils and mineral oils

1. Vegetable hair oils

Olive oil

Olive oil is a very hydrating hair oil and is strong in vitamin E, which is crucial for hair development. Antioxidants found in olive oil are abundant and beneficial for skin and hair. Lightweight and rich in oleic acid, olive oil readily permeates the hair shaft to seal in moisture. With frequent usage, olive oil produces touchably smooth and silky hair, making it the greatest natural conditioner on the market. This oil helps treat dandruff due to its anti-inflammatory qualities, which lowers hair loss and promotes new hair development.

Coconut oil

The best hair oil for smooth, shiny, and healthy hair is coconut oil, a natural conditioner that is high in antioxidants and vitamin E that helps to cure damaged hair. It is well known that coconut oil can enter hair follicles, promoting hair growth and hydrating parched hair. In addition to softening hair, coconut oil stops split ends. Also, coconut oil transforms into a wonder oil that treats all hair problems and speeds up hair growth when herbs like bhringa, brahmi, curry leaves, and other ayurvedic substances are added.

Castor oil

Minerals, proteins, and vitamin E are abundant in castor oil. It is difficult to remove the oil from hair due to its high viscosity. Dandruff and other scalp problems can be eliminated with the aid of castor oil's antibacterial qualities. Ricinoleic acid, found in castor oil, is a treatment for illnesses and inflammations of the scalp. Hair is softened and moisturized with castor oil, which keeps the moisture content of the hair stable. Castor oil promotes blood circulation, which accelerates the growth of hair. Since it has a hydrating quality, dry scalp can be treated with it. To use, thoroughly apply to the scalp, let it sit overnight, and then wash the next day with a gentle shampoo. Using castor oil on a regular basis results in thick, lustrous, nourished hair.

Sesame oil

Many ayurvedic medicines for hair growth, such as bhringraj oil, contain sesame oil as a base oil. Sesame oil heals several fungal and scalp problems because of its antibacterial properties. The ideal application for sesame is as a hot oil therapy. It eliminates dandruff, nourishes the scalp, conditions hair, and increases hair development because of the vitamin E in the oil.

Jojoba oil

The healing and moisturizing qualities of jojoba oil make it extremely advantageous for hair and skin. Frequent application of the oil leaves hair shiny and frizz-free. Jojoba oil promotes the development of new hair cells, which in turn promotes hair growth. It inhibits dandruff, which lowers hair loss.

Argan oil

It is a fantastic oil for lustrous hair. It deeply nourishes and hydrates hair by penetrating the hair shafts. Antioxidant-rich argan oil helps to restore damaged hair. The high levels of vitamins E and F help to restore damaged hair and give it shine. Split ends are also treated with argan oil. It is referred to as "liquid gold" because of its amazing effects on hair, especially damage caused by heat treatment.

Linseed oil

Linseed oil is has rich amount of omega-3 fatty acids and vitamin E. The presence of omega-3 fatty acids provide strength and elasticity to the hair, hydrates the scalp, and reduces the thinning and hair loss.

Almond oil

It is composed of oleic acid, linoleic acid, and monosaturated and polyunsaturated fatty acids. It also includes palmitic, stearic, and linolenic acids. It also contains a lot of vitamin E. Due to the high concentration of double bonds in its fatty acids, almond oil has been demonstrated to offer protection against UV radiation-induced hair damage. Because it bridges the space between cuticle cells, it has been shown to improve the flexibility of the hair. In addition, it imparts softness and moisturization to the hairs.

Mustard oil

It is composed of linoleic, arachidic, linolenic, oleic, behenic, erucic, palmitic, lignoceric, and myristic acid. It also consists of Tocopherol, carotenoids, and sinigrin. The thick viscosity and high vitamin E content of oil provide topical protection against strong UV radiation. It has demonstrated efficacy against *S. aureus*, *E. coli*, and *Candida albicans* and possesses a broad-spectrum antibacterial action. The antibacterial activity of the compounds may be attributed to the presence of phenol, flavonoids, alkaloids, sterols, and terpenes. In addition, the presence of amino acids in their composition provide anti-oxidant property also.

Fenugreek oil

Fenugreek contains a steroid sapogenin called diosgenin. Additional sapogenins include neotigogens, gitogenin, tigogenin, and yamogenin. Moreover, it contains alkaloids including gentianine, trigonelline, and carpine compounds. Social media has given fenugreek seeds a lot of attention as a plant-based antiandrogen. Diosgenin from fenugreek has been demonstrated to exhibit oestrogenic activity, which may result in the suppression of dihydrotestosterone, while the precise mechanism of action is unknown. In the scalp, flavonoids and trigonelline produce vasodilation. It has also been demonstrated that flavonoids have anti-inflammatory and anti-proliferative properties. The seeds extract have antifungal activity against *Aspergillus niger, Trichoderma viride*, *Aspergillus flavus* and antibacterial property against *E. coli*, *S. typhi*, *S. aureus*.

2. Mineral oils

Crude oil is processed industrially to generate mineral oil. Crude oil is refined into a slick fluid and utilized in many cosmetic products after going through a purification process. Crude oil contains a lot of chemicals and compounds that cause cancer, which makes this method problematic. Mineral oil should be depleted of these if they have been adequately distilled. On the other hand, some of these poisons may remain in mineral oil that is not made well. Because mineral oil is a processed product that must pass through several industrial processes before it can be found on store shelves, it cannot be regarded as a natural product. The benefits of mineral oils on hairs are very limited.

Benefits of Mineral oils on hairs

Ability to hold moisture

This is because it forms barriers over the cuticles, stopping the evaporation of moisture. Additionally, mineral oils keep moisture from reaching the hair strand. Therefore, it is best to thoroughly hydrate hair before using mineral oils. When it comes to hydrating hair, mineral oil outperforms other vegetable oils.

Curl formation

It improves how the curl forms. This is because mineral oil makes neighboring hair strands clamp together more effectively. In contrast to other hair types, African American hair, for example, is more brittle. Its lower moisture content explains this. On such hair, applying mineral oil promotes the production of curls.

Treatment of scalp conditions

Mineral oil generally lessens irritation overall and loosens the dry scales on the scalp. It might be helpful for cradle cap, psoriasis on the scalp, and dandruff.

Non-stickiness

When used, mineral oil is less greasy than other hair care products and does not cause the hair to look stringy. This is due to the lightness and lack of grease in mineral oil. It should only be applied sparingly though, as misuse could make hair oily.

Use with both conditional and unconditional hairs

Mineral oil is beneficial for both kinds of hair. It is important to use caution when applying mineral oil to hair that has a lot of conditioner in it, as this could lessen its effectiveness.

Economical

It is less expensive than other plant-based oils that have the same function.

There has been evidence connecting mineral oil to cancer. Although certain petroleum derivatives, such as certain polycyclic aromatic compounds, do contain carcinogenic elements, the mineral oil used in the cosmetic and pharmaceutical industries is extremely refined and pure. The US FDA and other international regulatory bodies are in charge of it. There is just no proof that mineral oil intended for cosmetic usage causes cancer. Mineral oil is unlikely to entirely block hair growth, although some research indicate that it may have an adverse influence on healthy skin growth.

Scalp scrub

A scalp scrub is a revitalizing hair care product with several advantages for the general health of hair, as it is made to wash and exfoliate the scalp. By successfully getting rid of accumulated debris, oil, and dead skin cells, it improves the environment for hair development. By thoroughly cleaning the scalp, hair care products are better absorbed by the hair, maximizing their effects and fostering general hair health. This exfoliation treatment reveals a whole new level of hair care advantages by unclogging hair follicles, decreasing dandruff, increasing blood circulation, and boosting the overall appearance and vitality of the hair and scalp. Regular shampooing concentrates on washing the hair strands; scalp scrubs, on the other hand, target the scalp more broadly. Scalp scrubs work by exfoliating the scalp to remove built-up debris, unclog clogged follicles, and encourage the growth of healthy hair by removing impurities that support a clean and revitalized scalp.

Benefits of scalp scrub

Buildup removal

By physically breaking down and lifting away debris, oil, and product residue from the scalp, scalp scrubs effectively eliminate buildup and leave the scalp feeling clean and renewed.

Unclogging of the hair follicles

By eliminating extra oil, dead skin cells, and other debris that might build up and clog the follicles, scalp scrub help to unclog hair follicles. By removing obstructions, the hair follicles receive better ventilation and nutrient delivery, which encourages healthy hair development.

Enhanced scalp circulation

By encouraging blood flow through the massaging action during application, scalp scrubs enhance scalp circulation. Because of the improved circulation, the hair follicles receive more essential nutrients and oxygen, which encourages stronger hair development and a nourished scalp.

Dandruff reduction

Dandruff causing dead skin cells and flaky buildup are removed from the scalp by gently exfoliating it using hair scrubs. This lessens the likelihood of dandruff flakes by fostering a better scalp environment and assisting in the regulation of oil production.

Improved absorption of hair care products

By eliminating accumulation and unclogging hair follicles, scalp cleaners improve the absorption of hair care products into the scalp. By doing this, hair care products are more effective and can benefit the hair and scalp in the ways that are intended.

Various cleansing and care products for scalp has been summarized in the Table 5.16.

Table 5.16: List of cleansing and care products for scalp.

Brand name	Active ingredient	Application	Type of product
Head & Shoulders Clinical Strength	Selenium sulfide	Dandruff and dry scalp	Shampoo
Jupiter Balancing Shampoo	Pyrithione zinc	Dandruff and hydration of scalp	Shampoo
Dove Dermacare Scalp	Pyrithione zinc	Dandruff	Shampoo
Briogeo Scalp Revival	Salicylic and lactic acids	Dandruff and dry scalp	Shampoo
First Aid Beauty	Pyrithione zinc	Dandruff	Shampoo
OUAI Detox Shampoo	Apple cider vinegar	Dandruff	Shampoo
Oribe Serene Scalp shampoo	Salicylic acid	Exfoliation	Shampoo
Biolage Scalp Sync shampoo	Pyrithione zinc	Dandruff	Shampoo
Selsun Blue Moisturizing shampoo	-	Yeast fighter	Shampoo
Nizoral shampoo	Ketoconazole	Yeast fighter	Shampoo
Dove Hydration Spa Therapy	Hyaluronic acid	Dry scalp	Shampoo

Table 5.16: ***Contd....***

Brand name	Active ingredient	Application	Type of product
Neutrogena T/Gel Therapuetic shampoo	Tar based	Dandruff	Shampoo
Neutrogena T/Sal Therapuetic shampoo	Tar based	Dandruff	Shampoo
Kiehl's Magic Elixir Scalp	Avocado, rosemary, and safflower oils	Deep moisturization, nourishment, and reduction of inflammation	Hair oil
Mielle Organics Rosemary Mint Scalp & Hair Strengthening Oil	Castor, rosemary, and peppermint oil	Dandruff, improved scalp circulation	Hair oil
Derma.E Scalp Relief Treatment	Tea tree oil, aloe vera	Cleansing and reduction of buildup on scalp	Hair oil
Philip B CBD Scalp + Body Oil	Olive oil, jojoba oil, and almond oil	Nourishing the scalp and reduction of inflammation	Hair oil
The Body Shop Ginger Scalp Serum	Ginger oil, birch bark oil	Balance the oil production	Hair oil
Rahua Founder's Blend Scalp & Hair Treatment	Rahua and palo santo oils	Reduction of irritation and hair growth	Hair oil
Carol's Daughter Goddess Strength 7 Oil Blend Hair & Scalp Oil	Castor oil and jojoba oil	Nourishing the scalp and support the growth of new hairs	Hair oil
Pattern Jojoba Oil Hair Serum	Jojoba oil, olive oil, safflower oil, and rosehip oil	Nourishing and anti-inflammatory effect	Hair serum
JVN Complete Pre-Wash Scalp & Hair Treatment Oil	Squalane, bisabolol, and basil root extract	Shining and healthier hairs	Hair oil
As I Am Dry & Itchy Scalp Care Oil Treatment	Olive oil and tea tree oil	Dandruff	Hair oil
Aveda Scalp Solutions Overnight Scalp Renewal Serum	Centella asiatica, Lactobacillus ferment, and hyaluronic acid	Prevent hair loss, drying of scalp, and shedding	Hair serum

Table 5.16: ***Contd....***

Brand name	Active ingredient	Application	Type of product
Tugain Essentials Scalp Cleansing Scrub	Salicylic acid, tea tree oil, and rosemary oil	Deep cleansing, unclogging of the pores, and promotes healthy scalp	Scalp scrub
The Body Shop Hair and Scalp scrub	Ginger essential oil and Vegan keratin protein	Exfoliation of scalp	Scalp and hair scrub
mCaffeine Anti Dandruff Coffee Scalp Scrub	Coffee powder, Natural AHA, and rosemary oil	Rid of dandruff and exfoliation	Scalp scrub

Cleansing and care needs for underarms

The underarm area has a higher number of sweat glands than other parts of the skin, which can cause an accumulation of bacteria on the skin. The distinct smell connected to underarms is caused by two types of bacteria: *Staphylococcus* and *Corynebacterium*. So the good care of underarms could lessen the growth of this bacteria. A person's general health can be inferred from their underarms. The underarm region is crucial to watch for changes since it can show symptoms of a number of diseases, including diabetes, hormone abnormalities, and cancer. Underarm care can help avoid a number of problems that are frequently brought on by underarm hair removal, including hyperpigmentation, odor, and dryness. The skin may eventually darken or become discolored as a result of inflammation, ingrown hairs, and dryness brought on by shaving, waxing, or using hair removal products. Additionally, using these hair removal methods can cause bacteria to build up and release offensive odors.

Care tips for underarms

- Deodorize regularly the underarms area.
- Prioritize regular cleansing of underarms area.
- Exfoliation of underarms area.
- Incorporation of the products which treat hyperpigmentation.
- Carefully razor the underarms area.

Cleansing and care products for underarms

1. Hair removal

There are various methods to remove the hairs from the underarm areas which include:

Shaving

For the purpose of removing underarm hair, shaving is arguably the most popular and accessible technique. Its ease of use and convenience make it the best method for most people to get rid of underarm hair. For individuals with hectic schedules, it's a great option because it provides a simple and rapid hair removal treatment. As it just requires a razor and shaving cream or gel, it's also a cheap choice. To sum up, shaving shouldn't hurt if done correctly and shouldn't cause any irritation or burns. But one major disadvantage of shaving is that hair regrows really quickly typically in a matter of days or two. Maintaining dependably smooth underarms requires frequent care. Furthermore, shaving could result in the formation of razor pimples. Ingrown hairs, often known as chicken skin beneath the arms, can cause discomfort and not look good.

Plucking

The hairs can be plucked out using tweezers. This hair removal technique targets specific hairs with precision. The results of plucking typically last longer, and no lotions or chemicals are involved in the process. However, plucking can be painful, unsuitable for larger areas like the underarms, and requires more accuracy and patience. It may also lead to ingrown hair and skin irritation due to improper use.

Waxing

Warm wax is applied to the underarm region and removed along with the hair during the waxing process. The wax can be taken off with a strip or, if it dries, it can solidify and come off by itself. The majority of people choose this technique since it produces results that last longer than shaving, even if hair development is usually slowed down. The benefits might continue for three to four weeks and can leave the skin smoother following treatment. Waxing can be uncomfortable, though, particularly for people with sensitive skin. Additionally, if the wax is applied incorrectly or is excessively hot, there is a chance of burns or skin irritation. Moreover, some people may find it inconvenient as waxing requires some regrowth in between sessions. This is particularly true the hair too short to wax your armpits for an upcoming function.

Sugaring

A sticky sugar paste is used in the natural hair removal technique known as "sugaring." Though stickier, this paste may have the consistency of most mild body scrubs. Because it only uses natural components, it's a good choice for anyone who are worried about being exposed to chemicals. Additionally exfoliating your underarms with the paste's sugar will leave your skin smooth. It is also thought to be less unpleasant and less likely to cause skin irritation than regular waxing. Conversely, applying and preparing sugaring can be messy. It could take some experimentation to get the paste's consistency just right. Additionally, waxing may be a more effective procedure for coarse hair.

Threading

Threading is the process of extracting individual hairs with a twisted thread. It's advisable to ask a friend or family member for assistance, as it could be difficult to do on your own. With threading, you can remove hair precisely and without using any products or chemicals. It can be applied to smaller regions, such as the underarms, and is safe for delicate skin. Threading is one of the greatest ways to eliminate underarm hair without darkening because of these advantages. But this approach can be difficult, especially for people who are not familiar with it. In addition, it takes a lot of time and could need expert knowledge to utilize well.

Depilatories

Depilatories are cosmetic preparations that are used to eliminate hair from the skin. They function by dissolving sulfur bonds in the keratin of the hair that are vulnerable to potent alkaline and deoxidation chemicals. The substance that actively breaks down the sulfur bonds is a thioglycolic acid salt. Strong alkalis, like sodium hydroxide, are employed to achieve a high concentration of hydroxide ions for maintaining thioglycolic acid as an active dianion in the product.

Thioglycolic acid is a strong chemical that can damage skin due to its high pH level. Because relatively modest amounts of chemicals are employed during chemical depilation, the dermal papilla is typically not destroyed. Hair can come again following chemical depilation. To reduce side effects, the active compounds are applied in a cream base that also contains a variety of additional components, including moisturizers, emulsifiers, antioxidants, and plant extracts. After depilation, the skin is carefully rinsed with water and treated with a variety of conditioners to bring its pH back to normal. They are easily accessible, offer a quick and painless way to remove hair, and do not cause the same cuts or discomfort that come with shaving. The formula for depilatories has been given in the Table 5.17.

Table 5.17: Formula for depilatories.

Ingredients	Quantity (%)
Calcium thioglycolate trihydarte	6
Calcium carbonate	21
Calcium hydroxide	1.5
Cetyl alcohol	4.5
Sodium lauryl sulfate	0.5
Sodium silicate solution	3.5
Perfume	Q.S.
Deionized water	Upto 100

2. Deodorants

The US Food and Drug Administration regulates and classifies deodorants, which are odor-eliminating products, as cosmetics. Deodorants frequently contain alcohol. While alcohol may momentarily kill bacteria, it also initially promotes sweating. Stearyl alcohol, sodium chloride, and sodium stearate are other active chemicals included in deodorants. Deodorants can be made with metal chelant substances like EDTA or with other, more potent antimicrobials that inhibit bacterial development, including triclosan. Deodorants can be scented with natural essential oils or perfumes to cover up the smell of sweat. Zinc oxide, ammonium chloride, sodium bicarbonate, formaldehyde, and acids were among the many skin-irritating or even cancer-causing substances included in deodorants in the past.

Deodorant products function in one of two ways: either they stop sweating completely or they let it happen but stop the bacteria that breaks down the perspiration on the skin. Certain natural materials can be used as deodorants in addition to the chemical chemicals found in deodorants. There are a few of the natural deodorants summarized in Table 5.18

Table 5.18: Herbal ingredients used for deodorants.

Herbal ingredient	Application
Baking soda	Odor neutralizer
Lavender and tea tree oil	Antibacterial
Witch Hazel	Skin care astringent, absorbs oils, and constricts the size of the pores of armpits

Over-the-counter deodorant crystals, often known as "natural deodorant crystal" or "crystal deodorant," are made of rock crystals that include potassium or ammonium alum to stop bacteria from growing on perspiration. Southeast Asia has been using potassium alum as a deodorant for hundreds of years. Over the past 30 years, crystal deodorant has gained popularity in Western countries. Its all-natural components, affordable price, and alleged health benefits—like a decreased risk of breast cancer—have helped it become more well-known. Despite potential concerns about aluminum exposure and contact dermatitis, these have become more and more popular as alternative health products.

There are several forms of crystal deodorant: spray, gel, roll-on, stone, and powder. Up to 24 hours could pass before crystal deodorant starts to work. Underarm odor causing bacteria are assisted in dying by the salt in crystal deodorant. Women frequently use vaginal deodorant, which comes in spray, suppository, and wipe form, to cover up vaginal secretions. They function by either absorbing perspiration that causes odor generation or by employing fragrance to mask odor. The choice of safe and appropriate components for this purpose establishes the safety of vaginal deodorants. Additionally, the possibility that vaginal deodorants could result in skin irritate or trigger an allergic response.

3. Antiperspirants

Antiperspirants are considered the first line of treatment for excessive sweating and can be used nearly anywhere on the body where sweating is a problem Antiperspirants are not Just for underarms, they can be used on hands, feet, face, back, chest, and even groin. While US FDA regulates most deodorants as cosmetics but classifies antiperspirants as over-the- counter drugs. The active components of antiperspirants, aluminum salts, dissolve in perspiration and other surface moisture when applied to the skin. The dissolved material turns into a tiny gel that forms a transient 'plug' at the top of the sweat gland, drastically lowering the quantity of sweat that is released onto the skin's surface. The flow is stopped by a feedback mechanism when the sweat duct becomes clogged. The plugs are washed away over time after remaining in place for at least a day. The antiperspirant can be safely removed by washing and taking a bath.

Because antiperspirants have an active ingredient that creates a layer of protection to prevent sweating in the region where they are applied, they help control perspiration. It's normally best to use antiperspirants right before bed. Antiperspirants lessen perspiration under the arms, but they have little effect on the body's innate thermoregulation system. Reapplying antiperspirants might help you stay fresh and minimize perspiration throughout the day. The quantity of sweat produced in the underarms is decreased when numerous sweat glands are blocked, yet this varies from person to person.

Along with being an antibacterial, the antiperspirant active helps get rid of body odor by destroying microorganisms that cause it. Antiperspirants and their contents are subject to strict safety requirements because the USFDA views the active ingredients as drugs. The FDA only permits the use of aluminum as the active ingredient in antiperspirant products due to safety concerns. Antiperspirants commonly contain aluminum chloride, aluminum chlorohydrate, and aluminum-pronun compounds, most notably aluminum zirconium tetrachlorohydrex gly and aluminum zirconium trichlorohydrex gly. In commercial antiperspirants, aluminum chlorohydrate and aluminum-zirconium tetrachlorohydrate gly are the most commonly found active components. Deodorants with antiperspirants agents are classified as drugs by the FDA in which antiperspirants prevent the sweat production while deodorants protects against bad odor.

4. Whitening creams

Various factors such as excessive production of melanin, plucking of hairs, shaving, excessive scrubbing, and deposition of sweat and dirt, hormonal changes, environmental factors lead to darkness of the underarm area. This darkness of underarms impart very unpleasant look mainly in the case of women. Hence underarm whitening creams or preparations are used to avoid the darkness of the underarms. The functions provided by underarm whitening creams include:

Targeting ingredients

Applying whitening lotion as prescribed on a regular basis can brighten the underarm region gradually over time, resulting in obvious improvements in clarity and brightness.

Exfoliation

Various whitening creams has exfoliating agents which remove dead skin cells, revealing brighter, smoother skin underneath.

Moisturization

Staying well hydrated is essential to having glowing, healthy skin. Moisturizing components found in whitening creams help to keep the underarm area supple and moistened.

Sun protection

Some formulations include SPF to protect the skin from further darkening caused by UV radiation.

Irritation reduction

Whitening creams can lessen the chance of additional skin discoloration from friction or shaving by relieving skin irritation and inflammation.

Consistent use

Applying whitening creams as prescribed on a regular basis can brighten the underarm region gradually over time, resulting in obvious improvements in clarity and brightness.

Various natural ingredients used in whitening cream along with their applications given in Table 5.19.

Table 5.19 Ingredients used in whitening cream along with their applications

Ingredient	Application
Lemon extract	Brighten the skin and reduction of dark spots
Bearberry extract	Inhibition of melanin production
Licorice extract	Prevention of pigmentation
Aloe vera	Soothing and hydration of the skin
Kojic acid	Inhibition of melanin production and reduction of dark spots
Papaya Extract	Exfoliation of dead skin cells
Vitamin E	Skin repair
Green tea extract	Protection against UV damage
Rosehip oil	Brighten the skin and promotes the collage formation

CHAPTER 6

Oral Cavity Related Cosmetics

Introduction

The oral cavity refers to the anatomical space within the mouth that is enclosed by the lips, cheeks, teeth, gums, hard and soft palates, tongue, and floor of the mouth. It serves as the primary entrance to the digestive system and is responsible for functions such as chewing, swallowing, and speaking. Additionally, the oral cavity plays a crucial role in taste sensation and oral hygiene.

Anatomy of Oral Cavity

The lips, two flexible muscular folds that stretch from the corners of the mouth to the base of the nasal columella above, and the mentolabial sulcus (fold above the chin) below, encircle the opening of the oral cavity (Figure 6.1). There are three anatomic zones on the lip. Similar to skin at other sites, the outer skin above and below the vermillion border has adnexal structures such as hair follicles, eccrine sweat glands, and sebaceous glands. The vermillion is a transitional zone that has an unusual reddish-purple color due to an increased number of cutaneous blood vessels and a thin stratum corneum. There are no sweat glands or hair follicles, however there may be ectopic sebaceous glands. The alveolar mucosa and the labial mucosa meet to cover the interior of the lip. It has a significant number of salivary glands that produce mucus. The labial frenulum attaches the lips to the surrounding gingiva. The tongue on the floor of the mouth, the cheeks and teeth laterally, and the arch of the hard and soft palates above combine to form the oral cavity. There is a small vestibule between the lips and the teeth. The smooth buccal and labial mucosa, which ranges in color from pink to light red, forms the sides of the oral cavity. It becomes one with the alveolar mucosa, which is connected to the periosteum beneath it only slackly. On the vestibule's buccal mucosa, across from the second molars, is a triangular papilla that serves as the opening of the parotid gland (also known as Tensen's duct). The dental occlusion line is marked by a pale-white to pink streak known as the linea alba, or occlusal line.

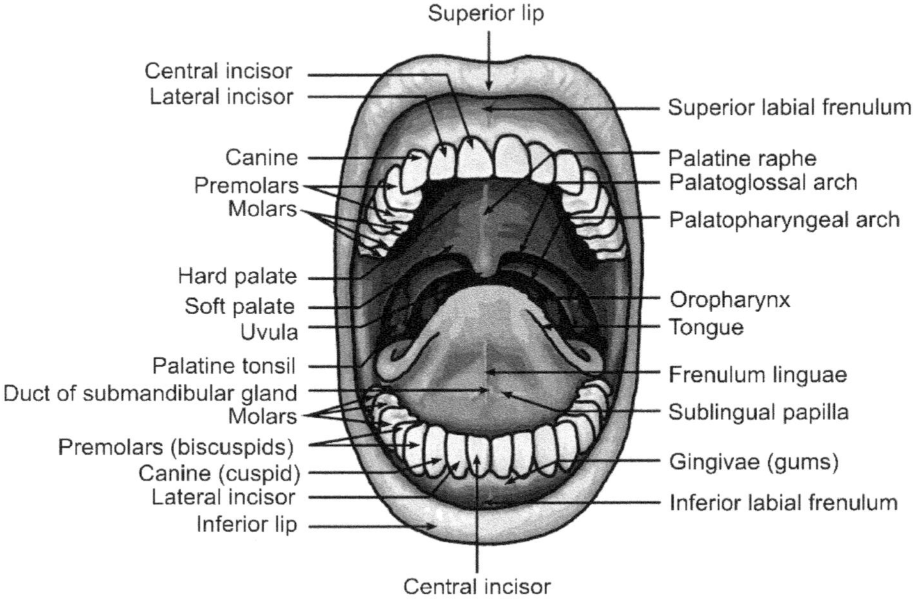

Figure 6.1: Structure of human oral cavity.

There are two types of gingiva: the free gingiva, which is next to the teeth and extends into the tissue that fills the space between them and the interdental papillae, and the fixed gingiva, which is attached to the alveolar process. While the free gingival tissue is typically not pigmented, dark-skinned people may have highly pigmented areas of the buccal mucosa and stippled gingiva connected to the skin.

The hard palate, which is made up of the two lateral and medial palatine processes, is the anterior two thirds of the palate. The mucosa on top has a median raphe, a rough look, and is attached to the underlying bone. The soft palate is a fold of muscle and mucosa that extends posteriorly along the roof of the mouth. It ends in the uvula in the middle and merges laterally with the tonsillar pillars and the tongue in the side. The anterior and posterior pillars are separated by the palatine tonsils. There is more lymphoid tissue at the tongue's base.

The tongue is made up of both inner and outside tongue muscles, which meet at various points. The lingual apex, a thin, narrow tip, is the endpoint of the front two-thirds of the tongue, which originate from the first pharyngeal arch. The lingual root refers to the posterior third of the tongue, which originates from the third and fourth pharyngeal arches. There is a V-shaped groove called the terminal sulcus that points toward the neck where the root and the remainder of the tongue meet. Marked by a V at its posterior end is the origin of thyroid gland's, the foramen caecum. The base is found in the ventral part of the tongue, whereas the dorsum, or surface, stretches from the tip to the epiglottis. Specialized papillae cover the dorsum of the tongue, which is designed for taste and mastication. The tongue has a rough texture due to the consistent distribution of filiform papillae, which resemble pointy spikes. Their main function is to control motor actions like licking. Red, mushroom-shaped structures called fungiform papillae are scattered throughout filiform papillae, with a greater concentration on the anterior surface. They are able to discriminate between salty and sweet tastes. The biggest and most noticeable papillae are the circumvallate papillae. They are responsible for detecting bitter taste and are found along the terminal sulcus. Usually connected to the lingual tonsils, the vestigial foliate papillae are seen on the posterior lateral part of the tongue.

The base of the tongue forms the floor of the mouth, while the lingual portion of the mandible forms the floor posteriorly. The lingual frenulum, which runs from the mandibular midline to the tongue's ventral tip, divides it in the middle. On the ventral side of the tongue, between the lingual frenulum and the lateral border, are symmetrical mucosal folds called plica sublingualis. They have a fringed free edge. The primary excretory duct of the submandibular gland, Wharton's duct, leaves the body at the sublingual caruncle that is located next to the lingual frenulum on both sides.

There are two sets of teeth in humans: twenty primary teeth and thirty-two permanent teeth. The eruption of main teeth typically starts at six months of age and lasts for two to three years, with one tooth erupting per month. By deducting six from the child's age in months up to two years old, one can approximate the typical number of teeth for a specific age. When the first molars erupt, usually around age six, the permanent teeth start to erode. The calcification of the permanent teeth starts at birth and lasts for eight to ten years, while the calcification of the primary teeth starts at three to four months in pregnancy. The structure of tooth is made up of the following components: pulp, which is loose connective tissue that contains blood vessels and nerves, cementum, which is similar to cement and ties dentin to the periodontal ligament, dentin, which is hard tissue that makes up the majority of teeth.

Oral health

The condition of the mouth, teeth, and orofacial structures that permits people to carry out basic bodily functions like breathing, eating, and speaking is known as oral health. It also includes psychosocial aspects like self-assurance, general wellbeing, and the capacity to interact with people and carry out tasks without experiencing pain, discomfort, or shame. From infancy to old age, oral health changes throughout life, is essential to overall health, and helps people fulfill their potential and engage in society.

Oral diseases comprise a variety of illnesses and ailments, such as dental caries, gum disease, tooth loss, oral cancer, orodental trauma, noma, and congenital abnormalities such cleft lip and palate. As per the WHO report 2022, about 3.5 billion people are affected by oral problems worldwide and 3 out of 4 peoples are affected by oral problems in middle income nations. Approximately 2 billion peoples are affected by dental caries of permanent teeth and about 514 million children are affected by dental caries. The prevalence of the major oral disorders is rising worldwide due to changes in living conditions and increased urbanization. The availability and affordability of foods high in sugar, inadequate exposure to fluoride (found in toothpaste and water supplies), and limited access to oral health care services in the community are the main causes of this. The promotion of sugar-filled foods and drinks, together with tobacco and alcohol, has resulted in an increase in the use of goods that aggravate oral health issues and other non-communicable diseases.

Dental caries (tooth decay) and periodontal (gum disease) are main two oral disorders affecting the population globally. It is now abundantly evident that there is a significant risk of prevention for each of these illnesses. Indeed, there has been a significant decline in the occurrence of dental cavities in Ireland since water fluoridation was implemented in the 1960s. Many people still experience significant levels of tooth decay despite this improvement. Other than dental caries and periodontal disease, other oral problems like dental trauma, oral cancer, tooth wear, dry mouth, mouth ulcers, tooth sensitivity, cold sores, and halitosis (bad breath) are also affecting the oral health throughout the world.

Dental cavity or dental caries

Dental cavity also known as dental caries or tooth decay is the main cause of tooth loss and oral pain and one of the most prevalent preventable diseases. It is a serious oral health condition that affects people of all ages and makes it more difficult to achieve and maintain good oral health. It is the term for the localized breakdown of dental hard tissues that are susceptible to acidic byproducts resulting from the fermentation of carbohydrates in food by bacteria. The majority of people have a sluggish progression of this chronic condition which is caused by an ecological imbalance in the balance between oral biofilms and tooth minerals. Variations in the pH of the plaque are caused by microbial activity within the biofilm. Bacterial acid production as well as the salivary and adjacent dental structure's buffering effects are the causes of this. Consequently, the tooth surface and its surroundings are in a state of dynamic balance. Enamel, dentine, or cementum demineralizes when the pH drops below a certain point, whereas remineralization happens when the pH rises above that point. Throughout the day, there are frequent instances of demineralization and mineralization. This procedure eventually causes caries lesions or the lesion to be repaired and reversed.

Symptoms of dental cavity

The symptoms of dental cavity may include tooth sensitivity, toothache, and difficulty in eating, chewing, smiling, and speaking because of missing, stained, or broken teeth, pits or holes in teeth, and staining on tooth surface.

Pathogenesis

The pathogenesis of dental cavity includes diet, host, and bacteria. Numerous facultatively and obligately anaerobic bacteria belonging to the genera *Actinomyces*, *Bifidobacterium*, *Eubacterium*, *Lactobacillus, Parvimonas, and Rothia* make up the varied microbial community associated with dental cavity. Other bacteria that can cause it include those belonging to the *Streptococci Mitis, Angiosus*, *Salivarius groups, Propionibacterium, Enterococcus faecalis, Scardovi, Prevotella Selenomonas, Dialister, Fusobacterium, Pseudoramibacter, Veillonella, Atopobium, Granulicatella, Leptotrichia and Thiomonas*. It is common for mucosal surfaces to harbor *Bacteroides, Prevotella, and Porphyromonas* species, which can be found in very high numbers in dental plaque, gingival crevices, and tonsillar crypts. Dental cavity is the result of fermentation of carbohydrate diet by the microorganisms present in the oral cavity which leads to formation of acid byproducts. These acid byproducts dissolves the hydroxyapatite structure of the tooth causing tooth cavity or caries as depicted in the Figure 6.2.

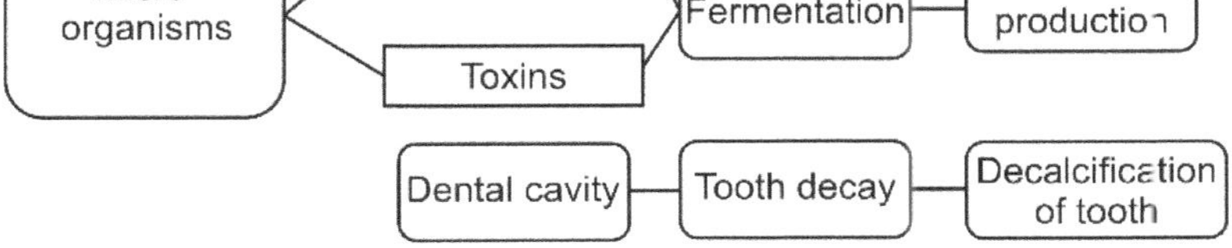

Figure 6.2: Sequential representation of formation of dental cavity or caries.

Risk factors

Various factors which increase the risk of dental cavity include xerostomia (dry mouth), genetic history of tooth decay, gum recession, eating foods having high sugar, starch, drinking between the food, and intake of fast food. The radiation therapy used to treat the neck and head cancer can also result into the dental cavity.

Types of dental cavities

Dental cavities can appeared on surface of any tooth. Common types of dental cavities along with their site include smooth surface, pit and fissure decay, and root decay (Figure 6.3). Dental cavity present on smooth surface erode enamel at slow rate. It can be easily prevented and reversed using proper oral hygiene. Most of the people of 20th century are prone to this type of dental cavity. Pit and fissure decay involves the formation of cavities on the chewing surface of the tooth. It mainly starts from teenage years and gradually increases. The people having receding gums are more prone to the root decay. Gum recession exposes the teeth roots to acid and dental plaque. This type of dental cavity is very difficult to treat and required the attention of dentist.

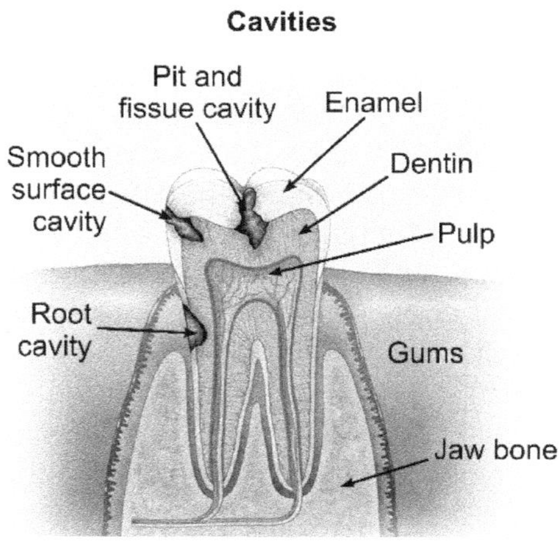

Figure 6.3: Types of dental cavities.

Control and prevention of dental cavities

The maintenance of oral hygiene using daily brushing and flossing are essentially required to control and prevent further decaying of the teeth. The proper brushing and flossing techniques offer the removal of plaque and dental biofilm production. Professional prophylaxis, or cleaning, and routine dental examination are also involved in the maintenance of oral hygiene.

It is advised to limit snacking since it provides a constant source of nutrients for oral bacteria that produce acid. Since sticky and chewy foods, like sweets or dried fruit, tend to stick to teeth longer, it is advised to brush your teeth right after eating. The American Academy of Pediatrics (ADA) and the Endocrine Purification Division (EAPD) advises against feeding newborns bottles to sleep with them and on a regular basis. Chewing gum that contains the sugar alcohol xylitol aids in the reduction of dental biofilm.

Foods high in calcium, such milk and green vegetables, are frequently advised to prevent tooth cavities. Fluoride binds to the hydroxyapatite crystals in enamel to help stop tooth decay. Enamel is more resistant to demineralization and, consequently, deterioration because of the added calcium. In order to protect the surface of teeth, topical fluoride such as toothpaste, mouthwash, or varnish is now more strongly advised than systemic intake, such as that provided by pills or drops. Rinsing should be avoided after using fluoride toothpaste. Fluoride has effects on preventing caries both before and after an eruption.

Bleeding gums

One of the initial sign of gum disease is frequently bleeding. Gingivitis is the initial stage of gum disease, characterized by bleeding along with red, swollen gums, soreness, poor breath, or tooth sensitivity. Bleeding accompanied by receding gums is also a common symptoms of gum disease.

Causes of bleeding gums

There are various causes of bleeding gums which include hard brushing, lack of vitamins intake, administration of blood thinner or other drugs, bleeding disorders, hormonal imbalance during pregnancy, mouth sores, dentures, and other diseases like diabetes mellitus, heart disease, scurvy, and leukemia.

Stages of bleeding gums

Bleeding gums is mainly due to the formation of plaque at the gum lines and the continuous deposition of plaque at the gum lines leads to a condition called as gingivitis. Extend of gingivitis in which plaque gets harder and transforms into tartar results in a condition called periodontitis. After it, the next stage involves the destruction of the bones and fibers supporting the teeth called as advanced periodontitis (Figure 6.4).

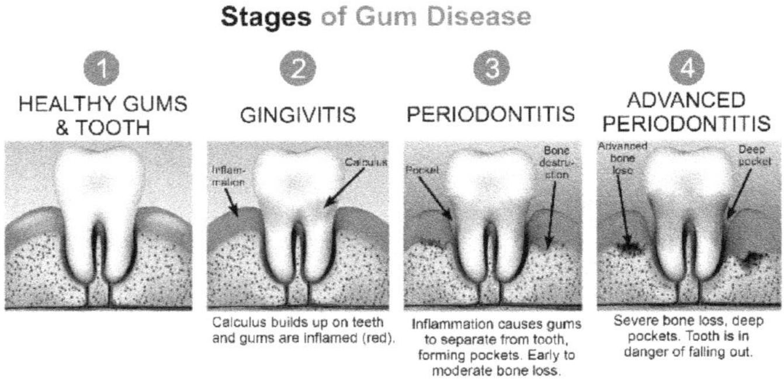

Figure 6.4: Stages of gum disease.

Treatment

The bleeding gums can be controlled and prevented by removing the plaque which is responsible for the gum diseases. The proper treatment of bleeding gums at their first appearance can avoid the problem of gingivitis and its further stages. Various treatment options such as scaling and root planing techniques can be used to slow down the progress of gum diseases. The third stage of gum diseases namely advanced periodontitis requires drug therapy and surgery in some cases depending upon the severity of the problem.

Therapy and care

Vitamin C is the greatest natural treatment for bleeding gums. However, if consuming citrus fruits does not produce the desired outcome, antimicrobial toothpaste is advised. Gingivitis is indicated if the gums bleed after brushing and are swollen and red. The main cause of gingivitis is bacteria that multiply and irritate the gums, making them uncomfortable, sensitive, and even bleed. *Plaque and tartar formation is aided by antibacterial toothpaste, which has a 12-hour germ fighting duration and helps shield against gingivitis.* The toothpaste can somewhat lessen tooth decay and effectively minimize bleeding gums, gingivitis, and plaque. Only supragingival plaque is affected by antimicrobial and plaque inhibitory compounds included in mouthwashes and toothpastes, which are intended to prevent or treat chronic gingivitis by inhibiting the production of bacterial plaque (Figure 6.5). They must be distinguished from substances that target subgingival plaque since the latter can be used to treat chronic periodontitis and requires access to the periodontal pocket at a high enough concentration to be effective. Numerous antimicrobial agents, which can be categorized as bisguanide antiseptics, quaternary ammonium antiseptics, phenolic antiseptics, other antiseptics, oxygenating agents, metal ions, and natural products, have been examined for the purpose of controlling supragingival plaque (Table 6.1).

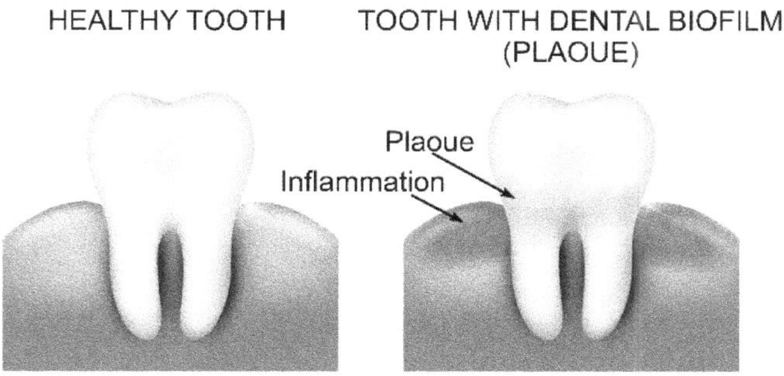

Figure 6.5: Representation of dental plaque.

Table 6.1: A summarized list of antibacterial agents used to various gum diseases.

Class	Examples	Key points	Category of product
Bisguanide	Chlorhexidine, octenidine and alexidine	Broad spectrum antibacterial agent. Chlorhexidine possesses greater and prolonged effect than other agents.	Toothpaste, mouthwash and gels
Quaternary ammonium compounds	Cetylpyridinium chloride	Impart moderate plaque prevention property. As compared to chlorhexidine, it has poor plaque and gingivitis inhibition property	Lozenges, mouthwash
Hexahydropyrimidine derivative	Hexitidine	Has low plaque prevention potential due to oral retention of 1-3 hours. The combination with zinc provides increased antiplaque property.	Mouthwash

Table 6.1: ***Contd....***

Class	Examples	Key points	Category of product
Iodine derivative	Povidone iodine	Not applied for prolonged used and can cause iodine sensitivity. It possesses no noteworthy plaque prevention potential when used as 1% mouthwash	Gargles
Amine alcohols	Octapinol HCl and delmopinol HCl	Delmopinol HCl prevents the growth of plaque and decreases the gingivitis. But it only reduces the salivary bacteria for half an hour.	Mouthwash
Metal ions	Zinc, copper	Provide plaque prevention activity. But they causes local side effects of staining	Used in combination with other antibacterial agents
Bisphenolic compound	Triclosan	Causes moderate plaque prevention potential on combination with zinc in mouthwash. Its oral retention can be improved by its conjugation with methoxyethylene and maleic acid. It also serves as anti-inflammatory agent.	Toothpaste, mouthwash
Salifour	Sn-octanoyl-3'-trifluoromethyl salicylanide	AAntiplaque, anti-inflammatory and antibacterial agent	Under clinical trials
Oxygenating agents	Hydrogen peroxide	Provides advantageous effects on ulcerative gingivitis mainly by preventing the anaerobic bacteria.	Mouth rinse
Natural derivatives	Sanguinarine (*Sanguinaria canadensis*)	It has iminium ion as active constituent which is responsible for its anti-plaque activity.	Toothpaste, mouth rinse

Tooth sensitivity

Tooth sensitivity also known as dentin hypersensitivity is a common dental condition marked by acute, transient pain or discomfort in one or more teeth in response to certain stimuli. These stimuli are extremes in temperature, sweet or acidic foods and beverages, and even brushing and flossing.

Mechanism of tooth sensitivity

The crowns of healthy teeth are shielded from damage by a layer of enamel, the body's toughest tissue. The tooth root beneath the gum line is shielded by a coating known as cementum. Dentin, a less dense portion of the tooth than cementum or enamel, lies beneath both of these layers. Tiny tubules, sometimes known as hollow tubes or canals, are present in the dentin. As the dentin loses its protective layers namely enamel and cementum, various stimuli such as heat, cold, acidic, and sticky foods can exposed to the dentin tubules. As per the hydrodynamic theory of pain, stimuli given to dentin tubules that are patent at the pulp and the oral surface induce the dentin fluid to move quickly and activate mechanoreceptors, which in turn causes pain (Figure 6.6). Variations in the fluid flow within the dentinal tubules may activate receptors on pulpal side neurons, causing a pain response. Dentin tubules may become visible following gingival recession brought on by periodontal disease or surgery, or as a consequence of enamel loss via mechanical attrition, erosion, and abfraction. Depending on pressure variations in the surrounding tissue, fluid within dentinal tubules in important teeth that have been exposed as a result of erosion, abrasion, dental treatment, or a tooth defect may flow inward or outward. The volume of the tubular fluid expands in response to heat and slightly contracts in response to cold stimuli. Fluid is pulled out of the tubules by strongly osmotic sugar or sour solutions.

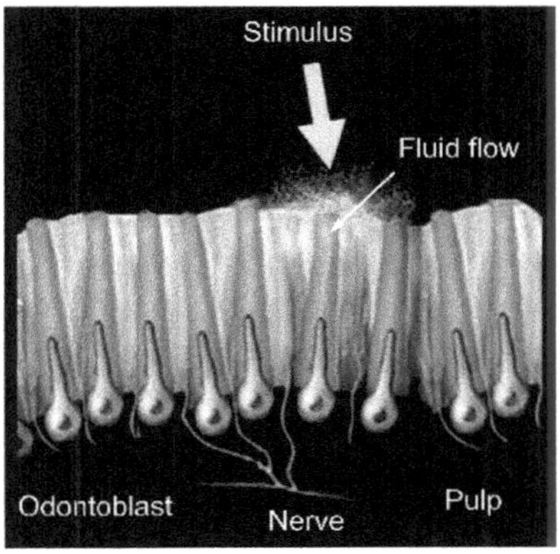

Figure 6.6: Fluid in or out of dentin based on stimuli.

Etiology of tooth sensitivity

The primary cause of tooth sensitivity is exposed dentin, which can arise from gingival recession linked to root surface exposure or from enamel loss brought on by dental wear or trauma. Tooth wear, which encompasses abrasion, erosion, attrition, and abfraction, is the term used to describe the permanent loss of tooth structure. The occurrence of occlusal hyperfunction and abrasion is frequently linked to wedge-shaped cervical lesions. Non-carious cervical lesions of dentin can have a variety of causes, but incorrect brushing is thought to be one of the main ones.

Sign and symptoms

Teeth sensitivity is indicated if eating or drinking hot, cold, sweet, or extremely acidic meals and drinks or breathing in cold air causes discomfort or sensitivity in a tooth. Tooth sensitivity is a condition that might come and go. Normal circumstances result in the enamel in the dental crown and the gums surrounding the tooth covering the underlying dentin of the tooth, which is the layer that directly surrounds the nerve. The enamel layer may get thinner with time and offer less protection. Additionally, in time, the gums may recede and reveal the dentin underneath the root surface.

Care for tooth sensitivity

The first step towards care for tooth sensitivity is to know the cause. If the sensitivity is due to the exposed dentin, there are various ways to reduce the tooth sensitivity which include:

- Apply a very soft bristle tooth brush.
- Application of tooth brush in correct manner to stop the abrasion of the enamel and gum recession.
- Application of anti-hypersensitivity agents like potassium nitrate and sodium fluoride to treat the sensitivity. Various other agents like calcium sodium phosphosilicate and casein phosphopeptide-amorphous calcium phosphate can be used as anti-hypersensitive ingredients.
- The dentists can apply a fluoride varnish on sensitive tooth to provide strengthening to the tooth and may prescribe the tooth paste having fluoride to use daily.

Bad Breath (Halitosis)

It is socially unacceptable to have bad breath. The primary cause of halitosis is an overabundance of volatile sulfur compounds produced by oral bacteria. The amount of sulfur compounds that are volatile in the breath can change significantly throughout the day depending on a person's eating, drinking, dental health, sleeping patterns, and how these activities affect saliva flow. According to studies, up to 50% of adults experience offensive mouth odor in the morning before eating breakfast or brushing their teeth. This is because, when saliva flow is decreased while we sleep, saliva incubates bacteria in the mouth. Because saliva and microorganisms in periodontal pockets incubate, people with periodontal disease have stronger odors. Certain unpleasant breath odors can also be caused by a number of systemic illnesses and disorders, including cirrhosis of the liver, diabetes mellitus, and chronic renal failure. The creation of a trustworthy apparatus to gauge the concentration of volatile sulfur compounds in breath is gaining traction. While some meals and beverages (such as coffee, alcohol, garlic, and onions) and tobacco can affect breath, their effects are felt in the lungs rather than in the mouth.

Etiology

Understanding the cause of halitosis is crucial since it usually requires multimodal therapy with a focus on the causal component. Based on where it originated, halitosis can be divided into two categories: genuine halitosis and delusional halitosis (Figure 6.7).

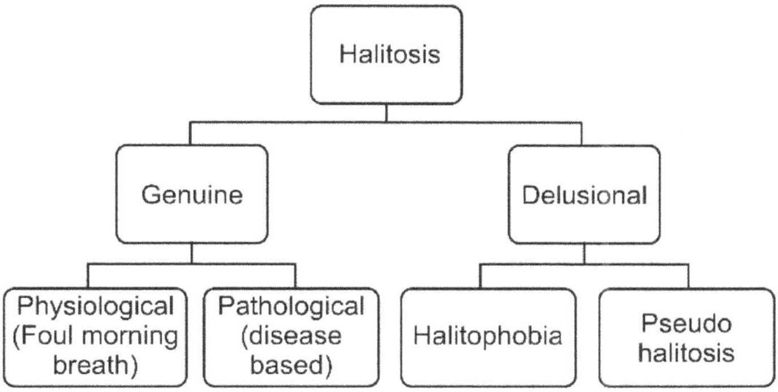

Figure 6.7: Various types of halitosis.

Physiological halitosis

The clinical manifestation of physiological halitosis (morning halitosis, foul morning breath) is characterized by a decrease in the frequency of fluid intake, saliva stagnation, putrefaction of trapped food particles, and desquamation of epithelial cells due to bacterial buildup on the tongue's dorsum.

Pathological halitosis

Various intraoral and extra oral pathological conditions lead to bad breath but 80-85% halitosis cases are mainly due to intraoral pathological conditions which include xerostomia, periodontal infections, odontogenic infections, and mucosal lesions. Extra oral pathological conditions include diabetes mellitus, liver failure, leukemia, sinusitis, respiratory tract infections, peptic ulcer, renal failure, and menstruation etc.

Halitophobia

In Halitophobia, the patient worries that people would think he smells bad and that this will not change even after treatment. In adults, this condition affects 0.5% to 1% of the population. After ruling out other organic explanations, it frequently necessitates rigorous counseling. Here, the olfactory reference syndrome merits particular attention. The patient feels that in addition to having bad breath, other areas of their body, such as their feet and armpits, smell bad is a serious fear of imaginary unpleasant breath.

Pseudo halitosis

The patient in this case claims to have bad breath but the clinicians and other people do not experience. Clinicians have noticed an upward tendency in this patient group in recent years. The reason for this can be the abundance of dental hygiene and cosmetic products that are widely advertised.

Prevention of bad breath

Halitosis can be reduced in a number of ways. Halitosis can be prevented, controlled, and concealed with the aid of oral hygiene products and plaque management measures meant to reduce periodontal disease and dental cavities. Halitosis will be lessened by periodontal therapy that reduces periodontal pocketing. The majority of research on volatile sulfur compounds focuses on how commercial mouthwashes affect halitosis reduction. The mouthwash's antimicrobial properties result in a decrease in mouth odor. However, some products only cover up halitosis instead of addressing the underlying cause. Tooth brushing, chewing gum and using specialized tongue-cleaning tools can all help reduce oral halitosis to a manageable degree, but the effects of these strategies are not as durable as those of antimicrobial mouthwashes.

Tooth discoloration

General tooth shade

A multitude of intricate elements, including illumination, translucency, opacity, light scattering, gloss, and the human eye and brain, interact to determine how a tooth looks and is perceived. The most significant of them is the intrinsic color of a tooth, which is influenced by both natural and hereditary causes. When light strikes a tooth, it is reflected, absorbed, and transmitted in different amounts by each layer of tooth material tissue. The way a tooth appears to the human eye is determined by reflected light. The outside surface of teeth is covered in a thin layer of enamel (Figure 6.8). The enamel layer, which is semitransparent and whiter, gives teeth their blue, pink, and green hues. The dentin layer underneath is less transparent, yellow-brown in color, and darker than the enamel. The majority of the tooth's composition, or dentin, is responsible for the tooth's overall color. The dental pulp, a soft connective tissue, is located at the center of the tooth. Because of its vascularity, the pulp is pink or crimson, but it is rarely visible through the layers of dentin and enamel unless tooth wear (or very rarely, internal resorption) reduces their thickness. The color of teeth varies depending on race, gender, and location.

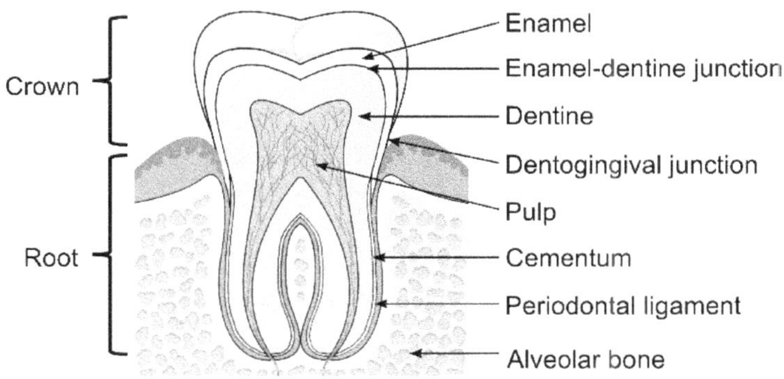

Figure 6.8: Diagrammatical representation of molar tooth.

Due in part to their smaller teeth and less bulky dentin, which is partially visible through the enamel layer, females typically have slightly whiter teeth than males. For the same reason, canine (cuspid) teeth and molars, which are larger teeth, typically have a darker hue. Because the ratio of enamel to dentin varies between baby teeth (deciduous teeth) and adult teeth, the former are often whiter than the latter.

Discoloration of tooth

Tooth discoloration, also known as tooth staining is an irregularity in the color, tone, or translucency of teeth. A collection of stains on the tooth's surface is known as external discoloration. Pigment particles that have absorbed into the tooth structure are the cause of internal discoloration. Tooth discoloration can be caused by a number of factors including:

Foods/drinks: Foods and beverages, certain fruits and vegetables (such potatoes and apples) as well as coffee, tea, colas, and wines can cause tooth discoloration.

Use of tobacco: Use of tobacco can cause staining of teeth.

Poor dental hygiene: Tooth discoloration can be brought on by inadequate brushing, flossing, and washing with an antiseptic mouthwash to get rid of plaque and stain-causing agents like coffee and tobacco.

Diseases: Tooth discoloration can result from a number of illnesses that affect dentin, the substance beneath enamel, and enamel itself. Certain medical treatments may also have an impact on tooth color. Chemotherapy and head and neck radiation, for instance, can discolor teeth. Additionally, some diseases in expectant moms might influence the development of enamel in the teeth, resulting in tooth discoloration in the offspring.

Drugs: It is well known that giving the medicines tetracycline and doxycycline to youngsters whose teeth are still growing (before age 8), can discolor their teeth. Teeth can also be stained by mouthwashes and rinses that contain cetylpyridinium chloride and chlorhexidine. Teeth discoloration can also be brought on by antipsychotic medications, antihistamines (such as Benadryl), and high blood pressure medications.

Dental materials: Certain dental materials, such amalgam restorations, particularly those containing silver sulfide, can give teeth a grayish-black tint.

Age: The teeth's outer coating enamel wears down with age, exposing the dentin's natural yellow color.

Genetics: the enamel of some people is inherently thicker or brighter than others.

Environmental conditions: Teeth discoloration can be caused by an excess of fluoride, which can come from the environment (high naturally occurring fluoride levels in water) or from excessive use (fluoride treatments, rinses, toothpaste, and oral fluoride supplements).

Trauma: Trauma due to any condition can disrupt the formation of enamel in children which results in discoloration of teeth.

Formulations for problems of oral cavity

Various formulations are used to address the above mentioned problems of oral cavity which include toothpaste, tooth powder, mouthwash, mouth spray, fluoride gels, fluoride varnishes, chewing gums, buccal films, and dental cones. All these formulations have been discussed in preceding section.

Tooth paste

Toothpaste is the most popular, widely acceptable formulation to address various problems linked with tooth like tooth sensitivity, bleeding gums, tooth decay etc. An explanation about the tooth paste has been detailed in the chapter 7.

Tooth powder

It is believed that tooth powder first appeared many thousands of years ago. Myrrh, burned eggshells, crushed animal bone ash, and oyster shells are among the substances that ancient humans may have employed to make powders that might polish and eliminate bad breath. The composition of tooth powder is about same as of tooth paste but difference is only that tooth powder does not have humectant, binder and preservative. Tooth powder may also contain medicated ingredients like fluorides, anti-caries agents, and anti-sensitivity agents to rid from various dental problems. Refer the formulation of tooth paste in chapter 7 for tooth powder also.

Mouth wash

Although mouthwash has a relatively recent history, its use is quickly increasing due to changes in lifestyle and the realization of the value of preventative dentistry and oral hygiene. Mouthwash serves to freshen the mouth, prevent halitosis, and clean the inside of the mouth. Dental cavities and periodontal disorders can be successfully avoided with mouthwashes that contain pharmaceutical ingredients. In Japan, mouthwashes that include fluoride to prevent dental cavities are considered pharmaceutical items even though they are easily found on the market in other countries. A few ingredients of mouthwashes include ethanol and other solvents, humectants, solubilizers, flavoring compounds, pH regulators, and humectants as given in Table 6.2. Instead of using liquid ingredients, the powder form uses sodium bicarbonate and additional dilution agents.

Table 6.2: Formulation of mouth wash.

Class	Ingredient	Application
Water	Purified water	Adjustment of viscosity and volume
Solvent	Ethanol	Dissolution of various water insoluble ingredients
Humectant	Glycerin	Retention of moisture
Solubilizer	Polyoxyethylene-polyoxypropylene glycol	Solubility enhancement
Preservative	Sodium benzoate	Inhibit the growth of microbes
Flavoring agent	Menthol	Impart flavor
Buffer	Citric acid ester	Maintain desired pH
Coloring agent	D&C approved	Impart desired color
Pharmaceutical agent	Bromelain, calcium fluoride, cannabidiol etc.	To treat various oral cavity related problems

Alcohol is a common ingredient in mouthwashes, and this could have a variety of negative effects. First and foremost, it's crucial to prevent accidentally consumption, especially by young children. Regarding this, reports of alcohol poisoning from this source exist.

Second, it has been proposed that regular use of mouthwashes containing alcohol may raise the risk of oral and pharyngeal cancer due to the established associations between alcohol consumption, tobacco use, and this type of cancer. Nevertheless, the evidence seems to be very poor, primarily due to the confounding effects of established etiological factors like alcohol and tobacco use in the study individuals, which impact the statistical tests used to determine the degree of link.

Thirdly, it has been proposed that using mouthwashes with alcohol in it may raise the amount of alcohol inhaled, which could alter the results of the police breath test. It was discovered that this effect was fleeting. Lastly, it has been demonstrated that mouthwashes with alcohol lower the hardness of restorations made of composite and hybrid resins; these effects appear to be correlated with the alcohol percentage of mouthwash. Additionally, it has been discovered that composite resins soaked in mouthwashes containing alcohol gain more weight than those soaked in mouthwashes without alcohol. This implies that a mouthwash ingredient likely alcohol is absorbed into the resin and could be the cause of the softening effect. Nonetheless, a study discovered that mouthwashes with or without alcohol decreased the hardness of glass ionomer cement and composite resin. Furthermore, it has been discovered that mouthwashes with alcohol may change the color of some hybrid composite resins.

Anti-plaque mouthwashes are primarily used to take the place of mechanical teeth brushing in the following circumstances:

- After oral or periodontal surgery and during the healing period.
- After intermaxillary fixation used to treat jaw fractures or following cosmetic jaw surgery. With acute oral mucosal or gingival infections when pain and soreness prevents mechanical oral hygiene.
- For mentally or physically-handicapped patients who are unable to brush their teeth themselves.

But these individuals can also be incapable of using mouthwash, in which case a caregiver's swabbing of the gingival borders might be the only course of action. It might not always be simpler for the caregiver to complete this. The main drawback of utilizing effective treatments over an extended period of time is that they might discolor teeth. Since anti-plaque mouthwashes are unable to penetrate heavy layers of established plaque or reach the subgingival environment, they are not useful in treating gingivitis or periodontitis. In these circumstances, they ought to be applied only after supra- and subgingival scaling has been completed, cleaning the tooth surfaces, to sustain this state of affairs for a brief duration during which the gingiva's discomfort can impede the efficacy of mechanical plaque control. Various commercial mouthwash has been compiled in the Table 6.3.

Table 6.3: Compilation of commercial mouthwash.

Brand name	Ingredients	Application
Listerine® Cool mint®	Eucalyptol, menthol, methyl salicylate, thymol and alcohol	Inhibits 99.9% germs causing plaque, gingivitis and bad breath
Listerine® ultraclean®	Zinc chloride and alcohol	Prevent plaque, gingivitis and bad breath
Listerine® Total care®	Sodium fluoride and alcohol	Prevents dental cavities, restores dental enamel and inhibit 99.9% bad breath causing germs
Colgate® Maxfresh peppermint fresh	Cetylpyridinium Chloride(CPC) and Sodium Fluoride	Provides freshness in oral cavity and keeps gum and teeth clean.
Colgate Maxfresh Plax	Sodium Fluoride	Prevents dental cavities, keeps healthier gums, antibacterial and remove bad odor

Table 6.3: ***Contd....***

Brand name	Ingredients	Application
Sensodyne Mouthwash Complete Protection+	Postassium Nitrate and Sodium Fluoride	Treat tooth sensitivity and dental cavities, protects enamel and provides freshness in mouth
Amflor	Amine fluoride and Cocamidopropyl betaine,	Strengthening of tooth enamel and treatment of dental cavities
Senquel AD	Potassium nitrate, sodium fluoride	Dental hypersensitivity
Hexlas	Chlorhexidine	Treat plaque, gingivitis and provides fresh breath
Fluocaril	Sodium fluoride, eugenol and sodium monofluorophosphate	Reduces dental plaque, remineralise enamel and prevents dental cavities
Oralsept	Cetylpyridinium and aromatic oils	Inhibits germs and provides freshness in oral cavity

Mouth sprays

Mouth Spray is sprayed into the mouth to cover up or temporarily get rid of bad breath and treat dry mouth. This spray solution is similar to breath mints, mouth rinses, and breath freshener candies in that it masks bad breath and hydrates your mouth for a short period of time roughly 4 to 6 hours. This is also known as mouth freshness spray. This product is very beneficial if someone is suffering from burning mouth syndrome (BMS). If someone is seeking for an easy solution to freshen your breath, it probably will meet his/her needs. These sprays are occasionally sold as products for tobacco dippers, smokers, and other people who wish to cover up the smell of cigar or cigarette smoke. Many individuals use mouth sprays because they are convenient to carry and come in a variety of flavors. Common varieties include peppermint, spearmint, and cinnamon. Company-specific tastes like "Ice Mint," "Cool Mint," and "Supermint" are also available.

Manufacturers of certain mouth sprays claim that their products which include zinc ions, essential oils, hinokitiol, chlorine dioxide, chlorhexidine, and cetylpyridinium chloride have antibacterial or anti-plaque qualities. Since alcohol is often a main component of breath sprays, some companies claim that their products are alcohol free. When mouthwashes or breath sprays containing alcohol are used excessively, it is believed that alcohol is the cause of dry mouth.

Additionally, several manufacturers support the use of sugar free formulations due to the detrimental effects of sugar on dental caries. The ingredients used in formulation of mouth spray has been compiled in the Table 6.4.

Table 6.4: Various ingredients used in formulation of mouth spray.

Class	Ingredient	Application
Solvent	Purified water and alcohol	Dissolves solid ingredient
Sweetener	Xylitol	Impart sweetness to the spray
Humectant	Glycerin	Retain moisture
Cooling & flavoring agent	Cinnamon, fennel, peppermint, spearmint, menthol	Provides cooling sensation and flavor
Preservative	Sodium benzoate	Inhibits the microbial growth
Antibacterial/ antiplaque agents	Chlorhexidine, cetylpyridinium chloride, zinc ions	Removes plaque and prevent dental cavities and other dental problems
Flavor modulator	Potassium acesulfame	Modify the sweetening and flavoring property

Mechanism of mouth spray

The substance leaves a moisturizing protective layer on the oral tissues when it is sprayed within the mouth. For a short while, this protective layer relieves dry mouth. The spray lacks the nutritious components found in normal saliva, despite acting as a saliva substitute.Generally speaking, bad bacteria are able to proliferate in our mouths due to a lack of saliva. Because the mouth sprays function quickly to treat this problem, they also stop bacteria from growing, which helps to eliminate the foul odor they release. A compiled list of mouth spray in market has been given in table 6.5.

Table 6.5: Compiled list of mouth spray for oral health.

Brand name	Key ingredients	Application
Spry moisturizing mouth spray	Oat Beta Glucan, xylitol and aloe vera	Relieves dry mouth
Vedshakti mouth protect spray	Clove, fennel, mint and star anise	Inhibits germs which protect the oral cavity
Glister mint mouth refresher spray	SD alcohol 38B	Fights dental cavities and plaque

Table 6.5: ***Contd....***

Brand name	Key ingredients	Application
eMIST Mouth freshener spray	Turmeric extract, clove extract, ginger extract, fennel extract and cinnamon extract	Protects from tooth decay, Easiness in toothache, and fights against oral germs
Emwet mouth spray	Sodium carboxymethylcellulose, potassium chloride, sodium chloride, Magnesium chloride, calcium chloride, potassium dihydrogen phosphate	Provides relief from dryness of mouth and throat
Listerine Pocketmist® Breath spray	Acesulfame, eucalyptol, tocopherol, thymol	Kills bad breath germs
Oraseptan oral spray	Cetylpyridinium chloride, lidocaine and zinc gluconate	Prevents gingivitis, inflammation or oral cavity and other oral problems
Lubricity dry mouth oral spray	Xylitol, sodium hyaluronate, potassium sorbate and sodium benzoate	Prevents dry mouth and other oral problems
Thera breath spray	Green tea, xylitol and aloe vera	Provides freshness in oral cavity

Fluoride varnishes

Fluoride varnish is generally acknowledged as the best treatment option for kids who are at high risk of developing dental cavities. Because of worries about fluoride intake from gels and foams, it is especially suitable for kids under 6 years. Fluoride varnish is a vehicle to hold fluoride in close contact with the tooth for a certain amount of time; it is not meant to be as permanent as a fissure sealant. Because varnishes are sticky, they should maximize fluoride contact with the tooth surface, giving them an advantage over other professional fluoride administration methods. Using large fluoride concentrations in little amounts of material is possible with varnishes. Although they were approved for use as cavity liners in the US in 1994, fluoride varnishes have a lengthy history in Europe and Canada. They are also used off-label to prevent dental cavities.

To keep up their cariostatic action, varnishes need to be reapplied frequently, and a dose-response pattern has been shown. Fluoride varnish is used in creative public health cooperation programs in the US to close the gap between dentistry and medical practice. The AAP5 and medical schools, as well as educational programs like Smiles for

Life124, are among the initiatives aimed at ensuring that doctors use fluoride varnish appropriately in their practices. Physicians who treat young children who are at-risk for dental caries in many states utilize fluoride varnish in exchange for Medicaid reimbursement.

The composition of fluoride varnish include sodium fluoride as main ingredient, alcohol as solvent, natural resins as bases, sweetening and flavoring agents as organoleptic additives. Various commercial fluoride varnishes used for dental problems has been summarized in the Table 6.6.

Table 6.6: Summarized list of fluoride varnishes for dental care.

Brand name	Key ingredients	Applications
Duraphat®	Sodium fluoride 5%	Used for dentine hypersensitivity
Prevident®	Sodium fluoride 50 mg in 1ml	Used for dentine sensitivity
3M ESPE Clinpro white varnish	Sodium fluoride 5%, tricalcium phosphate	Desensitization of teeth
Nupro™ varnish	Sodium fluoride 5%	Dentine hypersensitivity and teeth cavities
Enamel® pro varnish	Sodium fluoride, amorphous calcium phosphate	Used for entine hypersensitivity
F-Varnish	Sodium fluoride 5, calcium phosphate	Improves enamel strength and treat other dental problems
Copal-F® Varnish	Sodium fluoride	Protection of dentine
Cervitec® plus	Chlorhexidine and thymol	Used for dental cavities
Fagamin®	Silver diamine fluoride 38%	Used for dental cavities

Chewing gums

A chewable insoluble plastic that has been sweetened and flavored is called chewing gum. Chewing gum like substances have long been used by humans. Chewing betel and chewing coca leaf dates back 4,000 and 3,000 years respectively, in Asia and Oceania and the ancient Andes, respectively. Though chewing gum has been around for thousands of years, modern chewing gum was created and first sold in 1,848.

Chewing gum causes the salivary glands to contract mechanically, which raises the volume of pooled saliva and causes a high saliva flow rate. Gum flavors activate taste receptors in the mouth, which increases salivary flow. The removal of bacteria and food debris from the mouth, inhibition of plaque formation, neutralization of plaque acidity, promotion of remineralization of early enamel lesions, control of enamel demineralization, antibacterial action, maintenance of an environment saturated in calcium and phosphate, and provision of a buffering system (bicarbonate, phosphate, and protein) are the most significant roles saliva plays in relation to dental problems. According to clinical trials, dental caries are significantly reduced when sugar-free gum is chewed after meals and sugar-filled snacks. Chewing gum is also advised for patients with rapid development caries, individuals with physical or mental difficulties, limited salivation (such as those undergoing radiation therapy), and poor dental hygiene.

Clinical research have demonstrated that sugar containing gum can raise the incidence of dental caries by increasing plaque formation, adhesion, and acidity in contrast to the advantageous sugar-free gum. Compared to other carbohydrates, sucrose causes the largest pH decrease in plaque because it is easily digested by oral cariogenic bacteria. Chewing sugary gum can bring the plaque's pH down below the crucial 5.5, which is the point at which the minerals in the enamel start to breakdown. People who are more prone to caries are more vulnerable to drops in plaque pH than people who are more resilient to changes in plaque after consuming sugar. The formulation of sugar free chewing gums for dental problems has been summarized in the Table 6.7 and the commercial chewing gums for dental problems has been compiled in the Table 6.8.

Table 6.7: Various ingredients used in formulation of chewing gums for dental problems.

Category	Examples	Application	Concentration used
Elastomers	Polyisobutylene, chicle, nispero	Imparts elasticity to the gum base	15-45%
Elastomer solvents	Terpene resins, glycerol esters	Imparts softness to the elastomers	45-70%
Fillers	Calcium carbonate, magnesium and ground limestone	Help in compression of chewing gum	Less than 50%
Bulking agents	Polydextrose, insulin, oligofructose, indigestible dextrin	Used to improve bulk consistency in case of low calorie gums	Quantity sufficient

Table 6.7: ***Contd....***

Category	Examples	Application	Concentration used
Plasticizers	Lanoline, propylene glycol, glycerin, glyceryl triacetate	Imparts proper consistency and desirable texture to the gum base	Quantity sufficient
Softening agents	Lecithin, glycerin, oleic acid, linoleic acid	Improve mouth feel and chewing ability of chewing gum	0.5-15%
Sweetening agents	Xylitol (Main), mannitol, sorbitol and aspartame	Impart desired amount of sweetness	Less than 50%
Flavoring agents	Clove oil, fennel oil, cinnamon oil	Impart desired flavor	0.01-1%
Coloring agents	D&C approved colors	Impart desired color	0.1%
Antioxidants	Propyl gallate, butylated hydroxy anisole, butylated hydroxy toluene	Prevent oxidation of gum	0.02%

Table 6.8: Compiled list of commercialized chewing gums for dental problems.

Brand name	Key ingredient	Applications
Vitaflo CHX	Chlorhexidine	Inhibits tooth decay
Advanced +	Chlorhexidine	Inhibits tooth decay
HEXIT	Chlorhexidine	Inhibits tooth decay
Fluorette	Fluoride	Dental fluorosis
V6	Xylitol	Prevents dental caries
Epic	Xylitol	Prevents tooth cavities
B-Fresh	Xylitol	Provides freshness in breath

Buccal films and strips

In the realm of oral care, buccal films and strips have emerged as innovative vehicles for administering medications and nutrients directly through the buccal mucosa. This method offers several advantages over traditional routes of administration, including enhanced bioavailability, rapid onset of action, and improved patient compliance. Buccal films and strips are thin, flexible sheets composed of water-soluble polymers that adhere to the buccal mucosa upon contact with saliva. They can be loaded with various active ingredients such as antimicrobials, analgesics, anti-inflammatories, vitamins, and minerals. The close proximity of the buccal mucosa to the bloodstream allows for efficient absorption of these compounds, bypassing the gastrointestinal tract and first-pass metabolism.

Buccal films containing local anesthetics provide targeted pain relief for dental procedures, such as extractions, root canals, and periodontal treatments, without the need for injections. Antimicrobial buccal films combat oral infections, including gingivitis, periodontitis, and oral candidiasis, by delivering therapeutic agents directly to the affected area. Buccal strips enriched with vitamins, minerals, and antioxidants promote oral health by replenishing essential nutrients and supporting tissue repair and regeneration. Patients undergoing chemotherapy or radiation therapy often develop oral mucositis. Buccal films containing anti-inflammatory agents can alleviate pain and accelerate the healing of mucosal lesions. Various ingredients used in formulation of buccal films or strips have been given in Table 6.9 and the commercialized buccal films or strips has been compiled in the Table 6.10.

Table 6.9: Formulation of buccal films or strips for oral care.

Category	Examples	Applications
Active ingredient	Analgesic (lidocaine), antimicrobial (Chlorhexidine), anti-inflammatory (Cortisone), Vitamins (B_{12})	Provide therapeutic effect
Polymers	Hydroxy propyl methylcellulose (HPMC), polyvinyl alcohol (PVA), sodium carboxymethyl cellulose (NaCMC)	Serves as film forming agent
Solvents	Water and alcohol (ethanol, isopropyl alcohol)	Serves as vehicle for dissolving the active ingredients and other ingredients
Plasticizers	Glycerin, prolylene glycol, polyethylene glycol	Impart flexibility and mechanical strength to the film
Mucoadhesive agent	Carbopol, sodium alginate, chitosan	Provide mucoadhesion characteristic to the film
Sweeteners	Sucralose, aspartame	Impart sweet taste to the film
Flavors	Mint, menthol, or fruit extracts	Impart desired flavor to the film
Preservatives	Sodium benzoate, butylated hydroxytoluene	Inhibit the growth of microorganisms in the film
Surfactants	Sodium lauryl sulfate, polysorbate 80	Aid in solubilization

Table 6.10: Compiled list of buccal films or strips used for oral care.

Brand name	Applications
Listerine Pocketpaks	Kills offensive breath germs and refreshes the oral cavity
Freshmeltz	Maintains oral hygiene and provides freshness in the mouth
Crest whitestrips	Provide dental whitening
Advanced teeth whitening strips	Provide whitening of sensitive teeth
5D White	Decreases the sensitivity and whitening remove teeth stain
4Smiles	Decrease the sensitivity and improve the tooth whitening
Daybreak	Decrease the sensitivity and improve the tooth whitening

Dental cones

Dental cones are tiny tablets that are used to cover the area left by a lost tooth. It is usually used in conjunction with an astringent or coagulant to stop bleeding, or with a slow-releasing antibacterial drug to prevent bacteria from growing in the socket following such extraction. Sodium chloride, bicarbonate, or an amino acid are frequently the active ingredients in these pills. The composition of the tablet shouldn't contain any ingredients that could operate as a haven for bacteria. After the tablet is firmly placed in the extraction site, it should be given 20 to 40 minutes to gradually dissolve or erode in the presence of a tiny amount of serum or fluid. Dental cones are mainly used to provide therapeutic response at the place of tooth extraction. These are not used for general care of oral cavity health. Some dental cones available in market include Parasorb® Cone Genta, Parasorb® HD cone, R.T.R. cone, felt cones etc.

CHAPTER 7

Formulation Building Blocks

Formulation building blocks for cosmetics

These are ingredients which provides desirable characteristics to cosmetic or cosmeceutical product. Such ingredients can be classified as functional, aesthetic, and marketing ingredients. Functional ingredients impart particular function like cleansing property, hair conditioning, moisturizing property etc. cosmetic product example sodium lauryl sulfate, glycerine, propylene glycol, behentromonium chloride etc. These ingredients are also termed as active ingredients. Sometimes ingredients does not provide appealing effect to the cosmetic product, then aesthetic ingredients are added to the product. Aesthetic ingredients provide appealing or pleasant effect to the cosmetic product These ingredients include coloring agent, perfumes etc. Marketing ingredients are added in cosmetic product to support the marketing strategies of the product or to increase the sale of the product. These ingredient are not expected to perform any function in the formulation but only added to promote the marketing of the product. For example, consumer prefer to buy moisturizing cream with aloe Vera instead of petrolatum.

Main formulation building blocks for cosmetics and cosmeceuticals:

- Surfactants
- Emollients
- Rheological additives
- Antimicrobial agents

Surfactants

Surfactants are the most important and impactful ingredients among all ingredients used in cosmetic products. It is said that existence of cosmetic industries without surfactant is not possible because it acts as multifunctional ingredient in cosmetic products like foaming agents, cleanser, solubilizer, thickener, emulsifier, suspending agent, penetration enhancer, and antimicrobial agent etc. The main property of surfactant which makes it so important in cosmetic products is miscibility with oil as well as water. These reduce the surface tension or interfacial tension between two phases. solid phase and liquid phase enabling spreading of liquid easily over the solid surface leading to its solubilization these also reduces the interfacial tension between two liquid phases enabling their mixing. The surfactant is composed of two parts; hydrophilic head and hydrophobic tail to give on which are that determines surface tension or interfacial tension b/w two phases (figure 7.1).

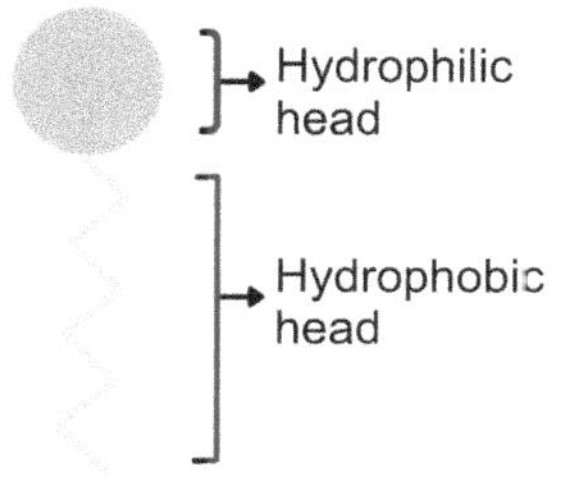

Figure 7.1: Structure of a surfactant.

Mechanism of surfactant

When a solution contains adequate concentration of surfactant molecules (critical micelle concentration), th en these molecules join together to create the structure called as micelles. On the creation of micelles, hydrophilic head of the surfactant aligns itself outside and hydrophobic tail aligns inside in case of oil-in-water while structure gets reversed in case of water-in-oil in which hydrophobic tail aligns itself outside and hydrophilic head aligns inside (Figure 7.2). The micelles act as unit to clean the dirt or debris. The hydrophobic tai s of the micelles attracted towards dirt or debris and hydrophilic head tends to pull surrounded dirt or debris from the surface into the cleaning solution. Then hydrophobic tails reconstruct the structure in which tails suspended the soil in the center of the structure (Figure 7.3).

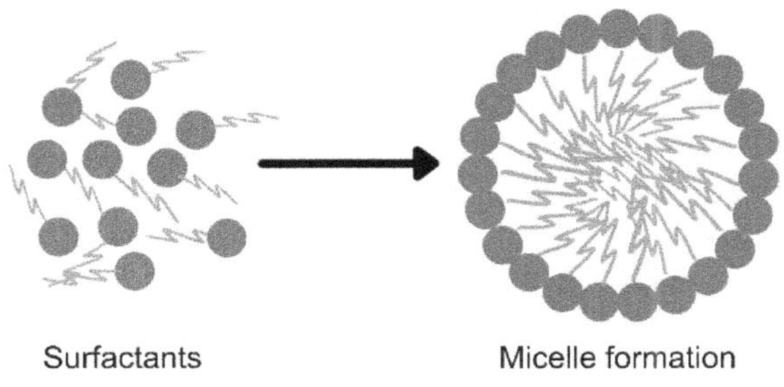

Figure 7.2: Micelles formation on critical micelle concentration.

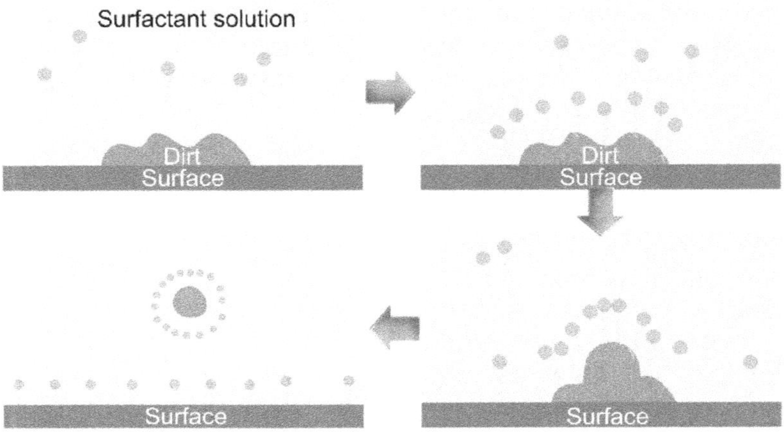

Figure 7.3: Mechanism for dirt or debris removal by surfactants.

Types of surfactants

Surfactants are basically classified depending upon the presence of polar head. Surfactants are classified into following classes depending upon the presence of charge on the polar head (Figure 7.4):

1. Cationic surfactants
2. Anionic surfactants
3. Non-ionic surfactants
4. Amphoteric or zwitterionic surfactant

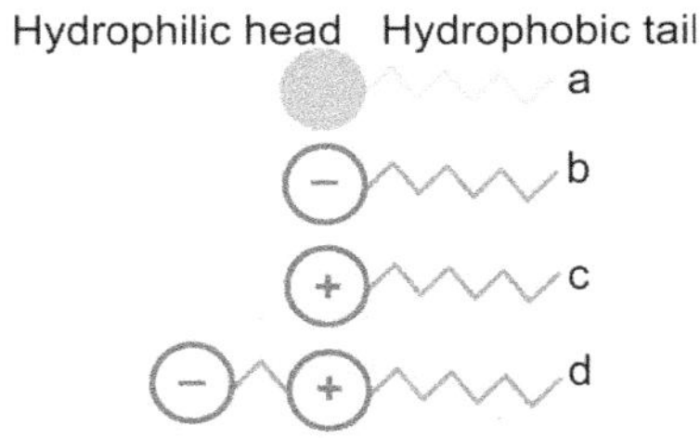

Figure 7.4: Types of surfactants.

1. Anionic surfactants:

These are the surface active agents having negative charge on their polar head. These are most widely used surfactant in cosmetic products especially for shampoos and cosmetics meant for cleansing purposes like body wash due to their higher foaming ability, greater cleansing property, and higher washing abilities in final product. These surfactant are best to remove clay, dirt, and various oil stains because these particles have positive charge while anionic surfactant possesses negative charge due to which strong binding between these particles and surfactants leading to effective cleaning. A number of anionic surfactants used in cosmetic and cosmeceutical products has been summarized into the table 7.1.

Table 7.1: Example of anionic surfactants used in cosmetic and cosmeceutical products.

Category	Examples	Comment
Harsh anionic surfactant	Sodium Lauryl Sulphate (SLS) Sodium Lauryl Ether Sulphate Ammonium Lauryl Sulphate Ammonium Laureth sulphate Sodium Myristyl Sulphate Sodium Myreth Sulphate Sodium Coco Sulphate TEA Lauryl Sulphate TEA-Dodecyl Benzene Sulphonate Sodium Alkylbenzene Sulphonate Ammonium or Sodium Xylene Sulphonate Sodium C14-16 Olefin Sulphonate	These surfactants must be avoided to use in cosmetics products
Mild and gentle Surfactant	Sodium Cocyl Isethionate Sodium Lauryl Sulphoacetate Sodium Socoyl Sarcosinate Sodium Lauryl Glucose Carboxylate Sodium Methyl Cocoyl Sodium Cocoyl Glycinate Dioctyl Sodium Sulphosuccinate Disodium laureth sulfosuccinate	These surfactants are safe to use in cosmetic products

Note: Anionic surfactants may cause skin irritation hence these are blended with amphoteric surfactants.

2. Cationic surfactant:

These are surface active agents having positive charge on their polar head. Due to possession of positive charge, these agents provide skin loving and nourishing property to the skin and body. These agents are not incorporated in cleansing formulations because these are not able to clean, rinse the surface and lack of foaming ability. These type of surfactants are primarily used as conditioner, hence also termed as conditioning agents. Human hairs possesses negative charge and with increase in damage of hair, negative charge on hair also increases. But these surfactants carry positive charge and hence attracted towards negative charged hair leading to adsorption on the hair shaft providing conditioning effect. This positive-negative interaction inhibits the removal of hair from the shaft. Mostly, cationic surfactants are used in combination with amphoteric or non-ionic surfactants but no used with anionic surfactants due to possession of opposite charge on them.

Various cationic surfactants which are most commonly used in cosmetic formulations have been summarized in table 7.2.

Table 7.2: Example of cationic surfactants used in cosmetic and cosmeceutical products.

Cationic surfactants	Cationic surfactants
Cetrimonium bromide	Stearalkonium chloride
Cetrimonium chloride	Isostearamidopropyl dimethylamine
Behentrimonium chloride	Quaternium-15
Behentrimonium methosulphate	Quaternium-18
Behenamidopropyl dimethylamine	Quaternium-22

3. Non-ionic surfactant:

These are the surface active agents which have no charge on their polar head. These agents lack foaming ability hence rarely used as prime surfactant in any cosmetic formulation. These agents have gentle cleansing activity and hence used in formulation of formulations like baby shampoo where gentle cleansing is required. These are used in combination with anionic surfactants to provide better foaming abilities, thickening property, and to reduce skin irritation by anionic surfactants. The polar group of non-ionic surfactant possesses the polyoxypropylene, polyoxyethylene, or polyol derivatives while hydrophobic group possesses saturated or unsaturated fatty alcohols or fatty acids. Various non-ionic surfactants used in cosmetic formulations have been summarized in the table 7.3.

Table 7.3: Example of Non ionic surfactants used in cosmetic and cosmeceutical products.

Non-ionic surfactants	Non-ionic surfactants
Decyl glucoside	PEG-10 Sorbitan Laurate
Laureth 10	Polysorbate 20, 21, 40, 60, 61, 65, 80, 81
Laureth 23	Steareth 2, 10, 15, 20
Laureth 4	Cocaamidopropylamine oxide

4. Amphoteric surfactants:

These are the surface active agents having both positive as well as negative charge on their polar head. These surfactants impart mild cleansing property and are combined with anionic surfactants to minimize the irritation caused by them. They also increases the foaming ability on addition with other type of surfactants. These surfactants are not used individually due to possession of poor cleansing property and hence always used as secondary surfactant.

These surfactants are costlier ten other classes of surfactant. Commonly used amphoteric surfactants in cosmetic formulations have been summarized into the table 7.4.

Table 7.4: Example of amphoteric surfactants used in cosmetic and cosmeceutical products.

Amphoteric surfactants	Amphoteric surfactants
Cocamidopropyl betaine	Sodium cocoamphoacetate
Disodium cocoamphodiacetate	Disodium cocoamphodipropionate
Coco betaine	Sodium Lauroamphoacetate

Applications of surfactants in cosmetic products:

Surfactant plays a vital role in preparation of cosmetic and cosmeceutical formulations. Surfactant has various important applications in cosmetic products without which it is not possible to formulate them. Surfactants provide various applications in cosmetic and cosmeceutical formulations which are following:

- Cleansing
- Wetting
- Foaming
- Thickening
- Emulsification
- Solubilization
- Conditioning
- Penetration enhancement
- Special effects

Cleansing

Cleansing is the main application of surfactant in cosmetic products. Commonly two types of dirt namely oil deposit and solid particulates are deposited on human skin and hair making them dirty. The oil deposit secreted from sebum produced in the hair follicles while solid particulates deposited from the environment and remain on human skin and hair through attractive forces. However, the some solid particulates can be removed from skin and hair using rinsing with water but oil deposits adheres to the more hydrophobic surfaces of the skin and hair. Then surfactants used in cleansing preparation provide freedom from these oil deposits. The hydrophobic part of the surfactant attracted to and align with the oil portion on surface of skin and hair while hydrophilic portion of surfactant align towards the surface of oil deposits leading to increase in hydrophilicity. It causes uplifting of the oil deposits from the surface of skin and hair and carried away using the rinsing with water.

Wetting

Surfactants also act as wetting agents because they decrease the contact angle between a thing placed on the surface and the surface itself. It allows the easy spreading of the surfactant on the surface and surfactant inject themselves in between the oil deposits present on the skin or hair and the skin or hair surface leading to uplifting the oil deposits from the surface which can be easily removed using rinsing. Wetting property also allows the spreading of the cosmetic product on skin or hair easily and prevents the balling up on the skin or hair surface of the product.

Foaming

This is another application of the surfactant provided in the cleansing products. Foam is formed on dispersion of air in continuous liquid medium and surfactant molecules tend to stabilize the foam by alignment. Foaming is not related to cleansing property of the product but consumers think that cleansing products provide good foaming and hence formulator has to add foaming surfactant in the cleansing formulation like shampoo.

Thickening

In aqueous solution, surfactant molecules align themselves in a structure termed as micelle. Micelle is a small structure in which hydrophobic tail align inwards while hydrophilic head align outwards. Micelles have crucial role in preparation of emulsion and to provide thickening property in the cosmetics. The thickness of a solution depends on closeness of the packing of micelles. More distance between the micelles leads to formation of thinner solution. Close packing between the micelles leads to formation of thick solution.

Emulsification

This is another main application of the surfactants to mix the oil and water leading to formation of emulsion. Cleansing products are used to remove oils from the skin but many cosmetic products are prepared to impart oily substances to the skin or hair. These substances cannot be used directly to skin or hair due to unappealing aesthetic properties, hence formulators prepare emulsions using the surfactants. Surfactants help in mixing of oil and water phase by minimizing the interfacial tension between these two phases leading to formation of emulsion. Various creams and lotions are based on the emulsion formation which can be either oil-in-water or water-in-oil type. When these products are applied on the skin or hair, then the micelles formed by surfactants break and deliver the oil substances to the skin. For example, cold cream is water-in-oil type while vanishing cream is oil-in-water type emulsion.

Solubilization

Most common problem is that emulsion produces opaque products. But when a clear product is required having oil in water, then surfactants help to do so by creation of so small particles that light easily crosses via them leading to clear formulation. These type of surfactants are termed as solubilization surfactants. These are also used to mix oily substances like various natural substances or fragrances into clear solution. An example of this type of surfactant is Polysorbate 20.

Conditioning

This is another application of surfactant in cosmetic products especially in hair shampoos. Due to the presence of hydrophobic part on their surface, surfactants possesses conditioning effect that help in improving the look and feel of the surfaces of hair or skin. Conditioning effect occur when surfactant left behind after rinsing with water. These types of surfactants possess positive charge on their polar head while hair possess negative charge. Hence the positive charge surfactant forms bond with negative charged hair leading to adsorption on the hair shaft and impart conditioning effect. Only cationic surfactants can be used to provide conditioning effect due to possession of positive charge on their polar head.

Penetration enhancement

Surfactant are also responsible for enhancement of penetration of various cosmetic products. It was recognized that due to possession of least toxicity and skin irritancy, non-ionic surfactants have been evaluated as powerful penetration enhancers for cosmetic products. These molecules penetrate into the intercellular areas of stratum corneum leading to increase in fluidity and eventually solubilize the lipid components.

Special effects

Despite of above applications, surfactants possess a number of other applications also that are more beneficial to formulator. For example, some surfactants can be used as preservatives in cosmetic products due to possession of antimicrobial effect. Some surfactants can be added in cosmetic products to provide a product having better elegancy, pearly effect leading to their aesthetic appeal. Some surfactants can be used to reduce the irritancy and improving the stability of product.

Surfactants in marketed cosmetic products:

Every type of cosmetic products available in market has various surfactants in single formulation which has been showed by some marketed cosmetic products in table 7.5.

Table 7.5: Surfactants in Marketed Cosmetic Products having diverse Blend in Every Formulation.

Category	Company	Surfactant	Uses
Moisturizing cream	Pond's	Behenic acid	Cleansing agent
		Ceteareth 20	Cleansing, emulsifying agent
Shampoo	Head & Shoulders	Sodium lauryl sulfate & Sodium laureth sulfate	Cleansing agents
		Cocamidopropyl, Betaine, Cocamide MEA	To aid foam, creamy, and easy to spread over the scalp
		Dimethicone	Hair conditioner & hair moisturizer
		Guar hydroxypropyltrimonium chloride, Polyquaternium-10	Conditioning agents
Shampoo	Dove	Sodium laureth sulfate	Cleansing and emulsifier agent
		Glycol distearate	Emollient, emulsifier, and viscosity enhnacer
		Cocamidopropyl, Betaine	Cleansing agent
		Dimethiconol	Emollient and moisturizer
		PEG-45M	Moisturizer
		Tea-dodecylbenzenesulfonate	Cleansing agent
		Cetrimonium chloride	Emulsifying, cleansing, and preservative
		Propylene glycol	Moisturizer
		Cocamide MEA	Cleansing and emulsifier agent

Table 7.5: ***Contd....***

Category	Company	Surfactant	Uses
Face wash	Clean & Clear	Myristic acid	Cleansing, emulsifying agent
		Lauric acid	Anti-acne, Cleansing, and emulsifying agent
		Cocamidopropyl, Betaine	Cleansing, viscosity modifier
		Lauryl phosphate	Emulsifying
Face wash	Pond's	Myristic acid	Cleansing, emulsifying agent
		Propylene glycol	Moisturizer,
		Palmitic acid	Emulsifier, emollient
		Stearic acid	Emollient
		Lauric acid	Anti-acne, cleansing and emulsifying agent
		Glycol distearate	Emulsifier, emollient
		Decyl Glucoside	Cleansing agent
Vanishing cream	Pond's	Propylene glycol	Moisturizer
		Dimethicone	Emollient
		Stearic acid	Emollient
Hair removal cream	Veet	Cetearyl alcohol	Emollient, emulsifying, and cleansing agent
		Ceteareth 20	Cleansing and emulsifying agent

Emollients

The word emollient is derived from Latin word "Mollire" which English meaning is "to soften". Hence these are the agents which are able to soften the dry, flakey, or rough surface making the feel of skin or hair better. These agents are also termed as moisturizers. These are the agents which provides smoothness and hydration to the skin on application by covering the skin with a protective film to trap in moisture (figure 7.5).

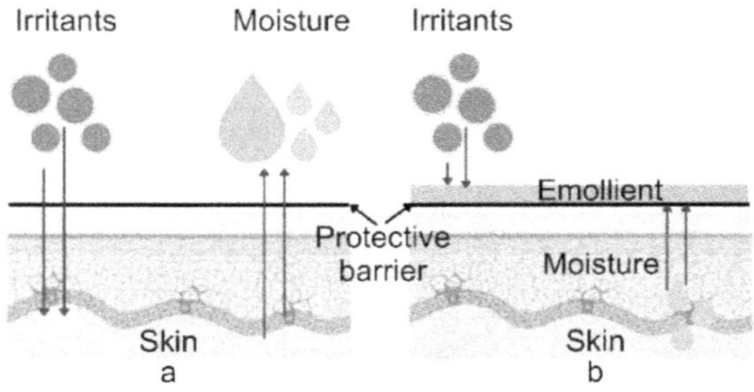

Figure 7.5: Mechanism for working of emollients.

There are main three functions of emollients:

1. Occlusion
2. Lubrication
3. Humectant

Occlusion

Occlusive agents form a covering of oil over the surface of skin providing a physical barrier that inhibit the water loss from the skin thus increase the water content of skin. For example, petrolatum, waxes, oils etc.

Humectants

These are the agents which retain the moisture of skin's surface by attracting the moisture from atmosphere as well as from the lower layers of the skin or increases the water holding capacity of the uppermost layer of the skin (stratum corneum). For example, glycerin, urea etc.

Lubrication

Lubricating agents are the agents which reduces the friction on rubbing of anything against the skin or aid in slippage or gliding over the skin.

Examples

Petrolatum, Cocoa butter, Lanolin, Mineral oil, Bees wax, Shea butter, Cetyl alcohol, Coconut oil, Sesame oil, Olive oil, Jojoba oil, almond oil, Triethylhexanoin etc.

Other ingredients

Various other special ingredients may also added in an emollient formulation like ointment or creams especially for skin disorders like psoriasis which are following:

Corticosteroids, Salicylic acid, Anthralin, Tacrolimus, Synthetic vitamin D, coal tar etc.

Types of emollients

There are following types of emollients which are available in market also:

- Leave-on emollients
- Wash-off emollients

Leave-on emollients

These are the emollients which are applied on the skin and left here to soak in. These are not washed off the skin. These type of emollients include;

Ointments

These emollients are greasiest and sometimes unaccepted by the people cosmetically. Because these are very effective in holding the water, hence widely used for dry and thick skin. These are not suitable for weeing eczema. These are generally prepared using the white soft paraffin and liquid paraffin and ideal for dry as well as thick skin. These are usually applied in the night and chances of skin irritation are less with ointments because they do not contain any preservative.

Creams

These are prepared using mixture of oil and water and feel cool and light on application. Hence people having eczema uses the cream in day time. These are less greasy than ointments so easier to spread on the skin. These preparations must be used frequently and abundantly to prevent the drying of the skin. These creams have preservatives in their formula hence chances of skin irritation increase but not in every case. Example: Aproderm® Emollient cream

Lotions

These preparations contain small amount of fat and more amount of water hence less effective in to keep moist the skin. But it is beneficial for the hairy part of the body like scalp and weepy skin. These also contain preservatives in their formula hence chances of skin irritation are more than ointments. Example: Parasoft® Emollient lotion

Wash-off emollients

These emollients are applied on dry skin by mixing with warm water followed by rinsing after sometime. These type of emollients mainly include soap substitutes.

Soap substitutes

Various skin care products like soap, shampoos etc can remove the oily layer from the skin rendering the skin dry and may also lead to skin condition which is termed as eczema. Hence soap substitutes can be used instead of these skin care products to avoid the dryness of the skin. Any emollient can be used by mixing with water for cleansing the skin because it does not remove the oily layer of the skin. Soap substitutes does not produce foam but clean the skin's surface as that of soaps. These can be used before bathing, washing, and showering. Example: Hydromol bath & shower emollient

Optimum amount of emollient

The required amount of leave-on emollient depends upon the size of the person and severity of the skin conditions or to treat the whole body, the required amount of emollient is approximately 600 grams/week for an adult and 250-500 grams/week for a child under 12 years. The required amount of different emollients to treat skin conditions has been given in table 7.6.

Table 7.6: Recommended Optimal Emollient Levels for Effective Skin Treatment.

Area of the body	Lotions	Creams and ointments
Face	100ml	120g
Hands	500ml	120g
Arms and legs	1000ml	500-1000ml
Trunk	1500ml	1000g

Selection of emollient

The selection of emollient should not only on the basis of cost but some other factors must also be taken into consideration which are following:

- Extent of dryness of skin, along with its severity
- Personal preferences of the user
- Previous experiences for allergic reactions like burning, stinging, and tingling which can occur due to presence of specific ingredient in the emollient
- Life style factors and time of year

- Type of skin because emollients in form of creams and lotions may beneficial for red and inflamed areas of the skin while emollients in form of ointments are preferred for dry skin than creams and lotions

Tips for application of emollient

The right method as well as right time for application of emollient are primary factor to obtain maximum benefit of it. The tips for application of medicated emollients used for various skin diseases or disorders are given by the doctor or prescriber. But the tips for application of over the counter emollient are following:

- Emollient should apply within 5 minutes of bathing because skin needs high moisture at that time.
- Emollients should be applied at least 3-4 times in a day or as directed by the prescriber or advisor.
- Emollient should be applied regularly to the hands or face because these are exposed more to the irritant elements than other parts of the body.
- Emollient should be applied lightly in direction of hair follicles after rubbing it in between the palms.
- Emollient should not rubbed on the skin because it may cause irritation leading to skin redness or any other skin disorder.
- Emollient should be applied before various activities like gardening, swimming because these activities may cause skin irritation.
- Emollients can be applied to the babies also before mealtimes to avoid sore from drink and food.
- Emollients should be applied quickly when you feel skin gets dry.
- Soap substitute should be applied lightly to avoid abrasion.

Side effects of emollients

Emollients can cause various skin problems which are following:

- A scorching, stinging, or burning sensation that persists after several days of treatment by emollient and mainly due to presence of any ingredient in emollient
- Inflamed or blocked hair follicle termed as folliculitis which can be due to presence of occlusive ingredients like petrolatum, mineral oils etc
- Contact urticaria which can be due to presence of preservative like sorbic acid and fragrances
- Acne which can be due to presence of occlusive oils used in emollient

- Allergic contact dermatitis which can be due to presence of ingredients like lanolin, propylene glycol, vitamin E etc.

Applications of emollient

Generally the skin gets irritated and dried especially during winter season and after washing the hands or face using cleansing cosmetics or soaps. Then emollients can be used to provide healing and soothing action for dried skin. Emollients also provide rid from dry skin in various skin disorders which mainly include:

- Eczema
- Psoriasis
- Atopic dermatitis
- Diabetes
- Hypothyroidism
- Kidney problems

Rheological modifiers

The optimum rheology is most important consideration in preparation of various cosmetic products. However the efficacy of cosmetic or personal care products mainly depends upon the concentration and choice of active constituent and excipients but the aesthetics and permeation of products through stratum corneum depends upon the rheology of product. Rheology is made up of two words namely rheo and logos which means flow and to study respectively. Hence rheology can be defined as the science or study of flow of things. It is prerequisite for cosmetic products that they must have adequate flow. The rheology is described in terms of viscosity which is the resistance of flow and described as:

$$\text{Viscosity} = \text{Shear stress} / \text{Shear rate}$$

The force per unit area applied is known as shear stress and the resulting velocity gradient is known as the shear rate. The way viscosity changes with different shear rates has a big impact on product stability and performance. A formulation which sustain its viscosity, nevertheless of shear rates is said to have Newtonian flow whilst a formulation whose viscosity reduces with shear rates is said to have pseudoplastic flow and a formulation whose viscosity increase with shear rate is said to have dilatant flow (Figure 7.6). The appropriate choice of rheological modifier helps to produce a formulation having ideal flow properties leading to achievement of thermostable rheology.

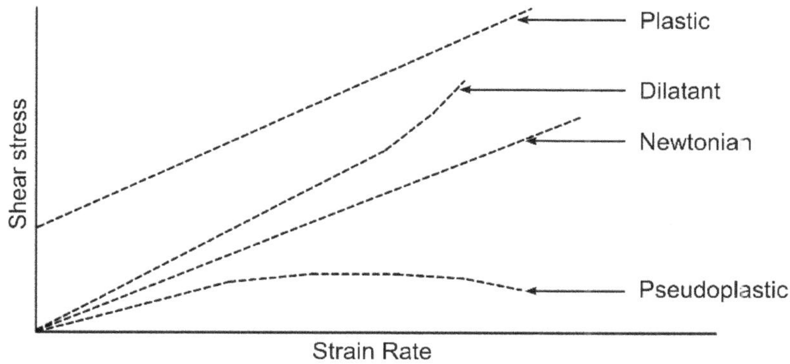

Figure 7.6: Change in viscosity with change in shear stress.

Rheology is involved directly or indirectly in every type of cosmetic product. For example, a cream should possess adequate viscosity so that it cannot be remove from the tube without squeezing but can be easily applied on the skin. Nail polish should possess sufficient viscosity so that it can suspend the large volume of pigment, not oozed from the brush but capable to provide an even covering of nail paint over the entire nail. Seeing the importance of rheology in cosmetic products, the rheological modifiers are added in cosmetic products which change or alter the viscosity or flow of a product. The terms Rheological modifiers, gelling agents, and thickening agents are near to same having slight different functionalities listed in table 7.7.

Rheological modifiers not only change the viscosity of the formulation but also impart specific functionality to the formulation. These specific functionalities include improvement in texture, body, hydration retention, suspendability of soluble pigments to provide stability, preventing syneresis, inhibiting bacterial attack, and resisting the shrinkage. The product can be Newtonian, psedoplastic, thixotropic, gel or a flowable liquid which will affect the appearance of the product in final container, its ease to pour or scoop from the final container, ease to apply on skin or hair shaft, ease to rinse or remove it from the surface after use. The appropriate rheological properties are necessary to formulate a product having better stability. To achieve these various characteristics in finalized product, various rheological modifiers are available in the market.

Table 7.7: Function of Rheological modifiers, gelling agents, and thickening agents.

Rheological modifiers	Gelling agents	Thickening agents
These are the ingredients which change or alter the flow or viscosity of a product along with altering the feel, increasing the slip, silkiness and behavior. Majority of rheological modifiers also cause improvement in rate of absorption, penetration as well as removal of dryness.	These are the agents that convert oil and aqueous phase into the gel having thick consistency but not stiffness. These gels cause preparation of thick products which can be shaken, stirred under high shear for easy application and pouring from the container.	These are the ingredients which only increase the viscosity of the product (like emulsion) without any change in performance of the behavior of product. These are mostly used to stabilize the formulation. These are generally occur in solid form instead of wax form.

Classification of rheological modifiers

Rheological modifiers can be classified on various parameters like their ionic charges, their application, their mechanisms for thickening etc. Traditionally, rheological modifiers are classified on basis of their chemical origin (inorganic or organic) either they are natural, synthetic or semi-synthetic (figure 7.7).

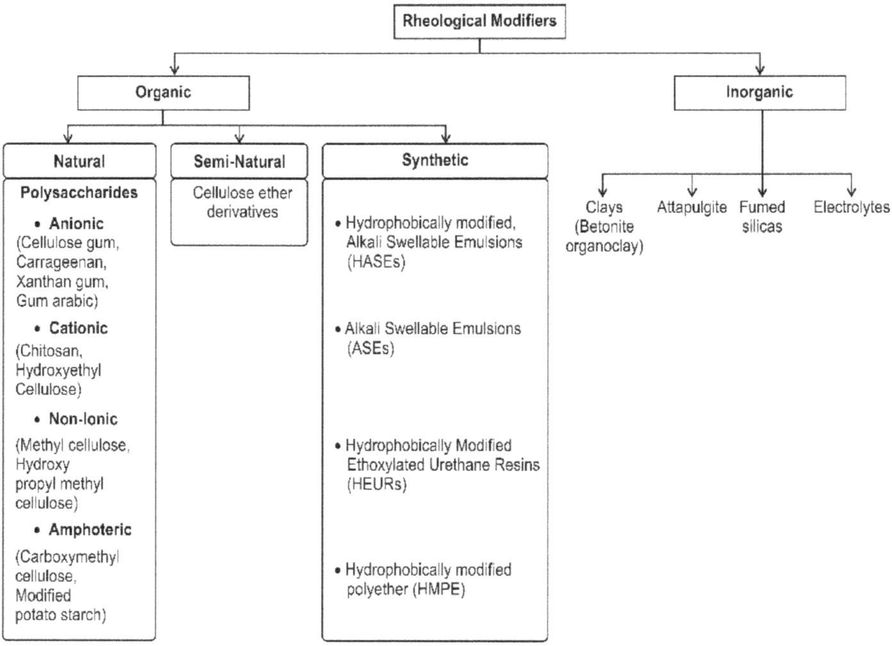

Figure 7.7: Classification of rheological modifiers.

Inorganic rheological modifiers

These are typically available in powder form and have a thixotropic shear thinning property as well as good yield values. This property is characterized by viscosity decreases with increasing shear rate and time-dependent recovery after shearing, characteristics that are particularly advantageous for suspending and gelling agents, which is the most common use of these type of rheological modifiers. Various types of inorganic rheological modifiers differs from each other on the basis of chemistry, crystallinity, particle size etc., even in same category. Various inorganic rheological modifiers are following:

Fumed silica

It is the most commonly used rheological modifier of inorganic nature. It is silicone dioxide (amorphous) having specific gravity of 2.2, particle size of 7-40 nm, and surface area of 50-380 m2/g. Fumed silica lacks internal surface area and thixotropic behavior is due to hydrogen bonding between the fumed silica particles forming loose lattice like structure which is responsible for increasing the apparent viscosity of the formulation. But this hydrogen bonding is weak in nature due to which lattice like structure is disturbed on applying the stress and quick recovery to initial form. It has greater surface area to weight ratio and added only in small concentration (1-5%) to the formulation. Fumed silica grades are classified as hydrophilic or hydrophobic based on their surface chemistry, which is linked to rheological properties. Hydrophilic silica is the standard grade, and it works best in nonpolar and medium polar formulations. Hydrophobic silica is more effective in medium polar to polar fluids and is commonly used to provide good moisture resistance in adhesives, sealants, and coatings.

Attapulgite

Attapulgite is a hydrated magnesium alumino-silicate and is crystalline in nature. It's a clay mineral that forms spontaneously and has a three-dimensional chain structure. It comes in a variety of grades, ranging from highly thermally activated attapulgite with a large surface area to fully hydrated attapulgites that thicken liquid systems without producing system swelling. Attapulgite compounds are effective rheology modifiers in both ionic and non-ionic aqueous solutions, primarily as thickeners, as well as in most organic liquids. Later, to achieve appropriate thickening and suspension qualities, attapulgites are dispersed with cationic and non-ionic surfactants.

Betonite clays

It is an aluminium silicate and mainly consist of montmorillonite, a smectite group mineral. Its structure is expressed as a "house of cards," with aggregates of flat platelets forming the foundation. Betonite's high specific surface area and numerous OH groups provide high absorption capability and ability to swell in water, and its flexible 3D network structure provides robust thickening effects and shear thinning thixotropic qualities. With a final formulation concentration of 1-2%, stabilizing effects can be achieved.

Organoclay

It is an organically modified phyllosilicate that is commonly used as a rheology modifier (bentonite). This alteration reduces betonite's natural absorption capacity in water while increasing its ability to absorb oil, grease, and other hydrophobic chlorinated hydrocarbons that are sparingly soluble. Transparency, which may be produced when the major particle size is around 8 to 10 microns, is a desirable feature of organoclays made from smectite type clays.

Organic rheological modifiers

Natural & Semi-natural organic rheological modifiers (polysaccharides)

These are mainly comprised of polysaccharides or amino acid building blocks. These polymers whether complete natural or semi-natural are obtained from plant, animal or microbial sources. Polysaccharides belong to natural polymers that possess wide application in cosmetics worldwide. These have been used extensively in personal care products due to possession of ready availability from natural sources along with their multifunctional property. Polysaccharides' interaction with other formulation elements, as well as their ease of chemical modification, could improve the qualities of personal care products. Finally, unlike synthetic-based polymers, these naturally occurring polysaccharides are renewable and have a long history of safe use. Depending upon the availability of charge, polysaccharides can be classified into anionic, cationic, non-ionic, and amphoteric.

Anionic polysaccharides

A large variety of naturally occurring compounds predominates in this class of polysaccharides which possess a negative charge. Commercially, cellulose gum (carboxymethyl cellulose) and carboxymethylchitin are two rheologically interesting derivatives for personal care. The carboxymethylation of naturally occurring cellulose and chitin, respectively, makes these derivatives anionic.

Cellulose gum (sodium carboxymethylcellulose; Na-CMC)

It is chemically modified derivative of cellulose widely available in all type of plants. β-D-(1,4)-glucose is the only repeating monosaccharide found naturally in cellulose. It is extremely crystalline and organised because to strong intermolecular hydrogen bonds, making it water insoluble. Derivatization of cellulose using sodium chloroacetate to produce Na-CMC is one technique to address this issue. The degree of substitution of commercially produced Na-CMC is usually between 0.7 and 1.2. Na-CMC is strongly anionic and has an acidity similar to acetic acid due to the presence of substituted carboxymethy groups. Most acid groups are deprotonated in the salt form at pH over 4.5, making Na-CMC water soluble. At pH below 4.5, CMC is water insoluble, with viscosity increasing first as chain tangling and phase separation rise. Carboxymethylcellulose solutions with concentrations up to 5% by weight are pseudoplastic but lack a yield value. With a modest amount of water added for increased solubility, it can dissolve in and thicken glycerin solutions. Na-CMC, like most anionic polysaccharides, binds strongly to multivalent cations like Ca2+ and gels as a result. With increasing degree of substitution, the flow behaviour of Na-CMC tends to flip from pseudoplastic to thixotropic. Its viscofying effects, on the other hand, are only stable in the pH range of 4–10 and at lower temperatures.

Xanthan gum

Xanthan gum is a polymer that is commercially generated during fermentation by precipitating the broth recovered from the exocellular coating on bacterial cell walls. It has a complicated structure with a -D-(1,4)-glucose backbone and branching trisaccharide side chains of -D-(1,2)-mannose and -D-(1,4)-glucuronic acid. The core chain's water solubility is due to the comb-like trisaccharide side chains. The carboxylic acid residues on D-glucuronic acid and the pyruvic acid moiety on the terminal D-mannose give xanthan gum its anionic charge. In the presence of cationic salts, xanthan gum forms helical coils, but whether or not double helices form is still a matter of debate. The creation of junction zones, which are thought to occur as a result of hydrophobic interactions on the helix, is required for the thickening and gelation mechanisms. Cations tend to "salt out" hydrophobic areas and strengthen junction zones, resulting in a modest increase in viscosity, even though the stiff backbone reduces the need for salts to generate solution viscosity. Because xanthan solutions' viscosity is derived from hydrophobic interactions, they have good temperature stability. Pseudoplastic xanthan solutions have a yield value below which the solution resists deformation. Water-insoluble particles or oily droplets can be stabilised or suspended using such solutions. This increases the formulation's shelf life and may lower the amount of primary emulsifiers required. At concentrations as low as 3.5 wt percent, xanthan gum generates cholesteric mesophase lyotropic liquid crystals in water, a growing area of interest in personal care due to their unique ability to form emulsifier-free suspensions. The salt concentration influences the formation of liquid crystals, with larger salt concentrations necessitating lower xanthan concentrations. The frequency and strength of junction zones are expected to increase with xanthan gum and gluco- or galactoannas (e.g. kappa carrageenan), resulting in increased solution viscosities. Anionic xanthan gum is incompatible with most cationic surfactants in terms of surfactant compatibility. Non-ionic surfactants have no effect on the viscosity of xanthan solutions, regardless of surfactant concentration. Anionic surfactants in concentrations more than 4% increase the viscosity of xanthan solutions, especially at low shear rates. This improves xanthan gum's capacity to suspend liquids. In addition, adding colloidal magnesium silicate to xanthan gum can improve its thickening efficacy synergistically.

Cationic polysaccharides

Synthetically modified polyglycans make up the majority of cationic polysaccharides of interest in personal care. They adhere tightly to anionic surfaces like human hair and skin because of their cationic nature. As a result, numerous cationic polysaccharides are used as conditioners or film formers in hair cosmetic formulations.

Chitosan

Chitosan is famous for being the only naturally occurring, commercially available polysaccharide with a catalytic charge. It's present naturally in insect exoskeletons and bacterial parasites, but it's made industrially by alkaline hydrolysis of crustacean chitin's acetamide. Chitosan is a random copolymer composed of two monosaccharides, N-acetyl—D-(1,4)-glucosamine and -D-(1,4)-glucosamine, which are commercially mixed in a 1:4 ratio. However, because chitosan is neutralised to a water soluble chitosonium salt at pH below 7.0, it is only cationic and water soluble. Commercially available chitosan is commonly neutralised with a carboxylic acid, such as lactic or glycolic acid, which are components of human skin's natural moisturising factor.

Chitosan has a high substantivity to negatively charged hair and skin in its salt form. It's also utilised in hair fixatives and shampoos as a film former. Because of the strong cationic charge on the chitosan backbone, it forms water-insoluble complexes with most anionic surfactants and some polyvalent metal cations (i.e. Cu2+). Because of its biocompatibility with the human body, it's been used in polysaccharide matrices for controlled drug delivery. Chitosan has also been proven to be mucoadhesive, binding to glycoproteins found in human tissue lining the eyes and throat. This shows that chitosan could be used in sophisticated cosmetics (also known as "cosmeceuticals") that entail the delivery of medications in the future.

Cationic hydroxyethyl cellulose (HEC)

It is a polysaccharide that has found the most success in hair care products as a conditioner. As previously stated, cellulose is water insoluble in its natural state, but it can be treated with the reactive alkylating reagent ethylene oxide in alkaline circumstances to produce hydroxyethyl cellulose, a water soluble cellulose derivative.

As an aqueous-based rheological modifier, it is widely utilised in personal care. Various cat- ionic reagents, which add quaternary charges randomly throughout the HEC backbone, can be used to further modify HEC. Polyquaternium-10 and polyquaternium-4 are two examples of commonly used cationic HEC derivatives, identified by their International Nomenclature Cosmetic Ingredient designations. Polyquaternium-10 is used as a conditioner in shampoo and conditioner formulations, whilst polyquaternium-4 is utilised in hair fixative formulations such mousses as both a conditioner and a fixative. Cationic cellulose-based polysaccharides are thought to interact weakly with cationic surfactants/surfaces. Cationic polysaccharides, such as cationic HEC, on the other hand, respond strongly to anionic surfactants/surfaces, even at concentrations well below the surfactant's critical micelle concentration.

The thickening efficacy of cationic HEC is determined by its molecular weight; as the molecular weight increases, the viscosity of the solution increases. The viscosifying effect is also proportional to the concentration. The anionic surfactant begins to neutralise the cationic charge on the polysaccharide in 1 wt% polyquaternium-10 solutions, causing a rapid increase in viscosity. As the surfactant concentration rises, the cationic HEC may redissolve or precipitate, depending on the surfactant type. The rheological contributions of cationic HECs are substantially overshadowed by the surfactant's larger contributions at high surfactant concentrations. Polyquaternium-10, like chitosan, possesses mucoadhesive characteristics, which expands its potential usage in personal care as ocular or oral treatments.

Non-ionic polysaccharides

Despite the fact that non-ionic polysaccharides do not have a formal charge, changes in solution polarity, the presence of salts, surfactants, polymers, and other components might impact their solution behaviour. Typically, they've been used as rheological modifiers in cosmetics, such as the ether-modified cellulose derivatives family.

Methyl cellulose (MC)

The gel point of methylcellulose (MC) is around 45°C. It precipitates from the solution at temperatures above 56°C, giving it a hazy, cloudy appearance. It is more lipophilic than hydroxypropyl cellulose. It can now dissolve and thicken a larger variety of organic liquids. Most surfactants are compatible with it. In shower formulations, MC has a unique capacity to improve foam formation and strength. MC approaches its gel point in hot/warm showers, increasing the viscosity of the films enclosing bubbles, making bubbles and foam more durable.

Hydroxypropylmethyl cellulose (HPMC)

It is comparable to methyl cellulose but contains hydroxypropyl groups, which compensate for the absence of hydrophilic domains in methyl cellulose. As a result, HPMC outperforms MC in several solvent systems. HPMC become fully expanded and the lipophilic domains are contained in surfactant micelles at very high surfactant concentrations. HPMC improves foam generation and strength in the same way that MC does. Even after heat sterilisation, the lipophilic and surface-active HPMC maintains the stability of o/w emulsions, allowing it to be used in the creation of sterile creams and lotions.

Amphoteric polysaccharides

Both cationic and anionic charges can be carried on the same chain in amphoteric polyglycans. Although amphoteric surfactants are widely employed in personal care products such as soaps, these polysaccharides are still relatively obscure and under utilised in cosmetics. Because of their ionic nature, they face numerous obstacles in formulation, including solubility, pH stability, and the presence of salts or surfactants. Typically, trial and error is the only viable approach for determining the best polysaccharide-containing composition.

Carboxymethyl chitosan

The most well-known amphoteric polysaccharide is carboxymethylchitosan, which comes in three varieties: N-, O-, and N,O-carboxymethylchitosan. N,O-carboxymethylchitosan is the simplest to make, requiring only a carboxymethylation reaction with chloroacetic acid. The fundamental benefit of an amphoteric chitosan is that it has a higher water solubility. Chitosan is generally only soluble in water under acidic conditions, however carboxymethylchitosan can dissolve under both acidic and alkaline conditions. At pH near 4.0, carboxymethylchitosan, on the other hand, is zwitterionic and water insoluble. It turns cat- ionic and redissolves at extremely low pH values.

Synthetic organic rheological modifiers

Synthetic rheological modifiers based on acrylic polymers have been classified into three major categories which are following:

I. Alkali-swellable or soluble emulsions (ASEs)
II. Hydrophobically modified, alkali-swellable emulsions (HASEs)
III. Hydrophobically modified, ethoxylated urethane resins (HEURs)

Alkali-swellable or soluble emulsions (ASEs)

These are carboxy functional copolymers prepared using the free radical polymerization of ethylenically unsaturated monomer units. These polymers are insoluble in aqueous phase at low pH values but possess thickening property on dissolution or swelling in aqueous media. It is anionic in nature and water insoluble on preparat on and before the application. These can be either non-associative (conventional) or associative depending upon the structure and structural divergence is supported by differences in the observed rheological behavior. Acrylic acid, methacrylic acid, itaconic acid, citraconic acid, maleic acid, fumaric acid, crotonic acid, maleic anhydride, and citraconic anhydride are some of the carboxylic acid functional monomers used in the manufacture of these thickening polymers.

Most conventional ASEs are two-monomer copolymers, and these thickeners are thought to have no associative characteristics. These ASEs must contain one or more hydrophobic co-monomers in addition to the more hydrophilic carboxyl-containing acid monomers for water insolubility at low pH. The hydrophobic monomers must also be present in sufficient quantities to achieve the optimum hydrophilic-hydrophobic balance, rendering the copolymer water insoluble prior to neutralisation while allowing swelling or solubility in aqueous conditions at a higher pH. Alkyl acrylates, alkyl methacrylates, styrene, vinyl acetate, ethylene, butadiene, and acrylonitrile are examples of hydrophobic monomers utilised in the manufacture of traditional ASEs. The most often mentioned chemical is ethyl acrylate. Associative ASEs have recently been created by modifying regular ASEs with monomers (macromonomers) possessing ethoxylation and terminal hydrophobe activity. Most associative monomers used to make associative ASEs have a long-chain hydrophilic section that is ended by a hydrophobic group (figure 7.8). Between the ethylenic unsaturation on one end of the molecule and the terminal hydrophobe on the other, the hydrophilic segment usually consists of polyethoxylation or poly(ethoxylation-propoxylation). The associative macro monomers are easily made by connecting the hydroxyl end group of a typical nonionic surfactant with a monomer having polymerizable ethylenic unsaturation in one common way of synthesis. The type of terminal hydrophobe, type of ethylenic unsaturation, ratio and degree of poly(ethoxylation-propoxylation), and component-linking functions are all used to create variation within the macro monomer structure.

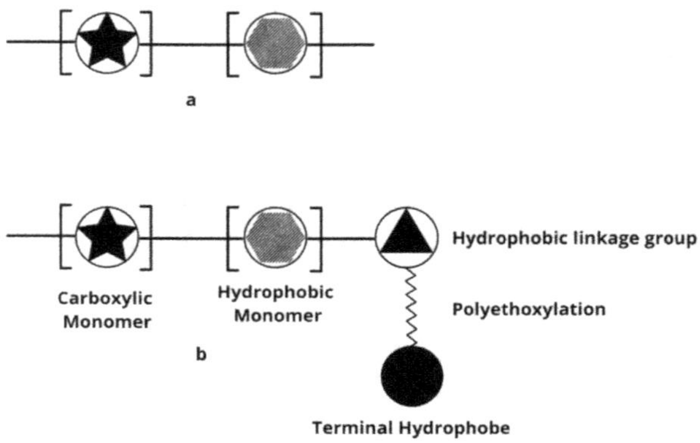

Figure 7.8: a showing conventional ASE & b showing associative ASE.

Hydrophobically modified, alkali-swellable emulsions (HASEs)

These are a type of ASEs which are obtained by addition of hydrophobic functional groups to the conventional ASEs rendering it associative polymer and hence it is commonly termed as associative thickener. Like conventional ASEs it is also anionic and water soluble in nature.

Hydrophobically modified, ethoxylated urethane resins (HEURs)

These type of polymers also belong to the associative thickeners and are non-ionic in nature. HEURs typically have a polyethylene glycol (PEG) backbone with alkylphenyl, fluorocarbons, or aliphatic alkyl chains end-capped. Urethane connections are formed when hydroxyl PEG end groups, hydrophobic alcohols, and diisocyanates react together to form urethane linkages (figure 7.9). When hydrophobic groups are solubilized in aqueous fluids above the critical aggregation concentration (CAC), intramolecular and intermolecular interactions produce flower-like micelles. The micelles are made up of a core of connected hydrophobic groups and floral loops of hydrophilic chains. Polymer chains begin to connect micelles together once the polymer concentration surpasses the critical percolation concentration (Cp), forming a physical transient network (figure 7.10). Under high shear rate, the dynamic network is destroyed and then reformed at rest resulting pseudoplastic behavior is realized.

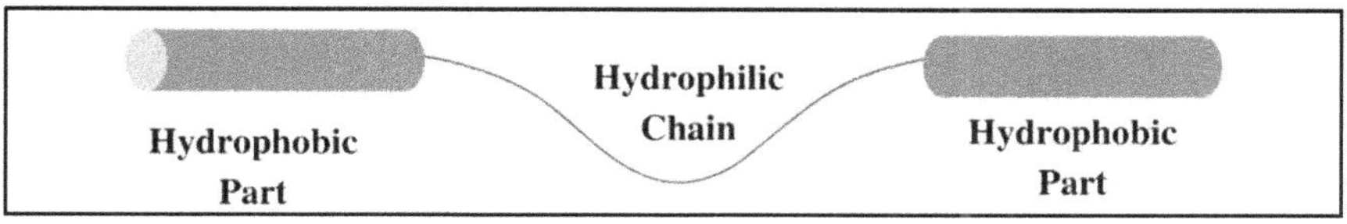

Figure 7.9: Structure of HEUR

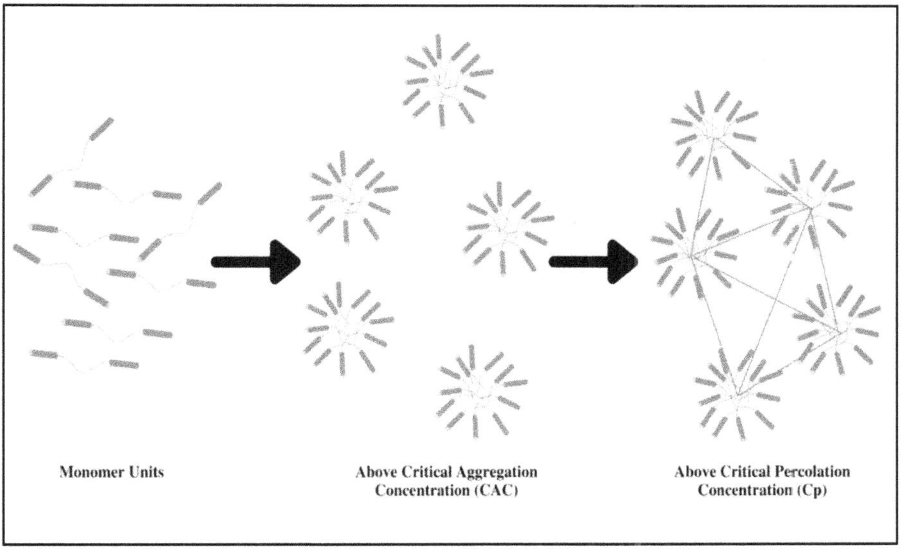

Figure 7.10: Mechanism for functionality of HEURs.

Mechanism of action of rheological modifiers

There are various ways by which rheological modifiers improve the rheological behavior of the formulation in which following mechanisms have predominance specifically:

Volume exclusion

This type of mechanism is exhibit by the water soluble polymers having swelling capability in water. For example, cellulose ethers, hydroxyethyl cellulose etc. This type of rheological modifiers improve the viscosity via chain entanglement mechanism (figure 7.11) as well as particle flocculation. The capability of improving the rheological behavior depends upon the molecular weight and amount of the polymers in the product. It means capability to improve the rheology of the product increases with increase in molecular weight as well as amount of the rheological modifier in the product.

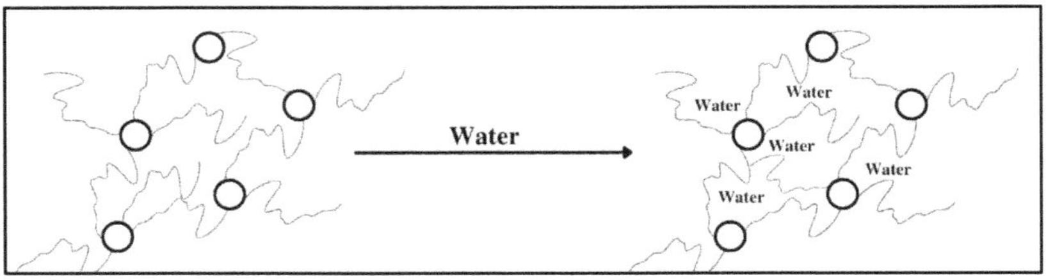

Figure 7.11:

Associative thickening

This mechanism is employed by water soluble polymers but do not cause thickening via water absorption. In this, polymers used as thickening agents possessed hydrophobic groups at both ends. Then, these polymers interact to each other as well as with the particles present in the formulation and on existence of sufficient concentration of these polymers, a dynamic three dimensional micelles like structure is formed causing thickening of the formulation due to restriction of the motion of the particles by this structure (figure 7.12).

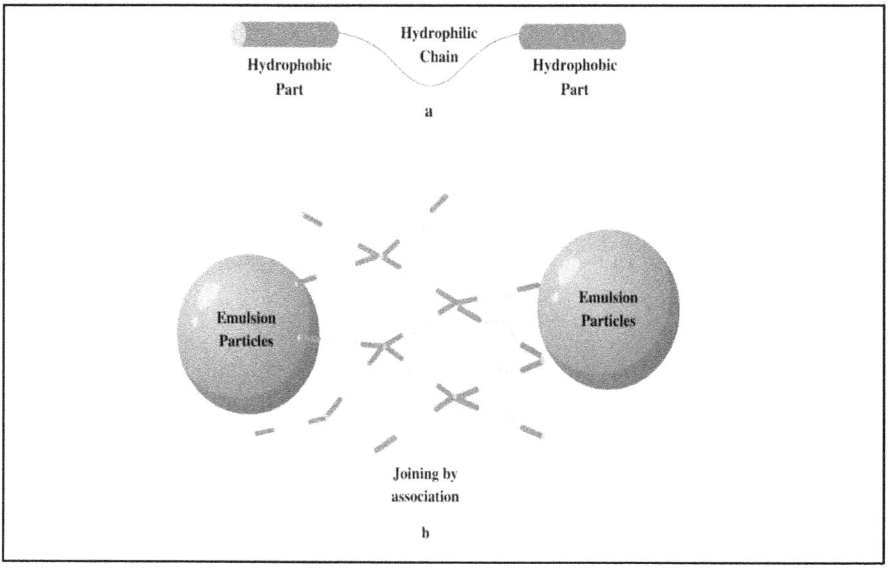

Figure 7.12:

Non-associative thickening

This type of thickening occur through hydrodynamic mechanism which means thickening is caused due to entanglement of aqueous based and high molecular weight polymer chains. The efficacy of the thickening agent belonging to this mechanism depends on molecular weight of the polymer. Formulations in which rheology is modified using the non-associative thickeners exhibit pseudoplastic rheology along with great elastic properties. But the formulations having this type of polymers possess restricted flow ability. Polymers having higher molecular weight may also cause compatibility problems like depletion flocculation sometimes.

An overview of different classes of synthetic rheological modifiers along with their thickening mechanisms has been summarized in Table 7.8.

Table 7.8: Overview of synthetic rheological modifiers and their thickening mechanisms.

Rheological modifier	Thickening mechanism	
	Associative	Non-associative
Polyacrylate thickeners	Absent	Present
Hydrophobically modified alkali swellable emulsions (HASE)	Present	Present
Hydrophobically modified polyether (HMPE)	Present	Absent
Hydrophobically modified Ethyleneoxide Urethane Rheology modifier (HEUR)	Present	Negligible
Cellulose ethers	Absent	Present
Hydrophobically modified Hydroxy Ethyl Cellulose (HMHEC)	Present	Present

Applications of rheological modifiers in cosmetics

The applications of rheological modifiers can be easily seen based on classification given in table 7.9.

Table 7.9: Applications of Rheological modifiers.

Class of rheological modifier	Examples
Lipid thickeners	Cetyl alcohol, carnauba wax, bees wax, stearic acid
Naturally derived thickeners	Guar gum, gelatin, xanthan gum, modified cellulose
Mineral thickeners	Silica, bentonite, aluminium magnesium silicate
Synthetic thickeners	Polyethylene glycol, carbomers
Ionic thickeners	Salt like sodium chloride

Lipid thickeners

These are primarily made up of lipophilic materials and provide natural thickness to the formulation. These type of thickeners are solid at room temperature whilst liquid on increasing the temperature and hence can be added into the emulsion based cosmetic formulations via heating them. These are commonly used in various creams and lotions.

Naturally derived thickeners

These ingredients work by absorption of water followed by swelling and lead to increase in viscosity. For example, hydroxyethylcellulose (cellulose derivative) is used in liquid cleansing products like shampoo and body wash. Other naturally derived thickeners include guar gum, xanthan gum, gelatin, locust bean gum etc. But these ingredients are used in the formulations having a large amount of water. These type of thickeners possess a disadvantage of inconsistency due to which clear formulation convert to cloudy formulations and appear sticky on touch.

Mineral thickeners

These are the naturally occurring, mined thickening agent having capability to absorb water as well as oil and cause increase in viscosity of the formulation. These type of ingredients can be used in water as well as oil based formulations. For example, bentonite, silica, aluminium magnesium silicate. Bentonite is used in calamine lotion a suspending agent.

Synthetic thickeners

These are the widely used thickening agents amongst all categories of rheological modifiers. These provide desirable features to the formulation which make them superior thickening agent than other categories of rheological modifiers. Carbomer is the example of synthetic thickening agent which is commonly and it is water swellable acrylic acid polymer.

Ionic thickeners

Addition of table salt (NaCl) to the formulation having anionic surfactant can cause increase in viscosity of the formulation. Salt is widely used as an adjusting agent during production of the formulation.

Antimicrobials as preservative

Degradation of cosmetic products is possible mainly due to presence of microorganisms or exposure of atmospheric oxygen to the product. Cosmetic products are more prone for growth of the microorganisms due to their organic nature and high water content. Microbial contamination in cosmetics poses a significant threat to consumer health since, under certain circumstances, contaminated products can cause irritation or illness, particularly when applied to injured skin, eyes, or newborns. To prevent the degradation of cosmetic products from microorganism and oxidation, basically two types of preservatives are used namely antioxidant and antimicrobials. Antioxidants prevent the oxidation of cosmetic product whilst antimicrobials inhibit the growth of microorganism in product. In regulatory terms, a preservative is a compound used to inhibit the growth of microbes either natural or synthetic. This inhibition should be effective across a wide range of activities and should last longer than the cosmetic product itself, equating to the projected shelf-life plus the consumption time. Furthermore, the antimicrobial action must be effective enough to avoid microorganism adaptation and resistance to the preservation system. Cosmetics are a nutrient-rich milieu that encourages the growth of microorganisms, which determines the efficacy of preservatives.

The amount of antimicrobial agent to be used in a cosmetic is determined by the desired function; high concentrations are used for active ingredients, while low amounts are used for preservatives. Antimicrobial cosmetics use the first, while most cosmetics require the second. The cosmetic business uses other preservation tactics, such as water activity and pH management, as well as multifunctional chemicals, in addition to antimicrobial agents.

Microbiological safety consideration of cosmetics

Microorganisms having capability to affect the safety and integrity of cosmetic products is mainly classified into three classes namely bacteria, yeast and molds. Bacteria also classified into two classes depending upon their differential techniques that are Gram-positive bacteria and Gram-negative bacteria. Gram-negative bacteria is more pathogenic whilst only few Gram-positive bacteria are pathogenic. Various Gram-negative and Gram-positive bacteria along with yeast and molds found in cosmetic products have been given in table 7.10. The microbiological contamination is possible to occur during manufacturing process (primary contamination) of cosmetics and during use of it by consumer (secondary contamination). Various causes, consequences, and various methods for prevention of against both types of contamination has been shown by the figure............ However, various sources of contamination can be identified and controlled using the four steps:

1. Proper inspection and control of raw materials
2. Method of manufacturing

3. Delivery of finished product
4. Use by the consumer

Table 7.10 : Examples of gram positive and gram negative bacteria.

Type of microorganism	Name of microorganism
Bacteria	*Pseudomonas aeruginosa* *Staphylococcus aureus* *Escherichia coli* *Klebsiella oxytoca* *Burkholderia cepacia* serratia marcescens
Yeast	*Candida albicans*
Fungi and molds	Aspergillus versicolor Clasdosporium cladosporioides Irpex lacteus Bjerkandera adusta Periconia byssoides

Ideal characteristics of a preservative

- It must have broad spectrum activity which means a preservative's ability to kill or prevent the growth of various types of microorganisms
- It must be efficacious at low concentration which will minimize the toxic effects of preservatives, cost, and will not affect the physical properties of the final product
- It must be stable under variable conditions of temperature, pH, humidity etc.
- It must be compatible with other ingredients of the product
- It must not affect the colour and odour of the finished product
- It must maintain activity throughout the shelf life of the finished product
- It must be easy to analyze in the finished product.
- It must be easy to handle
- It must be ecofriendly
- It must not show any toxic effect to human beings at optimum concentrations

Types of preservatives

Various types of preservatives are used in preparation of cosmetic products. These preservatives can be natural or synthetic. Natural preservatives are the agents which are obtained from the natural sources and possess efficiency of protecting the product against the microbial degradation. These natural preservatives can be plant originated and animal originated as shown in the table 7.11. Various commonly used synthetic preservatives have been summarized in the table 7.11.

Table 7.11: Biological sources and chemical constituents of selected natural compounds.

Common name	Biological Source	Chemical constituents
Ratanjot	Arnebia tinctoria	Naphthoquinones namely alkannin and isovalerylalkannin
Lipstick tree	Bixa orellana	Delta-tocotrienol
Smookebush	Buddleja madagascariensis	Mimengoside-A
Dalchini	Cinnamomum zeylanicum	Cinnamic aldehyde, trans-Cinnamaldehyde
Haldi	Curcuma longa	Curcumin
Wild granite	*Desmodium canum*	Isoflavanones namely desmodianones A, B, and C
Indian lotus	Nelumbo nucifera	Kaempferol 3-O-glucoside and luteolin 7-O-glucoside
African basil	Ocimum gratissimum	Thymol
Brimstone tree	Morinda lucida	Anthraquinone, alizarin –l-methyl ethers
Sausage tree	Kigelia pinnata	Naphthoquinones, isopinnatal, phenylpropanoids
Harmal	Rhazya stricta	Strictanol, rhazimanine, and akuammidine

Table 7.12: Biological sources and key constituents of essential oils.

Name	Biological source	Constituents
Cardamom oil	Elettaria cardamomum	Methyl eugenol, terpenes
Clove oil	Eugenia caryophylla	Eugenol, Isoeugenol
Cumin oil	Cuminum cymimum	Pinene, limonene, phellandrene
Birch oil	Betula alba	Betulin, betulinic acid, polyphenols
Fennel oil	Foeniculum vulgare	A-pinene, myrcene, 1,8-cineole
Thyme oil	Thymus vulgaris	Thymol, a-pinene, linalool
Sage oil	Salvia officinalis	Chlorgenic acid, flavones, flavonoid glycosides, cineole
Eucalyptus oil	Eucalyptus globulus	A-pinene, b-pinene, terpinen-4-ol, epiglobu ol
Oregano oil	Origanum vulgare	Phenolic acids, flavonoids

Table 7.13: Natural bioactive compounds, their sources, and uses.

Name	Source	Uses
Lard	Abdomen of hog Sus scrofa Linn	Preservative
Chitosan	Deacetylation of chitin present in fungal cell wall	Active against fungi, algae, and bacteria
Lactoferrin	Human milk, saliva, animal milk tears	Active against bacteria, virus, fungi
Pleurocidin	Isolated from mucus membrane of winter flounder	Active against bacteria, virus, and parasites

Table 7.14: Categories of preservatives, and their mechanisms of action.

Category	Name of preservatives	Mechanism of action	Comments
Organic acids	Benzoic acids, sorbic acids, anisic acid, levulinic acid, butyric acid, propionic acid	Acidification of external environment enabling unsuitable for growth of microbes Acidification of the cytoplasm of microbial cell Changing in the fluidity of the plasma membrane Prevention of the enzymes from cellular metabolism	Possess broad spectrum antimicrobial acitivity
Formaldehyde releasers	DMDM hydantoin, bronopol, and methenamine, Germall plus	Inhibition of microbial cell division and metabolism	Effective against bacteria but less effective against fungi Require low concentration
Isothiazolinones	Kathon	Produce oxidation of microbial proteins	Possess broad spectrum activity and effective over entire pH range, but can cause skin irritation

Table 7.14: ***Contd...***

Category	Name of preservatives	Mechanism of action	Comments
Phenoxethanol	Optiphen Optiphen plus	Possess antibacterial activity	Combined with sorbic acid/caprylyl glycol/EDTA to cause broad spectrum antimicrobial activity
Parabens	Methyl paraben, propyl paraben, butyl paraben, Germaben II	Inhibition of synthesis of RNA, DNA and some microbial enzymes	Widely used preservative and effective against fungi and some gram positive bacteria

Organic acids

These are pH dependent substances due to fact that they possess antimicrobial activity only in acid form. These are used in salt forms but salt itself does not possess antimicrobial activity until the pH is reduced to liberate the free acid. Example: Benzoic acids, sorbic acids, anisic acid, levulinic acid, butyric acid, propionic acid and their salts.

Advantages

- Effective against fungi
- Alternatives for natural preservatives

Disadvantages

- Possess weak efficacy for bacteria
- Required aqueous base for activity
- Used in combination with other organic acids for broad spectrum activity
- Undergo precipitation in presence of high water content
- Require acidic pH (2-6) for activity
- Required higher concentration which also lead to increase in costs

Isothiazolinones

These are a group of effective preservative used in various types of industries including cosmetic industries. These ingredients are heterocyclic derivative of 2H-isothiazolin-3-one having an active sulphur group which can oxidize thiol containing molecules, making it a stronger preservative. For example, isothiazolinones are available in market under the trade name Kathon CG (mixture of 2-methyl-3-

isothiazolinones and 5-chloro-2-methyl-3-isothiazolinones in ratio of 3:1). Cosmetic industries uses kathon CG in variety of leave on and rinse off products like shampoo, gels, skin care products.

Advantages

- Possess broad spectrum efficiency
- Best for rinse-off cosmetic products but also used for leave-on cosmetic products
- Possess activity over entire pH range
- Possess effectiveness at very low concentration
- Non-carcinogenic

Disadvantages

- Possibility for skin irritation

Parabens

These are the group of preservatives largely used in cosmetics and pharmaceutical industries. Chemically, these are the alkyl esters of 4-ydroxybenzoic acid. Most commonly used parabens include methyl paraben, propyl paraben, butyl paraben, isopropyl paraben, isobutyl paraben and benzyl esters but the iso and benzyl forms of the parabens have been banned by the European cosmetics regulations.

Advantages

- Widely used preservative
- Possess antifungal property but some antimicrobial property against gram positive bacteria
- Used for both leave-on as well as rinse-off cosmetics
- Antimicrobial activity enhanced on increasing the alkyl chain

Disadvantages

- Possess activity only in aqueous phase
- Possess pH dependent activity because higher pH cause dissociation of parabens
- Possibility to cause skin reactions
- Increased risks for reproductive disorders
- Possess esterogenic activity which is linked to various forms of breast cancer

Formaldehyde releasers

These are the chemical agents used as preservative in cosmetic and pharmaceutical industries. There are about 42 formaldehyde releasers which are found in various preparations like cleaning agents, cosmetics, toiletries preparations, adhesives, and paints etc. Formaldehyde releasers used in cosmetic products are DMDM hydantoin, ureas like imidazolidinyl urea (Germall 115), diazolidinyl (Germall II), quaternium-15, germall plus etc. According to European cosmetic regulations, all the products having formaldehyde and formaldehyde releasers must be labelled with the precaution "contains formaldehyde" if the concentration of formaldehyde in final product cross 0.05% concentration.

Advantages

- Formaldehyde release only when required so maintain low levels
- Ensures that actual concentration of free formaldehyde is very low but sufficient to stop the growth of microbes
- Release the formaldehyde slowly
- Effective against bacteria

Disadvantages

- Less effective against fungi
- Formaldehyde is carcinogenic

Phenoxyethanol

It is the widely used preservative in cosmetic products across the world. It is chemically stable and easy to use in various types of cosmetic products. Various phenoxyethanol derivatives include optiphen and optiphen plus used as preservatives in cosmetic and cosmeceutical products.

Advantages

- Possess better antibacterial activity
- Possess best activity against gram negative bacteria
- Chemically stable
- Stable over entire pH range
- Used in concentration upto 1%
- Milder alternative to conventional preservatives

Disadvantages

- Concern of carcinogenicity
- Used with other ingredients like sorbic acid, potassium sorbate, caprylyl glycol, EDTA etc to make it broad spectrum antibacterial agent

Factors affecting antimicrobial preservative efficacy

Preservative efficacy is the ability of the antimicrobial preservative agent to kill or inhibit the growth of microorganisms in a formulation. There are a variety of factors which can influence the activity of the preservatives which mainly include following factors:

- Interaction with components of formulation
- Effects of containers
- Properties of the preservatives
- Concentration
- Contact time
- Number of microorganisms
- Effect of pH

Interaction with components of formulation

The interaction of various components of a formulation with preservatives may cause reduction and enhancement in preservative efficacy of the preservative. For example, the interaction of various hydrocolloids like alginates, tragacanth, methyl cellulose etc. with preservatives causing decrease in their activity. Various emulsifiers used in preparation of various emulsion based cosmetics interact with preservatives leading to decrease in their activity. Various tablet excipients also pose a problem in preservation of tablets due to interaction with added preservatives. But the ingredients like alcohol, aldehyde, and acids in formulation cause enhancement in preservative efficacy due to possession of antimicrobial activity by these ingredients.

Effect of container

The material used for manufacturing of container intended for packaging of cosmetics also affect the activity of preservatives. Preservatives used in a cosmetic product can penetrate through the plastic container and interact with it causing reduction in preservative efficacy. Rubber used for manufacturing of the closures can also interact with the preservatives used in product leading to reduction in activity of a preservative while glass containers are able to retain the preservative efficacy of a preservative used in cosmetic product.

Properties of the preservatives

The properties of thee preservatives also affect the activity of a preservative. The distribution of the preservative must be homogenous or equal throughout the product and solubility of the preservative should be higher in bulk phase especially in case of multiphase system. Some preservatives like chlorobutol undergo hydrolysis on prolonged storage under the influence of unfavorable pH conditions. Preservatives also have tendency to interact with the substances leached out or remove from the container leading to loss in its preservative efficiency.

Concentration

The concentration of preservative also affect its activity. In general, increase in the concentration of preservative increases the activity. At higher concentrations, preservative behaves as cidal (kill the microorganisms) whilst at low concentration, acts as static (inhibit the growth of microorganisms). But higher concentration of preservatives are not advisable because higher concentrations of preservatives may cause toxic effects in the body. It must be remember that preservatives are used to kill the living cells hence at specific concentration it will also affect the skin whilst on other hand, too low concentration of preservatives may be ineffective enabling the stimulation of growth of microorganisms.

Contact time

Contact time of preservative with formulation may also affect its activity. Increase in contact time will enable the killing of large number of microorganisms. It is said that microbes are killed at a logarithmic rate and same percentage of microorganisms must be kill in each unit time under specific conditions.

Number of microorganisms

Presence of number of microorganisms in a formulation also affect the activity of preservative. Increase in number of microorganisms in a formulation, longer time will be taken by the preservative to decrease or reduce the number of microorganisms to an acceptable level in the formulation.

Effect of pH

The pH of the formulation also affect the efficacy of a preservative. A large portion of the preservatives is independent on pH of the formulation but some preservatives such as benzoic acid, parabens, and quaternary ammonium compounds are active in their acidic form.

Vanishing creams

These are the oil-in-water emulsion based cosmetics which look disappear on rubbing into the skin. These creams are made up of emollient esters, which leave a thin film on the skin and have a low oil phase percentage. Vanishing creams are based on stearic acid which melts at body temperature and crystallises in an imperceptible form, leaving a non-greasy film behind. Stearic acid also provides attractive appearance to the formulation. Due to stearic acid, these creams are white and hence these are also termed as "snow".

These creams possess stearic acid or one of its fats like hydrophilic esters as main emulsified ingredient along with small amount of other fats or oil ingredients. Stearic acid is the main ingredient of the vanishing cream. A good quality triple-pressed grade of stearic acid having melting point of 55°c is used. The important criteria for selection of stearic acid are high melting point, low iodine number, odourless etc. Stearic acid, alkali (potassium hydroxide or sodium hydroxide or triethanolamine) and water the main building blocks for preparation of vanishing creams. Generally distilled water, purified water and deionized water should be used but hard water must be avoided because it may cause inversion of cream due to formation of magnesium or lime soaps. The soap is formed due to the reaction in between the alkali and stearic acid.

The hardness or consistency of the cream depends on the amount of stearic acid neutralized or saponified by the alkali and type of alkali used. Normally 20-30% of stearic acid is neutralized by the alkali and it should not exceed 25% but best formulations are prepared when it is 16-20%. Sodium hydroxide used as alkali prepare the harder cream than potassium hydroxide. Besides potassium hydroxide and sodium hydroxide, triethanolamine can also be a good choice as alkali because it makes the preparation of creams easy and of viable nature. Borax can also be used to prepare very white cream but suffers from the drawback which is that preparation has a distinct tendency to grain.

Glycerin in concentration less than 10% also used in preparation of these creams to maintain the hardness or consistency of the preparation along with improvement in spreading ability. But it also suffers from the drawback of absorbing the moisture after use causing formation of globules of water due to hygroscopic nature. To overcome this problem, other glycols can be added in the preparation.

Satiny appearance (lustre, pearliness) assumed by these creams on standing, and hence various ingredients are added in the preparation to provide satiny appearance. The ingredients which are added to fulfill this purpose are castor oil, almond oil, cocoa butter, liquid paraffin, starch etc.

These creams possess a high amount of water due to which there are more chances for growth of microorganisms. Hence preservatives are added in the preparation to prevent the growth of microorganisms in it. The ingredients used as preservatives include methyl paraben, propyl paraben or combination of both.

Another ingredient used in vanishing cream is perfume. It is used to impart desired fragrance to the preparation. High attention must be given for selection of perfumes because improper perfume may cause discoloration of the cream. The perfumes used in vanishing creams include sandalwood, lavender oil, linalol, geraniol, terpineol, patchouli, bergamot etc. Various formulation building blocks used for preparation of vanishing creams are given in table 7.15.

Table 7.15: Formulation building blocks used in the preparation of vanishing creams.

Formulation building blocks	Examples	Functions
Main ingredient	Stearic acid	Main component & govern consistency of cream
Alkali	Potassium hydroxide, sodium hydroxide, triethanolamine, borax	Reaction with stearic acid to form soap which serves as emulsifier for cream
Humectants	Glycerin, propylene glycol, sorbitol	To maintain consistency and to enhance the spreading ability
Preservatives	Methyl paraben, propyl paraben	To inhibit the growth of microorganisms in cream
Perfume	Sandalwood, lavender oil, geraniol	To impart desired fragrance
Water	Purified water, distilled water, deionized water	Used a carrier

Table 7.16: Formulation of vanishing cream – ingredients, their quantities, and categories.

Ingredients	Quantity used	Category
Stearic acid	20gm	Main ingredient
Potassium hydroxide	1.4gm	Alkali
Glycerin	4gm	Humectant

Table 7.16: ***Contd....***

Ingredients	Quantity used	Category
Water	74.6gm	Vehicle
Perfume	q.s.	Fragrance
Preservatives	q.s.	Antimicrobial

Method of preparation

- Weigh the stearic acid and potassium hydroxide according to the formula in a china dish and heat at 70°c on water bath.
- Weigh the glycerin, preservative, and water in a beaker and heat also at 70°c on water bath.
- After it, mix the second mixture into first mixture dropwise with continuous stirring.
- Then add perfume when the temperature of the formulation drop to 35°c and mill it.

Sensory benefits of the vanishing cream

- It helps to keep the skin moist and hence in dry and cold areas, it saves the skin from dryness and scaly.
- It holds the skin's moisture causing fresh and clear look to the skin
- It is also used as base for application of make-up and acts as plain foundation.
- It saves the skin from harmful chemical in the cosmetics
- It also deal with the problem of sagging skin
- Another important benefit of vanishing cream is that it avoids the stickiness or irritation to the skin. It does not provide oily feeling to the skin due to vanishing effect by the skin
- It can be used without application of powder to minimize the effects of oiliness and shine on the skin due to possession of semi-matt finish

Limitations

- These type of creams cannot be used all the times. These are normally used in day time and hence also termed as "day creams"
- These creams do not remove marks of acne scarring
- These creams do not remove scars but heals the acne to very less extent

Table 7.17: Examples of commercial preparation of vanishing cream.

Commercial vanishing creams	Outer appearance
Pond's vanishing cream	
Garnier Skin active vanishing cream	
Johnson's healthy skin vanishing cream	
Cuticura vanishing creams	

Cold creams

These are the water in oil based cosmetic preparations intended to smoothen the skin and removal of the makeup. The name "cold cream" is driven from cooling sensation on slow evaporation of water phase from the skin. Traditionally, cold creams are of two types namely bees wax-borax type cold cream (white, emulsified) and translucent, liquefied, anhydrous cream having mixture of hydrocarbon oils and waxes.

Beeswax- Borax type cold cream

These are opaque, white, possess a great lustre, and easily spread on skin, but addition of almond oil still restricts the stability of cream. When mineral oil and petrolatum were used in formulation of cold cream rather than almond oil, cold creams were formulated having more stability, economical along with longer shelf life which makes them ideal formulation for large scale production at industrial level. These creams are basically formulated as water in oil (W/O) type emulsions which on application to the skin cause slow evaporation of water phase leaving oil phase behind to serve as solvent to remove the makeup. Beeswax is the main determining factor in formulation of this type of creams. Beeswax is the purified honeycomb of the bee, free from other type of waxes. Beeswax having the lowest melting point prepares the softest emulsions. It is natural, soothing, moisturizing, and non-comedogenic agent. Borax is another important ingredient of the cold cream. Borax forms boric acid and sodium hydroxide on dissolving in the water and then sodium hydroxide reacts with cerotic acid present in the Beeswax causing formation of an anionic emulsifier whilst boric acid serves as buffer agent for the cold cream. The produced anionic emulsifier is responsible for miscibility of oil phase and water phase leading to formation of emulsions.

Mineral oil (e.g. liquid paraffin) is a type of hydrocarbon which is stable, economical, odorless, and does not undergo rancidity. It serves as good solvent for the oil and grease binding the makeup to the skin. The cleansing power of a cold cream depends on its mineral oil content. It forms an occlusive layer on the top of the skin and prevents the removal of water from the skin providing moisture to the skin. Various formulation building blocks used for preparation of cold cream has been given in table 7.18.

Table 7.18: Various formulation building blocks used for the preparation of cold cream.

Formulation building blocks	Examples	Functions
Mineral oil	Liquid paraffin	solvent and emollient
Base	Beeswax	Main base, emulsifier, thickening agent
Emulsifiers	Borax	Emulsifier and provide whiteness
Moisturizers	Lanolin	Moisturizing effect
Humectant	Glycerin	To retain humidity
Preservatives	Methyl paraben, propyl paraben	To inhibit growth of microorganisms
Perfume	Sandalwood oil, lavender oil	Fragrance
Water	Deionized water	Carrier

Table 7.19: Formulation of cold cream – ingredients, quantities, and categories.

Ingredients	Quantity used (% w/w)	category
Liquid Paraffin	45	Solvent and emollient
Beeswax	16	Thickening agent & emulsifier
Borax	1	Emulsifier and give whiteness
Water	q.s. 100	Carrier
Preservative	q.s.	Antimicrobial
Perfume	q.s.	Fragrance

Sensory benefits of the cold cream

- It serves as moisturizer due to possession of mineral oil in their formula hence well preparation in winters especially who have very dry skin.
- It can also be used as substitute of the lip balm for very dry, and chapped lips.
- It also serves as cleanser and makeup remover.
- It also can be used as substitute of shaving cream.
- It can also be used for exfoliating the skin.

Limitations

- It is quite higher in consistency due to which people having oily skin feel it very greasy.
- People living in humid, hot weathers find this too heavy.
- It is mainly product of winter season.

Table 7.20: Examples of commercial preparation of cold creams.

Commercial vanishing creams	Outer appearance
Nivea Creme	
Pond's Cold cream Cleanser	
Garnier Nourishing Cold cream	
Ayur Herbal cold cream	
Dabur Gulabari Nourishing cold cream	

Toothpaste

It is most popular, widely accepted paste or gel like preparation (dentifrice) having complex composition used to clean the teeth using a toothbrush. These are used to maintain the health ans esthetics of the teeth. These are more expensive than tooth powder still more preferred due to various reasons which are following:

- Lesser wastage and spillage than tooth powder
- Uniform distribution in mouth
- Measured amount can be taken than toothpowder
- Easy to spread over the tooth brush
- More attractive consistency than tooth powder

Ideal characteristics of a tooth paste

- It must be able to clean the surface of teeth effectively without any scratching
- It must have appropriate consistency so that can be easily squeezed out from the container
- It must be easy to spread over the toothbrush but not sink into the toothbrush
- It must have constant consistency during entire shelf life
- It must not dry, especially quickly after opening it
- It must be non-toxic to the oral cavity
- It must not sensitize the buccal cavity
- It must be compatible with the material of the container

Formulation building blocks for toothpaste:

Various building blocks are used in preparation of toothpaste has been included in the Table 7.21.

Table 7.21: Various formulation building blocks used in the preparation of toothpaste.

Formulation building blocks	Examples	Functions
Abrasives	Calcium carbonate, aluminium hydroxide, hydroxyapatite, calcium hydrogen phosphates	Cleansing and polishing
Detergents	Sodium lauryl sulfate (SLS), sodium lauryl sarcosinate	Cleansing and formation of foams
Fluorides	Sodium fluoride, Stannous fluoride, sodium monofluorophosphate	Strengthen tooth enamel
Humectants	Glycerol, xylitol, sorbitol, polypropylene glycol	Prevention of drying out the product
Binding agents	Gum tragacanth, sodium alginate, carbopols	Buildup of consistency

Table 7.21: ***Contd....***

Formulation building blocks	Examples	Functions
Preservatives	Triclosan, zinc chloride	Antibacterial
Sweetener	Saccharine sodium	Provide sweetness
Flavoring agents	Peppermint oil, spearmint oil	Provide odor
Antisensitivity agent	Strontium chloride, potassium nitrate	Combat dental hypersensitivity
Anticalculus agents	Sodium polyphosphate, zinc citrate	Removal of dental calculus
Remineralizers	Calcium phosphate	Remineralization of teeth
Water	Purified water	Carrier

Abrasives or polishing agents:

These are main ingredients of a toothpaste which are also termed as cleansing agents. These ingredients work by removing the food particles or any other debris and stains from the teeth by enabling the friction and polishing enamel's surface. An abrasive agent must be present in powder form and sufficient hard but not cause scratches on the gums or enamels. Mostly water-insoluble abrasives are widely used but now water soluble abrasive agents are also used. The concentration of abrasive is about 50% in toothpaste which is just half of the total amount of the toothpaste. Most widely used abrasives in preparation of toothpaste are Calcium carbonate, aluminium hydroxide, hydroxyapatite, calcium hydrogen phosphates, magnesium trisilicate etc. Calcium carbonate (Chalk) is widely used abrasive agent and available in variety of grades, ranging from extra dense to light which differs in crystal form, density, particle size, and specific surface. Normally, the light grade of calcium carbonate is used in preparation of toothpaste because toothpastes prepared using lighter grade of calcium carbonate do not get so harder and possess sufficient consistency.

Dihydrate, dicalcium phosphate is superior and comparatively possess low abrasion power but not compatible with majority of the fluorides. It requires stabilizing agent to prevent caking, hardening, grittiness of the toothpaste on storage for long time. To fulfill this purpose, magnesium phosphate, tetrasodium pyrophosphate etc. are used.

Anhydrous, dicalcium phosphate possess comparatively higher abrasion property and used in small concentrations to enhance the abrasion property of the toothpaste but it is also not compatible with most of the fluorides. A wide range of abrasion property (mild to strong) can be achieved using the combination of dihydrate dicalcium phosphate and anhydrous dicalcium phosphate. Dicalcium phosphate is advantageous than calcium carbonate because it provides neutral pH whilst calcium carbonate imparts alkaline pH.

Sodium metaphosphate is another water insoluble agent having better abrasive property and used in combination with tricalcium phosphate. It is compatible with majority of the fluorides but comparatively costly.

Tetracalcium pyrophosphate is another widely used abrasive in toothpaste having stannous fluoride. But now, its use is continuously declining because mostly fluorides containing toothpastes are based on sodium fluoride or sodium monofluoro phosphate.

Hydrated silica is gaining more popularity as abrasive in toothpaste. It is mainly of two types namely abrasive silica and thickening silica. Abrasive silica is tasteless, odourless, non- absorbent, and dense. Its commercial grade in market is under the trade name "xerogels". It has better abrasive properties at small concentration and impart very little effect on the consistency of the toothpaste. Thickening silica is available commercially under the trade name "aerogels" having swelling property leading to increase in consistency of the toothpaste. It is unreactive and compatible with most of the fluorides. When used in combination with abrasive silica, then produce clear gel like toothpaste.

Aluminium hydroxide is also used as abrasive agent in combination with other abrasives in preparation of toothpaste. The powder of aluminium hydroxide possesses cleansing properties along with abrasive property.

Detergents or foaming agents

These are the agents which enhance the activity of the abrasives by minimizing the surface tension and wetting the surface of the teeth. They act by penetrating and loosen the debris followed by emulsification and suspending of it and thus remove from the teeth. These agents are also responsible for production of foams also and used in very low concentration in toothpaste which is about 0.5-2%. Sodium lauryl sulfate is most commonly used detergent in preparation of toothpaste. Besides it, sodium lauryl sarcosinate, diocetyl sodium sulfosuccinate, and sodium lauryl sulfoacetate also used as detergents in preparation of toothpastes. Soap is also used as detergent in toothpaste due to various advantages like dissolve the mucin, prevention of bacterial growth, possession of some emulsification property along with cleansing property and foaming ability.

Humectants

These are the liquid ingredients which are added in toothpaste to retain the moisture of product and to prevent the drying out of the product. These ingredients help in maintaining the consistency of the toothpaste. These are used in concentration of 5-10% but sometimes this concentration may be higher about 30% or more. The exact concentration depends upon the specific gravity of the powder mass and powder mass having lower specific gravity requires lesser concentration of humectant. Most widely used humectants include glycerol, sorbitol, and propylene glycol.

Glycerol is the most widely used humectant in toothpaste and gives glossy appearance as well as sweetness to the toothpaste but provides feeling of warmth to the mouth and costlier.

Sorbitol is another humectant used in toothpaste and sometimes preferred over the glycerol because it imparts more consistency and plasticity to the toothpaste as compared to glycerol. It is cheaper than glycerol and 70%w/v solution of sorbitol provides cooling sensation and sweetness to some extent.

Propylene glycol can also be used as humectant in toothpaste due to possession of superior solvent properties but it imparts low consistency and some bitterness to the toothpaste. It can be used as humectant in toothpaste in combination with glycerol and sorbitol.

Binding agents

These ingredients are added in toothpaste to hold various other solid and liquid ingredients in paste form or to avoid the separation of the paste. These are generally natural and synthetic gums which are used in toothpaste. These ingredients also added in toothpaste to improve and buildup the desired consistency of the paste. These are generally used in toothpaste in concentration of 0.9 – 2.0% of the total amount of paste. Various natural and synthetic gums, resins, and other hydrocolloids are used in toothpaste but most widely used binder is sodium carboxy-methyl cellulose (CMC) which is available in various grades. It must be remember that CMC must be avoided from the activity of cellulase enzymes which can destroy the consistency of the toothpaste. Besides it, various agents like carrageenan, gum karaya, sodium alginate, gum tragacanth magnesium aluminium silicate etc. are also used in toothpaste as binder.

Sweeteners

It is the most important ingredient of the toothpaste which mask the bitter taste of other ingredients used in toothpaste especially detergents and various oils used as flavors. Various synthetic sweeteners are used in toothpaste which include saccharine, cyclamates, and aspartame etc. These are used in concentration of 0.05-0.25% of total amount of the paste. The exact required concentration depends on other ingredients present in paste and sweetness of other added ingredients like glycerol. Saccharine sodium is most widely used sweetener amongst all available sweeteners.

Preservatives

These are the agents which prevent the growth of microorganisms in the toothpaste leading to increase its quality and stability. Toothpaste has greater chances for growth of microbes because it contain water and gums in its formula, hence preservatives are more important ingredients of toothpaste to maintain its shelf life. Although some antimicrobial property is provided by the flavoring oils and chloroform present in the toothpaste still separate preservative is needed to provide better stability. Most commonly used preservatives include methyl paraben, propyl paraben, methyl phenylhydroxybenzoate etc. A combination of methyl paraben and propyl paraben is used in concentration of 0.15% and 0.02% respectively as preservative in toothpaste. Sodium benzoate is not used as preservative especially in medicinal toothpaste due to its higher incompatibility with therapeutic ingredients present in the toothpaste.

Flavoring agents

These ingredients are added in toothpaste to impart fresh breathing sensation in the mouth after brushing. Various flavoring agents used in toothpaste include peppermint oil, spearmint oil, clove oil, anise oil, eucalyptus oil etc. these oils are used either separately or in combination as flavoring agent in toothpaste. These ingredients are used in concentration of 0.2-2% of total amount of the toothpaste. It must be remember that higher concentration of flavoring agent in toothpaste may cause irritation to the buccal mucosa.

Water

Deionised water is used which serves as carrier in the toothpaste. It is mainly used as solvent for other added ingredients and to support the binding agents in the paste which gets imbibe after adsorption of large portion of water. In clear toothpaste, the concentration of water must not exceed 10% which can cause loss of clarity of the paste. In this case, a balanced mixture of glycerol/sorbitol/water should be used.

Fluorides

Fluoride is natural mineral found in water, soil, rocks, and many other foods. It prevents the tooth decay which is major problem globally in children. Although it is preventable, still it is major cause for hospitalization of children. A wide variety of toothpastes are available in market having different concentration of fluorides. Toothpastes having concentration of 1350-1500 ppm is considered more suitable for prevention of tooth decay. But in children, the toothpaste having concentration of fluoride less than 600ppm are marketed to avoid the chances of dental fluorosis. Various fluorides such as Sodium fluoride, Stannous fluoride, sodium monofluorophosphate etc. are used in toothpastes to prevent the tooth decay and strengthening of enamel. Sodium fluoride and stannous fluoride are most commonly used fluorides in modern toothpastes. Sodium fluoride is preferred over stannous fluoride because it causes staining of teeth. Fluorides may also impose risks if used excessively. It may cause dental fluorosis in which color of the enamel gets change.

Antisensitivity agents

This is the main ingredient of antisensitivity toothpaste which prevent the dentin hypersensitivity. Potassium nitrate and sodium fluoride are widely used ingredients to prevent the tooth sensitivity. Besides them, other agents namely calcium sodium phosphosilicate, casein phosphopeptide-amorphous calcium phosphate can also be used.

Re-mineralizers

These are the agents which re-mineralize the tooth structure and provide more resistant power to the tooth against acid erosion and cavities. Re-mineralizers include calcium phosphate, hydroxyapatite etc. Many toothpaste manufacturer use hydroxyapatite rather than fluorides in their paste.

Anticalculus agents

These agents prevent the deposition of calculus on the teeth due to pyrophosphate present in it. Calculus is a sticky layer present on the surface of teeth having the bacteria which can lead to plague. The agents used as anticalculus include sodium pyrophosphate, and zinc stearate.

Table 7.22: Formulation of tooth paste- ingredients, quantities and uses.

Ingredient	Concentration (gm)	Use
Calcium carbonate	56	Abrasive
Sodium lauryl sulfate	1	Foaming agent
Glycerin	22	Humectant
Gum tragacanth	1.5	Binder
Water	19.4	Solvent
Saccharine	0.1	Sweetener
Oil of peppermint	q.s.	Flavour
Preservative	q.s.	Antimicrobial

Herbal toothpaste

These are the dentifrices which claim to possess herbs and vegetable oils for soothing, protecting, and clean the teeth and gums. It must not contain any artificial chemical, dyes, flavors, and preservatives. It must be made only using the natural ingredients. Herbal toothpaste are more in use in present days and various herbal toothpastes are also available in market like Dabur red paste, Dabur Meswak toothpaste, Patanjali Dant Kranti etc. These all toothpastes claim to have all natural ingredients having minimum side effects. The Dabur Red paste claims to be clinically tested for minimizing the plague, gingivitis, bad smell in the mouth. Patanjali Dant Kranti is a herbal fluorinated toothpaste having some herbs and ayurvedic ingredients which claims for betterment of the health of the teeth and gums by prevention of infections and cavities in the teeth.

Table 7.23: Examples of Commercial preparation of tooth paste.

Commercial toothpaste	Outer appearance
Colgate	
closeup	
Sensodyne	
Colgate Maxfresh	
Dabur red paste	
Dabur meswak	
Patanjali Dant Kranti	

CHAPTER 8

Soaps and Syndet Bars

Soaps

History of cleansing soap

The historical evidence of soap material can be traced to ancient Babylon in around 2800 BC. The formulation for soap inscribed on a Babylonian tablet constitutes cassia oil, alkali and water. Furthermore, the document Ebers papyrus (1550 BC, Egypt) validates that the Egyptians routinely bathed with soap like substance made of animal and vegetable oils combined with alkaline salts. In 300AD Zosimos of Panopolis, described soap making and soap. Galen also described lye based soap and prescribed regular washing to remove impurities from the human body and clothes.

Soap manufacturing from vegetation and herbs has been recorded in ancient China as well. However, soap made using animal fats, were not practiced in China until the modern era. In France, by the second half of the 15th century, the semi-industrialized professional manufacturing of soap was concentrated in a few centers. In contrast to soaps made with animal fat, soaps made from vegetable oils like olive oil, were produced in Europe from 16th century onwards. Castile soap is a popular example of the vegetable-only soaps derived by the oldest "white soap" of Italy. Eventually by late 18th century, industrially manufactured bar soaps appeared in the market as intense advertising campaigns in United States and Europe created awareness between health and cleanliness. With the passage of time, the soap recipes became popular, but it remained an expensive commodity because the ingredients were of natural origin.

The soap price significantly dropped in 1791 when a Frenchman LeBlanc discovered a chemical process that allowed bulk manufacturing of soap and afterwards the soap became inexpensive.

Almost more than two decades later, another Frenchman discovered the chemical reaction between fats, glycerin and acid that marked the initiation of modern soap making. By decade 1800, discovery of yet another soap making method resulted in significant price drop of soap. Since then no major innovations have been made and the same processes are being used by the soap manufacturers till date. With the advent of a variety of soap ingredients, soap for bathing became a separate commodity from laundry soap, by the middle of nineteenth century. Thus milder soaps were packaged with cosmetic appeal were sold for personal use. The liquid hand soaps are the invention of 1970s which positioned the soaps for places of public use. Today, a large variety of soaps for different purposes are available for personal, commercial and industrial use.

FDA definition of "soap"

By definition soaps are water soluble sodium or potassium salts of fatty acids. Soaps are prepared from oils and fats or fatty acids thereof, by treating them with strong alkali. The products that match with the definition of "soap" are exempted from the provisions of the Food Drug & Cosmetic Act because even though Section 201(i) (1) of the act includes "articles...for cleansing" in the definition of a cosmetic, Section 201(i)(2) does not include soap as a cosmetic.

Not every product marketed as soap meets the FDA's definition of the soap. FDA interprets the term "soap" to apply only when,

- The bulk of the non-volatile matter in the product consists of an alkali salt of fatty acids and the product's detergent properties are due to the alkali-fatty acid compounds, and
- The product is labeled, sold, and represented solely as soap [21 CFR 701.20].

The products that fulfill this definition of soap are regulated by the Consumer Product Safety Commission, and not by FDA. It is noteworthy that, if a product intended to clean the human body does not meet all the enlisted criteria for soap, it is then classified either as a cosmetic or as drug. For example: a cleansing product made of alkali salts of fatty acids or detergents and is intended not only for body cleansing but for other cosmetic uses also, it is then categorized as a cosmetic. Examples of cosmetic uses include enhancing attractiveness of the user, moisturizing the skin, imparting fragrance or serving as a deodorant. On the other hand, if a product is made of consists of alkali salts of fatty acids or detergents, and apart from cleansing is intended to treat or prevent skin disease; or to modulate the function or structure of the human body, it is then regulated as a drug, or both a cosmetic and a drug. Examples include cleansers intended to treat acne, antibacterial cleansers etc. If a product is intended for cleansing the human body only and has the characteristics associated with soap, and does not consist of alkali salts of fatty acids, it may be categorized as soap, but is regulated as a cosmetic.

Types of Soaps

Vegetable Soap

Vegetable soaps are considered to be natural and are devoid of chemicals of synthetic origin. Such soaps are typically termed as 'traditional' / true soap bars. The composition and performance of soap bars can be altered by adjusting the type and quantity of constituent fats and oils. Additives like Shea butter, Argan oil, cocoa butter may be incorporated to give moisturizing and cleansing effect on the skin whilst washing. The soap subsets along with their characteristics are listed below.

Glycerin bars/transparent bars	• Used rampantly in winter. • Contain humectant–glycerin to counter the drying effects of soap.
Superfatted soaps	• Contain greater amount of lipids such as triglycerides, lanolin, paraffin, stearic acid, or mineral oils which provide a protective film on the skin.
Deodorant soaps/antibacterial soaps	• Contain antibacterial agents such as triclosan, triclocarban, or carbanile to inhibit the growth of bacteria and thereby odor.

The Bureau of Indian Standards (BIS) categorizes bath/ toilet soaps as 'normal' soap as baby soap, transparent soap, and antibacterial soap. Except for normal soap rest are termed as soaps targeted for specific users. Soaps are graded in terms of total fatty matter (TFM). TFM measures the amount of fatty matter present in soaps, lends the product its soapy feel and TFM along with the insoluble matter in the soap is responsible for distinguishing the soaps from one another. On the basis TFM, toilet soaps can be classified into three grades.

Table 8.1: Classification of toilet soap on the basis of TFM.

Grade	TFM	Free salt (NaCl)	Moisture
I	More than 80	Max 0.7	Max 13.5
II	65-80	0.8	13 – 15
III	55-65	1.5	15 -20

Irrespective of variations in the TFM, free salt and moisture, all the three soap grades should contain not more than 0.05 % by weight of free alkali as sodium hydroxide, and less than 1% by weight of alkali carbonate. The maximum permissible free salt content in soap is 1.5 %. The Grade I toilet soap should have a TFM value more than 80 %, except in Ayurvedic soap. Any soap which has a TFM value less than 55 % is not considered as toilet soap. Today 85 % of bathing soaps available commercially are not toilet soaps.

Special processes are being investigated to upgrade the less expensive and readily available raw materials, in order to produce good quality toilet soap. The efforts include developing techniques to obtain ambient quality fatty acids from Neem oil, Sunflower oil, Jajoba oil, fish oil, Hazelnut oil and Karanja oil. An indigenous process to convert castor oil into textured castor oil for making transparent soap has already been developed.

Glycerin soaps

Glycerin soaps retain the natural glycerin and may also have pure glycerin added to them to increase the glycerin content. Opaque vegetable origin, high glycerin soap, sold globally is manufactured using vegetable oils. Glycerin soap is devoid of fragrances, alcohol or any other ingredients that have potential to irritate the skin. Glycerin can help lock in the skin's natural moisture and prevent over drying. This may be especially beneficial in skin conditions like acne, dermatitis, dry skin, psoriasis and rosacea. Glycerin may also have anti-aging benefits. It can help to even out the skin tone and texture. This may reduce surface blemishes and appearance of fine lines. Glycerin is non-greasy and the soap with glycerin is a good choice for anyone with oily or combination skin. Glycerin soap comes in available in bar and liquid formulas. In spite of its benefits, glycerin soap also has several drawbacks. It generally does not lather up like other soaps and may dissolve if it is left in water or attracts too much moisture from the air. Glycerin soap is expensive in comparison to most of other types of normal soap.

Herbal soaps

Herbal soaps are made using natural herbs and ingredients that are healthier and beneficial for the skin and are less likely to cause any damaging effect. Herbal soaps have high glycerin content and hence high absorbing water in the air and ensuring the protection and softness of skin. Herbs add texture, scent, and many other benefits for the skin. The skincare benefits offered by herbal soaps are (i) nourishing (comfort, healing and stress relief), (ii) aromatherapy, and (iii) relief from skin diseases (psoriasis or eczema can be benefitted from natural handmade soaps).

The herbs for herbal soap can be either of the following, Lavender, Chamomile, Calendula, Lemon Balm, Marshmallow root, Comfrey, Rosemary, Plantain, Rose, Burdock and Mint. The herbs are picked mid-morning after the sun has dried off the dew from flowers and leaves, but before the sun dries out the natural oils of the plant. The herb may be used a whole leaf, flower, it can be grounded. The herbs can be dried naturally in the sun, or in an oven or dehydrator to ensure zero dampness to avoid mold growth. The essential oils used in making herbal soaps can be from the list below.

- Olive oil - Rich in Vitamin E and works as a humectant for skin, produces silky bubbles
- Coconut oil - Rich in moisturizing properties and helps create a hard bar of soap with fluffy bubbles/lather
- Palm oil - Good for the conditioning of skin and helps make a hard bar
- Soyabean oil - Rich in vitamins A, E and K. Provides good natural antioxidant and moisturizing properties.

The selection of herbal soap depends on the skin type. For dry skin, herbal soap made of oatmeal and/or avocado extracts should be selected. These may also contain lavender, peppermint, and spearmint oils to get rid of impurities in the skin. For oily skin, herbal soap made with calendula oil or almond oil should be selected. Soaps made with tea oil are also considered to be effective in curing oily skin conditions.

Ayurvedic soaps

Unlike herbal soaps that use whole of powdered herb, Ayurvedic soaps are based on the use of medicinal plant extracts. Ayurvedic soap would have a base of vegetable oils, glycerin and then an assortment of healing oils. Coconut oil, ginger extract, orange oil and sandalwood oil are a few of the more common ingredients found in Ayurvedic soap. Some of the commercially available Ayurvedic soaps are listed in Table 8.2.

Table 8.2: A cross section of commercial Ayurvedic soaps.

Commercial Product	Claims	Manufacturer
Medimix Ayurvedic Classic 18 Herbs Soap	• Natural protection • Blemishes skin • Acne treatment	Medimix
Himalaya Ayurveda Clear Skin Soap India	• Made with kanakataila, a pure ayurvedic oil • Nourishes skin and helps improve the complexion, leaving skin healthy and clear, naturally • Help reduce blemishes and dark spots, and brighten, gently nourish and protect the skin.	Himalaya
Patanjali Haldi Chandan Kanti Body Cleanser	• Recommended for glowing skin • Protection of body, skin and hair	Patanjali
Chandrika Ayurvedic Handmade Soap	• Large amount of coconut oil and Ayurvedic herbs, which gently treat skin problems and gives clear, smooth and beautiful skin. • Protects from common skin problems like pimples, dark spots, rashes, pigmentation etc. • Provides radiant glow and keeps the skin healthy. Keeps skin naturally soft, supple and gently perfumed.	Chandrika

Ayurvedic soap cleans and refreshes the skin, with its specific ingredients determining its exact effects. Unlike traditional soaps Ayurvedic soaps are gentler on the skin, helping prevent rashes and blemishes while still being strong enough to cleanse. Manufacturers may also tailor certain Ayurvedic soaps to possess antiseptic or anti-inflammatory properties or to achieve specific cosmetic sensations such as enhanced skin relaxation or improved blood circulation for a sense of warming. However, owing to the constituent natural ingredients, an Ayurvedic soap is expensive than the traditional soaps.

Hair wash soaps

Washing hairs with soap bars is not uncommon and washing the hair with soap may not necessarily entirely wash off the hair, especially in hard water areas. The minerals in the hard water chemically react with the soap, deposit on the hair and can leave it feeling 'unclean' or 'waxy'. This is easily resolved by using a simple acidic rinse after washing the hair with soap. In soft water this is generally not a problem. Thus the effectiveness of hair washing with soap bar depends on various factors namely (i) Hair length and type (short/ dry/ curly hair); (ii) Scalp type (sensitivity hypersensitive/non-hypersensitive); (iii) Water quality and measures taken to mitigate against hard water; (iv) Technique; and (v) What the hair has previously been washed with.

Another product called as shampoo bar is also used for hair cleansing and is different from soap bar. The balance between the amount and type of oils and butters is the primary difference.

The shampoo bars usually contain more castor oil, which is an excellent hair care oil containing rich qualities of ricinoleic fatty acid. Gasfroil is a humectant, and contributes to the fluffy, bubbly lather. Shampoo bars may also contain Babassu and coconut oils that are good oils for hair and create a gentle and cleansing lather. Jojoba oil whose composition is resembles a liquid wax that resembles the natural sebum produced by the scalp, can also be used in shampoo bars. Jojoba, a lubricant and emollient, may help repair damaged hair shafts and offers protection from environmental damage as well. Incorporation of additional fats (butters or oils) to the soap mixture is called as superfatting. The amount of extra oil in shampoo bars can vary a lot depending on whether the bar is for dry, normal, or oily hair. The soap based shampoo bar is prepared via hot-press or cold-press method. The cold-pressed bars are smooth in appearance and take longer time to set whereas hot-pressed shampoo bars solidify quickly and have textured appearance. Remarkably, both processes require *sodium hydroxide/caustic soda/lye* to solidify the oils into a bar.

Baby Soaps

Gentle and natural, baby soaps are made using quality essential oils, herbs, fragrances, and other natural ingredients that can gently clean the skin of baby without irritating or drying it. Especially formulated for the delicate and sensitive baby skin, baby soaps are devoid of animal fats, preservatives, or dyes. These soaps are generally fortified with vitamin E, saponified olive, palm kernel, coconut, and food grade vegetable oils. Occasionally, butter milk, herbal extracts, spices, goat's milk and butters can also be incorporated in some of the baby soaps that renders dense and perforating thick lather with character and richness in every soap bar. Good quality baby soap should be gentle, hypoallergenic, non-toxic and Sandium layrylsulphate/or sulphate free.

Skin whitening soap

A whitening soap whitens the skin by inhibiting excess melanin production, which gives the skin the appearance of becoming lighter over a period of time. These soaps include ingredients like glutathione and kojic acid that reduce melanin production on exposure to sun, making the skin appear lighter. Sometimes, a skin whitening soap can also have exfoliating properties, making them ideal for removing tan. Such soaps have a slightly rough texture that removes dead skin cells. These soaps will help lift even the most stubborn dirt from the skin surface to reveal healthier and newly formed skin hiding underneath those dead skin cells. These soaps are especially made for the body and not for face. Facial scrubs with whitening properties may be opted.

Animal based soaps

In the past variety of animal fats were used to make soap. Lard is a fat from pig while tallow is usually fat taken from around the loins and kidney of a cow. Other sources of tallow are sheep tallow and deer tallow. Tallow for soap making will produce a harder bar that lathers better while using lard for soap making will produce a softer bar with conditioning properties. Both lard and tallow need to be rendered before these can be used to make soap. When tallow is mixed with an alkali substance, it can produce sodium, magnesium, or potassium tallowate. All three types of salt are used as soaps. Sodium tallowate helps easy clean the skin and hair by helping the water mix with dirt and oils readily and producing foamy lather. Tallow is on the FDAs list of Generally Recognized as Safe products as well as in the Cosmetic Ingredient Review list. It is considered safe for use in cosmetics and is not linked to any particular health issues. However, it needs to be understood that most soaps made from tallow, have a pH of 9 to 10 while the healthy skin has a pH balance of 5.4 to 5.9. Thus the possibility of disruption of skin's natural pH mantle on consistent use of tallow based soap cannot be ignored.

Sodium lardate is obtained by mixing lard with alkali to get lard soap. Lard soaps give creamy lather and have conditioning properties. Both lard and tallow based soaps are firm and produce persistent lather. Owing to these properties, both tallow and lard are commonly substituted for palm oil. Though, nowadays most soaps are synthetically made; however, one can still find soaps made from animal fat because some people prefer using traditionally made soaps since they often contain fewer chemicals. Animal fat based soaps generally make good hypoallergenic alternatives to other types of soap.

Skin benefits of soaps

1. Soaps are designed to cleanse the skin by removing sweat, dirt, oil and sebum from it.
2. Soaps also aid in the skin's natural exfoliating process by removing dead cells from the epidermis (the outermost layer of skin).

Bathing Bars

In India bathing bars, were introduced in 1985 and it was situation driven. AC that time, the country was facing acute shortage of vegetable cooking oils because much of the vegetable oils were being used by industry for soap manufacturing. In view of the vegetable oil scarcity, the government of India started importing palm oil from various countries. Additionally, to restrict the industrial usage of vegetable oils for soap manufacturing units, the government permitted soap manufacturers to introduce bathing bars.

According to Indian Standards BATHING BAR — SPECIFICATION (First Revision), IS 13498: 1997, The bathing bar shall be a product containing soap of fatty adds and synthetic surface active agents as active ingredients that could be used for bathing purposes in both soft and hard water. The REQUIREMENTS (Section 5) include:

5.1: The bathing bar should be firm and smooth. It should comply with the requirements given in Table1 of the standards.

5.2: The formulation when tested by the method given in IS13424 (1992) shall pass the dermatological safety test.

Types of bathing bars

The bathing bars can be categorized into two categories as follows-

1. Syndet bar – Completely made up of synthetic detergent, and
2. Combars- A combination of soap and synthetic detergent

1. Syndet bar

Syndet or cleansing bar / cleansing liquid is made up of synthetic surfactants. Syndet bars cannot be called as "soap," because the word "Soap" actually has a legal definition provided by the FDA. Since syndet bars are prepared using synthetic surfactants they do not conform to the FDA definition of soap. Since the advent of synthetic detergents, continual efforts have been put in to make "syndet bars". Syndet bars are soap-like bars made up entirely of synthetic detergent compositions or a combination of synthetic detergent and conventional toilet soap compositions. The success of the product has been hurdled by the fact that significant portions of synthetic detergents in toilet soap bars results in poor lathering, tackiness, poor firmness, high solubility and fabricating difficulties. Synthetic detergents are inexpensive, possess requisite cleansing lathering features and are more soluble than fatty acid salts used in making conventional toilet soap bars and are devoid of the plasticity of the latter. The solubility characteristic not only causes excessive wearing, but also leads to significant sloughing/slushing when a syndet bar is left wet and/or placed on a wet surface. Poor plasticity means poor physical strength, poor processing characteristics, cracking and crumbling during use. Some additional desirable characteristics are absence of grittiness, good dry and wet tactile properties ("feel"), absence of scum- or curd-forming characteristics. Another significant requisite is to avoid hydrolysis in aqueous solution at a pH of 10.2-10.4, which is characteristic of conventional soap.

The vast majority of cleansing products available in the market today are syndets. The word "syndet" is derived from "synthetic" combined with "detergent". Technically, syndet refers to the binding between different detergents/ surface active / tensioactive agents. These detergents solubilize oil, surround the dirt with rich foam and facilitate removal of these from the skin by water. Being a combination of detergents, syndets offer a plethora of formulations and are increasingly becoming popular for cleansing of healthy and diseased skin. Unlike the alkaline soaps that interfere with the cutaneous microflora, syndets do not alter the microflora and offer immense possibilities for addition of additives namely colorants and fragrances that is not suitable with soaps due to the alkaline pH that may degrade the additives.

Syndet soap bars are often commercialized as "dermatological bars" or "cleansing bars" and occasionally described as "soap free" or "soaps without soap." This may lead to confusion although aesthetically is correct. The irritancy potential of syndets is much lower than that of soap, thus are recommended for cleansing sensitive skin and even baby skin, as they are far gentler in pH terms than traditional soaps. However, the syndets made with anionic surfactants have potential to cause sensitization problems in reactive skins.

Syndet constitution

Syndet bars are made using blends of synthetic surfactants derived from oils, fats, or petroleum products. The synthetic surfactants position syndet bars as the mildest personal cleansing bars, often with pH neutral. The most famous and in fact first syndet soap bar was

Dove® launched in 1955. The U.S. Dove bar formulations of the 1990s are compared with the 2008 formulation in Table 8.3.

Table 8.3: Dove bar formulation(s) in USA.

Ingredient (%)	1992	2008
Sodium cocoyl isethionate	47-49	48-50
Free fatty acids (stearic acid + coconut acid)	23-25	23-26
Soap	7-10	9-11
Sodium isethionate	4-6	4-6
Alkyl benzene sulfonate	1-2	-
Cocamidopropyl betaine	-	2-3
Sodium chloride	0.5	0.5–1
Water	4-6	5-6

The formulation of cleansing bars is a skillful combination of scientific aspects and artistic creativity while selecting the ingredients to meet the consumer expectations of a broad range of qualities. To achieve all the requirements a suitable syndet/combo bar is essentially composed from a blend of ingredients as listed in Table 8.4.

Table 8.4: The ingredients of Syndet/Combo bars.

Ingredients range	(%)
Surfactants	30–70
Plasticizers, binders, emollients	20-50
Lather enhancers	0 -5
Mildness enhancers	0-5
Opacifying agent	0-0.3
Fragrance	0-1.5
Antibacterial, deodorant agents	0-2
Fillers	5-30
Water	5-12

An ingredient of the bar can have multiple and interchangeable functions. For example, a binder in addition to binding various ingredients together, plasticizes the mass, has capacity to absorb water, and can act as an emollient. Surfactants (anionic surfactants, non-ionic and amphoteric surfactants) in the bars are primarily responsible for cleansing and lathering. Depending on their HLB values, the non-ionic surfactants can also act as cleansers and plasticizers. Some surfactant compositions are listed below which illustrate the state of-the-art compositions for syndet/combars to meet consumer expectations.

- Soap (45–90%) + polyethoxylated fatty alcohol (1–8%)
- Soap (50–90%) + any surfactant (1–20%)
- Soap (75–85%) + polyhydroxy fatty amide (1–10%)
- Soap (70–85%) + alkyl ether sulphate (1–10%), alkyl polyglucosides (0.1–10%)
- Soap/fatty acid (10–50%) + any surfactant (20–65%)
- Soap/fatty acid (5–50%) + any nonionic/anionic surfactant (15–65%)
- Magnesium soap (5–50%) + any surfactant (20–50%)
- Alkyl glyceryl ether sulfonate (35–80%) + soap (1–25%)
- Aldobionamide (20–75%) + polylalkylene glycol (15–65%)
- Acyl isethionate (45–70%) + vegetable oil (0.5–2.5%)
- Long-chain alkyl sulfate (18–55%) + soap (1–20%)
- PEG (70–80%) + lauryl sulphate/amphoteric (8–30%)
- Sodium lauryl sulphate (70–90%) + binder

Performance and Appearance improving additives

One of the major drawbacks of the syndets is their solubility and mushiness in water, also known as *bar smear* or *bar slough.* This unattractive and unappealing property is due to high solubility of certain syndet surfactants and inappropriate formulation. Under extreme circumstances due to formulation failure the paste like mushy texture becomes non resilient and is unable to return to a solid state even after losing water from the mushy layer. One possible solution is to use potassium salts of alkyl sulfate syndets which reduces mushiness. Other low solubility enhancers are inorganic salts, such as sodium chloride and sodium sulfate. Aluminum triformate efficiently reduces water solubility of sulfosuccinate syndet formulations.

Zinc stearate and ethoxylated sorbitan ester have been incorporated in Extra Sensitive Dove brand, marketed in Europe to achieve slipping. Otherwise, preferred slipping agents are high molecular weight ethylene oxide polymers (e.g. as PEG14M). Sodium isethionate is incorporated in acyl isethionate syndet formulations to reduce the wear rate. To improve cosmetic appeal, like water retention and /or shrinkage prevention, Bar appearance aids are seldom incorporated from a list of water soluble organics, clays, salts and suitable waxes to impart skin mildness, firmness, plasticity, glossy look, smooth feel of the bar and processability. Antibacterial additives, such as triclosan and trichlorocarbanilide are successful additives for antibacterial and deodorant syndet bars.

Plasticizers and Binders

Plasticizers are incorporated in syndet bar formulation to facilitate extrusion and stamping. The plasticizers act by reducing the viscosity of the formulation material at the manufacturing temperature so as to facilitate flow of the material under pressure. The plasticizers most commonly used are polyol esters (glycerol monostearate, glycerol distearate and sorbitan stearate), long-chain fatty alcohols (higher than C16), stearic acid, sodium stearte, polyethylene glycol, fatty acid ethoxylate, paraffin wax, hydrogenated castor oil, fatty alkyl ketones, and a combination of hydrogenated triglycerides with fatty alcohols or acids. Plasticity problems are not encountered in soap manufacturing as the soap itself is a plasticizer. In syndet bar, both the plasticizers and the binders strongly influence mushing, lathering and wear characteristics. The binders in the formulation prevent separation of macroscopic agglomerates caused by local stress, facilitate cohesion and modulate the cracking behavior of the solid bar. Gums and gum resins may be used as binders to confer binding characteristics. Both, the plasticizers and binders have high melting points and high molecular weights. Their binding activity is manifested when the melting point of the syndet mass is simply increased.

Fillers

The fillers are inexpensive formulation ingredients incorporated to make the desired weight without escalating the product cost. In the case of syndet bars, the fillers are not inert ingredients but function to improve the internal structure and firmness of the finished product. Thus fillers can also be termed as additional binders. The ingredients employed as fillers are starch, dextrin and modified starch (ethoxylated). Talcum (1-40 %) as filler for syndets act as a colour of detergents, reduces the cost and also prevents mushiness; while buffered borax as filler reduces both, specific gravity and wear characteristics. While the fillers serve their purpose in the formulation, the negative characteristics attributed are loss of slip, rough surface texture, and loss of attractive overall appearance. Thus the concentration of the filler should be restricted to optimal limits. The list of fillers quoted by Hollstein and Spitz in 1982 includes sodium sulfate, calcium hydrogen phosphate, magnesium hydrogen phosphate, sodium hydrogen phosphate, dextrin, and mannitol. Others ingredients include aluminosilicate clays (0.5–25%), calcium carbonate and salt and salt hydrates (1–40%) of cations and anions. Wheat flour used as filler (25 to 65%) in acyl isethionate syndet bar is preferred to cornstarch since it confers an acceptable wear rate to the bar.

Other additives in syndet bars include moisturizers, emollients, and superfatting additives are included to provide skin conditioning benefits and to improve mildness. Some of them are presented in Table 8.5.

Table 8.5: Moisturizers/Emollients in Soap–Syndet (Combo) Bars.

Moisturizer	Purpose	Type of raw material
Occlusive	Deposit on skin surface Reducing rate of evaporation	Long chain fatty acids (25% moisture cream), ethoxylated/propoxylated ethers of lanolin alchol, Mineral oil or methyl glucose, vegetable oils.
Non-occlusive	Hygroscopic substances to stratum corneum, retaining water, improving lubricity	Glycerine, proplylene glycol, sorbitol, lactic acid, carboxylic acid, urea, L-proline, guanidine, isopropryl esters of adipic/ lactic, oleic/ stearic/ isostearic/ myristic, or linoleic acids, isotearyl2-lactylate, sodium capryl lactate, aloe vera gel, acetamide

The superfatting additives facilitate the formation of denser, creamier lather in the syndet/combo bars, which leave the skin smoother and softer. The superfatting agents include alkali soaps of Palmolive, cocoa butter, and fatty acids. These agents have a plasticizing effect on the base, thus the moisture content in the formulation needs to be reduced and the content of hardening agent has to be increased in the formulation.

Skin benefits of syndet bar

1. Routine cleansing with a mild syndet bar leads to significant enhancement in the appearance of skin such as texture, tone, clarity and brightness improvement.
2. Daily usage of syndet bars may reduce the appearance of fine lines/wrinkle.
3. Milder than soaps, syndet bars are widely used in a variety of skin conditions, including atopic dermatitis.
4. Syndet bar reduce the severity of eczematous lesions and maintain skin hydration.
5. Can be recommended as an integral part of patients' fundamental daily skin care regimen for a variety of skin conditions (e.g. acne, rosacea)

SOAP *versus* SYNDET

Evidence based clinical studies have depicted that soaps are generally irritating in comparison to syndets that can range from mild to harsh. Routine use of soaps and syndet bars has been linked with skin dryness and occasionally aggravation of dermatological conditions. Various factors, namely pH, chemical structure, and cleansing ability have been reasoned for these. The bars offer addition of various ingredients that can ameliorate its irritancy and provide skin benefits. The skin benefitting agents such as glycerin, mineral oil, lanolin or cocoa butter do not lower the irritancy potential of a bar since these are deposited in minimal amounts on the skin.

Table 8.6 enlists comparative features of vegetable soap with syndet bars.

Table 8.6: Comparison of vegetable and syndet bars.

VEGETABLE SOAP	SYNDET BARS
Vegetable based, natural, organic	Synthetic / Chemical
Offers oil benefits	No such benefit offered
High glycerin content	Glycerin may or may not be present
Skin additives may be incorporated	Wider range of additives may be incorporated
Less foam production	High foam production
Is alkaline in pH	Is neutral in pH
Drying on the skin	Minimal drying effect
Mild on skin	Relatively stronger on skin
Poor colour	Low colour
Easy processing	Offers processing challenges
Economical	Expensive

1. Combination Bars or Combars

Combination soap base or Combars are made using a combination of different types of surfactants, saponified oils and cleansers mixed in manner to maximize cleaning while minimize skin irritation. Primarily, these can be seen as structured toilet soaps. These combo soap bars are commonly combinations of traditional vegetable soap and syndet bar base. These contain 50 % Total Fatty Matter (TFM) and 30-35 % mineral material namely kaolin and talc. By formulating in this way combination bars are less irritating than traditional vegetable soaps, but less mild than syndet bars; a balance of the two. They lather up better and have a stronger cleansing action than milder syndet bars.

Gentle cleansers, such as Cetaphil® and Dove®, are examples of combination bars. Cetaphil® contains sodium cocoate, sodium tallowate and sodium cocyl isethionate (a mild synthetic surfactant), among other detergents. Commercial combo bar formulations are depicted in Table 8.7.

Table 8.7: Combo bar Formulations.

Ingredient (%)	Zest	Liver 2000	Ingredient (%)	Zest	Liver 2000
Sodium glyceryl ether sulfonate	12-18	-	Soap (tallow/coconut)	50-60	65-75
Sodium cocoyl isethionate	-	-	Magnesium soap	5-10	-
Sodium methyl sulfo laurate	-	1-3	Water	5-8	8-12
Free fatty acids	6-10	5-7			

2. Transparent/Translucent Syndet /Combar Cleansing Bars

The major challenge of the syndet/combar market is to design a consumer friendly extrudable transparent/ translucent of neutral pH. This target is yet to be achieved, therefore transparent combo bars made by casting (also called poured, molded) are ruling the market. Several commercial combo bases are offered on the market by different suppliers, such as Stephenson®, TensaChem® , Galaxy® and Unichema®. Commercially available transparent and translucent combars are made by incorporating C12–15 alkyl benzoate and non-oxynol-10-carboxylic acid to the soap syndet base. Cleansing bars based on sarcosinates or acyl glutamates (even of translucent appearance) are available commercially in past few years. An attractive round-shaped acyl glutamate syndet, is a gel soap containing TEA cocoyl glutamate; decyl glucoside, hydrolyzed collagen, dipotassium glycyrrhizinate, glycerine,urea, and isopropyl alcohol.

3. Syndet solid shampoo bars

Syndet solid shampoo bars are crafted from a combination of mild detergent based cleansers formulated to wash and care for hair. The types of detergents/surfactants used are from sulfate family, namely *sodium cocoylisethionate, sodium lauryl sulphate, sodium lauryl sulfoacetate.* The first on the list based on 'cocoyl' is derived from coconut oil but is synthetic, very gentle on skin and is found in various personal care products including baby products. Sulphates are able to draw out dirt and oils from hair and give a clean feeling. However, the downside is that these can be highly irritating to the sensitive skin. They are also being targeted as hormone/endocrine disruptors, which may have potential for adverse effects on scalp. Syndet shampoo bars cleanse the scalp free from dirt and oils. However, conditioners are required as the scalp gets stripped of precious sebum by the sulphates. Syndet shampoo bars produce a foamy lather better than liquid shampoos that get hair clean. These solid shampoo bars do not strip hair of oils and are gentle enough for even color treated hair.

Product performance evaluation

In addition to cleansing, color and odor, which are conceived as the main attributes for consumer acceptance, the bar performance evaluation parameters include

- Physical stability (wet and dry cracking)
- Chemical stability (odor, color, efflorescence)
- Hardness
- Mushiness/sloughing/smearing
- Erosion/wear/use-up rate
- Lathering (amount, stability, quality, density, speed of formation)
- Lather feel during washing
- Rinsability (from skin and bathtub)
- Skin feel (during and after rinsing/drying)
- Mildness/dermatological compatibility
- Processability/workability
- Packaging stability

Future Trends

Consumer appealing mild formulations with enhanced skin-care properties with an aesthetic appeal seems to be a major trend in the future. Special emphasis would be on the use of natural renewable raw materials, made exclusively from fatty materials of vegetable origin keeping in mind about environmental sustainability. A transparent, neutral pH syndet when perceived by customers as a pure harmless product targeted as a specialty bar is the real challenge of cosmeceuticals industry.

CHAPTER 9

Perfumes and Fragrances

The word perfume originated from the Latin word *"perfumare"* which means "to smoke through". Before 18th century, the perfume industry relied on naturally occurring want materials including leaf, flower, bark, and animal tissues that were collected, processed, and aged for a specific period of time. Thyme, lavender, peppermint, cedar, rose, almond oil, aloe, cinnamon, ox fat, cedar oil, myrrh, cassia, camphor oil, lemon, daisies, menthol, and myrrh are some of the often used sources to produce the perfumes. As a result of population growth and industrial revolutionization, cosmetic formulations that mimic naturally occurring items become more popular. However, Egypt is one of the biggest exporter of natural raw materials (80%) to cities across the world where perfume is made including Paris, London, New York and Moscow. National flower of Egypt, the "lotus" is used to create distinctive perfume which is special and rare in nation and a major draw for tourists to purchase and own.

Highly specialized science of perfume and fragrance chemistry necessitates understanding of the numerous components and how they combine to form the perceived aroma. While some perfumes quickly fade, others cling to the skin for longer. In order to get the desired outcome that results in a product with a pleasant appearance, the interaction of these features throughout time is crucial. Fragrance ingredients used in cosmetics must adhere to the same safety standards as other cosmetic ingredients. The safety of perfume ingredients is evaluated and controlled by International Fragrance Association (IFRA).

Cosmetic manufacturers obtain perfume mixtures from perfume houses to create their own exclusive blends. When perfumes are put to personal care products, they also contain a blend of substances that give the item an aroma and keep it stable. Few products identify the precise elements that go into a scent, despite the fact that many products have "fragrance" listed on the label. It is commonly recognized that few scent compounds are associated to major health issues like cancer, reproductive and developmental toxicity, allergies, and sensitivities, despite the fact that most fragrance chemicals are not reported to possess the same.

Expressing a perfume or fragrance

One way to describe a perfume, is to detail its fragrance notes. When a perfume is applied to the skin, certain scents are perceived, and they are described. These are categorized into three groups based on the fragrances that can be detected at various times after application namely top notes (head notes), middle notes (heart notes), and base notes (Figure 9.1).

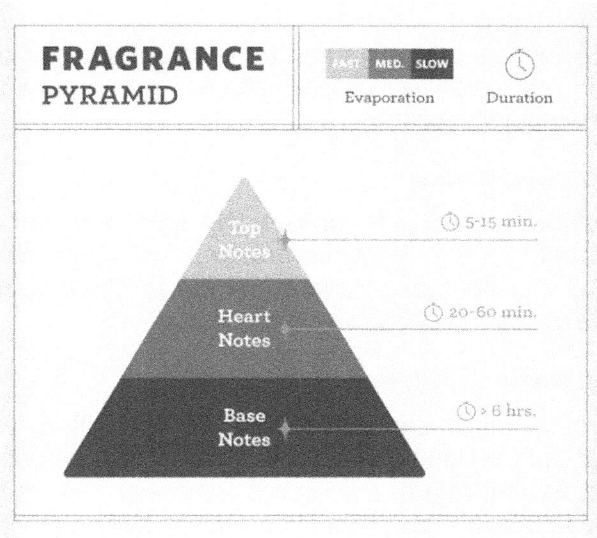

Figure 9.1: Three types of perfume notes.

Top notes

Top notes are those aromas that are most noticeable right away after applying perfume. These notes are produced by ingredients that contain tiny molecules that evaporate quickly. These notes are crucial for selling the perfume since they produce the aroma that customers smell immediately when they purchase the fragrance. Basil, eucalyptus, bergamot, cajeput, cinnamon, clary sage, grapefruit, lemon, tangerine, coriander, peppermint, thyme, and other smells are employed as top notes.

Middle notes

When top tones begin to fade, middle notes arise. Together with the base notes, they provide the perfume's dominant aroma and can be used to mask the underlying scent which can occasionally be unappealing at first. These are often more subdued notes and they can start to scent anywhere from two minutes to an hour after the perfume is applied. Aromas including those of pine, cardamom, lavender, rosemary, juniper, chamomile, marjoram, nutmeg, and even black pepper are utilized to lend medium tones to perfumes.

Base notes

The longest lasting notes in a perfume are the base notes which give it depth and substance. They can appear and last for up to 24 hours as middle tones start to fade. Ingredients used for base notes have molecules that dissipate very slowly and typically have a robust and rich smell. Perfumers utilize a variety of ingredients, including myrrh, frankincense, rose, vanilla, ginger, clove, and cedarwood, to give perfumes these potent aromas.

Classification of perfumes

There are various criterion to classify the perfumes namely gender, fragrance wheel, fragrance concentration, and place of application, time of origin, and sources. Various criteria to classify the perfumes have been discussed in preceding section.

Perfumes on basis of gender

On commercial basis, perfumes can be classified as feminine, masculine, or unisex. Unisex perfumes are in the minority. Perfumes classified as feminine are frequently described as fruity or floral, whereas those classified as masculine are typically described as spicy or tangy.

During in research on perfumes, the scents used as stimuli in perfume are typically found at the extremities of the gender spectrum. For instance, in a research, it was demonstrated that people who applied a traditional masculine scent were perceived as more competent than people who applied a traditional feminine scent. In another research, it was observed that people who were using typical feminine perfume were perceived as less macho than those who weren't. One more research demonstrated how teenage females were more competant with their daily lives when they wore their favorite perfume in comparison to alternate feminine perfumes.

Perfumes on the basis of fragrance wheel

Fragrance wheel classify the perfumes on the basis of way that a fragrance actually smells. The "fragrance wheel," a visual representation of assumed relationships across fragrance groups based on comparisons of their odours produced by American born author and fragrance specialist Michael A. Edwards. This wheel was derived from the "Fragrance Manual," a previous manual he published to help shops categorize perfumes and recommend fragrances to customers. Between 1983 and 2010, Edwards created 4 fragrance families, Floral, Oriental, Woody, and Fresh, which were further divided into 11 and later 14 separate classes (Figure 9.2).

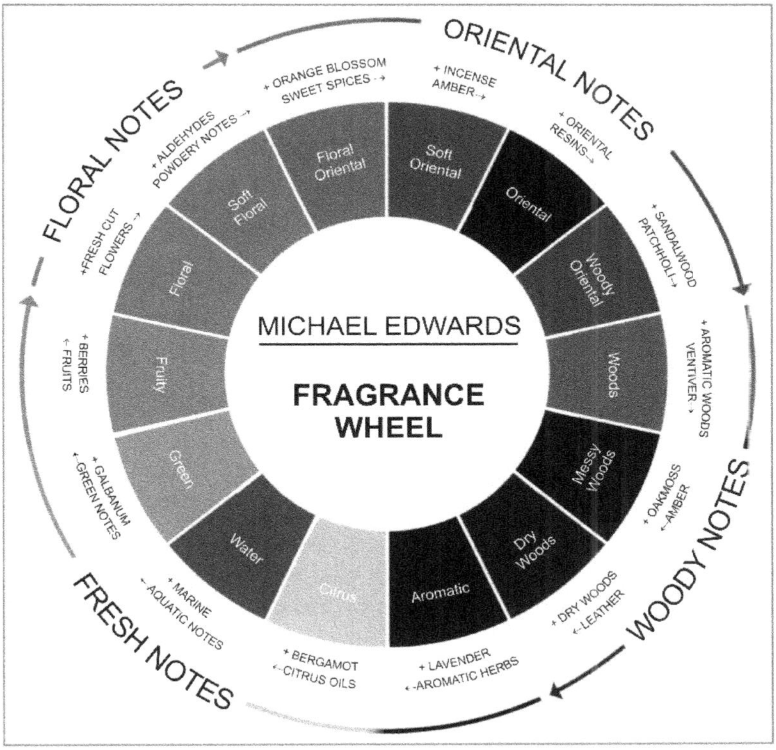

Figure 9.2: Four fragrance families on basis of fragrance wheel.

Perfumes on the basis of concentration

The concentration of fragrance utilized can also be used to objectively classify perfumes, especially liquid based ones. The terms Eau De Cologne, Eau De Toilette, Eau De Parfum, and lastly Perfume are used to describe the categories that result from the various levels of concentration (Figure 9.3).

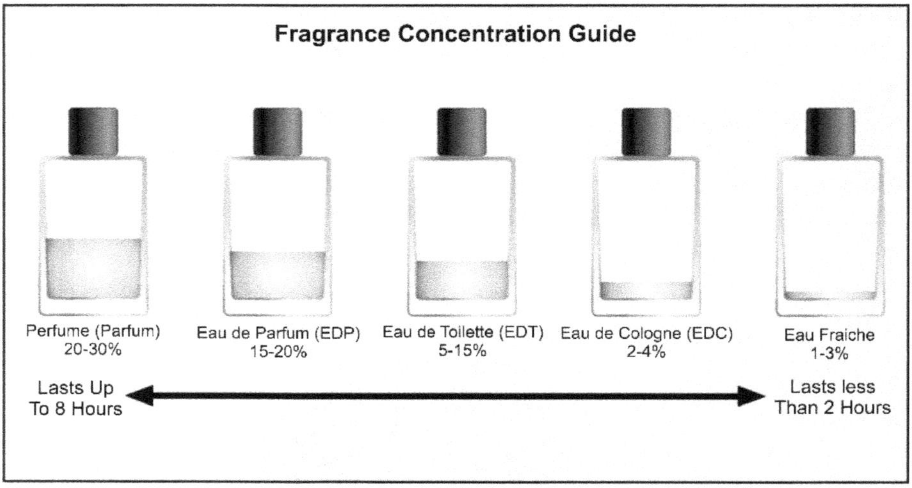

Figure 9.3: Perfumes on basis of concentration.

Perfumes on the basis of place of application

Location of application, where the perfumes are actually applied determines another application based classification for perfumes. Some perfumes are employed to freshen up the air in a room, while others are used to make someone smell pleasant. So, there are perfumes for the home and personal care purpose. Further these can also be sub-categorized, for instance, personal care items including perfumes which can be applied as body sprays whilst some perfumes are used for other purposes like breath fresheners, shoe deodorizers, feet fresheners, and even hair freshener sprays. The type of room in which a particular room freshener is used might also influence the type of freshener used. Different scents are employed in bathrooms, toilets, kitchens, and living areas. These sub-categories include niche marketing trends and target marketing topics once more.

On the basis of time of origin

On these basis of time of origin, perfumes can be classified as traditional and modern perfumes. The traditional perfumes were originated around 1900 having various categories of fragrances like amber, single floral, floral bouquet, woody, leather, fougere, chypre sub-types. The modern perfumes were originated around 1945 and include green, aquatic, ozonic, citrus, fruity, gourmand, aromatics, bright floral, and oceanic as sub-categories.

Perfumes on the basis of sources

Perfumes can be obtained from various sources such as plant, animal, microorganisms, and synthetic sources. Various part of plants from which perfumes can be obtained includes flowers, barks, fruits, leaves, twigs, roots, rhizomes, seeds, bulb and wood. Animal sources include musk, civet, honeycomb, ambergris, castoreum and hyraceum. Microbial sources include lichens, seaweed. Synthetic sources comprise calone (provide ozonous metallic marine aroma). Synthetic sources are mainly employed to obtain the compounds like coumarin, linalool which cannot be obtained from natural sources in sufficient amount.

Perfume ingredients listed as allergens in EU regulations

Based on the results of risk assessments, safety criteria need to be established for use of hazardous substances in consumer cosmetic products. In addition to using the terms "parfum" or "aroma," EU Regulation 1223/2009, which is applicable to cosmetics items supplied to European Union (EU) markets, mandates that the presence of any of the 26 compounds recognized as allergenic should be specified on the ingredients list. If any allergenic perfume used in leave-on products like creams, lotions in concentration more than 0.001% and in rinse-off products like shampoos, soaps in concentration more than 0.01%, they must be disclosed on the ingredient label. These 26 compounds include alpha isomethylionone, amyl cinnamal (Jasmonal A), amyl cinnamyl alcohol, anisyl alcohol, benzyl alcohol, benzyl benzoate, benzyl cinnamate, benzyl salicylate, butylphenylmethylpropional (lilial), cinnamal, cinnamyl alcohol, citral, citronellol, coumarin, eugenol, farnesol, geraniol, hexyl cinnamal (jasmonal h), hydroxycitronellal, hydroxyisohexyl 3-cyclohexene carboxaldehyde (lyral), isoeugenol, limonene, linalool, methyl 2-octynoate, everniafurfuracea (treemoss) extract, and everniaprunastri (oakmoss) extract.

The Scientific Committee on Consumer Safety (SCCS) of EU adopted SCCS/1459/11 (Opinion on fragrance allergens in cosmetic products) in December 2011 which came to the conclusion that more compounds beyond the 26 already specified in Regulation 1223/2009 were irritating to humans. Around 56 additional compounds were intended to be included in the regulation's preview. These additional allergenic perfumes include terpineol, menthol, linalyl acetate, vanillin, camphor, geranial, geranyl acetate, cinnamon oil, ylang-ylang oil (Canangaodorata flower oil), lavender oil and others.

The expansion of Regulation 1223/2009 was supposed to be adopted in 2020 however this has been delayed for a number of reasons including the COVID-19 pandemic. There is currently no clear indication of when expansion of regulation will take place. The increase is anticipated to take effect eventually though, so producers should make sure that their cosmetic goods are thoroughly evaluated and that the results are prominently shown on pertinent packaging. In the end, the expansion to include all 82 compounds will help both consumers who will have better access to information, and manufacturers, who will be able to improve the reputation of their brands by giving customers more confidence in the safety of their products.

Controversial Ingredients

Parabens

The widespread acceptance of parabens as preservative is mainly due to the efficiency and activity of parabens against a wide range of bacteria and fungus. In preserved items, they can prevent the growth of Gram positive (+) and Gram negative (-) bacteria, moulds, and yeasts. The antimicrobial activity of parabens enhances on lengthening of the alkyl chain in the substituent of paraben structure. Parabens inhibit the growth of microorganisms owing to inhibition of DNA and RNA synthesis, inactivation of bacterial enzymes, interference with lipid layers which leads to breakdown of microbial cell membrane. In addition, the activity of parabens across a wide pH range distinguishes them from other preservatives.

The European Union, the Scientific Committee on Consumer Safety (SCCS), and the Food and Drug Administration (FDA) all have regulations governing the maximum paraben concentration in cosmetics. The presence of parabens must be disclosed on the product package for manufacturers of cosmetics, and E symbols must be used when parabens are added to food products. It is considered safe to use parabens at concentrations lower than 0.4% for a single ingredient and 0.8% for mixtures (EC 1223/2009. 2009). The maximum concentration of propyl paraben and butyl paraben, however, is 0.14% for a single compound and 0.8% for a mixture with other parabens, according to Commission Regulation No. 1004/2014. In contrast, SCCS advises propyl paraben and butyl paraben as safe, provided that neither of their concentrations exceeds 0.19%. The use of long chain and branched parabens, including isopropyl paraben, isobutyl paraben, benzyl paraben, phenyl paraben, and pentyl paraben, is prohibited in countries that are members of the European Union (EC 358/2014. 2014).

There was a great deal of controversy about parabens after a study by British cancer researcher Philippa Darbre in 2004 which discovered parabens were present in malignant breast tumours. The study sparked a debate and raised more questions than it answered. The study, for instance, did not examine potential paraben levels in healthy, non-cancerous breast tissue and did not demonstrate that parabens themselves cause cancer or are dangerous in any way. Furthermore, it is uncertain if the discovery proves that parabens caused the tumour or if parabens only happened to accumulate in some malignant tissue.

Another issue with use of parabens is their endocrinic disruption property. However this estrogenic activity is very low. Cancerous tumours, congenital impairments, and other developmental diseases can be brought on by these disruptions. Although parabens are estrogenic compounds, their effects on the body are less powerful than those of natural oestrogens. The estrogenic activity of parabens increases with lengthening of alkyl chain. It is believed that propyl paraben is estrogenic to a certain limit but lesser than butyl paraben. It can be concluded that parabens have negligible estrogenic activity under normal use. Some researchers have shown that increased levels of paraben may cause reduced quality of male semen, obesity, and immunological disorders.

The Cosmetic Ingredient Review (CIR) Expert Panel stated in 2019 that the continued use of parabens as preservatives should be evaluated based on the most recent scientific findings. They emphasized the use of their potassium and sodium salts as cosmetic preservatives in addition to ordinary parabens (CIR. 2019).

In conclusion, parabens are widely accepted as preservatives. They never should any evidence of their carcinogenicity, genotoxicity, carcinogenic consequences, or endocrine disruption in humans. Additionally, compared to estradiol, their affinity for oestrogen receptors is 2.5 million to 10,000 times lower. Although a corpus of *in vitro* and animal *in vivo* evidence supports theoretical concerns about paraben activity, xenoestrogenicity, and toxicity, the impact, if any, on human health is still unclear. Additionally, there was no clear evidence of paraben related toxicity or a clearly established causal association when parabens were found in human tissue and bodily fluids.

As long as there is no conclusive scientific proof of paraben toxicity or endocrine disruption in humans, parabens will continue to be regarded as harmless. However, due to some uncertainties and the absence of fully developed scientific knowledge, measures should be taken when it comes to safety as well as the toxicity of parabens. However, further studying is required to close scientific gaps and the controversies surrounding them in order to give more precise answers to open questions, even if only hypothetical worries may be raised. The US FDA has concluded that there is no justification for consumers to be concerned about using paraben containing cosmetics. Additionally, the FDA has designated both methyl and propyl parabens as GRAS, which denotes that medical and toxicological professionals "Generally Regarded as Safe" them for use in food products and cosmetic items.

Formaldehyde liberator

Formaldehyde and formaldehyde liberating preservatives are used in various cosmetic products like shampoos, lipsticks, baby soaps etc. These preservatives which inhibit the growth of microorganisms in water based cosmetic products can be absorbed into the skin and can cause cancer and various skin allergic reactions. They are used in hair gel, body wash, body soap, nail paints, nail glue and other personal care products. Formaldehyde can be added directly or can be provided by addition of formaldehyde releasing chemicals like quaternium-15, DMDM hydantoin, imidazolidinyl urea, diazolidinyl urea, sodium hydrozymethylglycinate, glyoxal, brompol, polyoxymethylene urea. These chemicals release provides release of formaldehyde in small quantities over the time. As low as 250 ppm of formaldehyde might have negative effects on health. Hence slow release of formaldehyde in low amounts is also a matter of concern.

Due to these reasons, European union (EU) and GSO have imposed restrictions on exposure of formaldehyde. Formaldehyde in concentrations of maximum 0.2% w/w as preservative is allowed in all type of cosmetic products except oral hygiene products in which it is allowed maximum in concentration of 0.1% w/w. As per the Annex VI of the cosmetic directive 76/768 EC and Gulf Technical Regulation for Safety Requirements of Cosmetics and Personal Care Products (GSO 1943:2016). All the cosmetic products having formaldehyde or formaldehyde liberators must list the warning “contains formaldehyde” on the label on exceeding the concentration of free formaldehyde than 0.05% w/w. Japan and Sweden have prohibited the use of formaldehyde in various cosmetic and toiletries products whilst EU has allowed the use of quaternium-15 in concentration up to 0.2% as preservative in various cosmetic products.

Dioxane

In some cosmetic products, the substance 1,4-dioxane is a trace contaminant. Although it is not a cosmetic ingredient, it might be present in some cosmetics in very small concentrations. It is produced as by product during processing of some cosmetic ingredients. 1,4-Dioxane may cause cancer in people. The National Toxicology Programme (NTP) of the Department of Health and Human Services concluded in a report from 2016 that 1,4-dioxane is "reasonably anticipated to be a human carcinogen based on sufficient evidence of carcinogenicity from studies in experimental animals," despite the fact that the information from human epidemiological studies is insufficient to assess the connection between exposure to 1,4-dioxane and human cancer. The U.S. Environmental Protection Agency (EPA) has determined that 1,4-dioxane is "likely to be carcinogenic to humans," based on the observation that there is substantial evidence for the carcinogenicity of 1,4-dioxane in animals that have been purposefully exposed to it, but insufficient data for humans.

Hazard identification and risk assessment of exposure to 1,4-dioxane as a contaminant in cosmetic products has not been independently carried out by the FDA. However, the International Cooperation on Cosmetics Regulations (ICCR), an international group of regulatory authorities from the United States, the European Union, Japan, Canada, and Brazil, and the European Commission Scientific Committee on Consumer Safety (SCCS) have recently conducted two international scientific studies to examine the issue. Based on the existing safety assessments from Canada, Europe, and Japan, ICCR work group concluded that all of the values described in the current literature are within acceptable margins of exposure. The SCCS determined that 1,4-dioxane concentrations in cosmetic items are regarded as safe for consumers at trace levels of less than 10 ppm.

The FDA routinely checks the levels of 1,4-dioxane in cosmetic items, and we have seen that modifications made in the production process have caused these contaminants' concentrations to significantly decrease over time. Additionally, the FDA carried out skin absorption investigations, which demonstrated that 1,4-dioxane can penetrate both human and animal skin when used in specific preparations like lotions. However, additional FDA studies revealed that even in treatments that are left on the skin for hours, 1,4-dioxane rapidly evaporates, substantially reducing the already minimal amount accessible for skin absorption.

Since the late 1970s, the FDA has seldom checked for certain concentrations of 1,4-dioxane in cosmetic items. FDA carried out 10 surveys on the presence of 1,4-dioxane in final cosmetic items between 1981 and 1997. Despite the small sample sizes in these surveys, there was a decrease in the number of items with 1,4-dioxane concentrations above 10 ppm. In final cosmetic items, FDA discovered

1,4-dioxane on average at 50 ppm in 1981 and an average of 19 ppm in 1997, with a range of 6-34 ppm. The FDA carried out its 11th survey in 2008 utilizing a new analytical technique with a detection level of 1 ppm. The bulk (80%) of the items were found to be free of 1,4-dioxane, with only 6% of them having levels between 1 and 5 ppm, 6% between 5 and 10 ppm, and 8% between 10 and 12 ppm (highest amount discovers was 11.6 ppm).

The FDA tested 82 randomly chosen children targeted cosmetic goods for the presence of 1,4-dioxane in 2018; these products contained chemicals that have been linked to 1,4 dioxane contamination. Only 2 out of the 82 tested goods (or around 2%) had 1,4-dioxane concentrations higher than 10 ppm. Comparison to past results is inaccurate since this poll, unlike earlier studies, focused exclusively on products sold to children and utilized a newer and more sensitive detection technology.

Since the 1980s, FDA has advised manufacturers to reduce 1,4-dioxane by using the "vacuum stripping" method. The FDA will continue to keep an eye on data pertaining to 1,4-dioxane and its concentrations in cosmetics. If the FDA found a health threat, it would inform the industry and the public and assess the best course of action to safeguard consumer health and welfare from sub-standard cosmetics.

CHAPTER 10

Sun Protection and Sunscreens

Sun Damage

Repetitive cumulative exposure of the skin to the sun can lead to short-term and long-term changes in the structure of the skin. The short-term changes result in erythema (reddening) of the skin commonly termed as sunburn. Sunburn is inflamed, painful skin that feels hot to the touch. It often appears within a few hours of being in the sun too long. Erythema is followed by activation of melanocytes which increases their rate of melanin production darkening the skin appearance referred to as tanning. Sunburn symptoms often appear within a few hours after sun exposure. Within a few days, the body may start to heal itself by peeling the damaged skin's top layer. Bad sunburn may take several days to heal. Any lingering changes in skin color usually go away with time. Sunburn is more commonly seen in white-skinned people and young people with sensitive skin. The long-term effects of repeated exposure include irreversible loss of skin elasticity and may lead to the development of skin cancers, both melanomas and non-melanomas.

The extent of skin damage depends on the duration of exposure, seasonal variations in incident sunrays intensity, geographical location, and host dependent factors including age, skin colour, immune status and behavioral factors. The damage includes premature aging of skin (photoaging), precancerous skin lesions and skin cancer. The results of photoaging include weakening of connective tissues, which reduces the skin's strength and elasticity, deep wrinkles, dry, rough skin, fine red veins on the cheeks, nose and ears, freckles, mostly on the face and shoulders and dark or discolored spots (macules) on the face, back of hands, arms, chest and upper back – also called solar lentigines. Precancerous skin lesions are rough, scaly patches in areas that have been damaged by the sun. These often found on the sun-exposed areas of the head, face, neck and hands of people whose skin burns easily in the sun. These patches can evolve into skin cancer. They're also called actinic keratoses and solar keratoses. Excessive sun exposure, even without sunburn, increases the risk of skin cancer, such as melanoma. It can damage the DNA of skin cells. Skin cancer develops mainly on areas of the body most exposed to sunlight, including the scalp, face, lips, ears, neck, chest, arms, hands, legs and back. Some types of skin cancer appear as a small growth or a sore that bleeds easily, crusts over, heals and then reopens. With melanoma, an existing mole may change, or a new, suspicious-looking mole may grow.

Ultravoilet radiation

Sunrays consist of an array of wavelength ranges that vary in frequency and their energy profiles. The electromagnetic spectrum of sun is made up of cosmic rays, gamma rays, X-rays, UV rays, microwaves and radio waves in decreasing order of energy. Among these cosmic, gamma and X-rays are effectively filtered out of the earth's atmosphere and therefore present no potential for causing harm. The UV rays can penetrate the earth's atmosphere as can the rest of the lower energy spectrums. However, microwaves and radio waves do not cause skin damage.

UV radiation has broad spectrum, ranging from 40 to 400 nm (30–3 eV), which is divided into Vacuum UV (40–190 nm), Far UV (190–220 nm), UVC (220–290 nm), UVB (290–320 nm), and UVA (320–400 nm; (Figure 10.1), of which the latter two are medically important. There are two distinct subtypes of UVA radiation (i) Short-wave UVA (320–340 nm) and long-wave UVA (340–400 nm), the latter constituting most of UVA radiation. The amount of exposure to UVA usually remains constant, whereas UVB exposure occurs more in the summer.

The effects of UVA manifest usually after a long duration of exposure, even if the doses are low. UVA radiation damages skin by penetrating into the layers of skin and producing reactive oxygen resulting in acute and chronic changes. UVA upregulates the formation of matrix metalloproteinase, the enzyme that degrades the matrix protein's elastin and collagen, which if not prevented, can result in marked reduction in skin elasticity and increased wrinkling. UVA radiation can induce polymorphous light eruptions in sensitive skin. UVA can also cause exacerbation of cutaneous lupus erythematoses, whereas solar urticaria can be caused by both UVA and UVB radiation. UVA impairs the antigen presenting cell activity of the epidermal cells and thereby causes immune suppression, thus contributing to the growth of skin cancer due to the damage caused to DNA of human melanocyte. Thus, UVA radiation can cause nuclear and mitochondrial DNA damage, gene mutations and skin cancer, dysregulation of enzymatic chain reactions, immune suppression, lipid peroxidation (membrane damage), and photoallergic and phototoxic effects. UVB radiation can also cause acute changes, such as pigmentation and sunburn, and chronic changes, such as immune-suppression and photocarcinogenesis. Both UVA and UVB radiation can cause sunburn, photoaging reactions, erythema, and inflammation.

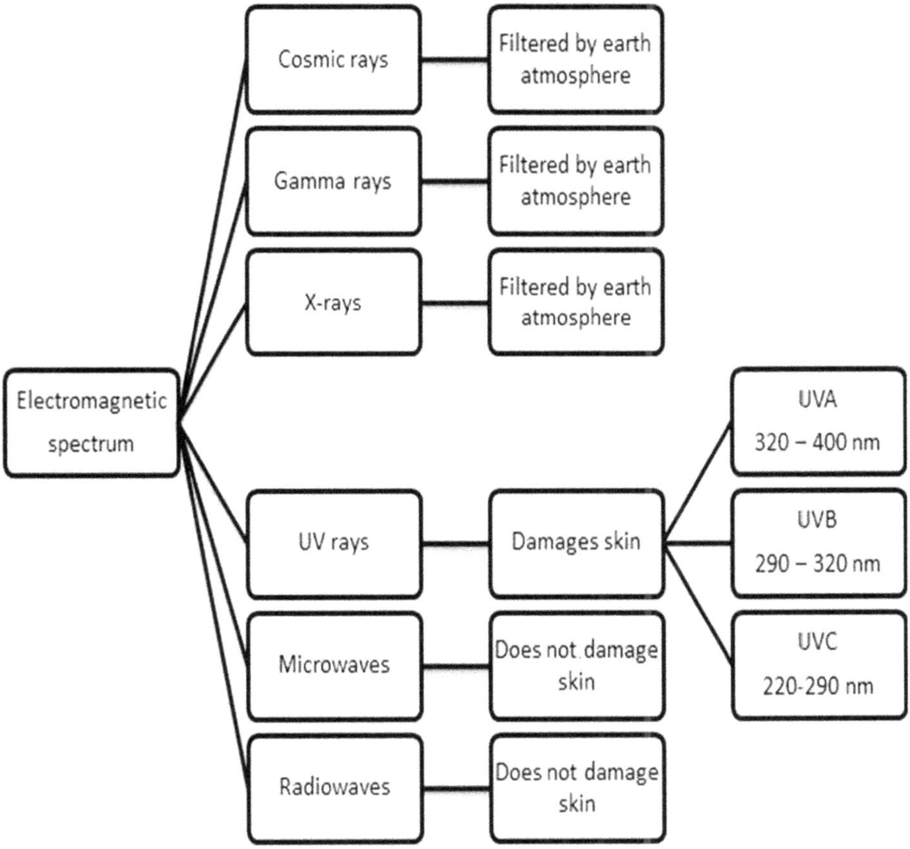

Figure 10.1: The electromagnetic spectrum of ultravoilet spectrum.

Ultraviolet-induced photoaging accounts for 80–90 % of visible skin ageing. The UVA radiation penetrates into the skin and reaches the dermis (Figure 10.2); provoking several damages such as immediate and delayed tanning reactions, loss of collagen, diminution in the quantity of blood vessels, alteration of the connective tissue of the dermis and skin photosensitization. Melanin and haemoglobin are the main absorbers of UVA.

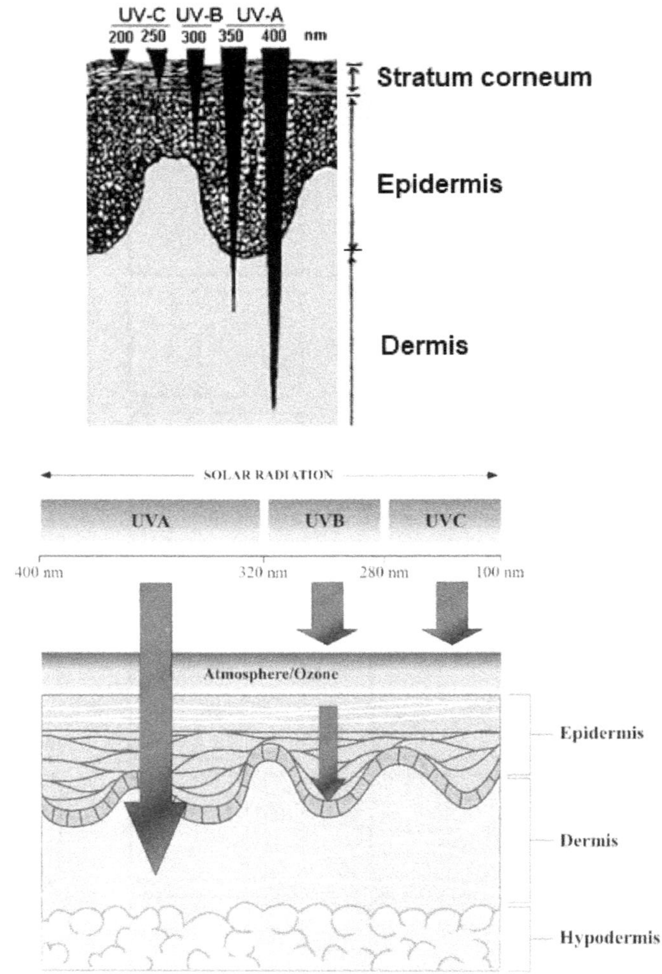

Figure 10.2: Penetration ability of various UV rays.

The UVB region is highly active biologically but cannot penetrate beyond the superficial skin layers. It is responsible for the tanning and immediate damage to the skin, which results in erythema or sunburn. In addition to these short-term effects it enhances skin ageing and significantly promotes the development of skin cancer. Most solar UVB is filtered by the atmosphere. UVC is the most damaging type of UV radiation. However, it is completely filtered by the atmosphere and does not reach the earth's surface. Although the UVC region has desirable properties such as germicidal activity, this spectral band also has been reported to be erythemogenic, mutagenic and carcinogenic.

Environmental factors affecting UV exposure

(i) Time of year and time of day

UV levels vary with the height of the sun in the sky and are highest in mid-latitudes during the summer months during the 4 h period around solar noon. During these times the sun's rays take the most direct path to earth. In contrast, during early morning or late afternoon the sun's rays pass at a greater angle through the atmosphere. Much more UV radiation is absorbed and less reaches the Earth.

(ii) Latitude

UV levels are higher closer to the equator as the rays have a shorter distance to travel through the atmosphere and therefore less of the harmful UV radiation can be absorbed.

(iii) Altitude

With increasing altitude, less atmosphere is available to absorb UV radiation. With every 1000 m in altitude, UV levels increase by approximately 10 %.

(iv) Ground reflection and clouds

Many surfaces reflect UV radiation and add to the overall UV levels experienced. While grass, soil or water reflect less than 10 % of incident UV radiation, sand reflects about 15 %, and sea foam about 25 %. Fresh snow is a particularly good reflector and almost doubles the UV exposure. Recurring incidences of snow blindness or photokeratitis in skiers emphasize that UV protective measures must take ground reflection into account. UV levels are highest under cloudless skies, and cloud cover generally reduces UV exposure. However, light or thin clouds have little effect and may even enhance the UV levels because of scattering giving sensitive person sunburn on a day with high UV levels.

(v) Ozone

Ozone is a particularly effective absorber of UV radiation. As the ozone layer gets thinner, the protective filter activity of the atmosphere is progressively reduced. Consequently, the people and the environment are exposed to higher levels of UV radiation, especially UVB. Ozone depletion is caused by human-made chemicals released into the atmosphere and will continue until the use of chlorine and bromine compounds is drastically reduced. International agreements, in particular the Montreal Protocol, are gradually succeeding in phasing out the production of ozone-depleting substances. However, the long life span of the chemicals already released will cause ozone depletion problems to persist for many years to come. A full recovery of the ozone level is not expected until 2050. The incidence of different types of skin cancer has been growing dramatically over the past decades. Some people claim that this is due to ozone depletion and enhanced levels of UV. However, most evidence now suggests that the major cause for the increased cancer rates is altered behaviour rather than ozone depletion. More outdoor activities and altered sunbathing habits often result in excessive UV exposure. Raised awareness and changes in life-style are urgently needed to alter ongoing trends. Ozone levels vary over the year and even across the day.

Photoprotection

Photoprotection is indicated for the reduction of UV radiation-induced skin damage and skin cancers. Photoprotection involves both primary and secondary protective factors. Primary factors are sunscreens; these include physical barriers that reflect and scatter light and chemical barriers that absorb light. Secondary factors include antioxidants, osmolytes, and DNA repair enzymes, which help to limit skin damage by disturbing the photochemical cascade that occurs with UV sunlight. In daily life, UV exposure is unavoidable; therefore sunscreen should be used regularly. Regular use of sunscreens has been shown to reduce the number of actinic or percutaneous keratosis and solar elastosis. Photoprotective agents protect the skin by preventing and minimizing the damaging effects of UV rays. They can be used as sunblock, which is opaque when applied over the skin and blocks a higher percentage of light as compared to sunscreens, which are translucent and require frequent reapplication for optimum efficacy. With the increased incidence in skin cancer cases, such as squamous and basal cell carcinomas, reported worldwide, use of photoprotective agents has increased over the years. There has been symptomatic improvement and inhibition of re-occurrence of these conditions when photoprotective agents are used either therapeutically or prophylactically, indicating the need to promote and regularize their application.

Sunscreens

Sunscreen, also known as suncream, sunblock or suntan lotion, is a lotion, cream, spray, gel, foam, stick or other topical product that absorbs or reflects some of the sun's ultraviolet radiation and thus helps protect against sunburn. Early civilizations used a variety of plant products to help protect the skin from sun damage. For example, ancient Greeks used olive oil for this purpose, and ancient Egyptians used extracts of rice, jasmine, and lupine plants whose products are still used in skin care today. Zinc oxide paste has also been popular for skin protection for thousands of years. Early synthetic sunscreens were first used in 1928, and the first major commercial product was brought to market in 1936, introduced by the founder of L'Oreal. The purpose of sunscreen products is to prevent or minimize the harmful effects of solar radiation or to assist in tanning the skin without any harmful effects. Suncare products available in market are in different form formats like cream, lotion, spray sunscreen, baby & kids sunscreen, sunless tanning, sports sunscreen, sunblock, sweat free sun block, sweat & water resistant sunblock, oil free sunscreen, sunscreen souffl'e, matte look sun screen, hydrophobic sun block and sunscreen stick. There are products for after sun exposure too, like soothing after sun gel.

Now-a-days, these products are marketed with herbal/natural actives. Many products have ingredients like Comfrey plant extract for anti-irritation properties, Sandalwood, Pineapple extract, Aloe vera juice, Seaweed extracts, Grape seed extract etc. Some plants have natural defenses against the damaging rays of the sun. For example the single-cell alga called *Dunaliella bardawil* that thrives in the Dead sea and the Sinai desert makes its own sunscreen. Scientists at the Weizmann Institute of Science in Israel isolated the protein that this plant produces when sunlight gets too intense. The protein acts as a solar deflector by funnelling the light. Search for many such harmless natural sunscreens is going on to meet the growing needs of consumer.

Classification of sunscreens

Ultraviolet filters also referred to as sunscreens, interfere directly with the incident solar radiation through absorption, reflection or dispersion of energy. They are classified into two categories based on their mechanism of action; organic or chemical sunscreens and inorganic or mineral-based sunscreens. Organic/chemical sunscreens absorb UV light and convert it into heat energy that is then released from the skin. Typical examples of chemical sunscreens include octisalate and avobenzone. The organic sunscreens afford better aesthetics upon application and are therefore more widely accepted, however they carry the potential for systemic absorption therefore sensitivity and untoward effects are more common with this group of sunscreens. Inorganic/mineral sunscreens also referred to as sunblocks act by reflecting and scattering the UV light thereby protecting the skin. Common examples of mineral sunscreens include titanium dioxide and zinc oxide. The FDA regulates sunscreen as an over-the-counter medication. Currently, 16 UV filters are listed, 14 organic filters, and two non-organic filters, including zinc oxide and titanium dioxide. The FDA has changed its guidelines to address broad-spectrum sunscreen use, which involves UVA and UVB coverage; water resistance, to indicate the time duration the sunscreen is effective; and sun protection factor (SPF). SPF-15 or higher is the recommended blocking strength, and manufacturers can label it as reducing the risk of skin cancer and early skin aging

Figure 10.3 represents an elaborative classification of sunscreens wherein the sunscreens are classified as topical and systemic and further the topical sunscreens are sub-classified into organic and inorganic. The topical organic sunscreens are classified into three categories based on the type of radiation blocked.

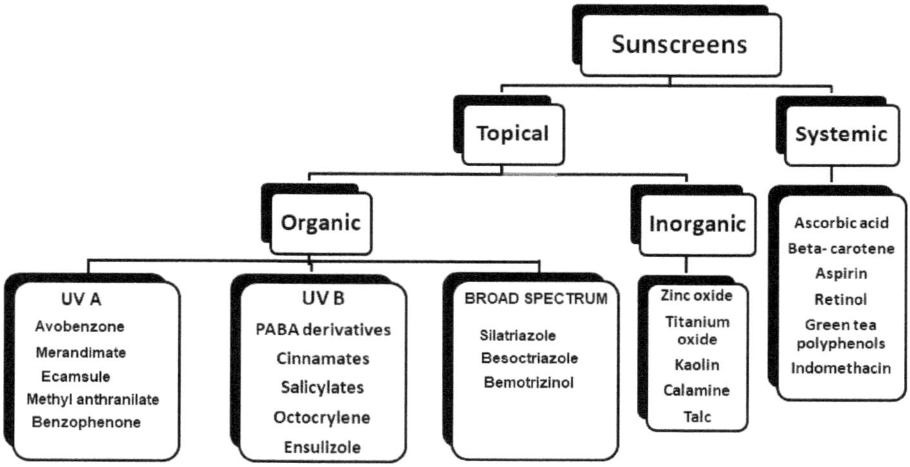

Figure 10.3: Classification of sunscreens.

Topical Sunscreens

The desirable chemical attributes of a topical sunscreen include; inertness, non-irritant, photostability, and compatibility with other ingredients. Physical characteristics include low viscosity to promote good spreadability, aesthetic appeal, small particle size, waterproof capability, appropriate solubility and non-odorous. Functional attributes include the ability to afford protection across a wide range of wavelength and limited systemic absorption through the skin to minimize sensitization. The products should also be readily available, inexpensive and contaminant free. The topical sunscreens can be classified into inorganic/mineral sunscreens and organic sunscreens. The classified description is in the following text.

A. Physical (inorganic/mineral) Sunscreens (Sunblocks)

Inorganic/mineral compounds were first used in cosmetics such as foundations, eye shadows, powders, pencils and as whitening agents. Titanium di oxide was reported as sunscreening agent in the year 1952. The ability of a mineral to block light may be determined by several physical properties: the refractive index, size of the particles, dispersion in the base and film thickness. The reflectant property of a sunblock is determined by the expression: Np/Nm, where Np is the refractive index of the pigment in question, and Nm is the refractive index of the adjacent medium, air in this circumstance. As the refractive index of air is almost constant, thus but by choosing a pigment with high refractive index, it is possible to increase reflection. Table 10.1 lists the refractive index of several inorganic pigments.

Table 10.1: Refractive index of inorganic mineral pigments.

Pigment	Refractive index	Pigment	Refractive index
Aluminium oxide	1.8	Talc	1.6
Barium sulphate	1.6	TiO_2 (rutile)	2.9
Calcium carbonate	1.5	TiO_2 (anastase)	2.7
Fumed silica	1.5	Yellow iron oxide	2.1
Magnesium oxide	1.7	Zinc oxide	2.0
Mica	1.6	Zirconium oxide	2.2

A sunblock which has strong reflecting ability is opaque on the skin and is white. Efforts to improve cosmetic acceptability have included adding brown color such as iron oxide (Fe_2O_3) pigments, which not only imparts better color, but also efficiently absorbs scattered light, thereby improving the effectiveness of the sunblock. The particle size of the pigment is also critical determinant of sunblock function. Fresnel's rules state that optimal reflection occurs when the diameter of the particle equals half the wavelength ($D = \lambda/2$). This expression helps in selecting the correct particle size. Standard TiO_2 particles of the cosmetic grade (rutile) are 200 – 500 nm in size, hence have excellent ability to reflect light, but are opaque, thus appearing white on the skin. Decreasing the size of particles leads to transparency to visible light, but reduces UV reflection and scattering. Reflection from the surface of microparticles is minimal. The maximum UVA and UVB opacities occur at different particle sizes, but by careful selection of intermediate particle size it is possible to provide good UV protection as well as cosmetic acceptability. Table 10.2 lists the advantages and disadvantages of sunblocks.

Table 10.2: Advantages and disadvantages of sunblocks (physical sunscreens).

Advantages	Disadvantages
• Offers protection against both UVA and UVB rays and is naturally broad spectrum • Protects from the sun as soon as it is applied. • Lasts longer when in direct UV light (but NOT when doing physical activities that cause the skin to get wet or sweat) • Less likely to cause a stinging irritation on the skin, making it better for sensitive skin • Better for those with heat-activated skin (like those with rosacea and redness) since it deflects the heat and energy given off by the sun away from the skin • Less likely to be pore-clogging, making it ideal for blemish-prone skin types • Longer shelf life	• Can rub off, sweat off and rinse off easily, meaning more frequent reapplication when outdoors is needed • May leave a whitish cast on the skin, making some formulas incompatible for medium to dark skin tones • May be too chalky and opaque for daily use under makeup • Can create an occlusive film, which results in increased perspiration during physical activities and, therefore, causes it to wear off more quickly • Can be thicker, which will require more effort to rub in • Can cause white drips to show on the skin when sweating • Can be less protective if not applied generously and accurately since UV light can get between the sunscreen molecules and get into the skin

Combinations of TiO_2 with other chemicals can lead to a marked reduction of UV transmission, both UVA and UVB. Sunscreens are now available with TiO_2 and ZnO alone, without organic chemicals, appearing to afford good protection across all wavelengths of UV. Combination of pigment particles gives broad spectrum protection. Increasing concentrations of TiO_2 give protection factors of 1.5± 2 for every 1% of sunblock used. However, with concentrations over 5%, sunblocks begin to look opaque on the skin.

Physical blockers have the added benefit of being water resistant. Not only do the pigmentary sunblocks reflect and scatter UV and visible light, but UV absorption may also occur. TiO_2 is photochemically active and particles of 10±100 nm absorb UV radiation in the UVB and UVA ranges. The rutile form of TiO_2 used in sunblocks is much less photochemically active compared with the anatase form. A further concern is that reactive species generated within the sunblock by sun exposure might degrade other ingredients within the sunscreen formulation leading to a less effective product. Degradation of the sunscreen formulation can be prevented if sunscreens are assessed properly not only for SPF and UVA protection but also for photostability.

The pigments can be micronized to get micropigments. Micropigmentary TiO_2 was first used in 1989 in commercial sunblocks and micronized ZnO was introduced in 1991. Particles of one-twentieth the size of conventional TiO_2 and ZnO are dispersed in a base, using technology to ensure even dispersion of the particles in a stable manner. It has been shown that micropigments may penetrate skin and hence cellular damage might occur. Table 10.3 enlists the positive and negative attributes of micropigment mineral sunblocks.

Table 10.3: Attributes of micropigment mineral sunblocks.

Positive attributes	Negative aspects
Non-allergenic	Relatively messy
Broad UV protection	Disaggregate easily
Relatively invisible	Visible pallor on dark skin
No clinical evidence of photoactivity	Photochemically active *in vitro*
	May penetrate skin

These micropigmentary sunblocks effectively block UV radiation by reflection and scattering. UV absorption may occur with microparticles. Historically, these products have behaved as inert agents on the skin. More research is required to demonstrate whether there are any *in vivo* adverse effects and whether sunscreens incorporating micropigments are more or less photostable compared with organic sunscreens.

A. Chemical Sunscreens (Sunscreens)

Sunscreens have been used to mitigate the harmful effects of the sun on the skin since medieval time. In ancient Egypt, women applied various natural products as sunscreens. These include; tirmis, yasmeen, zaytoon, sobar, aquatic lotus oil, almond oil, calcite powder and clay, rice bran extracts among many others. The Greek and other communities living in the Mediterranean were aware of the harmful effects of the sun rays and hence designed special hats to shield themselves from the harmful rays. There is documentary evidence of the use of oil in the Greek Olympics. In modern times commercial use of sunscreens was first reported in 1928 in the USA following the introduction of an emulsion containing benzyl cinnamate and benzyl salicylate. Formulations containing phenyl salicylate appeared in Australia in the early 1930s. Quinine oleate was used in the USA in the mid-1930s. Para aminobenzoic acid was patented in 1943, and numerous sunscreens containing PABA followed this. The US army developed specifications for sunscreens in the 1950s. Table 10.4 lists the advantages and disadvantages of chemical sunscreens.

Table 10.4: Advantages and disadvantages of chemical sunscreens.

Advantages	Disadvantages
• Tends to be thinner and, therefore, spreads more easily on the skin, making it more wearable for daily use • Less is needed to protect the skin because there is no risk of no spaces between the sunscreen molecules after application • Formula is easier to add additional treatment ingredients, such as peptides and enzymes, which offer other skin benefits	• Can possibly cause an increase in existing brown spots and discoloration due to a higher internal skin temperature. • Requires about 20 min after application before it begins to work • Increased chance of irritation and stinging (especially for those who have dry skin with a damaged moisture barrier) due to the multiple ingredients combined in order to achieve broad spectrum UVA and UVB protection • The higher the SPF (such as formulas of SPF 50 or greater), the higher the risk of irritation for sensitive skin types • The protection it offers gets used up more quickly when in direct UV light, so reapplication must be more frequent • Increased chance of redness for rosacea-prone skin types because it changes UV rays into heat which can exacerbate flushing • May clog the pores for oily skin types • Can cause stinging if it drips into the eyes from sweat

Chemical sunscreens contain organic (carbon-based) compounds that undergo a chemical reaction and work by changing UV rays into heat, then releasing that heat from the skin. They are often referred to as *chemical or organic absorbers*. Based on their structure, the chemical agents commonly used as sunscreens can be broadly classified into four categories as shown in Table 10.5.

Table 10.5: Chemical agents commonly used as sunscreens.

Class	Chemical agent	Attribute
Aminobenzoic acid derivatives	Para amino benzoic acid Padimate O- Methylanthranilite	Absorbs UVA radiation only Extensive UVB protection Extensive UVB protection, partial UVA protection
Benzophenones	Avobenzone Dioxybenzone Oxybenzone Sulisonbenzone	Extensive UVA protection, limited UVB protection Partial UVA protection, extensive UVB protection Partial UVA protection, extensive UVB protection Absorbs most UVB radiation, some UVA radiation
Cinnamates	Cinoxate Octocryline Octyl methoxy cinnamate	Limited UVA protection extensive UVB coverage Extensive UVB and limited UVA protection Extensive UVB and limited UVA protection
Salicylates	Homosalate Octyl salicylate Trolamine salicylate	UVB absorption only UVB absorption only Extensive UV B protection
Triazones	Ethyl hexyl triazone Diethylhexyl butamido triazone	Effective UVB protection with a peak protection at 314 nm UVA and UVB protection with a peak protection at 310 nm.

Based on the capability to block either UVA or UVB radiation or both, the chemical sunscreens can be classified in three categories. The description is given below

UVA Blockers

Typical benzophenones absorb mostly UVB; however, oxybenzone is considered a broad spectrum absorber as it can absorb UVA II as well. It is the most commonly used benzophenone. However, out of all the sunscreens, oxybenzone has the greatest likelihood of inducing contact or photo contact dermatitis. Oxybenzone is not considered photostable, and although not scientifically proven yet, there is a concern about carcinogenic and endocrine adverse effects. Other FDA-listed benzophenones include sulisobenzone and dioxybenzone.

Anthranilates are very weak UVB and UVA filters and are less effective than benzophenones. As a result, clinicians rarely use them. Avobenzones are considered broad-spectrum and have high efficacy against UVA I (>380 nm); however, they are very photo-unstable and lose from 50% to 90% of their particles after 1 hour of UV exposure. There are also reports that they degrade the UV filter octinoxate. UV absorbers such as octocrylene, benzophenones, salicylates, camphor derivatives, and micronized zinc oxide or titanium dioxide are used in combination to increase photostability. Ecamsule contains terephthalyidene dicamphor sulfonic acid, a very photostable product that is water-resistant with low systemic absorption. In animal studies, it prevented UVA-induced photoaging.

UVB Blockers

Aminobenzoates are the most potent UVB absorber but do not absorb UVA. Their use has declined due to para-aminobenzoic acid (PABA) sensitivity. PABA is a very effective UVB filter; however, it was reportedly the most common photoallergen and contact allergen. For this reason, it has limited use in sunscreen. Padimate O is the most commonly used PABA derivative; it has a good safety profile and is an effective UVB filter.

Cinnamates have replaced PABA as the next most potent UVB absorber and include octinoxate (OMC) and cinoxate. Octinoxate is the most commonly used UVB filter in the United States. It is not as potent a UVB absorber as padimate O; for this reason, other UVB absorbers are used in combination to increase the SPF. Octinaxate is not very photostable and degrades in the presence of sunlight after a short period. Cinnoxate is a less common choice.

Salicylates are used in high concentrations as they are weak UVB absorbers. They are also used to increase the effect of other UVB filters. Two salicylates that are FDA listed are homosalate and octisalate. They function to decrease the photodegradation of other UV filters, such as oxybenzone and avobenzone. A water-soluble salicylate is trolamine salicylate. Octocrylene is a very safe chemical associated with a decreased likelihood of irritation, phototoxicity, and photoallergic potential. When combined with other UV absorbers, it can increase the SPF formula. Ensulizole is a pure UVB filter and does nothing that affects UVA. It is a water-soluble compound commonly used in cosmetics for a lighter, less oily feel. Camphor derivatives are not FDA-listed but are moderately effective UVB filters. A camphor derivative that is also a broad UVA filter is terephthalyidene dicamphor sulfonic acid.

Broad spectrum sunscreens

Broad-spectrum sunscreens include methylene-bis-benzotriazolyl tetramethylbutylphenol (MBBT) and bis- ethylhexyloxyphenol methoxyphenyl triazine (BEMT). MBBT is advantageous as it is a large molecule that decreases the likelihood of systemic absorption or endocrine effects. It works as a combination of organic and inorganic filters, ultimately absorbing, scattering, and reflecting UV radiation. It decreases UVA transmission more than UVB. BEMT also does not affect the endocrine system and is photostable.

Systemic sunscreens

These are sunscreens that are absorbed into the body and accumulate in the skin affording protection from the UV rays. The use of systemic sunscreens for daily routine is minimal; as such the focus of this article is on topical sunscreens as these predominate in the market.

The reapplications of a sunscreen combined with the need to apply 2 mg/cm^2 of the product to ensure proper photoprotection are not always feasible. With this in mind, systemic sunscreens were developed. Beta-carotene can be prescribed in a dose of 0.5–1 mg/kg which comes up to 30–40 mg in total. Other alternatives are antimalarials, ascorbic acid, α-tocopherols (i.e., Vitamins A, C, and E), retinol, selenium, green tea polyphenols, PABA, antihistamines, aspirin, indomethacin, and corticosteroids. Antioxidants are less potent than sunscreens in preventing sunburn.

Green tea (*Camelia olifera*) polyphenols are systemic sunscreens. When ingested, these polyphenols help protect the skin against damage from the UV radiation that causes sunburn.

Polypodium leucotomos (PL), a South American species of fern, is a natural mixture of phytochemicals having powerful antioxidant and photoprotective properties. These include acids such as ferulic, caffeic, vanillic, p-coumaric, 3, 4-dihydroxybenzoic, 4-hydroxybenzoic, 4-hydroxycinnamic, 4-hydroxycinnamoyl-quinic, and chlorogenic. The commercially available PL capsules contain 240 mg of the extract and often additionally contain Vitamins C, E, and lycopene. The capsules have to be taken 30 min before sun exposure. With regular sun exposure, two capsules to be taken daily – one in morning and one mid-day, while for intense sun exposure, four capsules have to be taken – two in morning and two mid-day, 3 h after first dose. However, commercial capsules of PL contain gluten so should not be consumed by gluten-sensitive people.

The effectiveness of many of the agents in preventing UVB-induced sunburn reaction is mostly anecdotal and has not been evaluated. Some are obviously effective, but to a limited extent (e.g., melanin, urocanic acid, certain antioxidants). The three oral photoprotective agents of limited effectiveness are beta-carotene, chloroquine, and certain psoralens. Beta-carotene is recommended for the amelioration of photosensitivity reactions caused by visible radiation (400 to 760 nm) in patients with erythropoietic protoporphyria (EPP), erythropoietic porphyria (EP), and variegate porphyria. Only beta-carotene, which absorbs radiation in the visible spectrum of light (360 to 500 nm) with a maximum absorption at 450 and 475 nm, has been shown to be partially, if not totally, effective as a systemic photoprotective agent, particularly in patients with EPP who are extremely sensitive to visible radiation. Oral ingestion of synthetic betacarotene be regulated to maintain blood carotene levels between 600 and 800/g/100 ml (usually a dose of 120 to 180 mg/day for adults). In addition, the concomitant topical application of UVB and UVA absorbing sunscreens is also helpful, especially when the patient is likely to be exposed to solar radiation for periods longer than 1 h. Beta-carotene, when applied topically or given orally, is not an effective agent for preventing sunburn reaction induced by UVB radiation.

Antimalarials (chloroquine) have been used to treat many diverse entities other than malaria including lupus erythematosus (LE), polymorphous light eruptions (PMLE), solar urticaria, and porphyria cutanea tarda (PCT). The potential therapeutic benefits must be weighed against the potential toxicity of the drug. The recommended maintenance dosage is 200 mg/day for hydroxychloroquine, 250 mg/day for chloroquine, and 100 to 300 µg/day for quinacrine. Patients should not remain on antimalarials indefinitely, and as their disease improves, the drug should be discontinued. Antimalarials as topical sunscreen have also been tried. These drugs bind avidly to melanin and are deposited along the uveal tract and retinal pigment epithelium where they can remain for years. These drugs have been shown to inhibit a variety of enzyme systems, to be potent inhibitors of histamine, and to have anti-inflammatory properties. When used for cutaneous LE, PMLE, or solar urticaria, they are usually administered only when other measures have failed. However, a patient with the extensive facial scarring disease, LE, might be started on antimalarials. The recommended dosage is 250 mg/day for chloroquine, 200 to 400 rag/day for hydroxychloroquine, and 100 to 200 mg/day for quinacrine. The danger of retinopathy due to these agents can be avoided or at least recognized and minimized when the patients are examined regularly at 4- to 6-month intervals during the therapy.

The use of oral psoralens (e.g., 8-methoxypsoralen and 4,5',8-trimethylpsoralen) may help certain patients achieve an increase in tolerance to sunlight only when the administration of the drug is followed by exposure of the skin to sunlight or to UVA radiation emitted by artificial sources. In blonde or freckled persons with skin types I to III, and even in albino patients and vitiligo patients (idiopathic leukoderma) who suffer painful reactions to sunlight, 8-methoxypsoralen (8-MOP) can aid in increasing resistance to solar damage. Certain patients with polymorphic photodermatosis may also benefit by the indirect protective action of 8-MOP. This protective action appears to be related to an increase in the thickness of the epidermis (epidermal hyperplasia) and increased formation and melanization of melanosomes by the pigment-producing cells, the melanocytes.

Newer Sunscreen Approaches

Organic particulate sunscreens

Organic particulate sunscreens that mostly absorb UV light like organic chemical compounds, but contain multiple chromophores that reflect and scatter a fraction of light like inorganic particulates (eg. Bisoctrisole, marketed as Tinosorb M). Tinosorb® M is the first organic UV filter using microfine particle technology and acts as both a micropigment and an UV absorber. This product is a white dispersion, with a pH value of 10.5-12.0. The mode of action is about 90% by absorption and 10% by scattering. It dissolves poorly in both oil and water phase, and is applied as invisible particle. When formulated into a sunscreen, it has minimal skin penetration and it shows no estrogenic effects in vitro. It is approved in the EU and other parts of the world with maximum authorized concentration of 10% in cosmetics.

Polymeric sunscreens

Many molecular sunscreens penetrate into the skin causing photoallergies, phototoxic reactions and skin irritation. To overcome the deficiencies of sunscreen agent blends which are quickly removable upon contact with fresh or salt water, polymeric sunscreening agents have been proposed wherein the sunscreening agent is chemically bound in the polymeric backbone of the compound, thus making the compound more skin substantive.

Hybrid sunscreens

Effectiveness of organic sunscreens is limited by phototoxicity and degradation. Both of which can be significantly reduced by encapsulation in hollow particles or covalent incorporation into the solid structure of particles. New hybrid organic/inorganic polysilsesquioxane –silica particles have been reported as sunscreens. 2-Ethylhexyl salicylate was physically encapsulated in hollow silica nanoparticles prepared by oil-in-water microemulsion polymerization.

Encapsulated sunscreens

The purpose of encapsulating sunscreening agents is to separate different components to avoid incompatibility and the undesirable properties of the active sunscreening agent such as contact and photo-contact allergic dermatitis can be masked. Encapsulation also allows the use of the oil soluble actives in oil-free systems with a greater range of solubility. It transforms the organic sunscreen into particulates and isolates the sunscreen from skin. Finally, encapsulation produces a delivery system that decreases the amount of active needed and still maintains its efficacy. The ability to vary physical properties and the surface chemical properties through the manipulation of matrix composition can provide much greater flexibility when incorporating organic sunscreens even in to the most difficult formulations, whether new or existing.

As sunscreen preparations are often applied on large skin areas, even low penetration rates can cause significant amount of chemical UV absorber to enter the body. Therefore, sun-protecting preparations need to achieve a controlled release. For this purpose, microspheres have been used. In addition, it has been found that microspheres also act as physical sunscreens on their own, i.e. they have the ability of scattering or reflecting incoming UV radiations. Sunspheres are styrene/acrylate copolymers that do not absorb UV irradiation but enhance the effectiveness of the active sunscreen ingredients. The sunsphere polymer beads are filled with water, which migrates out of the particle, leaving behind tiny air-filled spheres, which have a lower refractive index (1.0) than the dried sunscreen film (1.4–1.5). As a result, scattering of UV radiation occurs, increasing the probability of contact with the active UV filters in the sunscreen. Sunspheres are also available in a powder form and can boost SPF by 50%–70% making it possible to reduce the concentration of active ingredients. Solid lipid nanoparticles were introduced as the new generation of carriers for cosmetics, especially for UV blockers, for the use on human skin and/or hair. These systems can be incorporated into gels, creams, liquids, ointments that release sunscreen depending on their temperature, moisture, friction, volatility of the entrapped ingredients or time.

Plant based sunscreens

In comparison to physical and chemical sunscreens, herbal sunscreens are mild, biodegradable and have low toxicity profile. The paste of Indian aloe (*Aloe barbadensis*), commonly known as the aloe vera, is an effective sunscreen. Sandalwood, known for its cooling properties, is an herbal sunscreen. Its diluted paste is applied on the skin for photoprotection. Rice bran oil has some anti-oxidizing as well as sunscreen properties and is used in sunscreen products and hair conditioners. *Ocimum sanctum* also contains polyphenols/flavonoids that can be effectively incorporated in cosmetic preparations as a potent sunscreen agent. Some of the other herbal sunscreens reported in literature include grapes (*Vitis vinifera*) and rhatany (*Krameria triandra*) extract.

The photosynthetic organisms that rely on sunlight for energy also need to protect themselves from the harmful UV radiation. In some plants, a thick, waxy cuticle forms a physical barrier that deflects UV rays. Recently, the wildflower meadowfoam has been investigated for sunscreening abilities. The white blossoms, meadowfoam is cultivated for its oil as an ingredient in shampoos and beauty products. The oil extraction process leaves behind lots of plant waste called seed meal, which is a rich source of glucolimnanthin, a glucosinolate compound. The derivatives of glucolimnanthin (Figure 10.4) in seed meal could offer photoprotection against UVB and may have anti-aging properties too.

(a) 3-Methoxybenzyl Isothiocyanate (Contains a 3-methoxybenzyl group attached to an isothiocyanate (-N=C=S) functional group)

(b) 3-Methoxybenzyl Nitrile (Features a 3-methoxybenzyl group with a nitrile (-C≡N) functional group

Figure 10.4: Derivatives of glucolimnanthin.

Meadowfoam seed oil is already commercially available, which suggests mass production of the glucosinolate derivatives is also completely feasible.

Marine sunscreens

Marine organisms produce chemical defense in the form of mycosporine-like amino acids (MAAs), a family of compounds that consist of a core cyclohexenimine or cyclohexenone ring with various functional groups attached. These compounds have sun protection capabilities due to their conjugated double bonds that absorb high-energy UV radiation and dissipate it as heat, similar to the organic sunscreens. MAAs are thus attractive sunscreens owing to their low molecular weight, water solubility and stability when exposed to light or heat.

Two European companies are marketing sunscreen products containing shinorine extracted from *Porphyra umbilicalis*, a type of red algae. The problem is that this species can take more than a year to grow before it can be harvested and the MAA extracted. By use of synthetic biology the shinorine synthesis genes isolated from *Fischerella* is overexpressed in *Synechocystis*, a cyanobacterium that takes only 2 weeks to yield enough shinorine to harvest. Shinorine (Figure 10.5) affords protection from UVB damage.

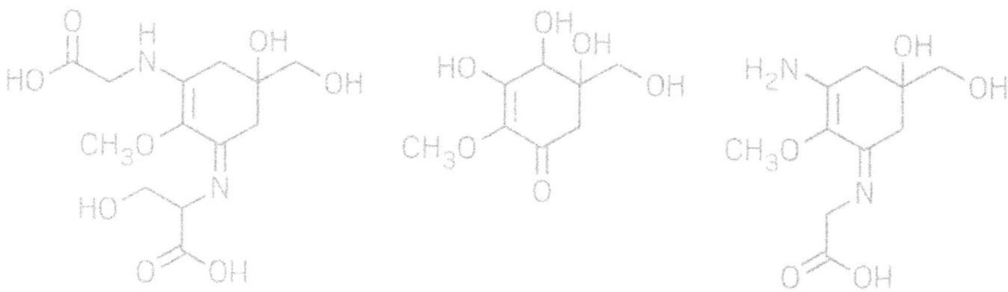

Shinorine **Gadusol** **Palythine**

Zebrafish, produces gadusol that is structurally related to MAAs and offers protection against UV-B. An MAA called palythine, has been extracted from the red algae *Chondrus yendoi* that can be harvested year-round, and offers protection from UV-A and UV-B.

Approved Sunscreening Agents

Sunscreening agents are used in some hair care products such as shampoos, conditioners and styling agents to protect against protein degradation and color loss. Currently, benzophenone-4 and ethyl hexyl methoxycinnamate are the two sunscreens most commonly used in hair products. The common sunscreens used on skin are rarely used for hair products due to their texture and weight effects. Following are the FDA allowable active ingredients in sunscreen formulations (Table 10.6).

Table 10.6: FDA approved sunscreen agents.

Active ingredient	Permitted maximum concentration (%)	Protection against	
		UV A	UV B
Oxybenzone	6 (US) 10 (AUS, EU) 5 (JP)	Yes	Yes
Menthyl anthranilate	5	Yes	No
Octyl methoxycinnamate	7.5 (US) 10 (EU, AUS) 20 (JP)	No	Yes
Sulisobenzone	5 (EU) 10 (US, AUS, JP)	Yes	Yes
Titanium dioxide	25 (US) No limit (JP)	Yes	Yes
Zinc oxide	25 (US)	Yes	Yes
Avobenzone	3 (US) 5 (EU, AUS) 10 (JP)	Yes	No

Other ingredients approved within the EU and other parts of the world that have not been included in the current FDA monograph, include those listed in Table 10.7.

Table 10.7: Sunscreens approved within EU.

UV filter	Maximum concentration
Tinosorb M	10%
Tinosorb S	10% (EU, AUS) 3% (JP)
Tinosorb A2B	10%
Benzophenone-9	10%
Uvinul T 150	5% (EU, AUS) 3% (JP)*
Parsol SLX	10%
Amiloxate	10%

Sun Protection Factor (SPF)

The concept of SPF was originally proposed by Prof. Franz J. Greiter of Austria, and subsequently adopted by the USFDA and certain pharmaceutical companies in Europe and America. It is based on the UV absorbing properties of the active ingredient(s) of a sunscreen product and is a measure of the effectiveness of that product. The SPF is defined as the ratio of the least amount of UVB energy (MED) required to produce a minimal erythema reaction through a sunscreen product film to the amount of energy required to produce the same erythema without any sunscreen application. A preparation containing 8% homo-menthyl salicylate (SPF 3.5 to 4.5) has been recommended as a standard to compare the SPF value of the test product.

$$\text{SPF} = \frac{\text{Minimal erythema dose in sunscreen protected skin}}{\text{Minimal erythema dose in non sunscreen protected skin}} \quad ....(10.1)$$

The minimal erythemal dose (MED) is defined as the lowest time interval or dosage of UV light irradiation sufficient to produce a minimal, perceptible erythema on unprotected skin. The higher the SPF, the more effective is the product in preventing sunburn. Nevertheless, it is necessary to standardize methods to determine the SPF of these products. Topical Analgesic Panel of the U.S. FDA has recommended that sunscreens be labeled for their effectiveness in terms of SPF based on MED tests performed on human skin, using either the natural sunlight or preferably a solar simulator equipped with a high-intensity xenon lamp which produces a range of wavelengths to approximate the spectral quality of sunlight in UVR spectrum.

The SPF on a package can range from as low as 2 to as high as 100 that imply the product's ability to screen or block out the sun's rays. For example, "SPF 15" means that 1/15th of the burning radiation reach the skin through the recommended thickness of sunscreen. It is a common mistake to assume that the duration of effectiveness of a sunscreen can be calculated simply by multiplying the SPF by the length of time it takes for an individual to suffer a burn without sunscreen, because the amount of sun exposure a person receives is dependent upon more than just the length of time spent in the sun.

If the skin would normally burn after 10 min in the sun, applying an SPF 15 sunscreen would allow one to stay in the sun without burning for approximately 150 minutes (a factor of 15 times longer). This is a rough estimate that depends on skin type, intensity of sunlight and amount of sunscreen used. SPF is actually a measure of protection from amount of UVB exposure and it is not meant to helps determine the duration of exposure.

For best protection, using a sunscreen of SPF 15, applying the proper amount (2 mg/cm^2 of skin, or about one ounce for full body coverage), and reapplying every 2 hours is recommended.

Most individuals under apply sunscreens, using ¼ to ½ the amount required. Using half the required amount of sunscreen only provides the square root of the SPF. So, a half application of an SPF 30 sunscreen only provides an effective SPF of 5.5 only. The SPF scale is not linear. Correspondingly, SPF 15 blocks 93% of UVB rays; SPF 30 blocks 97% of UVB rays; SPF 50 blocks 98% of UVB rays. Grossly speaking SPF 30 sunscreen affords 4% more protection than SPF 15 sunscreen. In terms of photons, SPF 15 (93% protection) allows 7 out of 100 photons through; SPF 30 (97% protection) allows 3 out of 100 photons through (Figure 10.5). Hence, while one may not be doubling the level of protection, a SPF 30 will block half the radiation that a SPF 15 would let through the skin. Most dermatologists recommend using a SPF 15 or SPF 30 sunscreen.

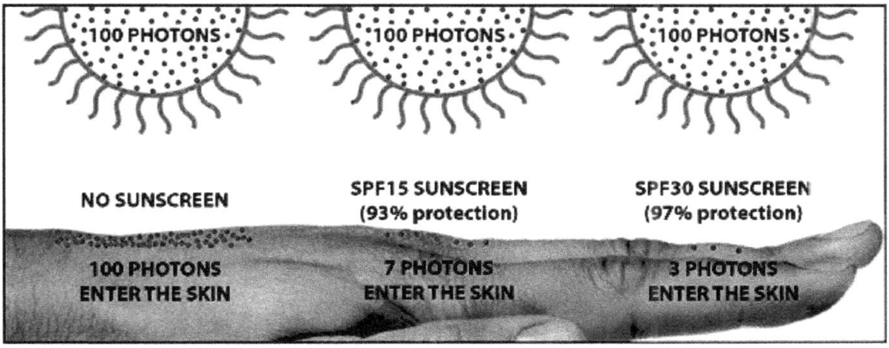

Figure 10.5: Depiction of the relation between protection and SPF.

Sunscreens with really high SPFs, such as SPF 75 or SPF 100, do not offer significantly greater protection than SPF 30 and mislead that they have more protection than they actually do. Additionally, in order to have broad spectrum protection, the UVA protection should be at least 1/3 of the UVB protection. High SPF sunscreens usually offer far greater UVB than UVA protection, thus offering a false sense of full protection. Table 10.8 classifies skin types and recommends the SPF.

Table 10.8: Skin types and recommended sunscreen protection factor.

Skin type	Sensitivity to UV	Sunburn and tanning history*	Recommended SPF
I	Very sensitive	Always burns easily; never tans	10 or more
II	Very sensitive	Always burns easily; tans minimally	10 or more
III	Sensitive	Burns moderately, tans gradually and uniformly (light brown)	8 to 10
IV	Moderately sensitive	Burns minimally; always tans well (moderate brown),	6 to 8
V	Minimally sensitive	Rarely burns, tans profusely (dark brown)	4
VI	Insensitive	Never burns; deeply pigmented (black)	None indicated

*Based on first 30 to 45 minutes' sun exposure after winter season or no sun exposure.

Products

Sunscreen can be formulated as a lotion, spray, gel or other topical product that absorbs or reflects some of the UV radiation and thus helps protect against sunburn. Skin-lightening products have sunscreen to protect lightened skin because light skin is more susceptible to sun damage than darker skin. A number of sunscreens have tanning powder to help the skin to darken or tan; however, tanning powder does not provide protection from UV rays.

Formulation of sunscreen involves four critical steps; selection of the target product design, choice of active ingredients and the delivery vehicle followed by product optimization. The primary objective of the formulation expert is to develop a product that forms a continuous film on the skin. Penetration of the organic ingredients into the skin should be minimized. Organic sunscreens are formulated as lotions and light ointments. On application, they form a thin film on the skin surface that affords UV protection. Other formulations include oils, gels, emulsions, mousses (fluid emulsions), aerosols, sticks, and powders.

Inorganic sunscreens are more difficult to formulate due to their particulate nature. Traditionally, they were formulated as creams that were sticky, oily and unpleasant to use. Nanonization has allowed spray formulations that form a translucent layer on the skin that affords protection while maintaining the aesthetics of the product. Currently no nanonized spray formulations of sunscreens have been approved for registration owing to safety concerns as these nanoparticles may be inhaled and therefore cause system toxicities. Inorganic sunscreens are formulated as pastes, emulsions, sprays, and ointments. Particle engineering approaches including micronization and nanonization of the particles are done to increase the aesthetic value of the products. The safety and convenience of the user guide the formulation approach. Any substance with potential skin irritancy and potential allergens must be avoided. Like other skin products, formulation requires the inclusion of adhering agents to promote skin adsorption as well as an appropriate vehicle into which the active substance is dispersed.

Among the challenges and concerns associated with topical sunscreens formulations involve the photostability of organic filters, broadening the effectiveness spectrum and parameters, incorporating active ingredients, improving cosmetic and sensory aspects, and individualizing vehicles. The ideal sunscreen formulation should take into consideration aspects including efficiency for the intended use, the scope of protection spectrum (UVA and UVB), safety and tolerability for topical use, stability, no staining of clothes, adequate cosmetics, pleasant fragrance, resistance to water, spreadability, high extinction coefficient, and affordable cost. Sunscreen formulations include the main sunscreen agents, excipients specific to the formulation type including an appropriate solvent or vehicle systems. The most common sunscreen actives; titanium dioxide, zinc oxide, avobenzone, benzophenone, octocrylene, and oxybenzone are used. To vary the amount of sun protection, the level of the active ingredient is adjusted. A synergy between organic and organic sunscreens demonstrates superior efficacy of products comprising of the two compared to those containing only organic or inorganic sunscreens. The FDA prescribes the maximum allowable concentration of each ingredient as well as the impurity content. It is common to find sunscreen being co-formulated with other skin products for value addition. A rationally designed and developed product enhances the compliance of the users while affording the necessary protection against the ultraviolet-induced skin damage.

Medical organizations such as the American Cancer Society, recommend the use of sunscreens because it aids in the prevention of squamous cell carcinomas. Many sunscreens do not block UVA radiation, which does not primarily cause sunburn but can increase the rate of melanoma and photodermatitis. The use of broad spectrum sunscreens can address this concern. A wide variety of different creams, dispersions, emulsions, gels, ointments, lotions, milks, sprays, tonics and hydrogels are available in the market using a variety of UV-filter systems. Many products contain broad spectrum sunscreening agents with a moderate SPF. Some products are designed to meet the requirements of a specific group of population like baby sunscreens.

The US Food and Drug Administration and The Skin Cancer Foundation recommend using sunscreen only on children older than six months; the Foundation further recommends keeping babies out of direct sun for the first six months. For children and infants above 6 months of age a sunscreen with SPF 15 or higher may be used. Using sunscreen on newborns is quite controversial. The infants' skin with a thinner stratum corneum, protects the body less effectively; thus the chemicals in sunscreen might penetrate deeper, making newborns more vulnerable to contact dermatitis (skin reactions, like rashes), allergies, or inflammation. Furthermore, the infants could very well lick the sunscreens off their fingers or any other reachable body area. That is the main reason, The Skin Cancer Foundation recommends avoiding sunscreen until baby is at least six months old.

Sunscreens and Cosmeceuticals

At present, there are moisturizers available with SPF in them. Moisturizers are typically reapplied every 10–12 h. However, the average sunscreen will need to be reapplied every 3– 4 h for maximum efficacy, especially with increased sweating as is characteristic of the tropical countries such as India. Using moisturizers like sunscreen together can be encouraged in patients in need of both; however, the patient must be advised to apply the moisturizer first. Applying sunscreen first may increase the dryness of the skin. Furthermore, application of the moisturizer will bridge any gaps in the stratum corneum and thus reduce any irritation. Concomitant use of makeup with sunscreen can be acceptable, provided the sunscreen is applied first as makeup tends to be opaque and has sun blocking properties. Thus, it is best kept outermost.

Regulatory requirements

Sunscreen is regulated as an over-the-counter medication by the US FDA and is indicated for the prevention of sunburn and skin cancer. Although the safety of mineral sunscreen filters has been established, the safety of chemical sunscreen filters has come under increased scrutiny in light of recent data from investigators at the FDA. An open-label, randomized clinical trial in 2019 demonstrated that, under maximal use conditions, chemical UV filters (avobenzone, oxybenzone, octocrylene, and ecamsule) were absorbed through the skin and achieved systemic levels exceeding the FDA threshold for safety testing (plasma concentration > 0.05 ng/mL). These were notable findings because systemic safety testing has not been previously documented for these common sunscreen ingredients. The study did not address key questions about sunscreen safety.

(i) First, what is the amount of systemic absorption after a single application of sunscreen?

(ii) Second, following the application of sunscreen, how long does it take for plasma concentrations of sunscreen ingredients to fall below the FDA threshold for safety testing?

(iii) This study also did not provide evidence of health risks associated with sunscreen absorption. However, data from animal studies and preliminary human data have previously indicated possible health risks associated with some of the sunscreen ingredients evaluated in this study, including endocrine disruption and reproductive harm.

The Sunscreen Innovation Act required the FDA to publish the rule finalizing the over-the-counter sunscreen monograph by November 26,

2019. This proposed date has now passed; thoughtful discussion will be needed to establish a reasonable compliance date to allow all stakeholders—including the FDA, sunscreen industry, scientists, the public, and most importantly, individuals who need access to sunscreen—to take necessary step.

Regulatory agencies seek to safeguard the safety and welfare of consumers using cosmetic products based on sound science. Different jurisdictions classify sunscreens as either therapeutic or cosmetic products. The USA, Australia, and Japan consider sunscreen as medicinal products subject to the strict requirement of manufacture under GMP conditions like other drugs. In the USA, cosmetic manufacturers are required to demonstrate the safety of each of the ingredients incorporated into their final products. The regulations also prescribe the maximum amounts of specific ingredients that have known toxicities while also providing a comprehensive list of substances that should not be included in the formulation. Cosmetic regulation is guided by the federal food drugs and cosmetic act of 1938. The sunscreen innovation act is the latest guide guiding the production of sunscreens and established the framework for approval of the next generation of sunscreens.

In the European Union (EU), cosmetic products are regulated under the Cosmetic Regulation (EC) No 1223/2009 which came into implementation in July 2013. The EU regulations are the first in the world to impose a complete ban on testing of cosmetic products on animals. Further the regulations proscribe the marketing of cosmetic products containing ingredient(s) tested on animals. Sunscreens are considered cosmetic products in the EU; however, the quality requirements are equally high. Regulation in emerging markets and developing countries is variable.

Safety Assessment

Before approval is granted for any sunscreen product, evidence towards its safe use must be established. The safety testing of sunscreen products is included in the laws regulating cosmetic products in general for the respective countries or regional jurisdictions where applicable. Cosmetic safety assessment takes into consideration the physicochemical properties of each ingredient included in the sunscreen formulation, as well as its potential to cause harmful effects over short-term, medium-term and long-term use. The toxicological studies aim to investigate both local and systemic effects. The endpoints generally considered include acute toxicity, repeated dose toxicity, skin and eye irritation, skin sensitization, mutagenicity, carcinogenicity, and effects on the reproductive system. Chemicals that may bear potential carcinogenic, mutagenic, or reproductive toxicity or those that may persist and accumulate in the body over time are particularly excluded from use in cosmetic products. The US food and cosmetic act CFR 21 which is implemented by the FDA declares that cosmetic products whose safety has not be substantiated prior to marketing be deemed misbranded unless the warning that the safety of the product has not been determined be conspicuously included on the principal display panel.

Labeling Requirement

The labeling requirements for sunscreens must comply with the guidelines issued by the specific regulatory authority. Labeling should include the following; Identity of the product and the key ingredients, excipients and their percentage composition. The list of ingredients should be in the order of predominance from the highest to the lowest. The label should include a statement on the name and location of the manufacturer or distributor of the product, cautionary warnings in case a patient is allergic to any of the formulation constituents, optimal storage conditions, appropriate use, frequency, SPF value and Water resistance. The EU cosmetic regulations require that certain ingredients such as nanomaterials to be included in the sunscreen products labelling. The EU and the Australia Therapeutics Goods Agency do require the inclusion of the products shelf life in the packaging label. In the USA some sunscreen products do not require expiration dating, this is in circumstances where the manufacturer provides documented evidence demonstrating that the product is stable for no less than 3 years. FDA does require the labelling to include the expiration date for sunscreens where the manufacturer cannot provide the stability data to this effect. A monograph reviewing the regulation of sunscreens comes into effect in the year 2019.

CHAPTER 11

Herbal Cosmetics

According to the research report presented by UnivDatos, the market for herbal personal care products in India is predicted to reach a value of USD 5.2 billion by 2027, rising at a manageable CAGR of 9.3% from USD 2.8 billion in 2020. Consumer interest in herbal personal care products has increased due to growing knowledge of the negative effects of chemicals like sulphates, fragrances, parabens present in traditional personal care products like skincare, haircare, body care. The younger generations are also well versed in recent innovations and the health advantages of herbal products in the beauty and personal care industries. The buying habits of consumers have also been significantly impacted by their increased awareness of animal welfare and efforts to avoid using personal care items that harm animals in any way. The demand for "safer" herbal and ayurvedic products like Himalaya, Biotique, Dabur, Lotus, Patanjali, and others is spurring development as people become more aware of the possible risks associated with using chemical formulations. To capitalize on the market's established players, numerous Indian and foreign brands have released a variety of items across different categories. In response to rising demand, super-premium and luxury companies including Kama Ayurveda, Forest Essentials, and Shahnaz Hussain all introduced products in this market. Depending upon the type of product, the cosmetic market is fragmented into various types namely hair care, skin care, body care, hand care, color cosmetics etc. The herbal ingredients used in these cosmetic products has been discussed in preceding section.

Herbal ingredients used in hair care cosmetics

All across the world, products that nourish and groom hair are becoming more and more common. Hair creams, tonics, lotions and conditioners are among the products available on the market for males, while for women, products like wave sets, hair sprays, specialty rinses, lotions and conditioners are popular choices. Many herbal plants are used in hair care formulations because of their advantageous properties. For example, Hibiscus, which contains calcium, phosphorus, iron, vitamin B, riboflavin, niacin, and vitamin C is used to promote the growth of thicker hair and prevent premature greying of the hair. Amla is abundant in vitamin C, tannins, and minerals like calcium, iron, and phosphorus that nourish hair and also encourage hair to darken. Prunus dulcis almond oil has a fat content of about 78% and just trace levels of omega-3 fatty acids. It strengthens, softens, and nourishes the hair. The following groups can be used to categorize the herbal plants used in hair care formulations:

1. Plants employed as hair cleaners
2. Plants employed as coloring agents
3. Plants employed as antidandruff agent
4. Plants employed as hair tonic

1. Plants employed as hair cleanser

Cydonia oblonga (Bihi), *Acacia concinna* (Shikakai), *Sapindus mukorrossi* (Ritha), *Trigonella foenum-graecum* (Methi).

2. Plants employed as coloring agents

Lawsonia inermis (Henna), *Eclipta alba* (Bhringraj), *Acacia arabica* (Kikkar), *Cydonia oblonga* (Bihi), *Hibiscus rosa sinensis* (Gudhal), *Haematoxylon campechianum* (Patang), *Juglans regia* (Akhrot), *Terminalia belerica* (Bahera)

3. Plants employed as antidandruff agents

Betula pendulo (Birch), *Arctinm lappa* (Great burdock), *Urtica dioica* (Stinging nettle), *Calendula officials* (Gule-abbas)

4. Plants employed as hair tonic

Morus alba (Shatoot), *Phyllanthus emblica* (Amla), *Annica montana* (Arnica), *Eclipta albo* (Bhringraj), *Nardostachys jatamansi* (Jatamansi).

Description of herbal ingredients used in hair care cosmetics

Aloe vera (Ghritkumari)

Aloe is the dried juice that is obtained by cutting into the bases of the leaves of several species of *Aloe vera* or *Aloe barbadensis* belonging to family *Liliaceae*. It primarily grows in the dry parts of Africa, Asia, Europe, and America. In India, it exists in Rajasthan, Andhra Pradesh, Gujarat, Maharashtra, and Tamil Nadu. It contains various active constituents including vitamins, enzymes, minerals, sugars, fatty acids, anthraquinones, and hormones responsible for various properties. It contains vitamins namely A, B, C, E, minerals namely copper, calcium, chromium, magnesium selenium, sodium, manganese, potassium, zinc, enzymes namely alkaline phosphatase, aliiase, bracykinase amylase, catalase, carboxypeptidase, cellulase, peroxidase, lipase, anthraquinones namely aloin, aloenin, emodin, fatty acids namely campesterol, cholesterol, lupeol, β-sisosterol, hormones namely gibberellins, auxins, and sugars namely mannose-6-phosphate, and glucomannans. It is an excellent conditioner and makes hair lustrous and silky. It encourages hair development, stops scalp irritation, lessens dandruff, and conditions hairs. *Aloe vera* gel has traditionally been used to treat baldness and promote hair growth after alopecia. The main ingredient that promotes hair growth without causing skin irritation is aloenin. There is no proof to support the idea that Aloe vera can heal brittle hair, despite this claim having been made in past.

Amla (*Embilica officinalis*)

Amla is the name given to the fruit of a leafy tree (*Emblica officinalis*), which a throughout India and bears an edible fruit. The precious ail, which is extracted from the fruit's seeds and pulp and used as a remedy for hair and scalp issues, is in addition to the fruit's high vitamin C content, one of the reasons it is so highly valued. Antioxidants stop the premature ageing and greying of hair. Apigenin, gallic acid, ellagic acid, chebulinic acid, quercetin, chebulagic acid, corilagin, isostrictiniin, methyl gall, and luteolin are only a few of the phytoconstituents found in this herb. Phyllaemblicin B, emblicanin A, emblicanin 8 punigluconin, and pedunculagin are among the tannins found in amla. Essential fatty acids found in amla powder aid in boosting hair development. Amla has many positive effects on hair:

- Nourishment of hair causing thicker and stronger hairs
- Providing lustrous to the hairs
- Controlling the premature ageing of hairs
- Moisturizing the scalp to aid with dandruff and other scalp-related problems

In traditional recipes for enhancing hair growth and pigmentation, Indian gooseberry, or amla, is a recognized hair tonic. Preferably in the shade, the fruit is dried after being sliced into pieces. Coconut oil is used to cook these pieces until the solid material is browned. This oil is quite effective at delaying greying. The water that dried amla pieces are steeped in overnight is beneficial to hair as well, and it can be used as the final rinse. Amla hair oil (coconut or sesame oil infused with dried amla pieces/powder) is one of the most promising herbal cosmetic used for of hair care rituals in the Indian culture. It has played a key role in nurturing and fulfilling dreams of thick and beautiful hair which every woman takes pride in. This wonderful hair oil acts as a natural conditioner, minimizes hair loss and greying, and encourages strong and healthy hair growth. Besides essential fatty acids, amla oil is rich in vitamin C, flavonoids, polyphenols, and also contain water, protein, carbohydrates, vitamins and minerals which are essentials for hair growth.

Use of amla hair oil may offer certain advantages, including antioxidant effects as well as antifungal and antiviral properties. Ayurvedic amla hair oil is also available with other potent herbal extracts: Reetha, Shikakai, Henna, and Methi, all prized for their natural cleansing, nourishing, and rejuvenating effect on the hair and scalp. Some hair darkening may also occur over time with repeated use, though this seems less likely than with amla powder.

Amla hair shampoo is also widely used hair care product in Asia market mainly in India. Amla shampoo in combination with other herbal ingredients like neem, bhringraj, heena is beneficial for scalp. It helps in eradication of pollutants from scalp. It causes the strengthening of hair from roots and growth faster. It also causes reduction in hair loss along with disease free scalp. Sometimes, conditioning agents are added in amla hair shampoo to make hair smooth, soft and silky.

Shikakai (Acacia)

It consists of the fruit of plant *Acacia concinna* belonging to family Leguminosae. It is a climbing shrub with Asian origins that is widespread in the tropical plains of central and southern India. The Pantoporia hordonia butterfly's larvae feed on this tree. It contains Lactone, Lupeol, Hexacosanol, Spinasterol, Spinasterone, Racimase-A, Calyctomine, Lupenone, Oleanolic acid, Betulin, Betulonic acid, Betulinic acid. It also possesses rich amount of vitamin C which is beneficial for hairs.The extract obtained from its pods is used to clean hair and treat dandruff. Shikakai naturally reduces pH levels while preserving the hair's natural oils and keeping them glossy and healthy. Additionally, it works well to condition and strengthen hair. Since amla, reetha, and shikakai complement one another, they are combined to produce healthy, lustrous hair. All hair types can benefit from Amla, Reetha, and Shikakai, which prevent split ends, hair loss, dandruff, greying, and other hair-related issues while making hair soft and silky.

Reetha (Soapnut)

It consists of the dried fruit of plant *Sapindus mukorossi* belonging to family Sapindaceae.. The plant is widely cultivated at altitudes between 200-1500 metres in the higher sections of the Indo-Gangetic plains, Shivaliks, and sub-Himalayan tracts. It is most treasured trees of tropical and sub-tropical region of Asia. It is a well-known component of ayurvedic shampoo, cleansers, and medicines for treating eczema, psoriasis, and eliminating freckles. It also has mild insecticidal properties and is traditionally used to get rid of lice from the scalp. Shampoos contain the dried powder of reetha as a foaming agent. It removes the greasy secretions from the skin and because it produces a natural lather, can also be used as a hair cleanser and tonic.

Brahmi (*Bacopa monnoria*)

It consists of the fresh and dried fruits of *Bacopa monnieri* belonging to family Scrophulariaceae. It is a tiny, prostrate or creeping annual herb that is glabrous, succulent, and grows throughout India in wet and damp areas. The genus Bacopa includes more than 100 species of aquatic herbs distributed throughout the warmer areas of the world, apart from India, Nepal, Sri Lanka, China, Taiwan and Vietnam and is also found in Florida and other southern states of the USA. A kaloids, brahmine, and herpestine were detected in Brahmi. Tetracyclic triterpenoid saponins, or bacosides A and B (a crystalline combination of multiple saponins), are the plant's main bioactive component. Bacoside A predominates among them. Bacosides A1 and A3 and bacopasaponins A, B, C, D, E, and F are additional saponins. Alkaloids (such as herpestine and Brahmin) and flavonoids (such as luteolin-7glucoside, glucuronyl-7-apigenin, and glucortonyl-7-luteolin, common phytosterols) are among the other minor substances.

Brahmi hair oil helps the hair by forming a natural protective layer around the hair follicles, which reduces dryness and split ends. By providing adequate hydration, it prevents dry hair and maintains the health of the hair fibres. It lessen hair loss and strengthen the roots of hair. Cortisol levels in body can be reduced by massaging brahmi oil into hair which is main cause for hair fall. Brahmi helps hair by nourishing the scalp, which it does by moisturising and exfoliating dry, dead skin cells. It regulates sebum production, which also aids in controlling pH levels. The scalp and hair follicles can benefit greatly from brahmi hair oil. They receive calcium, vitamin C, and zinc from it. These necessary nutrients increase blood vessel circulation which aids in promoting hair growth. It is excellent for treating a dry, irritated scalp. Using Brahmi oil to massage your scalp will reduce scalp irritation. Additionally, it has cooling properties on the scalp. It helps in increasing the volume of hair by providing essential nutrients and supplements to the hair. It also provide natural conditioning effect to the hair.

Bhringraj (Babri)

It consists of the leaves of plant *Eclipta prostrata* belonging to family asteraceae. It is indigenous to southwest America and India. The herb grows as a weed and is found in rice fields all over India. It is cultivated for medical uses in several regions of India. It is also available in China and Brazil. Bhringraj is referred to as "Keshraj" in Sanskrit, which means "the king of hair," because of its affinity for hair. When creating pure Bhringaraj oil, it is utilized as a fresh extract to promote hair development, stop hair fall, and treat early hair ageing. Additionally, it enhances the skin's radiance and complexion and guards against a number of skin conditions. It is regarded as an eye tonic and is also known to enhance vision. False Daisy is another name for Bhringraj in English. Bhringaraj contains a variety of bioactive components, including as flavonoids and phytochemicals such quercetin, wedelolactone, coumestans, polypeptides, polyacetylenes, thiophene derivatives, steroids, sterols like stigmasterol, heptacosanole, and hentriacontanol, and triterpenes. It is a traditional ayurvedic hair tonic that is very helpful for dandruff, grey hair, and hair loss. Along with helping the hair, it is also beneficial for headaches, mental weakness, and skin issues. Using bhringaraj oil to massage your hair has a relaxing effect on the head, improves memory, and stimulates blood flow to the scalp. It is one of the incredible hair oils that can successfully stop hair loss and encourage hair growth.

Henna

Lawson inermis, a member of the Lythraceae family of plants is the source of henna which produces a colour known as lawsone. The presence of gallic acid glucose, man lipids, resin (2%), mucilage, and traces of an alkaloid are the additional ingredients in addition to lawsone. Hennatannic acid and an oll green resin, both soluble in ether and alcohol, are produced by the leaves. Lawsone, a substance obtained from Lawsonia inermis leaves, has a notable antifungal and antibacterial activity. Henna causes various beneficial effects to hair which are following:

- Strengthening of hair
- Enhancement of hair volume
- Reduction in hair break
- Decrease in split ends of hair used as regular dye
- Antidandruff effect
- Removal of head lice
- Astringent property

- Antifungal and antibiotic effect
- Reduction in scalp inflammation

Tannin, an astringent, is present in henna. Henna application to the hair aids in tightening the scalp's surface, or the dye's molecule, which increases the follicles' grip on each hair, making hair stronger. Henna enters the hair shaft, fortifies it, smoothens the cuticle, increases hair thickness and volume, and makes hair more durable. The henna colouring strengthens hair while also assisting in UV radiation defence. There is only natural henna in a range of tones from orange to reddish brown; there is no black, neutral brown, auburn, or any hue of the rainbow. The quality and freshness of the henna, the length of time the paste was applied to the area of application, and the quality of the henna paste all affect how the henna stain on the skin and body turns out. It also depends on the levels of keratin in the hair, skin, and fibre.

Additionally, henna possesses antifungal and some established antibacterial properties. Tinea and nsolezzia are examples of fungal dermatophytes that can be removed with henna. These fungi have the ability to infect the skin, hair, and nails on a superficial level. Dandruff, ringworm, sports foot, and nail fungus infections are few examples. Additionally, henna helps treat some inflammatory conditions and get rid of head lice. To get good results with these straightforward treatments, all that is needed is to apply henna paste to the location of pain or infection and leave it on the skin long enough for the lawsone to permeate. When caused by Malassezia furfur, a fungus normally present on the skin surfaces of humans and many animals, henna helps get rid of dandruff. This fungus lives on skin oils and frequently infests the scalp of humans. Most people who routinely colour their hair with henna don't experience dandruff. People with M. furfur-related dandruff may observe a dramatic fall in dandruff after using henna for the first time. This is due to the fact that the top layer of the affected skin exfoliates when henna kills the fungus. Healthy skin persists and grows. In just one application of henna paste, most tinea dermatophytosis can be cured. Tinea pedis (athlete's foot), Tinea cruris (jock itch), which affects the groyne area, Tinea capitis, which affects the scalp, and Tinea barbae, which affects facial hair, can all be successfully treated with a single topical application of henna paste. Henna will stain hair and skin when applied to these areas. A single application is sufficient to nd the area of tinea until the stain has exfoliated. Repeated applications of henna paste can relieve Tinea unguium which affects the fingernails and toenails.

Henna has been used in cosmeceuticals for colouring hair for many years; in the past, kings and queens would combine it with potent medicines to dye their hair. Natural herbal powder known as henna is used not only to colour hair but also to soothe itchy scalps and reduce dandruff. It helps your hair develop and serves as a wonderful conditioner for them. There are now numerous products on the market that contain henna powder and are intended to colour hair. These items either contain henna powder by itself or a combination of henna powder and other natural plant powders including amla powder, shikaki powder, tulsi powder, and bringraj powder. Lemon juice and egg white are occasionally added to these products. These products typically make hair glossy, healthy, or voluminous when used twice a month (or more, depending on hair condition). The best and safest way to colour hair without ammonia, chemicals, or toxins is with these natural cosmetic items. The key to having great hair with henna is choosing the proper kind of henna from a reputable brand.

The next important and popular product of henna is henna oil for hair growth. Henna oil for natural hair is really useful that provides a healthy glow and volume to it and makes it shine with all its might Henna oil is prepared by extraction of henna powder in oils Gingili oil mustard oil castor oil coconut oil and some other vegetable oils can be used extraction of henna. Henna oil is for hair growth. It has properties that help to repair her cuticles, making hair strands thick and strong. Henna helps give volume to the hair shaft and improves hair texture making it to look beautiful silky and strong. It is a soothing conditioner for hair and scalp. It not only helps to add shine and volume to it, but also protects it from further damage by forming a protective coat over it.

Various herbal ingredients other than above mentioned ingredients used in hair care cosmetics have been summarized in the Table 11.1 and various marketed hair care products having herbal ingredients has been summarized in the table 11.2.

Table 11.1: A summarized list of herbal ingredients used in hair care cosmetics.

Name of herbal ingredient	Biological source & Family	Active constituents	Use
Basil (Tulsi)	Ocimum sanctum (Labiatae)	Eugenol, Cineol, Carvacrol, Vitamin A, Ursolic acid	Hair conditioning and antibacterial
Coconut	Cocos nucifera (Areacaceae)	Minerals, Amino acids, Sugars, Vitamins, Phytohormones	Moisturization of scalp and hair growth

Table 11.1: *Contd...*

Name of herbal ingredient	Biological source & Family	Active constituents	Use
Jasmine (African violet)	Jasminum officinale (Oleaceae)	Eugenol, Jasmone, Geraniol, p-cresol	Stimulation and revitalization of scalp as well as flavoring agent
Lemon grass (Sere grass)	Cymbopogon citratus (Graminae)	Limonene, Citral, Geraniol, Citronellal	Antibacterial and antifebrile
Neem	Azadirachita indica (Maliaceae)	Nimbin, Stigmasterol, Nimbinene, β-sitosterol	Prevention of scalp infection
Jojoba (Hohoba)	Simmondsia chinensis (Simmondsiaceae)	Alcohol, Esters, Acids, Tocopherol, Phytosterols	Decrease in hair fall, Moisturization of hair scalp, maintenance of pH
Olive (Oleum olivae)	Olea europaea (Oleaceae)	Triolein, Trilinolein, Tripalmitin, Tocopherol, Squalene	Hair conditioner, Moisturization of hair scalp
Deodar (Himalayan cedar)	Cedrus deodara (Pinaceae)	Centdarol, Dewarol, Himachalol, Dewarene	Antidandruff
Ricebran (Rice)	Oryza sativa (Graminae)	Vitamin C, Linoleic acid, Fatty acids, oleic acid, Tocopherols	Stimulation of hair growth
Gotukala (Indian pennywort)	Centella asiatica (Apiaceae)	Asiatic acid, Asiaticoside, Madecassica acid, Madecassoside	Prevention of scalp infections, antibacterial
Sunflower (Daisy)	Helianthus annuus (Asteraceae)	Tocopherol, Lecithin, Carotenoids, Waxes	Conditioning and smoothening agent
Patchouli	Patchouli cablin (Laminaceae)	Patchoulol	Reduction of headache
Nettle (Urticate)	Utrica diotica (Urticaceae)	Vitamins A. C, E, Minerals, Flavonoids	Stimulation of scalp, reduction of greying of hair
Vetiver (Khas khas)	Vetiveria zizanioides (Graminae)	Khusol, Azulene, β-vetivone	Antidandruff agent, flavoring agent

Table 11.2: Marketed herbal hair care products.

Type of product	Name of product	Use	Manufacturer
Hair oil	Dabur amla hair oil	Provides long, thick and silky hair	Dabur
Hair oil	Indulekha Bringha Ayurvedic Hair Oil	Provides hair growth and prevents hair fall	Hindustan Unilever
Hair oil	Sesa ayurvedic hair oil	Provides hair growth, reduces hair fall, and prevents bacterial and fungal infections on scalp	Sesa
Hair oil	Kesh King Ayurvedic hair oil	Promotes hair growth and reduces the hair fall	Emami
Hair oil	Mamaearth Onion hair oil	Provides stronger, smoother and shiny hairs	
Hair oil	Kesh Kanti Almond Hair oil	Provides strengthen, softer hairs and also reduces the hair fall	Patanjali
Hair oil	Kesh Kanti Advance Herbal Hair Expert	Supplies balanced nourishment to the hair roots and scalp to repair the damaged hairs. Also prevents the hair greying and reduces the hair fall	Patanjali
Shampoo	Himalaya Bhringraj Anti Hair Fall Shampoo	Stimulates hair growth and reduces the hair fall	Himalaya
Shampoo	Himalaya Gentle Natural Protein Shampoo	Strengthens the hair roots and reduces the hair fall	Himalaya
Shampoo	Ayur Amla Shikakai with Reetha Shampoo	Provides lustrous, health hairs and also reduces the dandruff	Ayur
Shampoo	Vatika Naturals Ayurvedic Shampoo	Maintains the healthy hairs and reduces the hair fall	Dabur
Shampoo	Kesh kanti natural hair shampoo	Hair cleanser and provides healthy and manageable hairs	Patanjali
Shampoo	Kesh kanti milk protein hair cleanser	Nourishes the scalp, repair dry dull hairs and reduces the hair fall	Patanjali

Table 11.2: *Contd...*

Type of product	Name of product	Use	Manufacturer
Shampoo	Kesh Kanti Aloe vera hair cleanser	Provides deep conditioning and nourishment of hair and scalp	Patanjali
Conditioner	Rice Water conditioner	Prevents split ends and reduces hair breakage	Mamaearth
Conditioner	Khadi Natural Neem & Aloe Vera Hair Conditioner	Provides healthy scalp by removing dead cells from the surface, reducing dandruff, and treating an itchy scalp	Khadi Natural
Conditioner	Red Onion Nutritive Hair Conditioner	Provides healthy nutritious and strong hairs. Provides soft, lustrous and creamy consistency	Lotus
Conditioner	Anti-Hair Fall Conditioner	Provides smooth and detangled hairs with hair fall reduction upto 96%	Himalaya
Conditioner	Kesh Kanti Hair Conditioner	Provides repairment and protection of dry and damaged hair	Patanjali
Conditioner	Natural Biotin Conditioner	Provides strength to hair, makes hair smooth and lustrous and prevents hair breakage	HK VITALS
Conditioner	Watercress Nourishing Conditioner	Strengthens and silkens the hair for good looking	Biotique
Hair color	Biotique Herbcolor	Provides stay of long lasting hair color for about 26 washes	Biotique
Hair color	Natural Shine Henna	Provides long lasting hair color	Himalaya
Hair color	Herbal Black Mehndi	Provides natural black color to the hair	Khadi Natural
Hair color	Kesh Kanti Hair Color	Imparts long lasting color intensity, natural shine and conditioning effect to hair	Patanjali
Hair cream	Onion Hair Styling Cream	Provides hold and shine, Reduces the hair fall and nourishes the hair	Mamaearth

Table 11.2: *Contd...*

Type of product	Name of product	Use	Manufacturer
Hair cream	Men Daily Nourish Hair Cream	Provides strong nourishment and prevents the hair from daily damage	Himalaya
Hair gel	Arata Hair Gel	Imparts lustrous to the hair	Arata
Hair gel	Kesh Kanti Aloe Vera Hair Gel	Provides hold and shine to hair	Patanjali
Hair gel	LILIUM Herbal Hair Gel Wet Look Hair Gel	Provides hold and shine to hair	LILIUM Herbal
Hair serum	Onion Hair Serum	Reduces frizz and tangles, minimizes hair breakage	Mamaearth
Hair serum	Mountain Ebony Vitalizing Sustainable Anti-Hairfall Serum	Stimulates hair growth, soothes the scalp	Biotique Natural

Herbal ingredients used in skin care cosmetics

An individual's skin beauty is influenced by their health, lifestyle, regular job, climatic conditions, and maintenance. During the summer, the skin will become dehydrated from overheating, which will lead to wrinkles, freckles, blemishes, pigmentation, and sunburns. Skin damage from the harsh winter includes cracks, wounds, maceration, and infections. The variety of procedures used to maintain the skin's integrity, improve its look, and treat skin disorders is known as skin care. This can involve good nutrition, avoiding too much sun, and using emollients as needed. The phytochemicals in herbal cosmetics for the skin influence the activities of the skin and give the nutrients required for healthy skin. These phytochemicals come from a variety of botanical sources. Herbs and essential oils used in cosmetics must not penetrate the skin's outermost layers and must not have any therapeutic effects, according to the Drug and Cosmetics Act. Herbal cosmetics are subject to the same legal requirements and regulatory processes as other chemical substances used in cosmetic compositions. The requirements for basic skin care include:

Cleansing agents

It clears the skin's pores of dirt, dead skin cells, and dust. Veggie oils including coconut, sesame, and palm oil are some of the popular cleansers.

Toners

The toners aid in skin tightening and shield the skin from various airborne toxins and other environmental pollutants. Witch hazel, geranium, sage, lemon, ivy burdock, and essential oils are a few of the herbs used as toners.

Moisturizer

The moisturizer makes the skin more supple and silky. Vegetable glycerin, sorbitol, rose water, jojoba oil, aloe vera, and iris are a few examples of herbal moisturizers.

There are various herbal ingredients which are used in skin care cosmetic preparation and has been classified into various categories depending upon their functions:

Herbs for Dry Skin Treatment

Aloe vera

It serves as moisturizer and skin softener due to which incorporated in skin preparations. The detailed note on aloe vera has been given under the herbal hair care cosmetics.

Coconut oil

It is obtained by crushing the copra having about 60-65% of the oil. It is derived from dried fruit or seed of the coconut palm tree *Cocos nucifera* belonging to the family Arecaceae. It has melting point of 24-25 °C due to which it can be easily applied in solid as well as liquid form on skin and hairs. It has excellent skin moisturizing and skin softener characteristics due to which applied as skin care ingredient.

Jojoba oil

It is obtained from the seeds of the *Simmondsiachinenesis* plant, a member of the Simmondsiaceae family, which grows in the desert. It has about 98% pure waxes namely wax esters, alcohols, free fatty acids, hydrocarbons along with vitamins, sterols, and some triglyceride esters. It can be simply processed to remove any odor, color and it is oxidative stable. It is mainly used in skin care cosmetics as moisturizer and carrier oil for exotic fragrances. Jojoba oil and sebum are almost same. Sebum guards the skin and provides moisturizing effect to the skin and hair but removed away by pollutants, chemicals, sun, age leading to dry skin and hair. Jojoba oil helps to replenish that dry skin and hair loses and help in restoration of their natural pH.

Sunflower oil

It is an easy and affordable oil. It is a non-volatile oil derived from the seeds of plant species *Helianthus annus* belonging to family the *Asteraceae*. It has lecithin, tocopherols, carotenoids, and waxes. It possesses smoothing characteristics and considered non-comedogenic. Due to possession of vitamin E, it provides antioxidant properties to the skin. It has various skin care properties such as unclogging of skin pores due to high absorption capacity and non-comedogenic property, sun protection effect, and wounds healing effect.

Olive oil

It is a fixed oil obtained from the fruits of *Olea europaea* belonging to the family oleaceae. It has triolein, trilinolein, tristearate, monostearate, triplamitin, squalene, triarachidin, tocopherol, and β-sitosterol as main chemical composition.

Skin Protecting Agents

Green tea

It is obtained from the leaves of tea plant *Camellia sinensis* belonging to family *Theaceae*. It contains four catechin derivatives namely epicatechin, epicatequinagalato, epigallocatechin-3-gallate (EGCG), and epigallocatechin. Due to possession of these chemical constituents, green tea provided antioxidant, anticancer, and anti-inflammatory effect. The polyphenols present in green tea in cosmetics impart superior skin penetration and retention ability due to which, green tea improve the skin performance by prevention of acute effects result of exposure of UVB radiation, decrease in inflammation, reduction of erythema and immunosuppression. Various other ingredients such as proteins, lipids, carbohydrates caffeine pigments like carotenoids and chlorophyll, vitamins like B, C, E, and minerals are present in green tea extract which provide extra benefits to the skin like skin moisturizer and skin protection effect.

Calendula

Calendula is derived from marigold flowers (*Calendula officinalis*) belonging to family *Asteraceae*. It is mainly consists of essential oil composed of α-pinene, α-thujena, T-muurolol, 1,8-Cineole, and dihydrotagetone. It is applied topically as a suspension or tincture to treat acne, lessen swelling, stop bleeding, and soothe sensitive skin. Radiation dermatitis can be effectively treated with calendula cream or ointment. It is mainly used to treat acne, decreasing the inflammation, controlling the bleeding and soothing irritated skin along with protection of skin. It also possesses good moisturizing property. It can also nourishes the skin due to presence of carotenoids in the oil.

Turmeric

It is obtained from roots and rhizomes of *Curcuma longa* belonging to the family *zingiberaceae*. It is a perennial plant that Hindus use in numerous festivities. It possesses various active constituents namely Demethoxycurcumin, Bisdemethoxycurcumin, Zingiberene, Curcumol, Curcumenol, Eugenol, Metatrihydrocurcumin, Triethylcurcumin, Curcumin, Turmererin, and Turmerones. The potential of turmeric in skin care includes anti-acne, masking of oily skin, anti-wrinkle, masking the signs of ageing, anti-stretching, anti-burn, removal of skin tanning, removal of dead cells from skin etc.

It functions as an analgesic, anti-inflammatory, antioxidant, anti-malarial, and insect repellant, among other things. Curcumin is the phytochemical present in the turmeric which provides yellow color to turmeric and is responsible for various therapeutic effects of turmeric. It may be the first known cosmetic due to the fact that women have historically applied turmeric to their skin. It is thought to reduce facial hair growth, clear up acne, and improve color complexation of the skin. It is said that many Tamil Nadu women still apply turmeric to their faces every day before taking a bath. An off-white hydrogenated version of curcumin known as tetrahydrocurcumin is applied topically as a cutaneous antioxidant. When added to moisturizers, it might stop lipids from going rancid.

In cosmeceuticals, various curcuminoids present in turmeric anti-inflammatory, antioxidant, and skin-lightening properties. Curcuminoids inhibit hyaluronidase, elastase, and collagenase *in vitro*. Curcumin gel has been shown to improve the appearance of photodamaged skin conditions such pigmentary changes, solar elastoses, actinic poikiloderma, solar lentigines, and actinic keratosis on prolonged use like six months. It might encourage cells with DNA damage to apoptose. It is being examined as a hair colouring agent that is friendly to the environment.

Anti-aging Agents

Carrot

It is derived from the plant *Daucus carota* belonging to the family *apiaceae*. It is a valuable herb since ancient time due to its richness in vitamin A along with other essential vitamins. The oil of carrot seed is employed as anti-aging, revitalizing and rejuvenating agent. It helps in reduction of wrinkles along with promotion of formation of new cells. It also serves as natural toner. The bright orange color of carrot is mainly due to possession of β-carotene along small amount of α-carotene and Ƴ-carotene.

Ginkgo

It is obtained from the tree *Ginkgo biloba* which belongs to the family *Ginkgoaceae*. The nuts and leaves of Ginkgo are utilized in China and Japan from ancient time for treatment of various conditions like poor blood circulation, poor memory, hypertension, male impotence, and depression. The chemical constituents present in Ginkgo leaves include terpene trilactones namely ginkgolides A, B, C, J, biflavones, flavonol glycosides, proanthocyanidins, alkylphenols, 6-hydroxykynurenic acid, polyprenols, and 4-O-methylpyrodoxine. It provides anti-aging, anti-inflammatory, vasodilator, anti-oxidant properties. The combination of Ginkgo extract with green tea provides moisturizing effect, enhanced cell renewal and increased skin elasticity. The Ginkgo extract EGb 761 obtained from leaves of Ginkgo plant is a natural mixture comprising of terpenes (6%) and flavone glycosides (33%) namely kaempferol and Quercetin which have provided the reduction in number of UVB induced sun burn cells in animal model.

Rhodiola rosea

It is a plant belonging to the family Crassulaceae which habitats in cold area throughout the globe. It is mainly grows in dry sandy ground at high altitudes in the arctic regions of the Asia and Europe. It is also known as roseroot, golden root, arctic root, aaron's root, orpin rose, and king's crown. The plant species of Rhodiola contains various chemical constituents like proanthocyanidines, flavonoids, tyrosols, glycosides, cinnamyl alcohol, alcohols, proteins, essential oils, and sugars. The polyphenolic content of *Rhodiola rosea is about* 41.4 ± 3.41%. Salidroside, tyrosol are the main constituents present in *Rhodiola rosea*. The Rhodiola rosea extract possesses the potential to modulate the skin melanogenesis process. Rhodiola rosea extract/L-carnosine-associated compound (RCAC) causes reduction of transepidermal water loss from sensitive skin of humans leading to improvement in skin barrier function. It serves as emollient and anti-ageing agent in skin care products. It is also used to reduced wrinkles and loss of firmness of skin.

Tamarind

It consists of dried ripe fruits of *Tamarindus indica* belonging to family fabaceae. It possesses fatty acids, amino acids, and various minerals. The sweet acidic taste of tamarind is mainly due to presence of tartaric acid. It is also a rich source of vitamin B along with presence of sugar in high quantity. It has antioxidant property which is mainly due to presence of polyphenolic content of tamarind. It can be used as face pack to provide nourishment to skin and prevention of skin damage from sun rays. The presence of alpha-hydroxy acid in tamarind provides skin exfiolating property due to which it unclog the pores, decreases the skin aging symptoms, and keep skin clear. It also have antioxidants due to which it guards the skin from free radicals. It has skin healing property.

Antioxidants

Vitamin E

It is the main hydrophobic antioxidant present in plasma membranes and tissues. It is a group of 30 naturally occurring compounds (4 tocopherols and 4 tocotrienols), all of which possess vitamin E activity. It acts by arresting the chain propagation and lipid peroxidation via scavenging lipid peroxyl radicals leading to protection of cell membrane from degradation. It serves as antioxidant, emollient, humectant, anti-inflammatory agent leading to younger skin.

Vitamin C

Vitamin C is the most prevalent and often water soluble nonenzymatic antioxidant in human tissues. Majority of plants and animals produce this vitamin in their bodies from glucose. However, it cannot be produced in humans due to lack of L-glucono-gamma lactone oxidase enzyme and hence supplied through diet. It serves as antioxidant by neutralizing the oxidative stress caused by various factors like pollutants, smoking, and solar radiations. It provides anti-aging effect, antipigmentary effect, and protection against photoaging. It also possesses anti-wrinkle effect. Various herbal ingredients used in skin care products has been summarized in the Table 11.3 and commercial herbal formulations for skin care has been summarized in the Table 11.4.

Table 11.3: A summarized list of herbal ingredients used in skin care.

Name of herbal ingredient	Biological source	Active constituents	Use
Aloe vera	*Aloe barabadensis (Liliaceae)*	Aloin, barbaloin, vitamin A,B,C,E, enzymes, and amino acids	Moisturizer, skin softener, cooling agent
Turmeric	*Curcuma longa (Zingiberaceae)*	Zingiberene, curcumol, curcumenol, eugenol, turmerin	Antiseptic, antibacterial, anti-acne, anti-wrinkle, and moisturizer
Neem (Margosa)	*Azadirachita indica (Maliaceae)*	Nimbin, nimbinene, stigmasterol, and beta-sitosterol	Antiseptic, antibacterial, and antifungal
Cinnamon (Dalchini)	*Cinnamomum zeylanicum (Lauraceae)*	Cinnamaldehyde, eugenol, mannitol, cuminaldehyde	Astringent, cooling agent, and stimulating agent
Eucalyptus (Lemon gum tree)	*Eucalyptus globules (Myrtaceae)*	Pinene, eucalyptol, camphene, phellandrene	Antiseptic and cleansing agent
Lavender (Hawthorn)	*Lavendula angustifola (Labiatae)*	Esters, linalyl acetate, cineol, geraniol, essential oils	Balancing and harmonizing action on both oily as well as dry skin
Apricort (Bittersweet)	*Prunus Americana (Asteraceae)*	Proteins, vitamin A, amandin, amino acids	Moisturizer, revitalizer, and exfoliating agent
Rose (Rosette)	*Rosa centifolia (Rosaceae)*	Quercetin, geraniol, kaempferol, citronell, essential oils	Cleansing and smoothening agent
Rosemary (Oleum rosemarini)	*Rosemarinus officinalis (Labiatae)*	Camphor, bornyl acetate, camphene, tannins, ursolic acid	Moisturizer and refreshing agent
Walnut (Burnt almond)	*Junglans renia (Junglandaceae)*	Cysteine, juglansin, tryptophan	Moisturizer and smoothening agent
Peppermint (Mint)	*Mentha arvensis (Labiatae)*	L-menthol, limonene, menthyl acetate, essential oil	Cooling and cleansing agent

Table 11.3: *Contd...*

Name of herbal ingredient	Biological source	Active constituents	Use
Ginkgo	*Ginkgo biloba (Ginkgoaceae)*	Ginkgolides, diterpenes, ginkgetin, bilobetin	Moisturizer, smoothening agent, and decrease roughness
Carrot	*Daucus carota belonging to the family apiaceae*	Vitamin A and other essential vitamins	Anti-aging, revitalizing and rejuvenating agent
Calendula (Marigold flowers)	*Calendula officinalis (Asteraceae)*	α-pinene, α-thujena, T-muurolol, 1,8-Cineole, and dihydrotagetone	Anti-acne agent, reduction of inflammation
Green Tea	*Camellia sinensis (Theaceae)*	Epicatechin, epicatequinagalato, epigallocatechin-3-gallate (EGCG), and epigallocatechin	Antioxidant, anticancer, and anti-inflammatory effect

Table 11.4: A summarized list of herbal commercial cosmetics for skin care.

Name of product	Ingredient	Biological source	Action
Vicco turmeric cream	Turmeric oil	Curcuma longa (Zingiberaceae)	Anti-inflammatory and antibacterial
Everyuth peel	Vitamin A	Lemon, citrus, fruits, sunflower oil	Antioxidant
Himalaya neem face wash	Neem oil	Azadirachta indica (Meliaceae)	Antimicrobial and antiseptic
Liquorice balm	Licorice extract	Glycyrrhiza glabra (Fabaceae)	Antioxidant, anti-inflammatory, skin whitening
Renova cream	Retinoic acid	Vitamin A	Promotion of cell renewal and smoothening effect
Loreal body conditioner	Rosemary extract	Rosemarinus officinalis	Antimicrobial, anti-inflammatory, and antioxidant
Thayers skin toner	Witch hazel	Hamamelis virginiana (Hamamelidaceae)	Skin toner
Seatonic stretch mark removing cream	Lupeol	Crataeva nurvula (Capparidaceae)	Skin conditioner and antioxidant

Table 11.4: *Contd...*

Name of product	Ingredient	Biological source	Action
Sandalwood face pack	Sandalwood	*Santalum album (Santalaceae)*	Glowing of skin
Margo/medimix	Neem	*Azadirachta indica (Meliaceae)*	Antibacterial and antifungal
Saffron skin cream	Saffron	***Crocus sativus*** *(Iridaceae)*	Anti-ageing
VLCC herbal sunscreen	Sandalwood & aloe vera extract		Provide nourishment to the skin
Aloe vera moisturizing cream	*Aloe vera*	*Aloe barbadensis (Liliaceae)*	Moisturizer and skin healing
Lotus herbal	*Aloe vera*	*Aloe barbadensis (Liliaceae)*	Skin softener
Patanjali aloe vera gel	*Aloe vera*	*Aloe barbadensis (Liliaceae)*	Repairment of skin dead cells
Saundarya face wash	Aloe vera, neem, tulsi, orange peel		Nourishment and healing of skin

Herbal ingredients in oral care

Personal oral hygiene is becoming more and more popular. In addition to toothbrushes and toothpaste, the general public also uses a lot of teeth powder, mouth washes, and other similar products. People brush and rinse their teeth in order to feel fresh, to prevent bad breath, dental caries, and oral ailments, as well as to have a pleasant smile. All people need to practice good dental hygiene, but it's especially crucial for children, pregnant women, people with immune system deficiencies, people receiving chemotherapy and radiation therapy. The association between oral health and diseases like diabetes, heart disease, and even death has also been demonstrated by numerous scientific investigations. Effective dental hygiene should be practised in order to remove plaque, prevent plaque production, and reduce strains in order to prevent the development of caries and periodontal illnesses. Throughout the world, dental caries, periodontal disease and oral infections are all quite prevalent. Oral illnesses and infections can be avoided with good oral hygiene. Various oral care products that contain antibiotics, fluoride, and chlorhexidine derivatives are effective against oral diseases such as infections and caries. But prolonged use of these chemical based oral hygiene products resulted in certain oral or systemic adverse responses.

In recent years, herbal oral care products which are frequently used in traditional medicine have drawn the attention of researchers. Various herbal ingredients including cloves and clove oil, coconut oil, pomegranates, green tea, *Salvadora persica (meswak), Aloe vera, and Acacia arabica* are traditionally utilized. Most of the active consituents identified from these species are antibacterial, anti-inflammatory, anticariogenic, and astringent. Various herbal ingredients used in formulation of products for oral care has been discussed in preceding section.

Miswak or Siwak

It is a traditional chewing stick obtained from tree *Salvadora persica* belonging to family salvadorecea. It is most popular traditional source of the substance for oral hygiene. Miswak is widely used in Islamic nations for basic oral hygiene because Islam has emphasized its use for this purpose. The ability of miswak's extracts to combat germs in dental plaque is well known and studied around the world. The main antibacterial component benzyl isothiocyanate and its derivatives were found to be present in miswak and their concentration indicated the effectiveness of the miswak. The applications of miswak as oral care attributes to following properties:

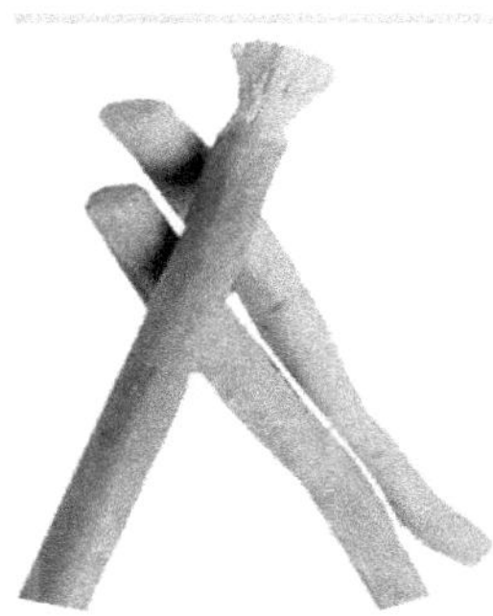

Figure 11.1: Miswak

- Fibrils are present in miswak like toothbrush hence serves as mechanical tool to remove dental plaque.
- The presence of silica in miswak serves as mild abrasive which helps in removal of stain.
- The presence of minerals and vitamins like vitamin C, calcium, chloride prevent the calculus formation, repairing the soft tissues, and improvement of the remineralization of hard dental tissues.
- The presence of essential oils in miswak like thymol, benzyl nitrite, eugenol, isotheymol, isoterpinolene, eucalyptol and g-caryophyllene provide antibacterial effects and bitter taste which aids in stimulation of salivary flow. Various active constituents responsible for oral care in miswak has been summarized in Table 11.5.

Table 11.5: Active constituents present in miswak for oral care.

Active constituent	Mechanism of action	Role in oral care
Benzylisothiocynate	Preventive agent	Inhibits against genotoxic and carcinogenic compounds
Fluoride	Antimicrobial	Inhibits dental caries
Vitamin C	Healing/repairing	Healing of oral soft and hard tissues
Silica	Abrasive	Removal of stains or plaque
Calcium	Prevents demineralization and promotes remineralization	Buffering action in oral cavity
Salvadorine (alkaloid)	Bactericidal	Stimulatory effect on gingiva
Tannic acid	Antifungal	Decreases *candida albicans*
Chloride	Inhibits calculus deposition on teeth surfaces	Buffering action in oral cavity

Green tea

It is obtained from the leaves of tea plant *Camellia sinensis* belonging to family Theaceae. It is consumed extensively worldwide and has been shown to have antioxidant and antibacterial benefits against bacterial colonies of dental plaque. Green tea polyphenols have been discovered to alleviate halitosis by altering the components of the odorant sulphur. In the presence of green tea polyphenols, oxidative stress and inflammation in the mouth caused by heavy cigarette and alcohol use significantly decreased. The application of green tea in oral care products is attributed to following characteristics:

- The presence of EGCG in green tea inhibits the growth of *prevotella intermedia, porphyromonas gingivalis*, and *prevotella nigrescens* on human buccal cells.
- The release of catechins present in green tea into the periodontal tissues leads to inhibition of metabolites of *P. gingivalis responsible for destruction of periodontal tissues.*
- Green tea possesses potent anti-inflammatory as well as antioxidant properties which is mainly due to reduction in the production of pro-inflammatory cytokines particularly interleukin 8.
- Green tea promotes the antioxidant capacity of gingival crevicular fluid along with potent anti-inflammatory and antiplaque effects.

- Green tea has capability to reduce pocket depth, gingival bleeding index and promote periodontal healing.
- Polyphenols in green tea leads to regeneration of periodontal tissues due to decrease in matrix metalloproteins (MMP 9), induction of apoptosis and suppression of osteoclast differentiation.

Neem

Since ancient times, the neem is known as wonder tree in the Indian subcontinent derived from *Azadirachta indica* belonging to family meliaceae. Each part of the neem tree possesses various therapeutic, biological, and pharmacological properties which are well documented. Neem is commonly used as a chewing stick throughout the world. Every component of the neem tree including the branches, twigs, bark, and oil has been utilized for generations in India to promote oral health. One of the ancient oral hygiene practises in India involves chewing neem leaves and seeds after meals and brushing with mango and neem branches. Nimbidin, Nimbibin, Nimbolid, Azadirachtin, Gallic Acid, Epicatechin, Catechin, and Margolone are the phytochemical components found in Neem. These all display strong antibacterial action. Azadirachtin which is an active antibacterial agent is the primary active component of neem. The application of neem in oral health is attributed to following properties:

- It imparts antibacterial property which is mainly due to its active constituents mainly Azadirachtin.
- Aqueous and ethanolic extract of neem exhibits anticandidial property against *candida albicans*.
- Chloroform extract of *neem* leaf prevents *Streptococcus salivarius and Streptococcus mutans* resulting in prevention of dental caries.
- *Neem* oil exhibits significant antibacterial effect and helps in treating the dental plaque.

Clove

It is derived from dried flower buds of *Eugenia caryophyllus* belonging to family Myrtaceae. It possesses various medicinal properties and generally referred as clove bud. It is used from ancient time in India and china followed by spreading in other parts of the world like Europe during 17th and 18th centuries. Traditionally, it is employed as antimicrobial agent and savouring agent in foods. It mainly consists of essential oil consisting of total 23 identified active constituents amongst eugenol, β-caryophyllene, eugenyl acetate, and α-humulene are main constituents. Due to possession of various properties, it can be used in formulation of various oral preparations like mouth wash and tooth pastes. Now-a-days various tooth pastes having clove in market are available in market like herbal colgate, dant kanti, dabar herbal etc. The role of clove in oral care is mainly due to following characteristics:

- The presence of eugenol in clove decorates it with antibacterial and anesthetic activities due to which it can be used in tooth pain or toothache.
- The oral administration of clove inhibits the *candida albicans* in oral cavity as well as alimentary canal.
- The extract of clove (in hot water) prevents the growth of *S. mutans.*
- Clove oil decreases the plaque deposition on hard oral tissues.
- The clove oil exhibits the antimicrobial activity against *Actinobacillus actinomycetemcomitans, Fusobacterium nucleatum, Porphyromonas gingivalis, Capnocytophaga gingivalis, Staphylococcus aureus, Candida albicans, Pseudomonas aeruginosa*, and *Escherichia coli*. Due to this effect, it can be used as adjuvant to periodontal therapy.
- The smell of clove helps in reduction of bad odor of oral cavity.

Liquorice

It is the root of *Glycyrrhiza glabra* belonging to family Fabaceae. It has great potential to treat various oral as well as dental ailments like dental caries, oral candidiasis, periodontitis, and recurrent aphthous. The main active constituent present in liquorice is Glycyrrhizin which is sweet in taste. Besides it, liquorice contains glabrin A & B, isoflavons, liquiritin, enoxolone, and liquiritigenin etc. The role of liquorice in oral care is mainly due to following characteristics:

- It stimulates production of saliva which is responsible for various tooth protection properties such as buffering action, antimicrobial action, remineralization action etc.
- It reduces the dental caries due to stimulation of salivation.
- It interferes with cariogenic bacteria namely *S. mutans.*
- Addition of Glycyrrhizin to phosphate-fluoride solution causes improved uptake of fluoride resulting its deposition in porosities of demineralized enamels.
- It also serves as flavoring agent in various oral care preparations like toothpaste.

Turmeric

It is obtained from roots and rhizomes of *Curcuma longa* belonging to the family zingiberaceae. It is a perennial plant that Hindus use in numerous festivities. It possesses various active constituents namely Demethoxycurcumin, Bisdemethoxycurcumin, Zingiberene, Curcumol, Curcumenol, Eugenol, Metatrihydrocurcumin, Triethylcurcumin, Curcumin, Turmererin, and Turmerones. The role of turmeric in oral care is mainly due to following characteristics:

- It serves as anti-inflammatory agent hence effective in pain reliving, periodontitis, and gingivitis.
- It serves as anticariogenic agent due to inhibition of growth of *S. mutans* by the essential oil derived from turmeric.
- It serves as coloring agent in pit and fissure sealant and dental plaque detection system.
- It can be applied in from of 2% gel as local drug delivery system in the treatment of periodontitis.
- It also serves as antimicrobial agent due to which helps in prevention of various oral infections.

Babool

It is also known as *Acacia arabica* which belongs to family Leguminosae. It is spiny, perennial tree having medium size mainly found in all over India. Currently, it is termed as Gum arabica because it is mainly imported to Arab countries. It mainly consists tannins and phenolic compounds like gallic acid, quercetin, dicatechin, betulin, hentriacontane, sitosterol, isoquercetin, chlorogenic acid, kaemopferol-3, and β-amyrin. The role of Babool in oral care mainly in teeth ailments such as plaque formation, gingivitis, and periodontitis is due to presence of gallic acid and tannins which provide antibacterial, astringent, haemostatic, anti-inflammatory, and antihistaminic properties. These properties help in management of various oral infections including teeth disorders. The regular use of babool provides strengthening to the gums along with reduction in inflammation of gums. Various herbal toothpastes having babool as ingredients are available in market such as Dabur's babool toothpaste, Patanjali Dant kanti.

Pudina

It is an aromatic herb derived from *Mentha spicata* belonging to family Labiatae. It is also termed as Spearmint in English and extensively used in India and Italy as cooking element. It consists about 0.5% volatile oil comprising of carvone. It also contains limonene, dihydrocarveol acetate, phellandrine, esters of acetic, butyric acids, resins, and tannins. Pudina is decorated with various therapeutic benefits. It possesses mouth freshener potential on chewing its leaves and use of its volatile oil in any oral care formulation such as toothpaste. The presence of volatile oil in pudina kills various anaerobic bacteria present in oral cavity. The presence of menthol in pudina also provides cooling and refreshing sensation on breathing. Herbal ingredients used in oral care has been given in Table 11.6 and commercial herbal formulations for oral care are given in Table 11.7.

Table 11.6: Various herbal ingredients used in oral care.

Ingredients	Biological Source	Active constituents	Use
Marigold	*Calendula officinalis* (Asteraceae)		Antibacterial, anti-inflammatory, antiviral
Miswak	*Salvadora persica* (Salvadorecea)	Benzyl isothiocyanate, Salvadorine, calcium, chloride, vitamin C, fluoride	Anticaries, antimicrobial, antiplaque
Clove	*Eugenia caryophyllus* (Myrtaceae)	Eugenol, β-caryophyllene, eugenyl acetate, and α-humulene	Relieve the dental pain, anti-inflammatory, antimicrobial, anticaries
Neem	*Azadirachta indica* (Meliaceae)	Nimbidin, Nimbibin, Nimboide, Azadirachtin, Gallic Acid, Epicatechin, Catechin, and Margolone	Antimicrobial, anticandidial, antiplaque, and anticaries
Babool	*Acacia arabica* (Leguminosae)	gallic acid, quercetin, dicatechin, betulin, hentriacontane, sitosterol, isoquercetin, chlorogenic acid, kaemopferol-3, and β-amyrin	antibacterial, astringent, haemostatic, anti-inflammatory, and antihistaminic
Liquorice	*Glycyrrhiza glabra* (Fabaceae)	Glycyrrhizin, glabrin A & B, isoflavons, liquiritin, enoxolone, and liquiritigenin	Buffering action, antimicrobial, remineralization action, anti-inflammatory action
Turmeric	*Curcuma longa* (Zingiberaceae)	Demethoxycurcumin, Bisdemethoxycurcumin, Zingiberene, Curcumol, Curcumenol, Eugenol, Metatrihydrocurcumin, Triethylcurcumin, Curcumin, Turmererin, and Turmerones	Antimicrobial, anti-inflammatory, pain reliever, and treatment of various teeth ailments like gingivitis, periodontitis

Table 11.6 *Contd...*

Ingredients	Biological Source	Active constituents	Use
Pudina	*Mentha spicata* (Labiatae)	Menthol, carvon, limonene, dihydrocarveol acetate, phellandrine, esters of acetic, butyric acids, resins, and tannins.	Refreshing agent, antimicrobial agent and provides cooling sensation on breathing
Green tea	*Camellia sinensis* (Theaceae)	Epicatechin, epicatequinagalato, epigallocatechin-3-gallate (EGCG), and epigallocatechin.	Antioxidant, anti-inflammatory, and treatment of various teeth ailments

Table 11.7: Commercial herbal oral care preparations.

Type of formulations	Name of product	Herbal ingredients	Use
Tooth paste	Dabur Herbal toothpaste	Babool, Lodhra, Clove oil, Bakul, Mint, Jamun and Akarkara	Antimicrobial, anti-inflammatory, and anticaries
Toothpaste	Dabur Meswak	Meswak extract	Decrease tooth decay, prevent plaque and inhibit gum diseases
Toothpaste	Dant Kanti	Clove oil, Babool, Tomar Seed Oil, Turmeric, Pippali Chhoti, Bakul, Pudina, Akarkara Root extract	Safeguard the teeth and gums from microbial attacks and prevents cavities formation.
Toothpaste	Colgate Swarna Vedshakti	Mint Oil, Clove Oil, Amla Extact, Neem Seed Oil, Aloe Vera Extract, Cinnamon Leaf Oil, Basil Oil, Fennel Oil, Honey Extract, Eugenol, D-Limonene	It safeguards the teeth from attack of microorganisms
Toothpaste	Dabur Red paste	Garik powder, Pippali, Maricha, Sunthi, Tomar beej, Kapoor, Clove oil, and Pudina	Helps in maintaining the oral health and keeps the teeth and gums healthy

Table 11.7: *Contd...*

Type of formulations	Name of product	Herbal ingredients	Use
Toothpaste	Glister Herbal toothpaste	Clove, Spearmint, Tea, Ginger, Camphor, Lemon, Mulethi, Neem, Tulsi, Eucalyptol, Peppermint	Whitens and strengthens teeth, minimizes surface stains and plaque, and lowers the risk of dental decay
Toothpowder	Charak GumTone Herbal Toothpowder	Babool, Khadir, Vajradanti, Kapoor	Inhibits bleeding gums, dental cavities, toothache and provides strength to the teeth and gums
Toothpowder			
Mouthwash	Himalaya Hiora Regular mouthwash	Bibhitaki, Nagavalli, Pilu, Peppermint satva, Gandhapura taila, Elaichi Yuvani satva	Antibacterial, anti-allergic, anti-inflammatory, , wound-healing and analgesic
Mouthwash	Bless-O-Fresh Mouthwash	Neem, clove, Liquorice, Cinnamon	Antibacterial, anti-inflammatory and pain reliever
Mouthwash	Dentup Herbal Mouthwash	Neem	Inhibition of germs and maintenance of oral hygiene
Mouthwash	KPNAMBOODIARIS Herbal Fresh Mouthwash	Menthol, Thymol, Tea oil, Clove extract, Nutmeg, Ginger, Cardamom, Mint	Fights against germs, prevents the cavities, and provide long lasting fresh breathing
Mouthwash	Himalaya Active Fresh Saunf Mouthwash	Fennel oil, Menthol	Eliminates 99.9% germs and provide fresh sensation on breathing

Review of guidelines for herbal cosmetics by private bodies like COSMOS

COSMOS referred to as COSMetic Organic and Natural Standards. It establishes certification standard for natural and organic cosmetics in Europe. The cosmetic industries recognize these standards globally. The Organic and natural cosmetics bearing COSMOS signature are trustable for the consumer to use. Currently, COSMOS trademark is present in over 34,000 items in 78 countries. COSMOS signature is present on more than 13,400 raw ingredients and COSMOS approved signature is present on more than 9,000 raw materials. Cosmetics marketers can verify that their goods satisfy industry standards for organic or natural products by using COSMOS signs, which are registered trademarks, on packaging. The COSMOS standard lays out the requirements that cosmetic industries must fulfill in order to guarantee to consumers that their goods are authentically organic or natural cosmetics made in accordance with the most advanced sustainable methods.

The Brussels based COSMOS standard AISBL is an independent, non-profit organization that oversees the COSMOS standard. The original members of the COSMOS standard, including the Soil Association in the UK, ICEA in Italy, Ecocert in France, BDIH in Germany, and Cosmebio in France, continue to contribute their collective experience to the standard's ongoing development and management.

Principles of COSMOS

- Encouraging the use of organic agricultural products while honoring biodiversity.
- Honoring the environment and making responsible use of natural resources.
- Utilizing clean, environmentally friendly manufacturing and processing techniques that respect people's health.
- Incorporating and expanding on the idea of "green chemistry".

COSMOS certification

COSMOS provides two signatures namely COSMOS ORGNAIC or COSMOS NATURAL for cosmetic items like skincare and cosmetics, which will always appear just beneath the emblem or symbol of the relevant certifier or association. The percentage of organic ingredients in the product will also be listed on the label. This indicates what proportion of the entire product is organic. However, you may also find the percentage of organic less these two ingredient groups, as certain products contain a lot of water and mineral elements, which can never be organic.

Products having the necessary percentages of organic components as outlined in the COSMOS standard and complete compliance with the COSMOS standard are eligible to bear the COSMOS ORGANIC signature. Products that meet the COSMOS standard in every way but fall short of the minimum organic percentage requirements are eligible for the COSMOS NATURAL signature.

Raw material certification and approval

Two signatures namely COSMOS CERTIFIED or COSMOS APPROVED are available for raw materials, which appear just beneath the trademark or mark of the relevant certifier or association, just like with items. The COSMOS CERTIFIED signature is offered for agricultural products with organic content that have been chemically or physically processed and satisfy the COSMOS standards while when non-organic raw materials are accepted for use in cosmetics goods certified to the COSMOS standard, they can bear the COSMOS APPROVED signature.

Certification bodies

If you are a producer of natural and organic cosmetics or raw materials for natural and organic products, your selected Certification Body will examine and certify your goods and raw materials before giving you a reputable official logo and COSMOS signature that customers will recognize. There are 12 COSMOS authorized Certification bodies which are following:

Certification Body	Location
ACO Certification Ltd.	Australia
BUREAU VERITAS CERTIFICATION	France
ECOCERT GREENLIFE	France
COSMECERT SASU	France
IONC	Germany
ICEA	Italy
CONTROL UNION KOREA Co., Ltd	South Korea
KOREA TESTING & RESEARCH INSTITUTE	South Korea
CAAE	Spain
EKOLOJIK TARIM KONTROL ORG.	Turkey
IFC GLOBAL	Turkey
SOIL ASSOCIATION CERTIFICATION	UK

The majority of Certification Bodies are global in scope, functioning either through national offices or local auditors in countries including Argentina, Brazil, China, India, Japan, the US, and the majority of EU member states.

Standard Documents of COSMOS

- The COSMOS Standard (The entire COSMOS standard paper, replete with glossary and definitions)
- Technical Guide (Extra clarification and interpretation to enhance the COSMOS standard)

- Labelling Guide (Outlines the COSMOS-standard label application process)
- Control Manual (COSMOS-standard certification and accreditation requirements)

Key sections of the COSMOS Standards

This Standard covers cosmetics with organic material as well as items branded as natural or organic. These products must meet the following requirements in order to receive certification:

- Origin and processing of ingredients
- Composition of total product
- Storage, manufacturing and packaging
- Environmental management
- Labelling and communication
- Inspection, certification and control.

Origin and processing of ingredients

As per COSMOS standards, the ingredients of a cosmetic product are classified into 5 categories:

1. Water
2. Minerals and ingredients of mineral origin
3. Physically processed agro-ingredients (PPAI)
4. Chemically processed agro-ingredients (CPAI)
5. Other ingredients

1. Water

- The water employed must have colony forming units (CFU) less than 100/ml and can be potable water, water obtained by osmosis, spring water, distilled water, and sea water. Water can be treated with the physical processes allowed in Appendix I of COSMOS standards.
- Following physical processes allowed in COSMOS standards (Appendix I):
  - Blending, centrifugation, decoction, bleaching, adsorption, desiccation, extraction, filtration, decoloration, deterpenation, purification, freezing, grinding, infusion, infusion, lyophilisation, maceration, microwave, percolation, pressure, roasting, shifting, settling & decanting, squeezing, crushing, sterilization by UV, ultrasound, sterilization by thermal means, vacuum, UV treatment.

2. **Minerals and ingredients of mineral origin**

   Minerals can be utilized as long as they are extracted using environmentally friendly methods and without intentional chemical modification. Minerals can also be treated with the physical processes listed in Appendix I of COSMOS standards.

3. **Physically processed agro-ingredients (PPAI)**

   Any physically processed product of plant, animal, or microbiological origin that meets the following requirements is included:

   - Only primary raw materials extracted via the physical processes specified in Appendix I, whether they are of plant, animal, or microbiological origin, are permitted.
   - The only main raw materials that comply with the Convention on International Trade in Endangered Species of Wild Fauna and Flora (CITES) are permitted.

4. **Chemically processed agro-ingredients (CPAI)**

   Any chemically processed product of plant, animal, or microbiological origin that meets the following requirements is included:

   - The primary raw materials that comply with the Convention on International Trade in Endangered Species of Wild Fauna and Flora (CITES) are permitted.

   Note: Fermentation by-products like alcohol and others are considered chemically processed agro-ingredients.

5. **Other ingredients**

   Other substances are permitted as long as there are no natural alternatives that work as well to protect consumer safety or product efficacy. The other ingredients listed in Appendix V are only permitted which has been given in Table 11.8.

Table 11.8: List of other ingredients listed in Appendix V of COSMOS standards.

Ingredients	Restrictions
Preservative & denaturing agents	
Benzyl alcohol	
Benzoic acid & its salts	
Dehydroacetic Acid and its salts	
Salicylic acid & its salts	
Sorbic acid & its salts	
Denatonium Benzoate and Tertiary Butyl Alcohol and other denaturing agents for alcohol (excluding phthalates)	Only as denaturing agent for ethanol – where required by law

Table 11.8: *Contd...*

Ingredients	Restrictions
Petrochemical solvents	
Annatto	
Absolutes, Concretes, Resinoids	
Betaine	
Carotenoids	
Carrageenan	
Lanolin	
Glycosphingolipids and Glycolipids	
Lecithin	
Oryzanol	
Phytosterol	
Tocopherol	
Ingredients having both petrochemical and natural origin	
Alkylamidopropylbetaine	
Alkylglucosidecarboxylate	
Alkyl amphoacetate/ diacetate	
Alkyl Methyl Glucamide	
Carboxy Methyl – Vegetal polymer	
Dialkyl Dimonium Chloride	
Dialkyl Carbonate	
Tetra Sodium Glutamate Diacetate	Only for the function of chelating agent of product/ingredient (liquid or solid) obtained through a saponification reaction
Vegetal polymer -Hydroxypropyl Trimonium Chloride	
Alkyldimonium Hydroxypropyl Hydrolyzed Vegetal protein	Use in hair/beard products only
Other ingredients	
Carmine	
Caramel	Only allowed if reagents and processes are compliant
Mother of pearl/Ostrea Shell Powder	Only from naturally dead shells, and only from wild harvest, not from food waste
Squalane	Vegetable origin
Silk	
CI 77288 (Dichromium trioxide, Chromic oxide; Chromium (III) oxide)	

Composition of total product

The COSMOS standards covers two types of products:

- Cosmetic products under Organic certification (Certified as COSMOS ORGANIC).
- Cosmetic products under Natural certification (Certified as COSMOS NATURAL).

Rules for Cosmetic products under Organic certification (Certified as COSMOS ORGANIC)

A. Ingredients

- Minimum 95% of the physically processed agro-ingredients must be organic.
- The remaining PPAI must be organic if they are given in Appendix VI of the COSMOS standards.
- The chemically processed agro-ingredients given in Appendix VII must be organic.

B. Total product

- Minimum 20% of the total product must be organic.
- By exception, at least 10% of the entire product must be organic for rinse-off products, non-emulsified aqueous products, and goods containing at least 80% minerals or substances of mineral origin.

Rules for Cosmetic products under NATURAL certification (Certified as COSMOS NATURAL)

- There is no requirement to use a minimum level of organic ingredients.
- Base formulations such as shampoo bases and soap bases that don't contain any organic material can't go through the standard approval procedure. Rather, they need to be COSMOS CERTIFIED sans organic%, which entails an on-site assessment.

Storage, manufacturing and packaging

Storage

- Storage spaces need to be properly labeled to prevent misunderstandings or threats to the products' integrity.

Manufacturing

- Different production processes need to be kept apart to keep organic or natural components from becoming contaminated.

- A quality control system needs to be in place, including components such as full traceability of inputs and finished goods, step-by-step manufacturing processes, testing of ingredients and products, and records of analysis, manufacture, and storage.

Packaging

The following requirements must be met by base formulae, certified raw materials, and primary and secondary packaging for finished cosmetic goods:

- To reduce direct and indirect environment impacts of packaging during the entire life cycle of product.
- All the material used for packaging of cosmetic products must be listed in Appendix IX of COSMOS Standards.

Environmental management

A. Environmental management plan

- It is necessary to implement an environmental management strategy that takes into account the entire production process, as well as any waste and leftover products.
- A waste management strategy that takes into account gaseous, liquid, and solid manufacturing waste must be implemented as part of the environmental management plan. The goal of the waste management plan should be to efficiently and rationally reduce, reuse, and recycle waste products.
- It must obey ISO 14000 guidelines.

B. Cleaning and hygiene

- Following cleaning and disinfectants agents are permitted in COSMOS standards:
    - o Acetic acid, 1-propanol, formic acid, glutaric aldehyde, iso-propyl alcohol, hydrogen peroxide, amphoteric surfactants, mineral acids and alkalies, ozone, peracetic acid.
- In addition, the following cleaning agents can be employed:
    - o Plant derived surfactants having biodegradability, plant derived cleaning agents certified as per standards listed in the Technical Guide document.
    - o Palm ingredients or derivatives not given in Certified Sustainable Palm Oil (CSPO), however appreciated to use CSPO.
- The client must guarantee that there are no cleaning product remains.

- The client must put in place an inspection mechanism to guarantee that compliance cleaning and disinfection solutions are used both before and after manufacture. Procedures, data records, and specifics of staff training must be included.

Labelling and communication

A. Labelling conditions for products under ORGANIC CERITIFCATION

- Products that have received organic certification must be labeled with the signature "COSMOS ORGANIC" next to the seal of the COSMOS-standard AISBL member organization as specified in the Labelling Guide.
- Products must indicate the certification body on the label.
- Products must indicate the percentage of organic sourced ingredients by weight in the total product, as "X% organic of total" on the label.
- The label must specify the percentages of ingredients of natural and organic origin with a maximum precision of two decimals.
- The products must use one of the following wording options in the INCI list to identify organic ingredients and those manufactured from organic raw materials:
    - "Made using organic ingredients" for chemically processed agro-ingredients and "From organic agriculture" for physically processed agro-ingredients or
    - "Organic" for organic physically processed agro-ingredients and "Organic origin" for organic chemically processed agro-ingredients.
- The product cannot be referred to as "Organic" unless it contains at least 95% organic ingredients as a percentage of the total product. Example: Organic shampoo.

B. Labelling conditions for products under NATURAL CERITIFCATION

- Products that have received natural certification must be labeled with the signature "COSMOS NATURAL" next to the seal of the COSMOS-standard AISBL member organization as specified in the Labelling Guide.
- Products must indicate the certification body on the label.

- Products must indicate the percentage of natural sourced ingredients by weight in the total product, as “X% natural of total” on the label.
- The label must specify the percentages of ingredients of natural and organic origin with a maximum precision of two decimals.
- The products must use one of the following wording options in the INCI list to identify organic ingredients and those manufactured from organic raw materials:
    - “Made using organic ingredients” for chemically processed agro-ingredients and “From organic agriculture” for physically processed agro-ingredients or
    - “Organic” for organic physically processed agro-ingredients and “Organic origin” for organic chemically processed agro-ingredients.
- If the formula has two qualities namely an organic raw material as the only component and a non-organic raw material in an extracts mixture with at least 95% organic quality, the label must have following statement:
    - Made using organic and non-organic ingredients or sources for chemically processed agro-ingredients
    - From organic and non-organic ingredients or sources for physically processed agro-ingredients

Inspection, Certification and Control

Inspection and certification

- It is essential to comply with the requirements given in the documents of the scheme to get certify by cosmetic products or cosmetic raw materials under organic or natural certification.
- An on-site inspection and documentation validation serve as the foundation for the certification that is provided by an accredited certifying body. It concerns the entire process, from verifying the end product to inspecting the ingredients.

Approval process

To get certify by cosmetic products or cosmetic raw materials under organic or natural certification, it is needed to:

- Have subjected the manufacturing operation and the ingred ents or products to inspection and certification by an authorized certification body; this includes any sub-contracted manufacturing plants that are used to process the ingredients or products hold a valid operational certificate from that body

- Undergo an on-site annual inspection cycle which may include possible unannounced inspections and other additional inspections, and
- Allow the certification body to take samples and carry out analysis using laboratories conforming to ISO/IEC 17025 for ingredients or contaminants either on a random basis or in case of suspicion.

Certification bodies certifying to COSMOS

- It must be member of COSMOS-standard AISBL.
- It must be accredited to ISO/IEC Guide 65.
- It must be authorized as per the requirements set out in the COSMOS-standard Control Manual.
- It must collaborate with other authorized certification bodies to guarantee common interpretation and implementation of this Standard.

COSMOS with respective to preservatives, emollients, foaming agents, emulsifiers, and rheology modifiers

COSMOS/ECOCERT certified Preservatives in Cosmetics

Name of preservative	Complaint with ECOCERT/COSMOS
Benzyl alcohol	YES
Benzoic acid & its salts	YES
Dehydroacetic acid and its salts	YES
Sorbic acid and its salts	YES
Salicylic acid & its salts	YES

Commercial preservatives certified by COSMOS/ECOCERT

Commercial name	INCI	Characteristics
Iscaguard 9093	Aqua, Sodium benzoate, Sodium dehydroacetate	Broad spectrum activity, used for both leave-on and rinse-off products.
Iscaguard BOA	Benzyl alcohol, dehydroacetic acid, benzoic acid, sorbic acid	Broad spectrum activity, suitable for acidic products, used for both leave-on and rinse-off products.
Iscaguard BSB	Benzyl alcohol, benzoic acid, sorbic acid	Broad spectrum activity, suitable for acidic products, used for both leave-on and rinse-off products.

Contd...

Commercial name	INCI	Characteristics
Iscaguard IAF	Aqua, Lactic acid, Propanediol, Citric acid, Tartaric acid, Gluconic acid	Aqueous mixture of naturally occurring fruit acids, suitable for both rinse-off and leave-on products.
Iscaguard NK12	Aqua, Sodium Benzoate, Potassium Sorbate	Broad spectrum activity, suitable for acidic products, used for both leave-on and rinse-off products.

COSMOS Approved rheology modifier for Cosmetics

Commercial name	Common name	Characteristics
Bentone Hydroclay™ 550	Magnesium Aluminium Silicate	High stability, low viscosity. Mainly used for serums, primers and face masks.
Bentone Hydroclay™ 2000	Hectorite	Thixotropic flow, improved emulsion stability, thermal stability, improved suspension capacity, and electrolyte tolerance are all benefits of this special organoclay.
Clearthix S	Cellulose Gum & Algin	Transparent, versatile, and economical.
Thixcin® R PC	Trihydroxystearin	Perfect for non-aqueous phase.
Sucrathix VX	Microcrystalline Cellulose & Cellulose Gum & Xanthan Gum	Completely organic water thickener. It can additionally enhance susceptibility and heat stability.

COSMOS/ECOCERT Certified or Approved emulsifiers

Name	INCI	Application
Akoline PGPR	Polyglyceryl-3 Ricinoleate (or) Polyglyceryl-3 Polyricinoleate	W/O emulsifier
Cosphaderm GMUD	Glyceryl Undecylenate	W/O & O/W type emulsifier
Dermofeel® NC MB	Polyglyceryl-3 Distearate; Glyceryl Stearate Citrate	O/W emulsifier
Axol ® C62 pellet	Glyceryl Stearate Citrate	O/W emulsifier
OLEAMULS® LOW	Polyglyceryl-6 Oleate, Potassium Olivate	O/W emulsifier
COLORMULS® XBASE	Polyglyceryl-4 Stearate Phosphate	Emulsifying agent for coloring agents
AVOMULS® LOW	Polyglyceryl-4 Isostearate, Persea Gratissima (Avocado) Oil, Olea Europaea (Olive) Oil Unsaponifiables	O/W emulsifier
OLEAMULS® WO	Polyglyceryl-4 Pentaoleate	W/O emulsifier
OLEAMULS® OW	Polyglyceryl-4 Stearate, Potassium Olivate	O/W emulsifier

COSMOS/ECOCERT Certified or Approved emollients

Name	Chemical description	Characteristics
Activonol-3	Propanediol	Serves as emollient, cosmetic solvent, humectant.
Activonol-5N	Pentylene Glycol	Provides moisturising effect, increases water resistance in sunscreens and serves as a co-emulsifier.
Beantree	Methylheptyl Isostearate	It is a low viscosity, clear liquid that feels comparable to volatile silicones. It has broad compatibility with sunscreen actives.
Castorlatum	Castor oil	Used in anhydrous preparations like lipstick and lip balms, and in creams and lotions.
Castorwax MP-80	Hydrogenated Castor Oil	Used in anti-perspirant sticks, cosmetic pencils, lipsticks, creams and lotions.
Naturechem CR	Cetyl Ricinoleate	Serves as emollient and moisturizer.
Akogel	Hydrogenated vegetable oil	Provides lower occlusivity and fast absorption.

COSMOS/ECOCERT Certified or Approved foaming agents

Name	INCI	Characteristics
ORAMIX™ NS 10	Decyl Glucoside	Non-ionic surfactant, high foaming capability, used in shampoos, shower gels, face cleansers.
ORAMIX™ CG 110	Caprylyl/Capryl Glucoside	Non-ionic surfactant, used in facial cleanser, shampoos, shower gels, and bubble baths.
PALMEROL 1299 Lauryl Alcohol	Lauryl Alcohol	Impart emollient effect, emulsion stabilization, and lubricity.
PALMEROL 1498 Myristyl Alcohol	Myristyl Alcohol	Used in preparation of detergents, pharmaceuticals and cosmetic products.

Challenges in formulating herbal cosmetics

Despite various advantageous features of herbal cosmetics, some challenges are imposed during formulation of herbal cosmetics which are listed below:

Ingredient Sourcing

Finding high quality herbal substances can be difficult because their strength and quality might vary based on various factors like location, climate, and harvesting methods.

Stability and Shelf Life

Due to the usage of natural ingredients, herbal cosmetics may have shorter shelf lives than synthetic ones. Keeping products stable and avoiding spoiling can be a challenge.

Standardization

It is crucial to retain consistency in quality and effectiveness across batches. The content of herbal substances can vary, thus it is important to standardize herbal formulas.

Safety and Allergies

Some individuals may have allergies or sensitivities to certain herbal ingredients. Formulators must consider potential allergens and conduct patch tests.

Regulatory Compliance

It can be difficult to comply with legal requirements for labelling, ingredient disclosure, and safety testing, especially since local laws may differ.

Preservatives

To stop microbial growth, preservatives are frequently needed n herbal cosmetics. It can be difficult to choose preservatives that are secure, efficient, and consistent with the natural branding.

Formulation Expertise

It can be difficult to get a thorough grasp of the qualities, compatibility, and synergy of herbs, which is necessary to produce stable and effective herbal formulations.

Texture and Aesthetics

It might be difficult to achieve desired textures and aesthetics in herbal cosmetics such as creams and lotions without using synthetic chemicals.

Efficacy and Consistency

Due to the variety of natural substances, proving the effectiveness of herbal cosmetics and assuring consistent results might be challenge.

Consumer Education

It can be difficult in a cutthroat industry to educate people about the advantages and proper use of herbal cosmetics. A mix of scientific knowledge, formulation skill, and a dedication to upholding strict quality and safety standards are necessary for the successful development of herbal cosmetics. Formulating herbal cosmetics can indeed present several challenges but with careful consideration and expertise, these challenges can be overcome. Following steps can be employed to overcome the challenges facing in formulation of herbal cosmetics:

Ingredient Selection

Select herbal substances that have a history of efficacy and safety. Make sure they are accessible and long-lasting.

Quality Control

Because natural substances might vary in composition, maintain strict quality control procedures to guarantee product consistency.

Stability

Herbal compounds might be sensitive to elements like light and temperature. To ascertain the shelf life and storage requirements of your items, conduct stability tests.

Preservation

Create efficient preservation systems that shield your products' natural and organic properties against microbial contamination.

Regulatory Compliance

Recognize and abide by national and international laws governing cosmetics, particularly those governing labelling, safety evaluations, and proof of claims.

Research and Development

Spend money on research to improve formulas and successfully handle particular skin or hair issues.

Consumer Education

To moderate their expectations, inform your customers about the advantages and restrictions of herbal cosmetics.

Packaging

Use appropriate packaging to shield your goods from the elements and preserve their quality.

Testing

Conduct consumer or clinical studies to get feedback and enhance your products..

Market Research

Keep abreast of consumer tastes and market trends to modify your formulations.

Partnerships

To improve your formulations, work with herbalists, dermatologists, and specialists.

Sustainability

To appeal to customers who are concerned about the environment, concentrate on sustainable sourcing of herbal ingredients and eco-friendly packaging.

Cost Management

To make your products competitive on the market, strike a balance between quality and price.

Marketing and Branding

To draw in a niche audience, develop a captivating brand narrative that highlights the natural and herbal components of your cosmetics.

HOTS (HIGH-ORDER THINKING SOLUTIONS)

Cosmetics – Regulatory Considerations:

1. How can regulatory provisions prevent the sale of spurious cosmetics in the market, and what challenges do enforcement agencies face?
2. Analyze the impact of strict import regulations on cosmetic product innovation in India.
3. Evaluate the pros and cons of India's labeling requirements for cosmetics in comparison to international standards.
4. What are the ethical considerations involved in the manufacturing of cosmetics under loan licenses?
5. Discuss the effectiveness of the penalties under Indian law in deterring the production and sale of misbranded cosmetics.

Cosmetics - Biological Aspects:

6. How does the structure of the skin influence the development of cosmeceutical products for treating pigmentation and wrinkles?
7. Analyze the relationship between hair structure and common hair problems like dandruff or hair loss. How can this knowledge guide formulation strategies?
8. What are the biological mechanisms behind acne development, and how do cosmeceuticals specifically target these mechanisms?
9. Propose a cosmeceutical formulation for addressing both dry skin and wrinkles simultaneously. What would be the key ingredients and their biological roles?
10. How can an understanding of the oral cavity's structure lead to the development of more effective dental care products?

Formulation Building Blocks:

11. Analyze how the choice of surfactants can affect both the performance and safety profile of cosmetic formulations.
12. Discuss the role of rheological additives in the formulation stability of shampoos and vanishing creams. How can they impact the user experience?
13. Critically evaluate the role of parabens as preservatives in cosmetics. Are there safer alternatives?
14. What are the formulation challenges in balancing microbial preservation efficacy and safety in cosmetic products?

15. How do different perfume allergens as per EU regulations influence the safety and marketability of a cosmetic product?

Cosmeceutical Products Design:

16. How would you design a cosmeceutical product that addresses both pigmentation and sun protection? Justify your choice of ingredients.
17. Analyze the role of antioxidants in cosmeceutical products designed to treat wrinkles. How do they biologically interact with the skin?
18. How can you reformulate a sunscreen product to comply with stricter regulatory guidelines without compromising its SPF efficacy?
19. How would you approach the development of a cosmeceutical product to treat dandruff without using synthetic active ingredients?
20. Evaluate the role of formulation strategies in addressing the complex problem of sensitive teeth in cosmeceutical oral care products.

Herbal Cosmetics:

21. How do the limitations of natural preservatives in herbal cosmetics impact product shelf-life? What strategies could be used to overcome this?
22. Compare and contrast the benefits and drawbacks of using herbal vs. synthetic foaming agents in hair care products.
23. Discuss how the challenges in maintaining consistency in herbal formulations can impact consumer trust in herbal cosmetics.
24. How can the COSMOS guidelines for herbal cosmetics shape global market access for Indian herbal cosmetic brands?
25. Propose a formulation for a herbal moisturizing cream that addresses both regulatory concerns and consumer expectations.

Challenges in Herbal Cosmetic Formulation:

26. How can formulators address the challenge of standardizing herbal cosmetic ingredients in the face of variability in plant sources?
27. What are the challenges of scaling up herbal cosmetic formulations for mass production without compromising quality?

28. How can formulators ensure the stability of emulsions in herbal cosmetics given the natural variability in herbal ingredients?
29. How can consumer demand for "natural" ingredients create challenges in ensuring the microbial safety of herbal cosmetics?
30. What are the strategies to balance cost-effectiveness and efficacy in the formulation of herbal skin care products?

Sunscreens and Sun Protection:

31. How would you optimize the formulation of a sunscreen to provide broad-spectrum protection while ensuring user compliance (e.g., comfort, appearance)?
32. How do the physical and chemical mechanisms of sunscreens differ, and how can formulators decide which type to use based on the target consumer?
33. Analyze the environmental impact of certain sunscreen ingredients like oxybenzone and how it affects regulatory guidelines.
34. How can new research on the biological mechanisms of UV damage influence the future design of sunscreen formulations?
35. How can you formulate a sunscreen that addresses both pigmentation and skin sensitivity concerns?

Skin Care Formulations:

36. How can cosmeceutical formulations be designed to treat multiple skin conditions like dry skin, wrinkles, and pigmentation simultaneously?
37. How does an understanding of the skin's microbiome influence the formulation of products for acne treatment?
38. Evaluate the formulation challenges in developing an effective anti-aging product for diverse skin types.
39. How can advancements in skin biology research impact the formulation strategies for treating prickly heat?
40. What role do humectants play in maintaining skin hydration, and how can formulators optimize their use in anti-wrinkle products?

Hair Care Formulations:

41. How does the hair growth cycle influence the long-term efficacy of hair care products designed for hair loss?
42. Analyze the formulation challenges of developing a shampoo that caters to both dandruff control and hair repair.

43. Discuss the impact of environmental factors on hair care formulations and how products can be designed to mitigate damage.
44. How can formulators develop a product that addresses scalp sensitivity and dandruff simultaneously?
45. What are the challenges in formulating a hair care product that is free from sulfates and silicones without compromising performance?

Oral Care Formulations:

46. Evaluate the role of fluoride in cosmeceutical formulations for preventing dental cavities. What alternatives exist for consumers seeking fluoride-free products?
47. How can formulators address both mouth odor and bleeding gums in a single oral care product? What key ingredients would you use?
48. What are the formulation challenges in developing herbal toothpaste that addresses sensitive teeth without synthetic active ingredients?
49. How does an understanding of the oral microbiome influence the development of more effective cosmeceutical oral care products?
50. Discuss the potential health risks associated with overuse of teeth-whitening agents in cosmeceutical formulations, and how formulations can be adjusted to prevent them.

QUESTION BANK

Short Type Questions (2-3 marks)

1. Define cosmetic products as per Indian regulations.
2. What are the regulatory requirements for labeling of cosmetics in India?
3. What is the meaning of "misbranded cosmetics" under Indian regulation?
4. What are "spurious cosmetics" as per the Indian regulatory framework?
5. Name any two regulatory provisions relating to the import of cosmetics in India.
6. What is a "loan license" in the context of cosmetic manufacturing in India?
7. What are the basic conditions required to obtain a cosmetic manufacturing license in India?
8. What is prohibited under the regulation concerning the manufacture and sale of certain cosmetics?
9. List two penalties for offenses related to cosmetic manufacturing.
10. What is the role of the Drugs and Cosmetics Act, of 1940 in regulating cosmetics in India?
11. What are the key layers of the skin and their functions?
12. Define the term "prickly heat" and its cause.
13. How is body odor caused and how can it be managed?
14. What is the structure of hair?
15. Name the phases of the hair growth cycle.
16. List common problems associated with the oral cavity.
17. How does dry skin occur and what are the potential remedies?
18. What are the biological causes of wrinkles in the skin?
19. What is pigmentation and how does it affect the skin?
20. Mention two cleansing needs for the lips and eye lids.

21. What are surfactants? Mention their classification.
22. Define emollients and state their role in cosmetic formulations.
23. What are rheological additives and why are they used in cosmetics?
24. Name any two antimicrobial preservatives used in cosmetics.
25. What are the demerits of using parabens in cosmetic formulations?
26. List two factors that affect microbial preservative efficacy in cosmetic formulations.
27. Differentiate between soaps and syndet bars.
28. Name two controversial ingredients used in cosmetics and briefly explain why they are controversial.
29. What are "perfume ingredients" listed as allergens in the EU regulation? Provide an example.
30. What are the building blocks of a vanishing cream formulation?
31. What are sunscreens? Provide their classification.
32. Mention two regulatory aspects related to sunscreen products.
33. How do cosmeceutical formulations address dry skin?
34. What are the key ingredients used in anti-acne cosmeceutical products?
35. Define prickly heat and state how cosmeceutical formulations can help treat it.
36. What cosmeceutical ingredients are used for skin pigmentation control?
37. How do cosmeceutical products address body odour?
38. What active ingredients are used in dandruff treatment formulations?
39. Name two cosmeceutical formulations used for sensitive teeth.
40. How can cosmeceutical formulations help manage wrinkles?
41. Name two herbal ingredients commonly used in hair care products.
42. What are the key herbal ingredients used in skin care formulations?
43. List two herbal ingredients used in oral care products.
44. What are the functions of preservatives in herbal cosmetics?

45. Define the role of emollients in herbal cosmetics.
46. Name any two foaming agents used in herbal cosmetic formulations.
47. What are emulsifiers, and why are they important in herbal cosmetics?
48. Mention one challenge in formulating herbal cosmetics.
49. What is the significance of rheology modifiers in herbal cosmetic formulations?
50. What does COSMOS certification regulate in herbal cosmetics?
51. Give an account of Syndet bars.
52. Write the difference between herbal soap and Ayurvedic soap.
53. Enumerate the differences between vegetable soap and Syndet.
54. How is product performance evaluated for syndets/combar?
55. Write a note on shampoo bar.
56. Highlight the importance of Total fatty matter in soaps. Classify soaps on the basis of TFM.

Long Type Questions (8-10 marks)

1. Explain the labeling requirements for cosmetics as per Indian regulations. What key details must be included on a cosmetic product's label?
2. Discuss the regulatory provisions related to the import of cosmetics into India. What are the steps involved in obtaining import clearance?
3. Define and differentiate between misbranded and spurious cosmetics. Provide examples to explain the distinction.
4. Describe the regulatory provisions governing the manufacture of cosmetics in India. What are the essential conditions to be fulfilled to obtain a manufacturing license?
5. Explain the penalties and offenses associated with the manufacture and sale of cosmetics under Indian law. What are the consequences of non-compliance?
6. Analyze the various types of licenses issued for the manufacturing of cosmetics in India, including the process of obtaining a loan license.

7. Elaborate on the prohibition of the manufacture and sale of certain cosmetics under Indian regulation. What products are covered under this prohibition, and why?
8. Describe the structure of the skin and discuss how different skin problems such as dry skin, acne, pigmentation, and wrinkles arise due to its structure.
9. Explain the hair growth cycle. Discuss common hair problems and the biological factors contributing to them.
10. Discuss the common problems associated with the oral cavity and explain the cosmetic care needs for oral health.
11. Outline the cleansing and care requirements for different body parts, including face, scalp, hands, feet, and under-arms.
12. Discuss the structure of the skin and hair and explain how it relates to cosmetic problems such as acne, pigmentation, and hair loss.
13. How do biological factors contribute to body odor, and what are the possible ways to control it using cosmetics?
14. Describe the specific care needs for sensitive areas like the neck, under-arm, and scalp. How do these needs differ from the care required for other parts of the body?
15. Discuss the classification and applications of surfactants in cosmetic formulations. Provide examples of each type.
16. Explain the role of emollients and rheological additives in cosmetic formulations. How do they contribute to product stability and effectiveness?
17. Analyze the antimicrobial preservatives used in cosmetics, including their merits and demerits. Discuss the factors that affect their efficacy.
18. Describe the formulation building blocks for a moisturizing cream, cold cream, and shampoo. Highlight the key ingredients and their roles in each formulation.
19. Compare and contrast the formulation of soaps and syndet bars. What are the advantages and disadvantages of each?
20. Discuss the classification of perfumes. What are the common perfume ingredients that are listed as allergens under the EU regulation?

21. Explain the controversial use of ingredients such as parabens, formaldehyde liberators, and dioxane in cosmetic formulations. What are the potential health concerns associated with these ingredients?

22. How do preservatives contribute to the microbial safety of cosmetic products? Discuss the factors that influence their efficacy in different formulations.

23. Elaborate on the formulation building blocks for toothpaste and shampoo. What are the essential ingredients in these formulations, and what role does each ingredient play?

24. Describe the formulation and key ingredients required for preparing a vanishing cream. How does it differ from cold cream?

25. Discuss the classification of sunscreens. Explain the regulatory aspects involved in manufacturing and marketing sunscreens.

26. Describe how cosmeceutical formulations can be designed to address skin conditions such as acne, wrinkles, and pigmentation. Mention the active ingredients commonly used.

27. Explain the formulation strategies to address dry skin. What are the key ingredients and their functions in a moisturizing cosmeceutical product?

28. How do cosmeceutical products provide sun protection? Discuss the types of sunscreens and their mechanism of action.

29. Discuss the role of cosmeceuticals in managing dental cavities, bleeding gums, and mouth odour. What ingredients are commonly used in dental care formulations?

30. Explain the formulation approach to treat dandruff. What active ingredients are effective in cosmeceutical anti-dandruff products?

31. Describe how cosmeceutical products can address sensitive teeth. What are the active ingredients and their mechanism of action?

32. What are the key considerations in designing a cosmeceutical product for sun protection? Discuss the formulation challenges and regulatory requirements.

33. Analyze the formulation and effectiveness of cosmeceutical products designed to treat prickly heat. What ingredients are commonly included, and how do they work?

34. Discuss how cosmeceutical products are formulated to manage pigmentation issues. What are the most effective ingredients used in these formulations?
35. Discuss the herbal ingredients used in hair care formulations. How do these ingredients benefit hair health?
36. Describe the common herbal ingredients used in skin care products and explain their roles in maintaining healthy skin.
37. Explain the formulation of herbal oral care products. Discuss the herbal ingredients commonly used and their functions.
38. Review the guidelines for herbal cosmetics by private bodies like COSMOS. Discuss how these guidelines affect the choice of preservatives, emollients, and foaming agents in formulations.
39. What are the challenges in formulating herbal cosmetics? Discuss how issues like stability, microbial contamination, and consistency affect product development.
40. Analyze the role of emulsifiers and rheology modifiers in herbal cosmetic formulations. Why are these components critical to the performance of herbal products?
41. How do herbal foaming agents differ from synthetic ones in cosmetic formulations? Discuss the advantages and limitations of herbal alternatives.
42. Discuss the challenges in maintaining the stability and shelf-life of herbal cosmetics. How can preservatives be used effectively without compromising the "herbal" label?
43. Explain how COSMOS certification influences the selection of ingredients and formulation strategies for herbal cosmetics. What are the key criteria that products must meet?
44. Describe the challenges involved in formulating herbal skin care products. How can formulators overcome the limitations posed by natural ingredients while ensuring product efficacy?
45. Give the FDA definition of soap. Explain the composition, classification and method of soap preparation.
46. Write a descriptive note on performance enhancement additives in syndets combar.
47. Write the notes on (a) skin whitening soaps, and (b) baby soaps
48. Give a description of bathing bars.
49. How do UVA and UVB damage the skin?

50. List the advantages of sunblocks. What are the advantages of micropigment mineral sunblock?
51. What is sun protection factor? Explain it significance.
52. Give an account of marine suncreens.
53. What are encapsulated suncreens. Specify their advantages.
54. What are systemic sunscreens?
55. Giving suitable examples, classify sunscreens. Elaborate their advantages and disadvantages
56. Describe the approaches for topical sunscreen formulations.
57. In context to newer sunscreen approaches, explain (i) Polymeric sunscreens, (ii) Plant based sunscreens.
58. What are the regulatory requirements of sunscreen products?
59. Elaborate the newer approaches for sunscreens.

INDEX

Q

R

S

T

U

V

W

www.ingramcontent.com/pod-product-compliance
Lightning Source LLC
Chambersburg PA
CBHW071223230926
51849CB00001B/14
* 9 7 8 9 3 4 9 5 6 2 7 6 9 *